Register f

solutions@syngress.com

Over the last few years, Syngress has published many best-selling and critically acclaimed books, including Tom Shinder's *Configuring ISA Server 2000*, Brian Caswell and Jay Beale's *Snort 2.0 Intrusion Detection*, and Angela Orebaugh and Gilbert Ramirez's *Ethereal Packet Sniffing*. One of the reasons for the success of these books has been our unique **solutions@syngress.com** program. Through this site, we've been able to provide readers a real time extension to the printed book.

As a registered owner of this book, you will qualify for free access to our members-only solutions@syngress.com program. Once you have registered, you will enjoy several benefits, including:

- Four downloadable e-booklets on topics related to the book. Each booklet is approximately 20-30 pages in Adobe PDF format. They have been selected by our editors from other best-selling Syngress books as providing topic coverage that is directly related to the coverage in this book.

- A comprehensive FAQ page that consolidates all of the key points of this book into an easy to search web page, providing you with the concise, easy to access data you need to perform your job.

- A "From the Author" Forum that allows the authors of this book to post timely updates links to related sites, or additional topic coverage that may have been requested by readers.

Just visit us at **www.syngress.com/solutions** and follow the simple registration process. You will need to have this book with you when you register.

Thank you for giving us the opportunity to serve your needs. And be sure to let us know if there is anything else we can do to make your job easier.

SYNGRESS®

SYNGRESS®

SYNGRESS
NO WAY TO FAIL!
WE'VE GOT YOU COVERED

CYA

Securing IIS 6.0

COVER YOUR A** BY GETTING IT RIGHT THE FIRST TIME

Chun Hai (Bernard) Cheah
Ken Schaefer
Chris Peiris Technical Editor

Syngress Publishing, Inc., the author(s), and any person or firm involved in the writing, editing, or production (collectively "Makers") of this book ("the Work") do not guarantee or warrant the results to be obtained from the Work.

There is no guarantee of any kind, expressed or implied, regarding the Work or its contents. The Work is sold AS IS and WITHOUT WARRANTY. You may have other legal rights, which vary from state to state.

In no event will Makers be liable to you for damages, including any loss of profits, lost savings, or other incidental or consequential damages arising out from the Work or its contents. Because some states do not allow the exclusion or limitation of liability for consequential or incidental damages, the above limitation may not apply to you.

You should always use reasonable care, including backup and other appropriate precautions, when working with computers, networks, data, and files.

Syngress Media®, Syngress®, "Career Advancement Through Skill Enhancement®," "Ask the Author UPDATE®," and "Hack Proofing®," are registered trademarks of Syngress Publishing, Inc. "Syngress: The Definition of a Serious Security Library"™, "Mission Critical™," and "The Only Way to Stop a Hacker is to Think Like One™" are trademarks of Syngress Publishing, Inc. Brands and product names mentioned in this book are trademarks or service marks of their respective companies.

KEY	SERIAL NUMBER
001	PO9873D5FG
002	829KMGG89G
003	88NJH2GHBN
004	2987GKGHNM
005	CVPL334522
006	VBP5T545BN
007	HJJJ997WD3
008	9J8N3F3MNB
009	629MPT8977
010	I5T6TFF497

PUBLISHED BY
Syngress Publishing, Inc.
800 Hingham Street
Rockland, MA 02370

CYA Securing IIS 6.0

Copyright © 2004 by Syngress Publishing, Inc. All rights reserved. Printed in the United States of America. Except as permitted under the Copyright Act of 1976, no part of this publication may be reproduced or distributed in any form or by any means, or stored in a database or retrieval system, without the prior written permission of the publisher, with the exception that the program listings may be entered, stored, and executed in a computer system, but they may not be reproduced for publication.

Printed in the United States of America
1 2 3 4 5 6 7 8 9 0

ISBN: 1-931836-25-6

Acquisitions Editor: Christine Kloiber   Cover Designer: Michael Kavish
Technical Editor: Chris Peiris   Copy Editor: Amy Thomson
Page Layout and Art: Patricia Lupien   Indexer: Rich Carlson

Distributed by O'Reilly & Associates in the United States and Canada.

Acknowledgments

We would like to acknowledge the following people for their kindness and support in making this book possible.

Syngress books are now distributed in the United States by O'Reilly & Associates, Inc. The enthusiasm and work ethic at ORA is incredible and we would like to thank everyone there for their time and efforts to bring Syngress books to market: Tim O'Reilly, Laura Baldwin, Mark Brokering, Mike Leonard, Donna Selenko, Bonnie Sheehan, Cindy Davis, Grant Kikkert, Opol Matsutaro, Lynn Schwartz, Steve Hazelwood, Mark Wilson, Rick Brown, Leslie Becker, Jill Lothrop, Tim Hinton, Kyle Hart, Sara Winge, C. J. Rayhill, Peter Pardo, Leslie Crandell, Valerie Dow, Regina Aggio, Pascal Honscher, Preston Paull, Susan Thompson, Bruce Stewart, Laura Schmier, Sue Willing, Mark Jacobsen, Betsy Waliszewski, Dawn Mann, Kathryn Barrett, John Chodacki, and Rob Bullington.

The incredibly hard working team at Elsevier Science, including Jonathan Bunkell, Ian Seager, Duncan Enright, David Burton, Rosanna Ramacciotti, Robert Fairbrother, Miguel Sanchez, Klaus Beran, Emma Wyatt, Rosie Moss, Chris Hossack, and Krista Leppiko, for making certain that our vision remains worldwide in scope.

David Buckland, Daniel Loh, Marie Chieng, Lucy Chong, Leslie Lim, Audrey Gan, Pang Ai Hua, and Joseph Chan of STP Distributors for the enthusiasm with which they receive our books.

Kwon Sung June at Acorn Publishing for his support.

David Scott, Tricia Wilden, Marilla Burgess, Annette Scott, Geoff Ebbs, Hedley Partis, Bec Lowe, and Mark Langley of Woodslane for distributing our books throughout Australia, New Zealand, Papua New Guinea, Fiji Tonga, Solomon Islands, and the Cook Islands.

Winston Lim of Global Publishing for his help and support with distribution of Syngress books in the Philippines.

Authors

Chun Hai (Bernard) Cheah (MCP+I, MCSE, MCDBA, CCSE) is a Microsoft Most Valuable Professional (MVP) specializing in IIS Server. He is currently a contract solution consultant working on Internet solutions analysis, design, and consultancy as well as implementation. His primary focus includes online e-commerce system security and high availability features. He is pursuing his masters in IT business strategy at the University of Portsmouth, UK.

Ken Schaefer is an experienced systems administrator who has worked with IIS for over six years. He currently works for the University of New South Wales in Sydney, Australia. He has experience with WinNT 4/2000 server, SQL Server (6.5, 7, 2000), IIS (3, 4, 5) and MacOS (6+), as well as development experience with ASP, ASP.Net, ADO, ADO.Net, VB, SQL Server, and Access. Ken participates in numerous support forums, and provides a broad assembly of troubleshooting resources on his website, www.adopenstatic.com. He was recently honored with a Microsoft MVP distinction in the Windows Server (IIS) category. Ken received a bachelor's degree in commerce at the University of New South Wales, where he is currently pursuing a master's degree in business technology.

Technical Editor

Chris Peiris (MVP, MIT) works as an independent consultant for .NET and EAI implementations. He is currently working with the Commonwealth Bank of Australia. He also lectures on distributed component architectures (.NET, J2EE, and CORBA) at Monash University, Caulfield, Victoria, Australia. Chris was awarded the Microsoft Most Valuable Professional (MVP) for his contributions to .NET technologies by Microsoft, Redmond. Chris has been designing and developing Microsoft solutions since 1995. His expertise lies in developing scalable, high-performance solutions for financial institutions, G2G, B2B, and media groups. Chris has written many articles, reviews, and columns for various online publications including 15Seconds, Developer Exchange (www.devx.com), and Wrox Press. He is co-author of *C# Web Service with .NET Remoting and ASP.NET* and *C# for Java Programmers* (Syngress Publishing, ISBN: 1-931836-54-X), and study guides on MCSA/MCSE Exams 70-290 and Exam 70-298, also from Syngress. Chris frequently presents at professional developer conferences on Microsoft technologies.

His core skills are C++, Java, .NET, C#, VB.NET, Service Oriented Architecture, DNA, MTS, Data Warehousing, WAP, and SQL Server. Chris has a bachelor's in computing, a bachelor of business (accounting), and a masters in information technology. He is currently under taking a PhD on web service management framework. He lives with his family in ACT, Australia.

Chris dedicates this book to his mentors: Dianne Hagan, Brian Simpson, Christine Mingins, Keith Howie, Robert Morgan, Greg Stone and Charles Sterling. In his own words "this is a token of my gratitude for all your guidance, assistance and your vision. You all contributed to my career in a very significant way… Thank you for the opportunities."

Contents

About the Book xvii

Chapter 1 Introducing IIS 6.0 1
  In this Chapter 1
  IIS 6.0 Enhancements 2
    Increased Reliability and Availability 2
    Manageability Improvements 3
    Scalability and Performance Improvements 5
    Increased Security 7
  Understanding IIS 6.0 Architecture 10
    Services Provided by IIS 6.0 10
    HTTP.SYS Kernel Mode Driver 12
    Inetinfo.exe Process and the IISAdmin Service ...12
    The World Wide Web (WWW) Publishing
      Service 14
    Application Processing Modes 14
      IIS 6.0 Worker Process Isolation Mode 14
      IIS 5.0 Isolation Mode 17
  Your A** is Covered if You... 19

Chapter 2 Hardening Windows Server 2003 ..21
  In this Chapter 21
  Get Secure and Stay Secure 22
    Networking Environment 23
    Patches and Updates 25
    Windows Services 28
    User Accounts and Groups 29
    File System 30
    Auditing and Logging 32

Staying Secure 34
Secure IIS Checklist 35
A Final Word on Security 37
Knowing the Enemy and What They Want 38
Your A** is Covered if You... 38

Chapter 3 Installing Internet Information Services (IIS) 6.0 39
In this Chapter 39
Installing IIS 6.0 Using the Configure Your Server
  Wizard 40
Installing or Modifying IIS 6.0 Using the
  Add/Remove Programs Control Panel 44
Installing IIS 6.0 Using Automated Installation
(Unattended Setup) 49
  Installing IIS 6.0 During the Windows 2003
    Server Setup 50
  Installing IIS 6.0 After the Windows 2003
    Server Setup 54
Upgrading IIS 5.0 to IIS 6.0 55
  Post-Installation Information 56
After Installation: Locating the Administrative Tools ..59
  IIS Manager 60
  Application Server MMC 61
  The Remote Administration Website 62
  Sharepoint Administration Website 62
Your A** is Covered if You... 64

Chapter 4 Configuring Basic Web Server Security 65
In this Chapter 65
Enabling and Disabling Web Service Extensions 66
Configuring Multipurpose Internet Mail Exchange
  Types 70
Configuring IP Address Restrictions 75
Setting Website Permissions 81
Securing Web Resources 87

Enabling and Securing Web Access Log Files 98
Your A** is Covered if You... 114

Chapter 5 Advanced Web Server Security Configuration 115
In this Chapter 115
Configuring Authentication 116
   The Authentication Process 117
   Configuring Anonymous Authentication 118
   Configuring Basic Authentication 120
   Configuring Digest Authentication 122
   Configuring Advanced Digest Authentication . .125
   Configuring Integrated Windows Authentication 126
   Configuring UNC Authentication 131
   Passport Authentication 132
   Configuring SubAuthentication 132
   Configuring Delegation 133
Configuring IIS User Accounts 135
   IIS 6.0 Running in Worker Process Mode 136
      Changing the Process Identity of a Web
         Application Pool 138
      Other User Accounts – IUSR_
         <machinename> 139
   IIS 6.0 Running in IIS5 Isolation Mode 139
      IWAM_<computername> Account 141
      ASPNET Account 142
      IUSR_<machinename> 142
Configuring URLScan 142
   Configuring URLScan.ini 143
      Other Sections 148
Configuring Your Server to Use SSL 150
   Generating a Certificate Request 153
   Submitting a Certificate Request 156
   Installing an Issued Certificate 158
   Managing your Website Certificates 160
   Configuring IIS SSL Options 161

Configuring URL Authorization with the
  Authorization Manager 163
    Creating the Authorization Store 164
    Configuring Access to the Authorization Store ..166
    Creating a New Application 166
    Creating an Operation 167
    Creating a Scope 168
    Creating a Role 169
    Configuring IIS 6.0 172
    Testing the Authorization Store 175
Configuring Custom Error Messages 175
    The Default ASP Error Message 176
    Configuring a Basic ASP Error Message 178
    Configuring a Custom ASP Error Message 179
    Configuring a Custom ASP.NET Error Message 182
Securing Include Files 184
Disabling Parent Paths 187
Configuring IP Address, TCP Port and Host-
  Header combinations 189
Your A** is Covered if You... 192

Chapter 6 Securing Application Pools 195
In this Chapter 195
Application Pools 196
    Creating Application Pools 198
    Configuring Application Pools 198
        Configuring Application Pool Identities 200
Isolating Web Applications 203
Understanding User Impersonation 207
Your A** is Covered if You... 209

Chapter 7 Securing FTP Sites 211
In this Chapter 211
Configuring FTP Sites 212
    Relocate the Default FTP Root Path 213
    Configure FTP Messages 214

Configure the FTP Directory Output Style 216
Securing FTP Resources 216
Configuring FTP User Isolation 221
    Do Not Isolate Users 222
    Isolate Users 223
    Isolate Users Using Active Directory 224
Securing the FTP Connection 227
Enabling and Securing the FTP Access Log File . . .232
Your A** is Covered if You... 238

Chapter 8 Securing SMTP and POP3 Services .239

In This Chapter 239
Configuring SMTP Virtual Servers 240
    Creating Additional SMTP Servers 241
    Configuring Additional Domains 242
    Configuring SMTP Server Folders 244
    Enable Logging 246
    Other Configuration Options 249
SMTP Virtual Server Security 252
    Configuring Authentication 253
    Configuring Connection Controls 254
    Configuring Transport Layer Security 256
    Configuring Relay Controls 257
Configuring and Securing the POP3 Server 260
    Initial Configuration 262
    Configuring Mailboxes 265
Your A** is Covered if You... 267

Chapter 9 Securing NNTP Virtual Servers 269

In this Chapter 269
Configuring NNTP Virtual Servers 270
Managing NNTP Newsgroups 279
Securing NNTP Newsgroups 287
Enabling and Securing NNTP Access Log Files 296
Your A** is Covered if You... 302

Chapter 10 Securing Certificate Services 303
In this Chapter 303
Understanding Certificate Services 304
    Certificate Authority and its Structure 306
Configuring Certificate Services 308
    Configuring Your Certificate Authority 308
Securing Certificate Services Web Enrollment
   Support 317
    Web Enrollment Virtual Directory Permissions .318
    Authenticating Web Enrollment 319
    Restricting Access to Protect your Web
      Enrollment 320
Monitoring Certificate Services Web Enrollment
   Access 323
Your A** is Covered if You... 324

Chapter 11 Securing Web Publishing 327
In This Chapter 327
Configuring and Securing WebDAV Publishing 328
    Installing and Enabling WebDAV 328
    Configuring and Securing WebDAV 330
Configuring and Security FrontPage Server
   Extensions 335
    Installing FrontPage Server Extensions 336
    Enabling FPSE Authoring 338
    Securing your FPSE Virtual Host 342
Your A** Is Covered If You... 347

Chapter 12 Securing Internet Printing 347
In this Chapter 347
Configuring Internet Printing 348
Securing Internet Printing 354
Monitoring Internet Printing Access 357
Your A★★ is Covered if You... 359

Chapter 13 Monitoring Internet Information Services (IIS) 6.0 361
In this Chapter 361
Monitoring Site Activities Logging 362
Monitoring Event Viewer Logging 367
Monitoring HTTP API Error Logging 373
Monitoring URLScan Logging 380
Your A★★ is Covered if You... 384

Index 385

About the Book

Network System Administrators operate in a high-stress environment, where the competitive demands of the business often run counter to textbook "best practices". Design and planning lead times can be non-existent and deployed systems are subject to constant end-runs; but at the end of the day, you, as the Administrator, are held accountable if things go wrong. You need help and a fail-safe checklist that guarantee that you've configured your network professionally and responsibly. You need to "CYA".

CYA: Securing IIS 6.0 is part of the new *CYA* series from Syngress that clearly identifies those features of IIS that represent the highest risk factors for attacks, performance degradation and service failures; and then walks the reader through step-by-step configurations to assure they have been thorough and responsible in their work.

In this Book

This book fills the need of Networking professionals responsible for configuring, maintaining and troubleshooting the security of Microsoft's Internet Information Server 6.0. It will provide:

- A comprehensive "checklist" to all of the security related configuration consoles in IIS.

- A clear presentation of Microsoft's recommended security configurations/policies based on the business needs of your network.

- A warning of the drawbacks of some of the recommended practices. The promise is essentially that you won't get busted for being negligent or irresponsible if you follow the instructions in the book.

The book is organized around the security services offered by IIS. The table of contents reflects the hierarchy of topics within the IIS MMC, and covers any configuration option within IIS that relates to security. In some instances, references are made to non-IIS services, but only as they relate to or support the IIS service being discussed.

In Every Chapter

There will be several introductory paragraphs with a **By the Book** configuration check list. This section identifies, according to the product manufacturer, the function/benefit/protection of the feature that you are about to configure. There are also sections entitled **Reality Checks** that provide you with insight into situations where **By the Book** may not be the only solution, or where there are hidden costs or issues involved with the **By the Book** solution.

Additional Reading

Additional reading for this book can be found at www.syngress.com/solutions. There you will find an appendix to the book as well as the configure options that will especially help while reading Chapters 4 and 5.

Your A** is Covered if You…

At the end of every chapter, you are provided with a bullet list of items covering the most essential tasks completed within the chapter. You will use this section to make sure you are ready to move on to the next set of configurations in the following chapter.

Chapter 1
Introducing IIS 6.0

In this Chapter

Released as part of the Windows 2003 Server family, Internet Information Services (IIS) 6.0 is the latest incarnation of Microsoft's Internet server. In the six years since IIS 1.0 was released (as part of Windows NT 3.51), IIS has rapidly developed, adding new features and scaling to new levels of performance. IIS 6.0 is no different. It offers significant improvements in scalability, security, manageability, reliability and performance over previous versions of IIS. However, it is the improvements in security and scalability that will probably most impress systems administrators.

By the end of this chapter, you will be familiar with the major components of IIS 6.0, how IIS 6.0 differs from previous versions, and the workings of the internal architecture of IIS 6.0.

IIS 6.0 Enhancements

This section serves as an introduction to the new and/or enhanced features in IIS 6.0, and how they compare to features in previous versions of IIS.

Increased Reliability and Availability

IIS 6.0 has been extensively redesigned to improve reliability and availability, in particular the components involved in serving and managing the Web server. A new fault-tolerant architecture detects and restarts failed web-based applications, while a new request system reduces dropped user connections by queuing incoming user requests until a restarted web application is able to process them.

Table 1.1 lists the major reliability and availability improvements in IIS 6.0.

Table 1.1 IIS 6.0 Availability and Reliability Improvements

Feature	Explanation
Application Pools	IIS 6.0 introduces web application pools. Websites (and web applications within websites) can be isolated into individual web application pools, each of which is served by one or more Windows processes (these are visible in Task Manager as w3wp.exe). These particular processes are called *worker processes*. Because web application pools are isolated from each other, a failure in one pool cannot affect any other pools or the web applications that those other pools host. Additionally, the worker processes hosting the application pools run all user code, ensuring that faulty user code is unable to affect the core IIS 6.0 services. This includes Internet Server Application Programming Interface (ISAPI) filters, which previously ran in the core Inetinfo.exe process. For more information on the new IIS 6.0 architecture, see the "IIS 6.0 Architecture" section in this chapter.
Health Monitoring	IIS 6.0 periodically checks the health of web application pools. If the pool does not report itself as healthy within the configured timeout period, corrective action can be taken. More information on application health monitoring can be found in the IIS 6.0 online help. Chapter 6, "Securing Application Pools", discusses accessing and configuring application pool settings.

Continued

Table 1.1 IIS 6.0 Availability and Reliability Improvements

Feature	Explanation
Process Recycling	Web application processes can be recycled based on a flexible set of criteria, including CPU utilization and memory consumption. While a process is being recycled, incoming web requests are queued until a new process is ready to accept requests.
Rapid Fail Protection	IIS 6.0 can restart an application pool if fails or is marked unhealthy. If a pool fails many times in a short period of time, IIS 6.0 can be configured to prevent the pool from restarting again. In this case, an "HTTP 503 Service Unavailable" error will be displayed to users who attempt to access the pool.
Orphaning Worker Processes	When an application pool fails, IIS 6.0 normally terminates the worker processes servicing the pool. However, IIS 6.0 can be configured to allow the worker process to continue running and to have a program (for example, a debugger) run, or send notification to an administrator. Configuring this feature requires setting a metabase entry. See the "IIS Architecture" section in this chapter for more information on the metabase.

Manageability Improvements

Management of your Internet server is easier and more flexible in the new IIS 6.0. The IIS metabase (where IIS stores its settings) is now in an XML-based settings store, allowing for easier editing. IIS also has full support for Windows Management Instrumentation (WMI), as well as previously supported Active Directory Service Interface (ADSI) classes. Most IIS settings can be edited on the fly, with the changes taking effect immediately. Table 1.2 summarizes the major manageability improvements.

Table 1.2 IIS 6.0 Manageability Improvements

Feature	Explanation
New HTML IIS Administration Interface	IIS 6.0 includes a revamped HTML administration website that improves on the functionality of that offered in IIS 4.0 and IIS 5.0. See Chapter 3, "Installing IIS 6.0", for more information on the administrative tools available for IIS 6.0.
XML-Based Metabase	The metabase stores most of IIS' settings, in a similar way to how the Windows registry is used to store settings for many applications. The metabase was created to provide for quicker and easier access to IIS' settings (the metabase, being smaller than the registry, can be loaded completely into memory). In IIS 4.0 and IIS 5.0, the metabase was stored in a proprietary binary format. In IIS 6.0, this becomes an XML-based format, and comprises two files: Metabase.xml and MBSchema.xml.
Metabase History	IIS 6.0, by default, creates backup copies of the metabase every time the metabase is edited. These are stored in %windir%\system32\inetsrv\history. By default, the last 10 versions of the metabase are kept. These can be used to restore IIS to a previous configuration on the same machine. Note that these versions cannot be used to restore IIS 6.0 to another machine (or to the same machine if Windows 2003 has been reinstalled) because sensitive data in the backup file (such as passwords) are encrypted with the machine key.
Metabase Backup and Restore	The metabase can now easily be exported and restored, even to other machines, directly from the IIS Manager or by using the supplied iiscnfg.vbs VBScript file. If a password is supplied when creating the backup, the backup can be restored on another machine. If no password is supplied, the current machine key is used to encrypt sensitive information in the backup file, and the backup can only be restored to the current Windows 2003 installation.

Continued

Table 1.2 IIS 6.0 Manageability Improvements

Feature	Explanation
Edit While Running Capability	The metabase can be edited while IIS is running, and in many cases, the new settings can be applied without having to restart IIS or any of its subcomponents. One notable instance that requires restarting IIS 6.0 is when you switch application processing modes.
Administration Interfaces	IIS 6.0 supports the same ADSI-based administration capabilities as previous versions. In addition, a new WMI provider provides an additional interface for programmatically manipulating IIS 6.0. A number of new administrative scripts (located in %windir%\system32\) are provided that use the new WMI interfaces.

Scalability and Performance Improvements

A new internal architecture and a number of smaller enhancements are combined in IIS to dramatically improve the performance and scalability that IIS 6.0 offers, particularly in the area of website hosting. In particular, a new kernel mode driver receives requests for web pages and routes them to the appropriate worker process for execution. In previous versions of IIS, this task was done by the user-mode Inetinfo.exe process (which also had to handle a number of other tasks), forming a potential bottleneck when running extremely busy websites.

Table 1.3 lists the major performance and scalability improvements.

Table 1.3 IIS 6.0 Performance and Scalability Improvements

Feature	Explanation
Kernel Mode HTTP.SYS Driver	IIS 6.0 introduces a new kernel mode driver, called HTTP.SYS, which is integrated directly into the Windows Transmission Control Protocol/Internet Protocol (TCP/IP) stack. Its purpose is to route website requests through to web application pools. In IIS 5.0, this task was performed by the Inetinfo.exe process. Additionally, HTTP.SYS maintains a cache that can be used to serve requests for content without having to switch out of kernel mode.

Continued

Table 1.3 IIS 6.0 Performance and Scalability Improvements

Feature	Explanation
Web Gardens	Web application pools can be serviced by multiple worker processes. This setup is called a *web garden*. If all the threads in one worker process are busy (for example, by long running tasks) or deadlocked, then requests can still be routed through the other worker processes allocated to the application pool.
Processor Affinity	On a multiple-CPU machine, application pools can be tied to particular processors. This improves performance by maximizing the chance of CPU cache hits.
Persisted ASP Template Cache	In IIS 5.0, Active Server Pages (ASPs) were compiled into templates the first time they were requested. These were stored in memory and lost if the server was restarted. In IIS 6.0, these pages are persisted to disk, and can be reused even if the server is restarted.
Advanced HTTP.SYS Caching Heuristics	IIS 6.0 uses advanced heuristics to determine which responses can be cached in the high-speed kernel mode cache maintained by the HTTP.SYS driver. Requests served from this cache greatly improve performance, as the overhead of routing the request through to a user-mode worker process is avoided.
Website Scalability Improvements	IIS 6.0 can shut down application pools that have been idle for a configurable amount of time, releasing the resources used by the worker process servicing the pool. Additionally, when the Web server is started, resources are not allocated to application pools until a request comes in for a resource (for example, a web page) that is served by that pool. This allows more websites to be run on a single machine because not all websites are required to have resources allocated to them at all times.
Web Server Resource Limits	If you run services other than the Web server on your machine, you can limit the bandwidth used by websites (bandwidth throttling) as well as limit the CPU usage of application pools, so that other processes are not starved of network bandwidth or CPU time.

Continued

Table 1.3 IIS 6.0 Performance and Scalability Improvements

Feature	Explanation
Logging Improvements	IIS 6.0 can now log the HTTP substatus codes that it uses internally for different types of errors. These are visible in the IIS Web server logs, and can help you to identify and troubleshoot the causes of service errors. Logs can be stored on remote servers to centralize log storage and backup. A new binary log format allows IIS 6.0 to store logs for all websites in a single binary formatted file. This is useful in situations where many thousands of websites may be hosted on a single server and writing an individual logfile for each site will have a significant performance impact.

Increased Security

IIS 6.0 incorporates a large number of security changes designed to make IIS 6.0 a more secure application server. Internally, the processing architecture for the Web server functionality has changed significantly, both to improve performance, and to make IIS 6.0 more resilient to faulty user code and malicious external attacks. IIS 6.0 is no longer installed by default when installing Windows 2003 Server (except for Windows 2003 Server Web Edition). Additionally, a new IIS 6.0 installation only includes a minimum level of functionality, and administrators are required to explicitly enable specific functionality. This helps guard against attacks that exploit features that administrators may not even be aware are running on their IIS server.

Table 1.4 lists the major security enhancements in IIS 6.0.

Table 1.4 IIS 6.0 Security Enhancements

Feature	Explanation
IIS Not Installed by Default	By default, IIS 6.0 is not installed when Windows 2003 Server is installed. You can override this behavior by using an unattended installation and customizing the answer file. The exception to this is Windows 2003 Server Web Edition, where a number of IIS 6.0 components are installed by default. See Chapter 3 for more information, including unattended installations.

Continued

Table 1.4 IIS 6.0 Security Enhancements

Feature	Explanation
Installed in Locked-down" Mode	IIS 6.0 is installed in *locked-down mode*. While File Transfer Protocol (FTP), Simple Mail Transfer Protocol (SMTP) and Network News Transfer Protocol (NNTP) services are fully functional, the Web server will only serve static content. Dynamic content (such as ASP.NET, or WebDAV authoring) must be specifically enabled. The exception to this is Windows 2003 Server Web Edition, where ASP functionality is enabled to allow administration via the HTML administration website. WebDAV is explained in more detail in Chapter 11, "Securing Web Publishing".
IIS Installations Can be Disabled Using Group Policy	Windows 2003 Server includes new administrative templates that can be used in group policy objects. These templates allow domain administrators to prevent IIS from being installed on machines within the domain, thus enhancing overall domain security by restricting the establishment of unauthorized IIS servers.
Web Service Extensions Can be Enabled and Disabled	IIS 6.0 allows administrators to quickly enable and disable defined web service extensions. Web service extensions serve dynamic content and include ASP, ASP.NET and WebDAV. By default, all web service extensions are disabled upon a clean install of IIS 6.0. For more information on administering web service extensions, see Chapter 4, "Web Server Security".
Only Recognized MIME Types are Served	For files to be available via the Web server, a Multi-Purpose Internet Mail Extension (MIME) type must be defined. This prevents attackers from downloading sensitive operating system files if those files do not have a defined MIME type. Common document types have MIME types set by default. For more information on MIME types and their configuration, see Chapter 4.
Command Line Tools Cannot be Executed	The default user accounts used by IIS 6.0 no longer have permissions to run command line tools, such as batch files and executables. This helps prevent attackers from gaining access to cmd.exe and similar tools.

Continued

Table 1.4 IIS 6.0 Security Enhancements

Feature	Explanation
Support for Advanced Digest Authentication	Advanced digest authentication allows the new IIS 6.0 worker processes to run as low privilege accounts while still supporting digest authentication. Additionally, user passwords no longer have to be stored in Active Directory using reversible encryption. For more information on advanced digest authentication, see Chapter 5, "Advanced Web Server Security".
ASP Global Events Run in User Context	ASP global events, such as Application_OnEnd, now run under the impersonated user account of the last user of the application, rather than the process identity of the worker process. Previously, if the identity of the process hosting the application had elevated privileges, a malicious user could perform actions that the impersonated user might not have been able to.
SubAuthentication No Longer Installed By Default.	SubAuthentication allows IIS to log on the configured anonymous user account even if IIS did not have the current anonymous user password. This was a security risk, and is disabled by default in IIS 6.0. See Chapter 5 for more information on SubAuthentication.
Constrained Delegation	Constrained Delegation is a new feature in Windows 2003 Server domains, and allows delegated access by IIS 6.0 (on behalf of a user) to remote resources that can be constrained to a single remote service (for example, access to a particular remote SQL server is permitted, but not to any other remote service). See Chapter 5 for more information on enabling delegation.
FTP User Isolation	A new feature exists in the IIS 6.0 FTP server to allow administrators to create home directories for each user underneath the FTP server's root folder, while simultaneously preventing the user from navigating outside his or her own individual directory.

Understanding IIS 6.0 Architecture

IIS 6.0 provides a new processing architecture that differs from previous versions of IIS. While the FTP, NNTP and SMTP services are managed the same way as in previous versions of IIS, the way that web requests are handled is significantly different. To make things a little more complex, two separate processing models are available to handle web requests: worker process isolation mode (the native IIS 6.0 mode), and IIS 5.0 isolation mode (for backward compatibility with web applications that may not work in the new worker process isolation mode, but do work under processing model that is used by IIS 5.0 or earlier).

This section will provide an overview of all the major components of IIS 6.0, and how they tie together. For someone new to IIS, or even someone with a familiarity with the older pre-IIS 6.0 architecture, this can be a little daunting. However a good understanding of the IIS 6.0 components and how they operate will help you troubleshoot errors and ensure that your IIS 6.0 installation is secure.

Services Provided by IIS 6.0

IIS 6.0 provides four Internet servers that can be used to provide services to clients. These are:

- A Web server that is used to handle HyperText Transfer Protocol (HTTP) requests.
- An FTP server that can be used to transfer files to and from the server by users.
- An SMTP server that can be used to deliver mail to remote destinations. Applications on your server and client e-mail applications can use the SMTP server to send mail out. Windows 2003 Server also includes the option of installing a Post Office Protocol v3 (POP3) server, which allows hosting of e-mail mailboxes for users. The POP3 server itself is not managed by IIS.
- An NNTP server that you can use to distribute network news messages to NNTP servers and to NNTP clients (news readers). NNTP provides for the distribution, inquiry, retrieval, and posting of news articles.

To manage these servers, IIS 6.0 uses the following five Windows services (Table 1.5). They can be managed using the **Services Admin Tool**, which you can access by selecting **Start** | **Administrative Tools**. If certain servers are not installed, the corresponding services will not exist.

Table 1.5 Services used by IIS 6.0

Service Name	Description	Service Short Name	Core Component	Host Process
World Wide Web Publishing Service	Delivers Web publishing services.	W3SVC	Iisw3adm.dll	Svchost.exe
File Transfer Protocol	Allows file uploads and downloads from remote systems.	MSFTPSVC	Ftpsvc2.dll	Inetinfo.exe
Simple Mail Transfer Protocol	Sends and receives electronic mail messages (e-mail).	SMTPSVC	Smtpsvc.dll	Inetinfo.exe
Network News Transfer Protocol	Distributes network news messages.	NNTPSVC	Nntpsvc.dll	Inetinfo.exe
IISAdmin Service	Manages the metabase.	IISADMIN	Iisadmin.dll	Inetinfo.exe

We will look at the Web publishing service and the IISAdmin service in more detail later on.

HTTP.SYS Kernel Mode Driver

One of the major IIS 6.0 enhancements over previous IIS versions is the inclusion of a new kernel mode driver (HTTP.SYS), which sits inside the TCP/IP network stack. HTTP.SYS is responsible for handling requests for web resources (both HTTP requests, and Secure Sockets Layer (SSL)-encrypted requests). As each request comes in, HTTP.SYS first determines if the request is valid (for example, whether the request is destined for a website hosted on the server). Next, HTTP.SYS determines whether the request can be served from its own internal cache. If it can't, HTTP.SYS determines which worker process queue it should be placed into for processing. HTTP.SYS uses an internal namespace routing table to determine where to route requests. This routing table is managed by another component – the Web Service Administration and Monitoring (WSAM) component, which we will examine shortly.

HTTP.SYS also performs a number of other functions. It is responsible for writing the text-based web request logs, implementing Quality of Service (QoS) functionality (such as bandwidth throttling, connection limits, and connection timeouts), and for maintaining a kernel mode cache of responses. Future requests may be served out of this kernel mode cache, thus increasing performance because the request does not have to be routed all the way through to a worker process.

HTTP.SYS does not process any user code whatsoever. This makes the Web server much more robust than in previous versions of IIS. If faulty user code does manage to adversely affect a worker process, HTTP.SYS will queue requests for that process until a new process can be started to replace the failed one.

Inetinfo.exe Process and the IISAdmin Service

The Inetinfo.exe process hosts a number of IIS 6.0 components. As in earlier versions of IIS, the non-Web services (SMTP, FTP and NNTP) are run inside Inetinfo, and Inetinfo.exe is responsible for managing the IIS metabase (via the IISAdmin service). The metabase is a hierarchical XML-based repository of almost all of IIS' settings. It exists as two files in %windir%\system32\inetsrv (metabase.xml and mbschema.xml). It may be helpful to think of metabase.xml as the file that stores your IIS server's settings, and mbschema.xml as a master list of all possible configurable options and their possible values. When the IISAdmin service is started, the metabase is read off the hard disk and converted to a high-performance, in-memory binary format using Admin Base Objects (ABO). When changes are made to IIS' settings, the IISAdmin service is responsible for flushing them back to disk. If the physical metabase files are edited directly, the IISAdmin service is responsible for propagating the new settings into the in-memory copy.

So what is different about Inetinfo.exe in IIS 6.0? In previous versions of IIS, Inetinfo.exe was responsible for routing incoming HTTP requests to the process hosting the website in question. This routing functionality is now the responsibility of HTTP.SYS.

Inetinfo.exe also previously hosted the Web publishing service, which is responsible for configuring and managing websites. The Web publishing service has now been separated and lives inside an svchost.exe process instead. We will examine this service shortly.

Another major feature offered by Inetinfo.exe prior to IIS 6.0 was the hosting of *in-process* web applications. These web applications ran inside the Inetinfo.exe process, so IIS did not have to marshal the request across a process boundary to an external process. Running a web application in-process thus offered the highest level of performance, but a faulty application could bring down the Inetinfo.exe process, subsequently crashing the entire IIS server. When using the new IIS 6.0 worker process isolation mode, no web application can run inside the Inetinfo.exe process. Instead, all applications must live inside separate worker processes, ensuring that a faulty application cannot bring down IIS itself, only its own worker process.

Finally, Inetinfo.exe previously hosted all ISAPI filters. ISAPI is a set of APIs that enable developers to extend the functionality of IIS. ISAPI filters can intercept raw HTTP requests prior to any processing by IIS and alter the incoming request (for example, to reroute requests if your website structure has changed). Additionally, they can examine and modify outgoing responses after IIS has finished processing them. A faulty ISAPI filter could, in previous versions of IIS, crash IIS itself. In the new IIS 6.0 worker process mode, ISAPI filters reside in the worker processes as well, ensuring that a faulty ISAPI filter is not capable of crashing the core IIS services. Common ISAPI filters used in IIS 5.0 included URLScan (a security tool from Microsoft), as well as ISAPI filters for SSL and for MD5/Digest authentication. In IIS 6.0, SSL encryption and decryption is now handled by the core Local Security Authority Subsystem (LSASS) process, and MD5 encryption is handled by IIS 6.0.

The World Wide Web (WWW) Publishing Service

The Web publishing service now resides inside its own separate svchost.exe process. Just like the HTTP.SYS component, the Web publishing service does not run any user code when using the new IIS 6.0 worker process isolation mode. Since this service is responsible for monitoring the health of worker processes, the exclusion of user code (which may be unstable or faulty) is a necessary feature. The main component of the Web publishing service is the Web Service Administration and Monitoring component. This component is responsible for:

- **HTTP Administration** The WSAM component interacts with the metabase to determine which web applications are hosted on the machine. It initializes the HTTP.SYS namespace routing table with one entry for each application. HTTP.SYS then uses the routing table data to determine which application pool responds to each incoming request. If a worker process does not already exist to service a request, WSAM is responsible for starting one up to service the incoming request.

- **Worker Process Management** WSAM is responsible for managing worker processes, including starting them and maintaining information about them. WSAM also determines when to recycle a worker process and when to restart a worker process if it becomes blocked and is unable to process any more requests. Finally, WSAM is responsible for invoking rapid fail protection if the application pool that the worker process is serving is continually failing in rapid succession.

Application Processing Modes

As mentioned previously, IIS 6.0 offers two application processing modes: the native IIS 6.0 worker process isolation mode, and the IIS 5.0 isolation mode. Depending on which processing method you choose, the IIS 6.0 processing architecture for web applications varies.

IIS 6.0 Worker Process Isolation Mode

When using IIS 6.0 worker process isolation mode, the administrator defines a set of web application pools. Each web application on the server is assigned to an application pool. An application pool can host multiple web applications, but each web application can be assigned to one web application pool only.

By default, each website created on the server is a single web application; however it is possible to define subsets of a website as additional, separate, web applications. See Chapter 6 for more information on web applications.

Each web application pool is serviced by one or more worker processes. Each worker process is hosted inside a separate instance of w3wp.exe, as shown in Figure 1.1. The Windows security subsystem (LSASS.exe) provides SSL encryption and decryption capabilities.

Figure 1.1 IIS 6.0 Worker Process Isolation Mode

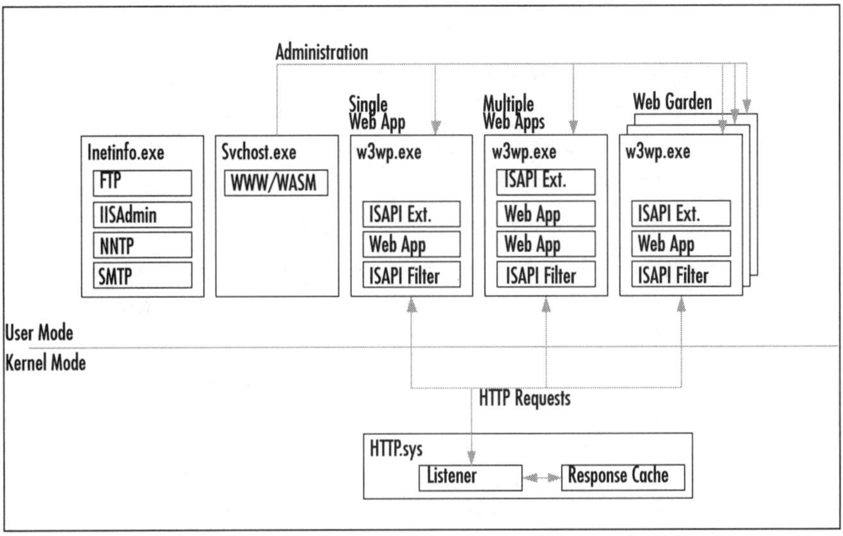

The following are benefits of using worker process isolation mode:

- **Application Isolation** By hosting each web application pool inside a separate worker process, faulty code in one application cannot affect applications hosted inside separate worker processes.

- **Increased Scalability and Performance** Web application pools allow certain performance settings to be applied to a subset of the web applications hosted on the server. For example, each web application pool can be configured to unload itself from memory if no requests are received within a certain timeout period. This allows IIS 6.0 to host many more low traffic websites, since each website does not require dedicated resources continuously. However, if you have some web applications that are high traffic, these can be placed into one web application pool, and the low traffic applications into another.

- **Web Gardens** When more than one w3wp.exe worker process is assigned to a web application pool, this is known as a web garden. Having multiple worker processes allows requests to be served even if all the threads in one of the processes are deadlocked, or are performing long running actions. However, memory is not shared between these processes, so if your application relies on in-memory session state management (such as an ASP application that uses the intrinsic ASP session object), your application will not work as expected.

- **Application Health Monitoring** When using worker process isolation mode, the Web service can detect an unhealthy pool and restart the worker process serving it. The Web service can detect an unhealthy pool when:
    - the worker process quits unexpectedly.
    - all the threads in the process are busy or blocked, and the worker process thus fails to respond to a ping from the Web service.
    - the worker process notifies the Web service that it's unhealthy.

- **Process Recycling** IIS 6.0 can be configured to periodically recycle worker processes, based on time or number of requests served. This can be an overlapped recycle, where a new process is started and begins servicing new requests while the old process is allowed to finish processing existing requests. When the old process is finished, it is shut down. If this doesn't occur within a specified timeout period, IIS 6.0 forcibly terminates the old process.

- **Multiple Application Pools** In IIS 5.0, there is only a single medium isolation pool where multiple web applications could be hosted. All other applications had to be hosted independently of each other in high isolation. Using web application pools allows multiple pools that each can host multiple web applications.

- **Increased Security** Each web application pool's worker process can be configured to run under different user accounts. This can further help isolate web applications from each other by using different user accounts for each pool and then restricting the access to system resources that each account has.

- **Processor Affinity** Processor affinity is an application pool property that forces worker processes to run on a specific set of one of more CPUs. Processor affinity applies to all worker processes that serve a particular application pool and allows you to take advantage of more frequent CPU caching. To set up processor affinity, configure the SMPAffinitized and SMPProcessorAffinityMask metabase properties. See the IIS online help for more information on setting these properties.

REALITY CHECK...

While faulty web application code can no longer bring down the IIS server, this is not necessarily true about the other services that IIS provides. A fault in the FTP, SMTP, or NNTP servers can possibly crash the Inetinfo.exe process. Since Inetinfo.exe also hosts the IISAdmin service that manages the metabase, a failure in Inetinfo.exe will also cause the Web server to fail. The IISAdmin service can be configured via the Services Administrative tool to automatically restart when it has failed.

For mission-critical web applications, it is recommended that a careful analysis of the need for any of the other non-Web servers be undertaken to ensure that these are not running unnecessarily on the IIS server, just in case they bring down the Web server as well.

IIS 5.0 Isolation Mode

IIS 5.0 isolation mode is designed to be used only in cases where an existing web application relies on certain aspects of the IIS 5.0 architecture and is incompatible with the new IIS 6.0 worker process isolation mode. You can find more information on which types of applications are incompatible in the "Upgrading from IIS 5.0" section of Chapter 3.

In IIS 5.0 isolation mode, web applications can run in-process; that is, inside the Inetinfo.exe process, in medium (pooled) isolation inside a dllhost.exe process with other pooled applications (though there can only be one such pool), or in high isolation (in which case the application runs inside a dedicated dllhost.exe process).

Web applications running in-process run as LocalSystem, which means that if malicious attackers can subvert the application, they potentially have full access to the system. Additionally, because in-process applications are running inside the core IIS process (InetInfo.exe), faulty application code can crash the entire IIS server. This is not possible in IIS 6.0 worker process isolation mode because no user code runs inside any of the core IIS processes.

Web applications running in medium (pooled) isolation run inside a single dllhost.exe process that has the IWAM_<machinename> account as its default process identity. All pooled applications are protected from applications running in high isolation, but not from each other. Only a single pooled application, dllhost.exe process can exist on the server.

Web applications running in high isolation run inside dedicated dllhost.exe processes. By default, these processes use the IWAM_<machinename> account as their process identity. All high isolation applications are protected from other applications.

When using IIS 5.0 isolation mode, there is only a single kernel mode request queue. All requests are routed to the Inetinfo.exe process, which then determines where the request should be forwarded. ISAPI filters all run inside Inetinfo.exe (as shown in Figure 1.2).

Figure 1.2 IIS 5.0 Isolation Mode

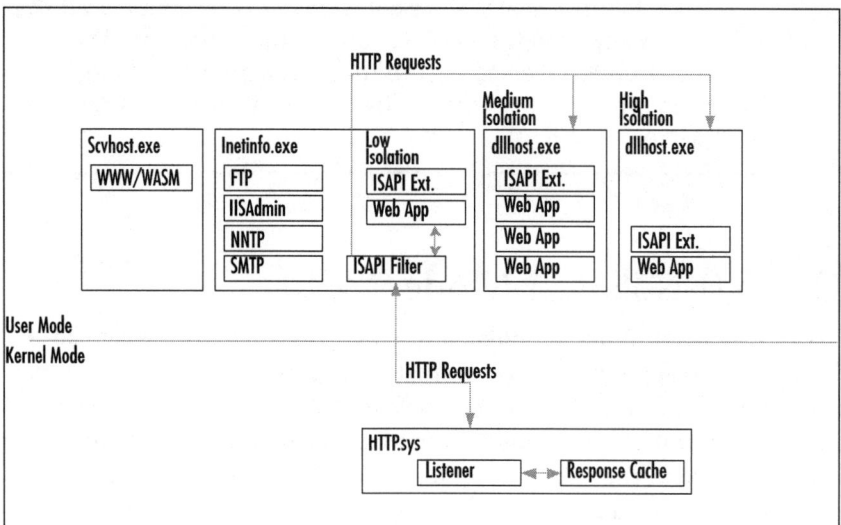

It should be noted that IIS 5.0 isolation mode does not provide many of the new features that IIS 6.0 worker process isolation provides, such as application health monitoring, process recycling and rapid fail protection. As such, IIS 5.0 isolation mode should be used only if required by existing applications. It is not possible to run both application modes simultaneously. If you wish to use IIS 6.0 worker process isolation mode and IIS 5.0 isolation mode, you will need two separate IIS servers.

IIS 6.0 worker process isolation mode is the default mode when performing a new installation. If you are upgrading a Windows 2000 Server running IIS 5.0, then IIS is placed into IIS 5.0 isolation mode by default. For more information on upgrading IIS 5.0 to IIS 6.0 (including switching to worker process mode), see Chapter 3.

Your A** is Covered if You...

- ☑ Are aware of the major reliability improvements in IIS 6.0, including process recycling, application health monitoring, rapid fail protection, and process orphaning.

- ☑ Are aware of the major manageability improvements in IIS 6.0, including the new XML-based metabase, new backup and restore features, and the automatic metabase versioning system.

- ☑ Are aware of the new performance and scalability improvements, including the new HTTP.SYS kernel mode driver, support for web gardens, support for processor affinity, support for persisted ASP templates, and the new kernel mode cache.

- ☑ Are aware of the major security enhancements, including the fact that IIS 6.0 is not installed by default, and when installed it is running in locked-down mode, user code no longer runs inside core IIS processes, unknown MIME types are not served, and web service extensions can be selectively enabled and disabled.

- ☑ Are aware of the major changes to the IIS architecture, including the fact that web applications can no longer be hosted inside Inetinfo.exe, but inside separate worker processes instead. Also, Inetinfo.exe no longer manages websites; rather, the Web publishing service and the WSAM component exist in a separate Svchost.exe and continuously monitor the health of worker processes.

- ☑ Are aware that IIS 6.0 offers a backward-compatible processing architecture that can be used for existing applications that are not compatible with the new processing architecture. However, using the IIS 5.0 process isolation mode incurs a performance penalty, and you lose access to many of the new features available in IIS 6.0.

Chapter 2
Hardening Windows Server 2003

In this Chapter

Before your install, configure and secure Internet Information Services (IIS) 6.0, it is important that the underlying operating system is properly configured in a secure fashion. Though Windows Server 2003 comes with many new built-in security initiatives that are highly integrated with IIS 6.0, there are still different aspects that you will want to consider before you start securing IIS 6.0. It is beyond the scope of this book to cover every area of the rich operating system. However, as you read this chapter, we will also provide you with additional references that will give you further detail and information on what must be done and where you can locate more information to assist you further.

- Get Secure and Stay Secure
- Secure IIS Checklist

By the end of this chapter, you will have a hardened Windows Server 2003 and will have prepared yourself for the next chapter on Installing IIS 6.0. You will get to know more about different areas of the operating system that relate to IIS server. You will equip yourself with knowledge of getting secure and staying secure with Windows Server 2003. Finally, you will have a good overview and roadmap covering the different IIS components in this book.

Get Secure and Stay Secure

The idea of *getting secure* is to make sure you have a secure Windows Server 2003 and a healthy networking environment for your IIS server. It starts with the networking environment and operating system itself, as the networking setup will be the communication channel where requests will be coming in and the operating system will be the base where IIS will on. *Staying secure* is the next step; this will ensure your operating system is always secure after first hardened exercise. In order to have a secure IIS server, you must first ensure that you have hardened Windows Server 2003.

BY THE BOOK...

Microsoft created an initiative called Trustworthy Computing, dedicated to helping to build computing systems that are as reliable, secure, and trustworthy as the infrastructure utilities that we all depend on for daily living. This is a long-term goal; in the shorter term, Microsoft's approach to improving the security of its products is based on four pillars, as defined by Microsoft:

Secure by design Security, privacy, and protection are taken into consideration during design stage.

Secure by default Security, privacy, reliability and configuration settings are optimized in every product.

Secure in deployment Setup and product deployments are defaulted to secure mode. Guidelines, whitepapers and other resources are available to assist customers.

Communication Constantly listening and communicating internally with employees and externally with customers.

Windows Server 2003 family is the first set of operating systems based on these initiatives. Hence, IIS is not installed by default (except on the Web edition); this is taking a proactive stance, where administrators need to manually install the component if it is needed. For more information about Trustworthy Computing, refer to http://www.microsoft.com/mscorp/innovation/twc/.

Although Windows Server 2003 comes with a number of security improvements, there are several areas that you must implement to ensure that a secure operating system is running for IIS 6.0. This book will focus on areas specifically related to IIS services. The context of discussion will be based on securing IIS 6.0 as an Internet Web server. On the subject of getting secure, we will look at the following:

- Networking environment
- Patches and updates
- Windows services
- User accounts and groups
- File system
- Auditing and logging

Next, the subject of staying secure will focus on the security issues within your server and ensuring that it is always updated with latest patches and fixes to prevent any successful attacks via newly discovered exploits.

Networking Environment

Before you deploy a machine into your network, you must ensure that the network is safe and protected, as your server will be connected to different client machines from both inside and outside your local area network. It is recommended that you block access to any newly deployed Windows Server 2003 so that you can first ensure that it is securely configured. You should specifically pay attention to the following areas:

- Router
- Firewall
- Intrusion Detection System

A router can be either a software application or a hardware device that is responsible for forwarding IP packets among connected networks. One example is Cisco, a well-known vendor for hardware-based routers that are in charge of routing both incoming client request packets to your server and outgoing server response packets to a client machine.

A typical router setup will include the access control list (ACL), which controls packet flows between the external and internal networks. The ACL can be configured to block or filter any unwanted traffic to your internal hosts. It is recommended that you configure the ACL to block access to your new Windows Server 2003 machine before it is configured and protected. You can consult your router's vendor setup documentation for details on the ACL configuration. If you do not have a router in your setup, or if you have a managed circuit provided by your Internet Service Provider (ISP), you should always contact ISP support to have it configured.

It is strongly advised that you have a firewall in place to further protect and filter malicious requests to your server. For example, Checkpoint, Microsoft, and Symantec all sell firewalls in their product range. The main responsibility of a firewall is to block access in more complex manner than that provided by ACLs. Firewalls allow you to specifically allow traffic on one or more sets of protocols while blocking others, and it gives you the ability to filter traffic based on well-known or custom port access.

Windows Server 2003 comes with a very basic internal software firewall called the Internet Connection Firewall (ICF). This facility is disabled by default. If you enable it, the firewall can be configured to enable or disable protocol access to IIS. The protocols in question that relate to IIS include Hypertext Transfer Protocol (HTTP) and File Transfer Protocol (FTP). Table 2.1 includes a full list of the ports that relate to IIS services. It is important to note that FTP passive mode ports can be configured in IIS 6.0 (see Chapter 7 for more details). IIS 6.0 will not function correctly if the ICF is enabled and the relevant protocols are disabled. For example, the IIS 6.0 Web server will not function if the HTTP protocol is blocked by ICF.

Table 2.1 IIS Well-Known Ports

Service	Port Number
Hypertext Transfer Protocol (HTTP)	80
HTTP Secure (HTTPS)	443
File Transfer Protocol (FTP) Control Channel	21
FTP Data Channel	20
Simple Mail Transfer Protocol (SMTP)	25
Post Office Protocol v3 (POP3)	110
Network News Transfer Protocol (NNTP)	119
Secure NNTP	563

Microsoft recommends that you use the ICF for small- to medium-sized web project development if you do not have a more sophisticated firewall solution (such as Microsoft Internet Security and Acceleration (ISA) server) deployed. ICF is adequate to protect Internet traffic on most websites. However, large organizations should consider ISA or another heavy-duty firewall product. You do not need to enable the ICF if you have a corporate firewall to protect your Web servers. For more information about configuring ICF, refer to the Windows Server 2003 help documentation. If you are running ISA or third-party firewall product, consult the manufacturer's product documentation.

An intrusion detection system (IDS) is a device or application that is able to detect attack patterns on your network segment. The IDS will pick up traffic and analyze it to determine if a request should be categorized as a symptom of an attack. IDS is normally coupled with firewall products (such as an IDS from CheckPoint). With intrusion detection, your networking environment is actively monitored by the application; it will detect possible attack patterns and identify the source of the attack. This approach is recommended, as intrusion detection not only monitors incoming requests traveling through the network, but it also provides internal network monitoring as well. This can help ensure that you have a healthy network. For more details about configuring IDS, refer to the product documentation.

Combining different networking hardware and software applications will effectively protect your network from being abused by other users. Attacks such as Denial of Service (DoS), IP spoofing and session hijacking are very common in today's interconnected networks. However, it is beyond the scope of this book to cover these topics; for more details about network security, refer to www.microsoft.com/technet/security/guidance/secmod88.mspx.

The following is a list of best security practices when securing your network:

- Filter traffic based on protocols and ports. For example, if you are only supporting web browsing on your IIS server, it is recommended that you only allow HTTP and HTTPS protocol traffic.
- Disable Internet Control Message Protocol (ICMP) requests. By disabling ICMP, attackers will not be able to ping your server, thus minimizing the risk of a ping flood attack.
- Disable NetBIOS over TCP/IP. Disabling NetBIOS over TCP/IP prevents NetBIOS services from using TCP Port 139, thus stopping all NetBIOS sessions.
- Enable logging and audit log files on a routine basis.
- Update and patch devices accordingly.
- Limit physical and remote access to networking equipment.

Patches and Updates

Security fixes, patches, and updates are critical to ensuring that the operation system and IIS are running with the latest components and files. An un-patched server may suffer attacks that target certain known exploits and vulnerabilities. For example, in Windows Server 2000, a buffer overflow condition exists in an unpatched Microsoft Indexing Server, which can result in a hacker executing arbitrary code, resulting in server compromise. It is vital to your keep your system patches up-to-date.

It is recommended that you always test patches and updates on a test machines before you deploy them on live production machines, as they may themselves contain flaws that could adversely affect your applications and other components. The first step in patching your operating system is to determine which patches and fixes are needed for your server (you must therefore be aware of which components and services are running on your operating system). For example, if you are not running Microsoft SQL server, there is no need to deploy any updates or service packs related to that product. After determining your system's needs, download the patches from a trusted source, typically from Microsoft's website, then test the updated files on a test server before rolling it out to your production machines.

The following list includes the IIS-related components that you should especially be aware of:

- **Core operating system patches, updates, and service packs.** These are especially important, as IIS is highly integrated with Windows Server 2003, so any attacks at the operating system level could bring down the entire Web server.

- **Microsoft Data Access Component (MDAC).** Typically, this component is used as part of your web application to access different data sources and database servers. Windows Server 2003 is shipped with the latest MDAC version (currently version 2.8).

- **Windows Scripting engine.** The scripting engine includes Microsoft VBScript and JScript and is used by Active Server Pages (ASP) written in either of these two languages. Windows Server 2003 is shipped with latest Windows Scripting engine (currently version 5.6).

- **The .NET framework related to the .NET application being hosted on your IIS server.** Updates to this component typically relate to Common Language Runtime (CLR) and .NET framework class libraries. Windows Server 2003 ships with the latest .NET framework (currently version 1.1).

If you are running other applications, such as Microsoft Exchange and Microsoft SQL Server, you need to make sure that all related patches and updates of the products have been updated as well, as vulnerabilities in one of these components may eventually allow attackers to take over the entire server. It is vital to have the most up-to-date information about patches and security fixes. There are few ways to stay current about patch information:

- **Security Bulletins** To get the latest information about the Microsoft operating system and other products, you can visit www.microsoft.com/security/. You can also sign up to receive security bulletin alerts via e-mail at www.microsoft.com/security/security_bulletins/alerts.asp. You will receive notification via e-mail when Microsoft releases a new security bulletin. From the bulletin, you will get more technical information about the patch or update, as well as information about which products will be affected by the patch or update.

- **Windows Automatic Updates** This is an application that keeps your server up-to-date with latest patches and enhancements. There is no need for you to search for patch information, as the application will auto-detect the applications installed on your server and download related patches for you. It is recommended that you turn off automatic installation of this update service, as you might want to test out the new patches before you actually deploy them on live production boxes. However, you should enable Windows automatic update to notify you when there is new update available. For more information about Windows automatic updates, refer to the Windows Server 2003 help documentation.

- **Windows Updates** This is similar to an automatic update, except that you will have to visit http://windowsupdate.microsoft.com/. When you browse this site, your computer will be remotely scanned to determine if any related patches or updates are needed, based on the configured application and components running in your machine. You will then be prompted to install related patches. For more information about Windows updates, visit the Windows update website. It is important to note that some applications, such as Microsoft Office, are not detectable via Windows updates or automatic updates. For patches related to Microsoft Office products, visit http://office.microsoft.com/officeupdate/.

- **Microsoft Baseline Security Analyzer (MBSA)** This is an application that is able to detect patches or updates that are not currently installed on your server. It detects missing patches and prompts you for a course of action. One major advantage with MBSA is that it allows you to remotely scan any client computers in your network. It also checks for other security settings, such as the number of administrator accounts, weak password, and more. For more information about MBSA, visit www.microsoft.com/mbsa/.

It is vital for you to remember that patches and updates do not pertain only to the server(s) on your network; rather, they apply to every single machine and hardware device (such as firewalls, routers, and hubs) on your network.

The following is a list of best security practices relating to patches and updates:

- Stay current with patch and update information.

- Only download patch files from trusted sources, for example, Microsoft.com.

- Do not accept any e-mail updates. Always verify the integrity and credibility of these updates before using them.

- Always test patches and updates before deploying them on production machines.

- Understand the details about the products affected by a patch and what changes a patch will make to your system(s).

Windows Services

Windows services are applications that run in the background providing continuous functionality or features to the operating system, or applications running on the server. Some of these services are core services, such as Remote Procedure Call (RPC), which provides an RPC endpoint interface for many operating system functions. By disabling unwanted services, you can reduce the attack surface of the server.

To enable or disable particular services, select **Start | Administrative Tools | Services**. In Services tool window, click on a service's name to read its description. You can restart, stop and change the startup type of the service. Service startup type can be one of the following:

- **Automatic** The service automatically starts when the operating system starts.

- **Manual** The service is not started when the operating system starts. It can be started by administrators and applications.

- **Disabled** The service is completely disabled. It cannot be started until the startup type is changed to Automatic or Manual.

It is recommended that you disable all unnecessary services running in the operating system to make it a more secure server. For example, if you do not need a configured local or shared printer in the server, you should disable the Print Spooler service.

In chapter 3, you will see a more detailed discussion on IIS components, and you will be able to determine which components to install based on your requirements. For example, if IIS server is only being used to host ASP.NET applications, but not Active Server Pages (ASP), you should install the ASP.NET component, but not the ASP component. The following is a list of best security practices when configuring Windows services:

- Do not install unneeded components and services.
- Disable unnecessary Windows services.
- Do not install additional third-party applications if they are not needed.

User Accounts and Groups

Windows user accounts require that users provide a unique user ID in order to access server resources. User credentials are sensitive and must be kept confidential to avoid illegal or unwanted access to your network. It is recommended that you implement a strong password policy to avoid any weak passwords being disclosed under brute force or dictionary attacks.

One of the first tasks you will perform after you set up the operating system is to rename the Administrator account. This account is subject to malicious abuse by attackers, who can gain full control of the system by renaming the original local Administrator account and creating a new 'shell' administrator account. It is recommended that you assign a strong password to the original administrator account and audit logon events for the shell administrator account; auditing logon events allows you to track suspicious attempts to log on using the fake administrator account.

For easier user administration, it is suggested that you group related users into groups. For example, if you have four system administrators in charge of a system backup, you can group the four system administrators into a single "Backup Operator" group. The following is a list of best security practices for user accounts and groups. For more information about how to implement these changes, refer to the Windows Server 2003 help documentation:

- Remove unused accounts.
- Disable temporary accounts when an account has to be deactivated for a while.
- Disable guest accounts.
- Rename the Administrator account.
- Enforce strong password policies.
- Implement account lockouts.
- Log on to the system with fewer privileges.
- Disable null session logons.

File System

To enable file-level security, it is recommended that you format each operating system partition using the NT file system (NTFS) format. This will allow full access control at the folder and/or file levels. File-level security is the last level of access control before a request is fulfilled by the operating system.

The server applies file-level security in the following ways:

- **Network File Share** When a user accesses a remote file via a network file share, the OS first checks to see whether the user has appropriate share permissions. Possible share permissions are *full control, change* and *read access*. Alternatively, a user can be explicitly denied access to a resource. If the user has an appropriate share permission, then NTFS File and Folder permissions are checked. If any of these checks fail, the request will be rejected. When there is conflict in permission settings, the most restrictive permissions are applied. For example, if a user has full control over a network share, but only has read permissions on a targeted file, the effective user permissions for the file will be read only.

- **IIS Request** First, IIS checks the requesting client's IP address. If that IP address is allowed access, IIS will determine if the anonymous access for the content is allowed. After that, IIS checks against the configured web permissions and then, finally, the NTFS permissions. If any of these checks fail, an access-related error message will be returned to the client. Again, the most restrictive permissions are applied for this type of request. For example, if the web permission is configured as read, but the NTFS permissions is configured as deny read, the request will be rejected. For more information about access control in IIS, refer to Chapter 4.

File system access control is the most powerful control setting that is available for you to limit and control access to resources. It is recommended that you configure proper NTFS permissions to secure your operating system and sensitive data. For easier administration, it is suggested that you group related file types and resources into a single folder and further customize NTFS permissions on the folder and file levels.

The system registry is the repository for many critical system settings. It is recommended that you disabled remote registry access to protect the configuration from being modified remotely. By default, only the administrators group and backup operators can remotely access the system registry. To disable remote registry access, disable the Remote Registry service.

Next, to further ensure that you have a clean file system, you can deploy an antivirus solution to ensure that your operating system is virus-free. Viruses can harm your system in many ways, by either completely bringing down your server, or causing permanent loss of your valuable data. It is recommended that you have at least one antivirus solution installed on your operating system. Antivirus vendors such as Symantec and McAfee are well-known third-party antivirus manufacturer that offer a range of antivirus products to suit different organizational needs. It is important to note that you must always keep the virus definition file up to date; this will allow the antivirus applications to detect the latest virus and worms, which are developed and released everyday. For more information on updating virus data definition files, consult the vendor's product documentation.

The following is a list of best file system security practices:

- Use NTFS format for disk partitions; this will enable you to configure file-level security.

- Group related files into one folder and configure strong NTFS permissions.

- Restrict the Everyone group's access and configure specific users or user groups to control resource access.

- Always grant minimum permissions. Do not grant full control to any non-system user; always grant minimum permissions to users and user groups. Grant permissions on an as-needed basis.

- Deny write access permission for IIS anonymous users; this will prevent anonymous user from uploading malicious scripts. If write permission is required, grant it at the minimum file or folder level.

- Restrict access to system command line tools. By default, in IIS 6.0, anonymous users do not have access to system command line tools such as cmd.exe. If you are customizing your own anonymous users, ensure that they do not have access to such tools. You can apply this restriction by applying the deny read access for the user accounts.

- Do not install any sample files on a production machine.

- Remove unnecessary network shares.

- Deploy an antivirus solution.

Auditing and Logging

Logging keeps track of access activity on your server, while auditing allows you to understand and detect any unusual activity related to each access. While auditing and logging do not provide you with a way to prevent attacks or unauthorized access to your system, they do provide valuable information about the access activity on your server. They can provide you with details such as when, where, and how the access occurred and whether the request was successfully processed or rejected by the server.

In addition to the server and its components, it is recommended that you also enable logging for every component and hardware device on your network. These include router access, firewall policy, IDS, and others. However, it is important to note that by enabling logging on these devices, you will create additional traffic that may prove to be a burden to your network environment. Therefore, you should only log important traffic based on a request or protocol type. Log files are vital to trace the tracks left by attackers; by combining different log files you can obtain more information about particular attacks. Log files can help in troubleshooting access errors as well. For example, when determining at what level a request was dropped before reaching the IIS server, you can check the router and firewall log file to investigate whether the request was dropped at that level and identify why the request was blocked.

It is recommended that you secure and protect these log files, as attackers may try to delete logs in an effort to erase their tracks. Auditing log files routinely enables you to detect intrusion or attack patterns. Based on this information, you can take the next course of action to deal with the attacks. For example, if you notice continuous buffer-overflow attacks from a particular IP address, you can block access to that IP address using the IP restriction features in IIS, or by implementing firewall-level filtering.

The following outlines different log sources to which you should pay particular attention:

- **Event Viewer** Event viewer records related service events in IIS and Windows operating systems. These events can be logged in three major categories: system, security, and application.

- **IIS Site Activity** Logging site activities helps you to keep track of client access requests. This type of log provides you with details about who, when, where, and how contents are being accessed. Information that can be logged includes the visitor's IP address, the user account accessing the contents, a timestamp of when requests were made, the server status reply to the request, the requested resource location, the amount of bytes used in the request, and more.

- **HTTP API Error** HTTP Application Programming Interface (API) error logs are generated by HTTP.SYS. This new kernel-mode driver handles HTTP requests and routes them to the related application pool. Errors occurring in this driver will trigger a log entry in the HTTP API error logs.

- **URLScan** This is an Internet Server API (ISAPI) filter that can be installed in IIS 6.0. URLScan monitors incoming HTTP requests based on a set of rules. If requests do not comply with the URLScan rule sets, IIS replies with a "404 File Not Found" error to the client and writes an entry in the URLScan log file More information on URLScan can be found in Chapter 5.

The following is a list of best security practices when configuring auditing and logging. For more details on configuring auditing, refer to the Windows Server 2003 help documentation:

- Enable auditing for failed logon attempts.
- Enable IIS site activity logging.

- Relocate the default IIS log file and secure it with proper NTFS permissions.
- Backup and archive old log files.
- Enable auditing for failed access to important system files.
- Audit log files on a routine basis.

Staying Secure

Staying secure is the next task after securing the operating system. This is important, as attack patterns can range from known exploits to newly discovered vulnerabilities. It is important to keep every single component in the operating system secure, as a successful attack on the server can eventually damage it, or worse, create access channels (commonly known as *back doors*), which allow attackers to gain full control of your server.

To help you keep your server secure, use the following:

- **Auditing** Establish log file auditing procedures to check and review different log sources. An external IT audit done by an expert may help to uncover additional aspects that you may have overlooked.
- **Security Updates** Always stay current with latest security update information. Subscribe to security notifications via e-mail from Microsoft or other major security mail listings.
- **Security Assessment** Review your current setup and requirements from time to time to determine if you have to modify any security-related configurations.

> **REALITY CHECK...**
>
> Ensure that you start off with the best practice guidelines provided to secure your server. Follow up by staying secure to properly protect your server. A secure server provides a protected foundation to host IIS applications; it is recommended that you follow every procedure in this section to have a secure web server.
>
> For more details about securing Windows Server 2003, you can download the Windows Server 2003 Security Guide from www.microsoft.com/downloads/details.aspx?FamilyId=8A2643C1-0685-4D89-B655-521EA6C7B4DB.

Secure IIS Checklist

Once you have hardened your Windows Server 2003 operating system, the next step will be deploying IIS correctly. We will talk about installing IIS 6.0 in greater detail in Chapter 3; this section will entail a brief checklist that you should follow when securing IIS 6.0.

> **BY THE BOOK...**
>
> IIS is one of the most popular solutions for private and commercial Web servers on the Internet today. Because of its popularity, and the overall prevalence of Windows-based machines on the Internet, IIS has become a favorite target of hackers and virus/worm authors. One of the major goals of Microsoft's Secure Computing Initiative was to improve the security of Microsoft software in three areas: by default, by design, and by deployment. IIS 6.0, the version of the Web server software that's bundled with Windows Server 2003, is one of the first major services to reflect this initiative. As opposed to previous releases of the server operating system where IIS was turned on by default, an administrator now needs to install and enable IIS on a Windows Server 2003 machine, and manually enable support for technologies such as ASP and the Network News Transfer Protocol (NNTP).

Microsoft recommends using the following checklist when securing the IIS server:

1. **Patches and Updates** Focus on staying secure to ensure the operating system and its components have the most up-to-date patches to prevent any known exploits.

2. **IIS Lockdown** To be more specific, running URLScan in IIS 6.0. Understand the differences between built-in and URLScan filters. See chapter 5 for more information.

3. **Services** Minimize component installation based on requirements and disable unwanted services.

4. **Protocols** It is recommended that your remove unused component in IIS.

5. **Accounts** It is important that you be aware of how user accounts are related to IIS services, as well as the risks of having many administrator accounts on one server.

6. **Files and Directories** This relates to file system format and the best practices for configuring NTFS permissions.
7. **Shares** Focus on network shares consideration and planning. It is recommended that you remove unused network resources.
8. **Ports** This is related to port communication between client and server and networking detail to secure communication.
9. **Registry** The system registry holds configuration information for the operating system, as well as IIS-related settings. It is recommended that you disable remote registry access.
10. **Auditing and Logging** This refers to enabling different types of log files and developing routine procedures to analyze and detect intrusion or attacks patterns.
11. **Site and Virtual Directories** Involved moving of site content directory to non system partition, configuring site permissions and as well as authentication methods. See chapter 4, 5(Web), 7(FTP), 8(SMTP and POP3), 9(NNTP), 10(Certificate Services), 11(FrontPage) and 12(Internet Printing).
12. **Script Mappings** Concerning web service extensions and removing unwanted scripting engine mapping. See chapter 4.
13. **ISAPI Filters** Remove unnecessary Internet Server Application Programming Interface (ISAPI) filters.
14. **IIS Metabase** The metabase file holds vital information for every IIS component. It is recommended that you restrict access to the metabase file. Additional information on the IIS Metabase can be found at www.syngress.com/solutions.
15. **Server Certificates** Focus on digital certificate issues.
16. **Machine.config** This pertains to the configuration settings for .NET framework applications. It involves removing unused HttpModules, protecting resource access with HttpForbiddenHandler, and more. For more information on securing ASP.NET application, refer to http://msdn.microsoft.com/library/en-us/secmod/html/secmod92.asp.
17. **Code Access Security** Control code access security using the security.config file. Remove access permissions from both local intranet and Internet zones. Fore more detail information on code access security, refer to http://msdn.microsoft.com/library/en-us/secmod/html/secmod82.asp.

It is recommended that you follow this checklist when securing IIS server. It is important for you to know what needs to be done and why;

it is not wise to disable services or components before you analyze your needs and requirements. For additional checklist items, refer to http://msdn.microsoft.com/library/en-us/secmod/html/secmod104.asp.

> **REALITY CHECK...**
>
> Before you connect an IIS server to the Internet, you need to ensure that it is fully hardened. This includes securing the operating system, securing other application running on the same machine, and finally, securing IIS itself.
>
> It is important that you follow each checklist item outlined in this section and study your needs carefully before performing any actual configuration. Always have a system backup before introducing any major changes; it is recommended that you have a test machine to test your security changes before you modify the production machine.
>
> Finally, web application testing and code verification is very important. Having unverified application codes running on a secure IIS server is equal to having a non-secure IIS server. Techniques such as SQL injection allow attacks to execute remote queries by submitting requests for non-validated web forms. For more information on writing secure code, refer to http://msdn.microsoft.com/security/securecode/default.aspx.

A Final Word on Security

There is no such thing as the perfectly secure system, only systems that are more secure than others. As a system becomes more resistant to attack, it generally becomes harder to use. An ultra-secure system might not be connected to any network (requiring you to bring your work in on floppy disk), in a secured room, where only one person can use it at a time. Compare that to the ease-of-use of the average office desktop system. Because of this security/usability tradeoff, many experts say that security is about *managing risk*. Since you can spend almost limitless amounts of money, and place innumerable hurdles in the way of attackers, it is not practical (or affordable) to build the ultimate secure system. Instead, you need to evaluate the risks that you face, the likelihood of each risk, the cost if one of those risks eventuates, and develop cost-effective strategies to ameliorate each risk.

Knowing the Enemy and What They Want

In determining the security risks you face, you should keep in mind that attackers can be internal or external and inasmuch, present different threats. The greatest difference between an outsider and an insider is the motive. An outsider may be looking to deface a site for fame, gather credit card numbers, get free software or services, or perhaps build a cache of high-bandwidth boxes for launching other attacks. The insider, on the other hand, may be engaged in corporate espionage, gathering information for insider stock trading, or, if leaving the company, copying proprietary source code or customer lists. But insider attacks are not always outright malicious. An insider may just be snooping around to read a supervisor's e-mail or see what others get paid. Although certainly not any less significant, the attacker's motivation in that case would likely be more of curiosity than criminal intent.

It is also important to know what attackers don't want. An internal attacker is unlikely to try and launch a Denial of Service attack against your server, or deface your corporate Intranet homepage. On the other hand, an external attacker is unlikely to expend a significant amount of effort breaking in just to snoop on everyday email. As such, your security measures internally and externally, need to reflect the types of threats that each group of attacker is likely to pose. While this book can tell you the various configuration options you have for securing your IIS installation, you will need to make the final decisions on which settings are best for you.

Your A** is Covered if You…

- ☑ Get secure by hardening Windows Server 2003.
- ☑ Stay secure by ensuring the operating system and installed components contain up-to-date patches.
- ☑ Have a good understanding of each best security practice outlined in this chapter.
- ☑ Have a good understanding of each IIS security checklist item.
- ☑ Understand the importance of writing secure code.

Chapter 3

Installing Internet Information Services (IIS) 6.0

In this Chapter

Windows Server 2003 is the first major platform released by Microsoft to implement the "secure by design, secure by default, secure in deployment" paradigm. Unlike previous versions of Microsoft Windows, where a lot of options were installed by default, Windows 2003 requires the administrator to deliberately install and enable many services, including Internet Information Services (IIS). The exception to this is the new Windows 2003 Server Web Edition, which installs some IIS components by default. There are a number of ways to install the various components of IIS 6.0.

- Installing IIS 6.0 Using the Configure Your Server Wizard
- Installing or Modifying IIS 6.0 Using the Add/Remove Programs Control Panel
- Installing IIS Using an Automated Installation (Unattended Setup)
- Upgrading IIS 5.0 to IIS 6.0
- Locating the Administrative Tools

By the end of this chapter, you should be aware of the components that make up IIS and what each component is used for, which components are installed as part of the Application Server and Mail Server roles, and how to modify, add, or remove components as required. Finally, you should be aware of the location of the various administrative tools used to manage IIS and its related services.

Installing IIS 6.0 Using the Configure Your Server Wizard

Windows Server 2003 provides a *Configure Your Server* wizard that can be used to quickly configure your server to perform one or more roles. Configuring your server to perform a role installs and configures the necessary components for the server to provide those services. Roles include *File Server, Domain Controller* and *DHCP Server*. Overall, there are 11 preconfigured roles included in the *Configure Your Server* wizard. The exception to this is Windows Server 2003 Web Edition, which does not have this wizard, as it is designed primarily to be a Web Server.

The *Configure your Server* wizard is loaded from the *Manage Your Server* tool. This loads automatically when you logon to a Windows 2003 Server, and can also be found in the **Administrative Tools** program group in the **Start** menu.

> **BY THE BOOK...**
>
> Configuring your server to perform a defined role installs a necessary minimum set of common components to allow the server to perform functions related to that role. For example, configuring your server as a Domain Controller installs Active Directory and the Microsoft DNS Server.
>
> We will use the wizard to configure the server to perform the Application Server role, which includes the minimum components required to run IIS.

To configure the Application Server role, perform the following steps:

1. If the *Manage Your Server* tool is not already displayed on the screen, launch it by selecting **Start | Program Files | Administrative Tools | Manage Your Server** (see Figure 3.1).

Figure 3.1 The *Manage Your Server* Administrative Tool

2. Click **Add or remove a role**.
3. Check that your server meets all the requirements on the **Preliminary Steps** page and click **Next**.
4. Select **Custom Configuration** and click **Next**.
5. Select **Application Server** from the list of available roles and click **Next** (see Figure 3.2).

Figure 3.2 Selecting the *Application Server* Role

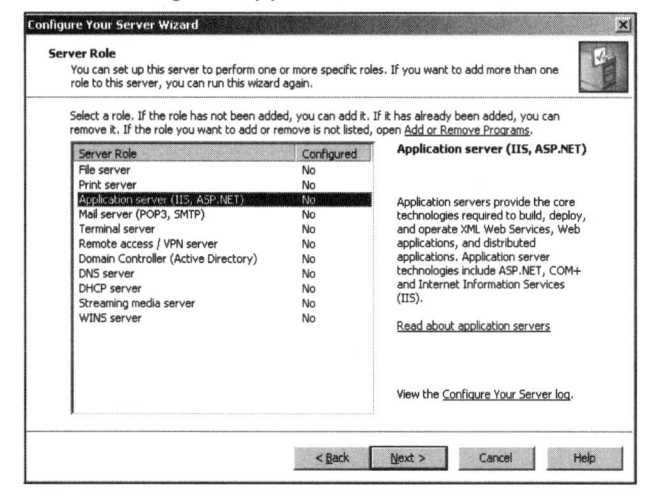

6. You now have the option to install the Frontpage Server Extensions (FPSE) and/or enable ASP.NET. These components will be explained in the next section. Do not do install either at the moment; click **Next**.

7. Review the list of items to be configured on the **Summary of Selections** screen and click **Next**. Windows will now copy files from your installation media, and configure IIS.

This process installs the minimum components to have IIS functional, plus some administrative tools. These components are:

- The IIS core files (including the IISAdmin service).
- The World Wide Web Publishing service.
- A default website, located in c:\inetpub\wwwroot\ (where c:\ is the drive containing Windows).
- The IIS Manager (a Microsoft Management Console (MMC) snap-in for managing core IIS services)
- The Application Server Manager (another MMC snap-in, which includes the IIS Manager, plus snap-ins for Component Services and .Net Framework Configuration). You can run this MMC snap-in by selecting **Start** | **Run** and typing **appsrv.msc**.
- ISAPI (Internet Server Application Program Interface) extensions including Active Server Pages (ASP via asp.dll), Server Side Includes (via ssinc.dll) and the Internet Data Connector (IDC via htppodbc.dll) are installed, but not enabled.
- Network COM+ and Distributed Transaction Coordinator (DTC) access is enabled to allow your server to host COM+ objects that may be used in a distributed application, and to allow the DTC to manage distributed transactions.

Note that if you are using Windows 2003 Server Web Edition, the following components are automatically installed as part of a default installation:

- The IIS Service core files, the World Wide Publishing Service, and default website mentioned in the previous list.
- An administration website that can be used to administer IIS. A shortcut to this website is placed in the Administrative Tools folder

- The Simple Mail Transfer Protocol (SMTP) service (for delivering mail).
- The ASP ISAPI extension is installed and enabled (ASP support is required for the Administration website to function).
- Other ISAPI extensions, including SSI and IDC are installed, but not enabled.
- Network COM+ access is enabled to allow your server to host COM+ objects that may be used in a distributed application.

Notes from the Underground...

Disabling or deleting the Default Web Site

With previous versions of IIS, a common recommendation was to disable or delete the default website, due to the number of pertinent security threats. With the new locked-down default installation of IIS 6.0, this is no longer required.

We would recommend against deleting the default website, since a number of add-on products actively look for the default website during installation, and may fail if the default website does not exist (for example, Microsoft's SQL Server Reporting Services). If you delete the default website, you can recreate it by creating a new website named Default Web Site. You may also need to set the website identifier to 1 by editing the IIS Metabase. The IIS Metabase is examined in Chapter 1.

If you would like to configure your server as a mail server, you can rerun the *Configure Your Server* wizard to add the Mail Server role, which installs the Post Office Protocol 3 (POP3) service, the SMTP service, and the POP3 administration tools (the SMTP service is administered through the IIS Manager that was previously installed). If you prefer to install the SMTP service only (for example, to allow your web applications to send mail out), then use the steps in the following section.

Installing or Modifying IIS 6.0 Using the Add/Remove Programs Control Panel

Unlike the *Configure Your Server* wizard, which installs a set of components depending on the role you have selected, the *Add/Remove Programs* Control Panel allows you to add or remove individual components (as shown in Figure 3.3). To change the installed components of your server, select **Start | Control Panel | Add/Remove Programs | Windows Components**. The IIS components are located under the option titled **Application Server**. Click the **Details** button at any time to see which subcomponents are available for the selected component.

Figure 3.3 Windows Components Wizard

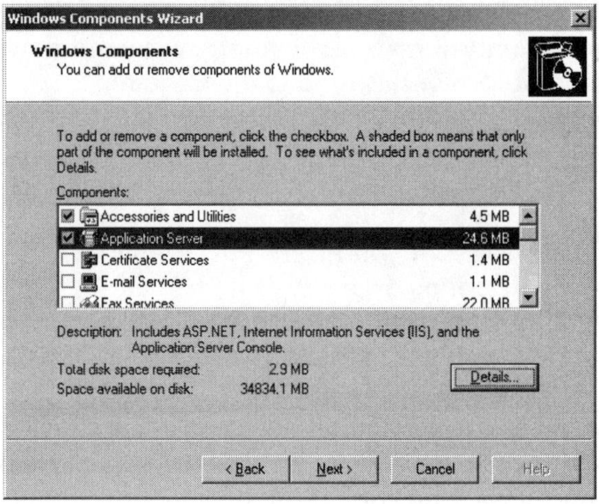

The following components, shown in Table 3.1, are available for IIS.

Table 3.1 Hierarchy of Components in the Control Panel

Component	Sub-Component	Description
Application Server Console		A saved MMC that contains a number of snap-ins for managing IIS functions. The snap-ins include the IIS Manager, .Net v1.1 Configuration, and Component Services configuration. You can load the Application Server Console by typing selecting **Start**	**Run** and typing **appsrv.msc**
ASP.NET		Configures appropriate handlers in IIS to allow processing of ASP.NET-related files such as ASPX pages, web handlers and modules and .Net based web-services. Installing this component also enables ASP.NET web service extension processing (see Chapter 4).
Enable network COM+ access		Enables your server to host COM+ components that are part of a distributed application.
Enable network DTC access		Enables the Distributed Transaction Coordinator to manage network transactions. If an application running under IIS enlists a transaction that spans multiple computers, then this feature allows the DTC to manage this transaction.
Message Queuing		Installs the Message Queuing service, which supports guaranteed messaging between applications.
Internet Information Services	BITS (Background Intelligent Transfer Service) Server Extensions	Enables support for throttling and restarting data transfers. The BITS server extensions allow the BITS service on a client operating system (OS) such as Windows XP to upload or download files using Hypertext Transfer Protocol (HTTP). BITS supports the ability to resume interrupted file transfers, and to transfer files in the background even if the calling application has exited. After installing the BITS Server Extensions, you can configure it using the IIS Manager on a website or virtual directory. For more information on BITS visit the library at msdn.microsoft.com.

Continued

Table 3.1 Hierarchy of Components in the Control Panel

Component	Sub-Component	Description
Internet Information Services	Common Files	Core IIS files, including the IISAdmin service.
Internet Information Services	File Transfer Protocol (FTP) Service	Adds support for an FTP Server, commonly used to upload and download files.
Internet Information Services	Frontpage 2002 Server Extensions	Enables authoring and administration of websites using FPSE-compatible clients such as Microsoft Frontpage, Microsoft Visual Studio.Net and Microsoft Visual Interdev. You can administer your server's FPSE by using the **Microsoft Sharepoint Administrator** shortcut that is placed in the **Administrative Tools** folder.
Internet Information Services	IIS Manager	An MMC console that allows administration of IIS services. The IIS MMC snap-in is also added to the **Computer Management** console, which can be accessed from the **Administrative Tools** folder, or by right-clicking **My Computer**, selecting **Manage** and expanding the **Services and Applications** node.
Internet Information Services	Internet Printing	Enables printer management and printing over HTTP.
Internet Information Services	NNTP Services	Adds support for a Network News Transfer Protocol (NNTP) server, which can be used to host newsgroups.
Internet Information Services	SMTP Services	Adds support for an SMTP server, used to deliver mail. Windows 2003 Server also provides a basic POP3 server, which you can add by selecting **Email Services**.

Continued

Table 3.1 Hierarchy of Components in the Control Panel

Component	Sub-Component	Description
World Wide Web Service	Active Server Pages	Enables the ASP web service extension. The ASP files are always installed (asp.dll). Selecting this option is the same as enabling the ASP Web Service Extension via the IIS Manager (see Chapter 4). ASP is an older technology, first introduced with IIS 3.0, and has now been superseded by ASP.NET.
World Wide Web Service	Internet Data Connector	Enables the IDC web service extension. The IDC web service extension is seldom used now, but is included for backward compatibility. IDC files (httpodbc.dll) are always installed. Selecting this option is the same as enabling the IDC web service extension via the IIS Manager (see Chapter 4).
World Wide Web Service	Remote Administration (HTML)	Provides a web-based method of administering IIS. Using the Remote Administration website requires the ASP web service extension to be enabled.
World Wide Web Service	Remote Desktop Web Connection	Provides a web page with a hosted ActiveX control that can be used to connect to the server's Remote Desktop service (known as Terminal Services Admin mode in Windows 2000). Clients without the Remote Desktop Client installed can use the remote desktop web connection instead. Remote Desktop allows the server to be interactively controlled from a remote machine as if the user was sitting at the server console. Accessing this functionality requires the Remote Desktop client (installed by default on Windows XP).
World Wide Web Service	Server Side Includes	Enables the Server Side Includes (SSI) web service extension. SSI files (ssinc.dll) are always installed. Selecting this option is the same as enabling the SSI web service extension in the IIS Manager (see Chapter 4).

Continued

Table 3.1 Hierarchy of Components in the Control Panel

Component	Sub-Component	Description
World Wide Web Service	WebDav Publishing	Enables the WebDev Publishing web service extension. WebDav Publishing files (httpext.dll) are always installed. Selecting this option is the same as enabling the WebDev Publishing web service extension in the IIS Manager (see Chapter 4).
World Wide Web Service	World Wide Web Service	The core World Wide Web (WWW) Service files.

Note that Windows 2003 Server introduces a new POP3 server. A POP3 server is used to host mailboxes for individual users. The counterpart to POP3 is SMTP, which is used to deliver mail to the POP3 mailboxes. The SMTP service is part of IIS, even though the POP3 service is listed separately under **Email Services**. Installing the POP3 service also installs and enables the IIS SMTP service.

REALITY CHECK…

While Microsoft has made great strides in fixing the number of security vulnerabilities in IIS (compared to its predecessors), it is a cardinal rule of security that you should try to minimize the *attack surface* of your server. In short, this means you should only install those services that you actually need, rather than installing every service. By restricting what is running on your server, you reduce the number of potential vulnerability points that can be exploited by an attacker.

Installing IIS 6.0 Using Automated Installation (Unattended Setup)

Automated installations offer faster, less expensive and more consistent installations than manual installations performed by operators. Windows 2003 Server offers three methods of automated installation:

- Unattended installations
- Installations using RIS (Remote Installation Service)
- Installations using SysPrep

The most common of these three is the unattended installation. We will look at installing IIS 6.0 as part of an unattended installation.

For information on all three methods of installation, the Windows 2003 Server Deployment Guide provides a comprehensive coverage of the design, test and deployment process for automated installations: www.microsoft.com/resources/documentation/WindowsServ/2003/all/deployguide/en-us/Default.asp?url=/resources/documentation/WindowsServ/2003/all/deployguide/en-us/ACIBB_OV_OVERVIEW.asp

> **BY THE BOOK...**
>
> IIS 6.0 is not installed by default when you install the Microsoft Windows Server 2003 operating system. To simplify the setup process on multiple computers, you can set up IIS 6.0 while the server is unattended. To do so, you can either create and use an answer file to install IIS 6.0 at the same time that you install Windows Server 2003, or you can perform an unattended installation of IIS 6.0 after you install Windows Server 2003.

Installing IIS 6.0 During the Windows 2003 Server Setup

An unattended installation of IIS during Windows 2003 Server setup requires ONE of the following:

- A distribution point (usually a network share) and an answer file that contains answers to questions that would normally be presented to the user during setup.

- Bootable original installation media (usually a CD), and a special winnt.sif answer file located on a floppy disk. When booting from CD, setup will check for the presence of a floppy disk containing a winnt.sif file, and use the information in that file to answer questions usually presented to the user during setup. This method can only be used to install a new copy of Windows 2003 Server, not to upgrade an existing version of Windows.

The Windows 2003 Server CD contains a sample answer file (unattend.txt) located in the \i386 folder. Additionally, a Graphical User Interface (GUI) tool (setupmgr.exe) that can generate an answer file based on user-supplied details is located in \support\tools\deploy.cab.

To use the answer file in a 16-bit environment (for example, MS-DOS), start the Windows 2003 Server setup by entering the following:

`winnt.exe /unattend:<answerfilename> /s:<InstallSource>`

To use the answer file in a 32-bit environment (for example, if you are upgrading an existing Windows NT or Windows 2000 installation), start the Windows 2003 Server setup by entering the following:

`winnt32.exe /unattend:<answerfiename> /s:<InstallSource>`

For more information on preparing the installation source, consult the deployment help file (Deploy.chm) located in \support\tools\deploy.cab on the Windows 2003 Server CD and in the Windows Deployment Guide.

In the answer file, you will need to add entries in the **[Components]** section to specify which IIS components should be installed. You can optionally include an **[InternetServer]** section that allows to you control some of the properties of IIS 6.0.

The following parameters are valid in the **[Components]** section (see Table 3.2). To add a parameter, edit the answer file:

```
[Components]
aspnet = on
complusnetwork = on
```

Table 3.2 Parameters in the Components Section

Parameter	Description
aspnet = on/off	Enable ASP.NET.
complusnetwork = on/off	Enable network COM+ access.
dtcnetwork = on/off	Enable network DTC network access.
bitsserverextensionsisapi = on/off	Enable the BITS Server Extensions ISAPI.
bitsserverextensionsmanager = on/off	Enable the BITS Server Extensions snap-in.
iis_common = on/off	Install Common Files.
iis_ftp = on/off	Enable the FTP service.
fp_extensions = on/off	Install Frontpage 2002 Server Extensions.
iis_inetmgr = on/off	Install IIS Manager.
iis_nntp = on/off	Enable the NNTP service.
iis_smtp = on/off	Enable the SMTP service.
iis_asp = on/off	Enable Active Server Pages.
iis_internetdataconnector = on/off	Enable IDC.
tswebclient = on/off	Enable remote desktop web connection.
iis_serversideincludes = on/off	Enable server-side includes.
iis_webdav = on/off	Enable WebDAV publishing.

Continued

Table 3.2 Parameters in the Components Section

Parameter	Description
iis_www = on/off	Enable the WWW service.
appsrv_console = on/off Console.	Install the Application Server

The parameters given in Table 3.3 are valid in the **[InternetServer]** section:

Table 3.3 Parameters in the InternetServer Section

Parameter	Description
SvcManualStart = www and/or ftp	If WWW or FTP is present, those services will be set to manual start. If you specify both **www** and **ftp**, separate them with a comma (,). When installed, the default service state is to start automatically.
PathFTPRoot = path to FTProot	Alternative path in which the FTP service is installed. The default is *systemroot*\Inetpub\Ftproot.
PathWWWRoot = path to WWWroot	Alternative path in which the WWW service is installed. The default is *systemroot*\Inetpub\Wwwroot.
ApplicationDependency = *ApplicationName, GroupID, GroupID*	Adds application dependencies. For example, the following entries: **ApplicationDependency = CommerceServer, ASP, IndexingService ApplicationDependency = ExchangeServer, ASP60 ApplicationDependency = MyApp, ASP.NET v1.1.4322** make the Commerce Server dependent on ASP and the Indexing Service, Exchange Server dependent on ASP, and MyApp dependent on ASP.NET v1.1.4322.

Continued

Table 3.3 Parameters in the InternetServer Section

Parameter	Description
ExtensionFile = <Enabled Flag>, <File Path>[,<UI Deletable Flag> [,<Group ID> [, <Description>]]]	Specifies an extension file. This parameter allows you to add additional Web Service Extensions, which will be visible in the **Web Service Extensions** node of the IIS Manager (see Chapter 4 for more information on Web Service Extensions and securing them). The **UI Deletable Flag, Group ID**, and **Description** settings are all optional. However, if you specify any of the optional settings, you must include all of the previous settings. The parameters represent the following: **Enabled Flag** is set to **0** for disabled and **1** for enabled. **File Path** is the path to the file, and it can contain environment variables. **UI Deletable Flag** specifies whether the item can be deleted using IIS Manager. Set to 0 to disable deletion and 1 to enable deletion. **Group ID** allows you to group different dynamic-link libraries (DLLs) and Common Gateway Interfaces (CGIs) and have dependencies for the applications. **Description** is the description of the extension file.
DisableWebServiceOnUpgrade = True/False	By default, when upgrading from Windows 2000 Server, the World Wide Web Publishing service will be placed into a paused state unless the IISLockDown tool has been run (see the next section on Upgrading IIS 5.0 to IIS 6.0). This parameter can be used to override this behavior.

Installing IIS 6.0 After the Windows 2003 Server Setup

If you do not install IIS 6.0 during the Windows 2003 Server setup, you can always return later and install IIS 6.0 once the Windows 2003 Server setup is complete. This may be useful if certain operations have to be completed prior to installing IIS 6.0. To install IIS 6.0 after Windows 2003 Server setup has completed, use the sysocmgr.exe application:

```
sysocmgr.exe /i:sysoc.inf /u:<path_to_answer_file>
```

The answer file is in the same format as the one used for installing IIS 6.0 as part of the Windows 2003 Server installation. In addition to the parameters listed for the **[Components]** and **[InternetServer]** sections, an additional **askit_web on/off** option is available under **[Components]**. This option installs the RemoteAdministration Website (HTML). Note that this feature is not available on 64-bit editions of Windows 2003 Server.

You also have the option to call sysocmgr.exe automatically from your unattended installation answer file, either by making an entry in the **[GUIRunOnce]** section, or by using the cmdlines.txt file located in the OEM folder of your distribution share. For more information on configuring these two options, refer to "Designing Post Installation Tasks" in the Windows 2003 Server Deployment Guide located on the Microsoft website.

REALITY CHECK...

An unattended installation is the only way to configure the location of the WWW and FTP server root folders as part of the IIS 6.0 installation. Installing IIS 6.0 interactively requires you to manually move the default website and the default FTP site's root folders.

While IIS 6.0 hasn't been found to be vulnerable to canonicalization bugs (such as those exploited by the Sadmind/IIS worm) that allow attackers to move outside the default website's root folder, some organizations may mandate this as part of their server security configuration. Using the parameters in the **[InternetServer]** section of the unattended setup's answer file allows you to specify an alternate location when IIS 6.0 installs.

For more information on the Sadmind/IIS worm see: www.cert.org/advisories/CA-2001-11.html and www.microsoft.com/technet/security/bulletin/MS00-078.mspx.

Upgrading IIS 5.0 to IIS 6.0

To upgrade an existing Windows 2000 Server running IIS 5.0 to Windows 2003 Server running IIS 6.0, you need to ensure that your hardware meets the minimum requirements for the OS version that you are installing. Verify that any third-party applications you may have installed will run under Windows 2003 Server, and ensure that you have drivers for any software that is not on the Windows 2003 HCL (Hardware Compatibility List).

BY THE BOOK...

Upgrading an existing server to IIS 6.0 does have some advantages over performing a clean install. Upgrading can reduce the amount of time it takes to deploy a new server. Additionally, the upgrade process preserves many of the current settings of your IIS services (such as your website directory structures and permissions), so that you do not have to manually recreate them.

An upgrade from IIS 5.0 to IIS 6.0 maintains almost all of the server's functionality. For example, all allowed ISAPI extensions (for example ASP) that were allowed under IIS 5.0 will still be allowed under IIS 6.0. In contrast, a default installation of IIS 6.0 does not allow any ISAPI extensions. Table 3.4 summarizes the changes to IIS functionality following an upgrade. The upgrade process also maintains existing user configured settings including virtual directories, custom error pages, and default documents.

Table 3.4 Changes to IIS Functionality Following an Upgrade

Before Upgrade	After Upgrade
The IISAdmin virtual directory exists.	The IISAdmin virtual directory is removed and a default web page is placed in the directory.
If the IISLockDown tool was installed, and this disabled any extensions, then those extensions are mapped to 404.dll.	All extensions mapped to 404.dll are disabled in the Web Services Extension node of the IIS Manager. All other extensions are enabled.

Continued

Table 3.4 Changes to IIS Functionality Following an Upgrade

Before Upgrade	After Upgrade
If the IISLockDown tool was installed, then Web Distributed Authoring and Versioning (WebDAV) is disabled by removing permissions via NTFS file system permissions.	NTFS permissions are changed to allow proper WEBDAV operation, and WebDAV is added to the Web service extensions list as *prohibited*.
If the IISLockDown tool was installed, the Indexing Service is disabled by using NTFS permissions.	Indexing Service remains disabled with the same NTFS permissions.
Web services hosted on IIS 5.0 are enabled.	Web services supported by the WWW service are disabled.
FrontPage 2000 Server Extensions are supported.	FrontPage 2000 Server Extensions are not supported. Upgrade all web sites to FrontPage 2002 Server Extensions.

To perform the upgrade, insert the Windows 2003 Server CD. Enable the **Check System Compatibility** option to ensure that your hardware will support Windows 2003 Server. If everything is OK, choose to install Windows 2003 and follow the on-screen prompts.

Post-Installation Information

If you have previously run Microsoft's IISLockDown tool on your IIS 5.0 installation, then the World Wide Web publishing service will remain running when the upgrade finishes. If you have not previously run the IISLockDown tool, the World Wide Web Publishing service will be placed into a paused state when the upgrade finishes. You should manually review the configuration of your IIS server to ensure that nothing is enabled that you do not want, and then change the **WWW Publishing** service's startup type in the **Services Administrative Tool**, as shown in Figure 3.4.

Figure 3.4 The World Wide Web Publishing Service Disabled after Upgrade from Windows 2000

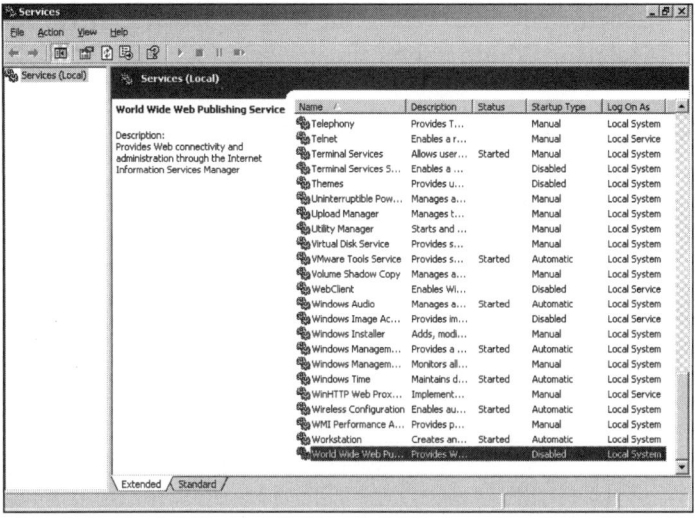

You can disable this behavior, and force the World Wide Web Publishing Service's startup type to be automatic by adding the following registry key prior to the upgrade: **HKLM\System\ CurrentControlSet\W3SVC\RetainW3SVCStatus\do_not_disable**. Ensure the **DWORD** value is **1** (or any other non-null value). If you are using an unattended setup answer file, then add the following line in the **[InternetServer]** section:

```
DisableWebServiceOnUpgrade = False
```

You should also note the following about the upgrade from IIS 5.0 to IIS 6.0:

- The IIS 5.0 HTML Administration website is removed and replaced with an HTML page explaining that you need to install the new IIS 6.0 Remote Administration HTML website. The IIS 5.0 HTML administration website is not compatible with IIS 6.0.

- All ISAPI extensions that were allowed under the previous IIS 5.0 installation are allowed (by default) in the upgraded IIS 6.0 installation, including unknown ISAPI Extensions and Unknown CGI extensions. You should review this list and determine which ones are not required (refer to Chapter 4).

- IIS will initially be running in IIS 5.0 isolation mode. To change the server to IIS 6.0 worker process isolation mode, open the IIS Manager in the **Administrative Tools** folder, right-click the **Web Sites** and select **Properties**. On the **Service** tab, disable the **Run WWW Service in IIS 5.0 Isolation Mode** option (Figure 3.5).

Figure 3.5 Changing IIS from IIS 5.0 Isolation Mode to IIS 6.0 Worker Process Isolation Mode

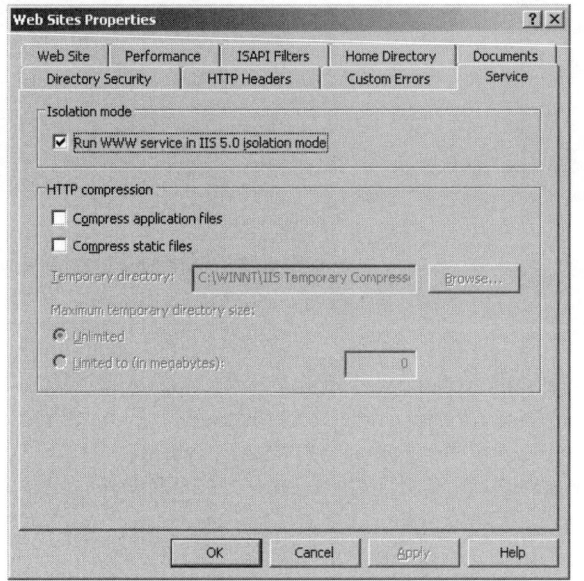

REALITY CHECK...

Deciding between an upgrade and a clean install can be a difficult decision. If your current server OS is currently experiencing any instability, or has had a number of programs installed and then uninstalled, a clean installation is recommended.

Microsoft has an IIS 6.0 migration tool that can help you move your websites from an existing server to a new server if you decide against the upgrade path. You can download the Migration tool from:

www.microsoft.com/downloads/details.aspx?FamilyID= 56fc92ee-a71a-4c73-b628-ade629c89499&DisplayLang=en

Chapter 9 of the Microsoft IIS 6.0 Resource Kit discusses this tool in depth, including its usage, benefits and limitations. You can download this chapter from:

www.microsoft.com/downloads/details.aspx?familyid= 80A1B6E6-829E-49B7-8C02-333D9C148E69&DisplayLang=en

After upgrading to IIS 6.0, existing applications should be evaluated to ensure that they are compatible with IIS 6.0 worker process isolation mode before changing from IIS 5.0 isolation mode. If your application relies on any of the following conditions, it will be incompatible with IIS 6.0 worker process isolation mode, and IIS must be run in IIS 5.0 isolation mode instead:

- The application has to run inside dllhost.exe or inetinfo.exe. In IIS 6.0 worker process isolation mode, all code execution occurs inside w3wp.exe.
- The application requires access to v1.0 of the .Net framework. IIS 6.0 supports v1.1 of the .Net framework only in worker process isolation mode. Applications that require v1.0 of the .Net framework can only run in IIS 5.0 isolation mode.
- The application relies on ISAPI filters that may be incompatible with the new IIS 6.0 processing model (for example, they rely on recycling provided by IIS 5.0).

After Installation: Locating the Administrative Tools

Following a successful IIS 6.0 installation, you will want to familiarize yourself with the administrative tools available to you. We will be using these tools throughout subsequent chapters of the book to make configuration changes that enable or disable IIS functionality.

BY THE BOOK...

Microsoft provides numerous methods of administrating IIS services. There are the GUI tools such as the MMC snap-ins that we will look at shortly. In addition, there are programmatic interfaces for manipulating IIS, including ADSI (Active Directory Services Interface) and WMI (Windows Management Instrumentation). Microsoft also provides a number of scripts (located in c:\inetpub\adminscripts\ and c:\windows\system32\) that can be called from a command line or scripting environment to allow manipulation of IIS. These are examined in detail in Appendix A.

IIS Manager

IIS Manager is the most popular IIS management tool, and it is installed as part of the Application Server role. It is installed by default on Windows 2003 Server Web Edition, and is located in the **Administrative Tools** program group on the **Start** menu.

The IIS Manager (shown in Figure 3.6) allows the administrator to configure websites, FTP sites, and the SMTP and NNTP servers. You can also configure Web Application Pools, and Web Service Extensions from this snap-in. There are links from this snap-in to the Sharepoint Administration website (if you have installed Frontpage Server Extensions). If a website has not already been configured for FPSE, you can right-click the website in the websites node and select **All Tasks | Configure Server Extensions**. If you have already configured a site for FPSE, you can access a link to the Sharepoint Administration website by right-clicking the website and selecting **Properties | Server Extensions 2002**.

BY THE BOOK...

Microsoft recommends that you do not use an account with administrative privileges for day-to-day operations. For performing administrative tasks, the **runas** command can be used to run programs with elevated privileges when required.

To open the IIS Manager using administrative privileges you can either right-click the **IIS Manager** shortcut and select the **run as** option, or you can select **Start | Run** and enter **runas /User:AdminAccountName "mmc %systemroot%\system32\inetsrv\iis.msc**, where *AdminAccountName* is the name of a user account with administrative privileges. The same procedure should be followed for invoking any of the other administrative tools that we will use throughout this book.

Figure 3.6 The IIS Manager

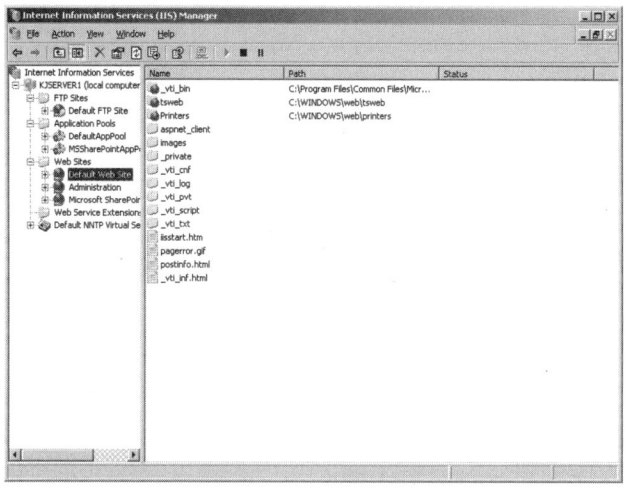

Application Server MMC

Installed as part of the Application Server role, the MMC can be accessed by selecting **Start | Run** and typing **appsrv.msc**. Alternatively, you can click the **Configure This Role** link in the *Manage Your Server* administrative tool. The Application Server MMC (shown in Figure 3.7) includes the IIS snap-in that is included in the IIS Manager, as well as snap-ins for managing ASP.NET and Component Services. In this sense, it is a superset of the IIS Manager.

Figure 3.7 The Application Server MMC

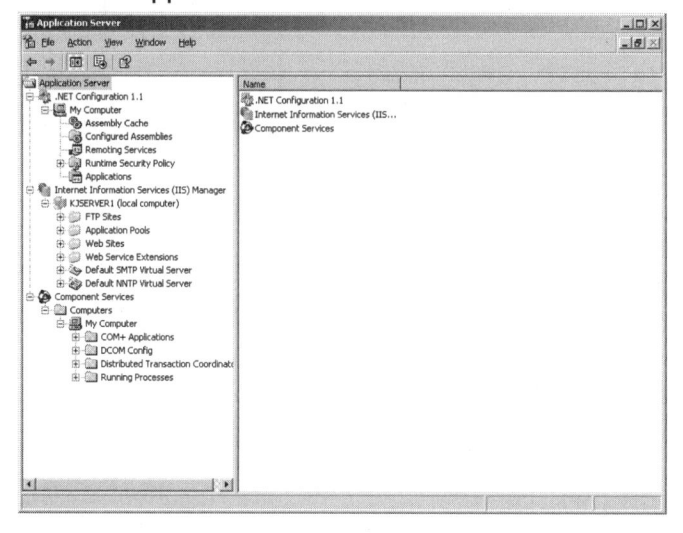

The Remote Administration Website

The Remote Administration website (shown in Figure 3.8) is an HTML-based administration website that can be used to perform many of the same functions that the IIS Manager does. In addition, you can use it to perform a few additional tasks, including managing the Windows event logs, managing local users and groups, and configuring various network properties. The Remote Administration website is installed by default on Windows Server 2003 Web Edition, and you can access it by selecting **Start | Administrative Tools Web Interface for Remote Administration**.

Figure 3.8 The Remote Administration Website

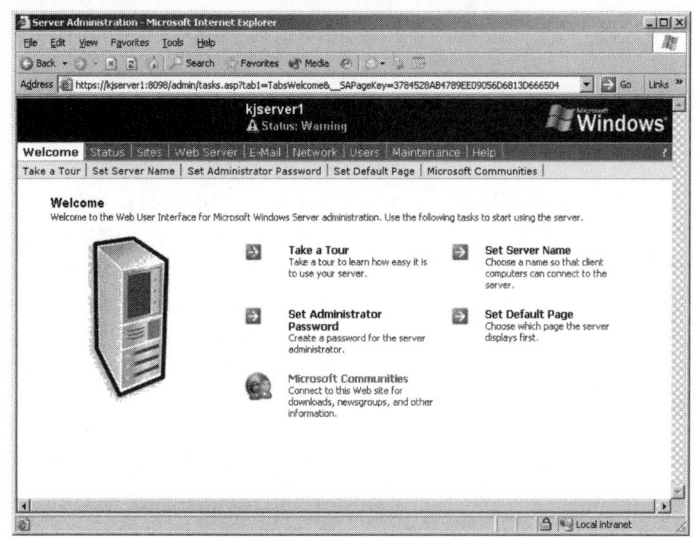

Sharepoint Administration Website

The Microsoft Sharepoint Administration website (shown in Figure 3.9) is used to manage Frontpage Server Extensions. This includes determining which sites can be authored by FPSE clients such as Microsoft Frontpage and Visual Studio.Net, as well as determining which Windows user accounts have which FPSE permissions. The Sharepoint Administration website can be accessed by selecting **Start | Administrative Tools | Microsoft Sharepoint Administrator**.

Figure 3.9 The Sharepoint Administration Website

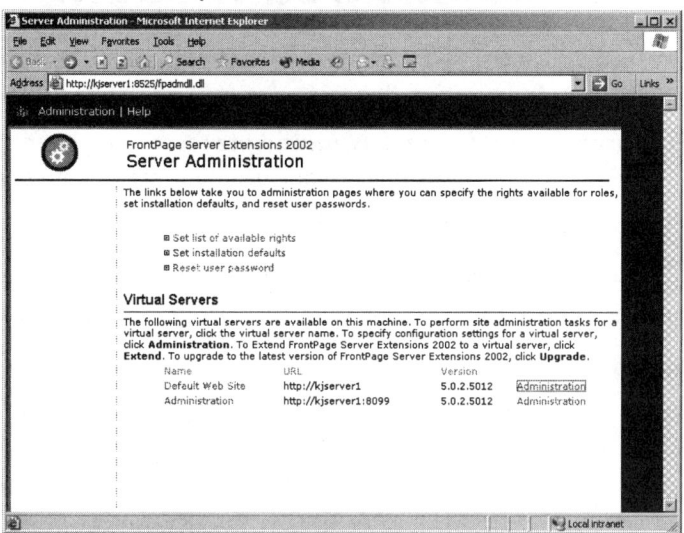

Your A** is Covered if You...

- ☑ Familiarize yourself with the various components that comprise Internet Information Services.
- ☑ Survey your requirements, identifying those components that will be required to support your planned Internet applications.
- ☑ Install only required components.
- ☑ Familiarize yourself with the available IIS Administration tools.

Chapter 4
Configuring Basic Web Server Security

In this Chapter

Now that you have a hardened Windows 2003 Server running IIS 6.0, you can focus on a few basic security configurations. The information in this chapter will help you secure your newly deployed IIS 6.0 server, provide you with a basic understanding of new security changes in IIS 6.0, and prepare you for the more advanced configurations discussed in Chapter 5.

- Enabling and Disabling Web Service Extensions
- Configuring Multipurpose Internet Mail Exchange
- Configuring IP Address Restrictions
- Setting Website Permissions
- Securing Web Resources
- Enabling and Securing Web Access Log Files

By the end of this chapter, you will understand how to secure your Web server by enabling the required dynamic application extensions and configuring Multipurpose Internet Mail Exchange (MIME) types. You will also understand how to prevent resource access by configuring website properties and NT File System (NTFS) permissions.

Enabling and Disabling Web Service Extensions

In order to take a more proactive stance against malicious attacks, IIS 6.0 is not installed by default on most operating systems in the Windows Server 2003 family (the exception is Windows Server 2003 Web Edition). Furthermore, once you do install IIS, its default behavior is to serve only static content (such as Hypertext Markup Language (HTML) and image files), and to block all requests to dynamic applications. If you want IIS to run dynamic applications, you can configure it by creating web service extension access lists, which control the type of dynamic content that the IIS server will provide to its clients.

> **BY THE BOOK...**
>
> To ensure that Windows administrators do not face unnecessary security threats upon installation, IIS 6.0 is installed with request-handling for static web pages enabled, and with all other request-handling features disabled. From the moment IIS is installed, the locked-down security profile of IIS 6.0 minimizes the attack surface available to intruders.
>
> Configuring web service extensions allows you to specify which types of dynamic applications will be provided by the IIS server. This setting is *per binary basic*, meaning that IIS forwards executable file requests to the processing application hosted in IIS server. Creating a web service extensions access list allows you to specify which request handlers are to be made available for users accessing your IIS server. This provides a more proactive means of defending against attackers who may try all possible ways to gain access to your server.
>
> Minimizing the types of dynamic contents that IIS will process can also help to conserve system resources; disabled web service extensions are not loaded into memory since IIS does not require them to process the dynamic content requests.

Notes from the Underground...

Profiling and Worms

In *profiling*, attackers will gather as much information as they can from your web server using techniques such as port scanning and banner requests. These techniques allow attackers to collect valuable system-level information including IIS versions, operating system version, server name, and web application details. Attackers can then use this information to prepare for more significant attacks against any known weak points.

A *worm* works by sending malicious requests to the IIS server and self-replicating from one server to another. For example, by using the buffer overflow vulnerability in the default indexing engine in previous version of IIS, the notorious "Code Red" worm was able to cause a large amount of damage. Worms are typically hard to detect, as they do not normally create file footprints; however, most worms can be detected once they begin to consume system resources and begin to slow down the system or halt other system programs.

To protect the IIS server from worm and profiling attacks, you must:

- Ensure the latest security fixes and service packs are installed on the system.
- Disable any unused system components and services.
- Block all unnecessary ports at the firewall and host levels.
- Enable only the required web service extensions.
- Deploy antivirus programs and Intrusion Detection Systems (IDSs).

When using web service extensions, you can either choose from one of the predefined extensions, or you can create and customize your own. Table 4.1 lists the predefined web service extensions and when they should be enabled.

Table 4.1 Web Service Extensions

Web Service Extension	Enable when...
Active Server Pages (ASP)	Websites contain ASP applications
ASP.NET	Websites contain ASP.NET applications
FrontPage Server Extensions	Websites require FrontPage extensions
Internet Data Connector (IDC)	Websites contain .idc and idx files for IDC connection
Server Side Includes (SSI)	Websites use SSI directives to insert reusable content
Web Distributed Authoring and Versioning (WebDAV)	Websites need to support clients publishing and managing content via WebDAV

For more details about each service extension and its functions, you can refer to Chapter 3 on Installing Internet Information Services (IIS) 6.

Perform the following steps to enable and disabled built-in Web Service Extensions:

1. In IIS Manager, expand the local computer and click **Web Service Extensions**.

2. In the right-hand details pane (shown in Figure 4.1), click the web service extension that you want to enable or disable.

Figure 4.1 Enabling and Disabling Web Service Extensions – Web Service Extensions Node

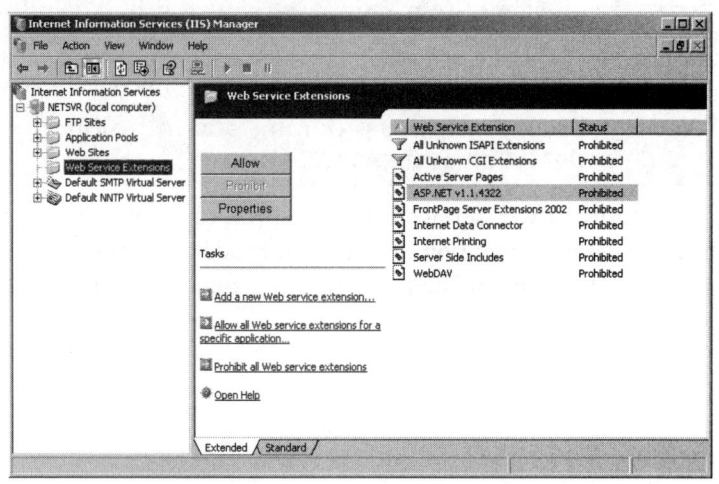

3. To enable a disabled web service extension, click **Allow**. To disable an enabled web service extension, click **Prohibit**.

Configuring Basic Web Server Security • Chapter 4   69

4. Click **OK**

You may need to create your own web service extensions if the dynamic application you need is not in the predefined the list, such as a customized Internet Server Application Programming Interface (ISAPI) extensions written by your development team or a Common Gateway Interface (CGI) extension (such as a Perl script). Perform the following steps to create customized web service extensions:

1. In IIS Manager, expand the local computer and click **Web Service Extensions**.
2. In the right-hand pane, click the **Add a new Web service extension** link.
3. In the **New Web Service Extension** dialog box (shown in Figure 4.2), enter a name for the extension in the **Extension Name box** field.

Figure 4.2 Creating New Web Service Extensions – New Web Service Extension Dialog Box

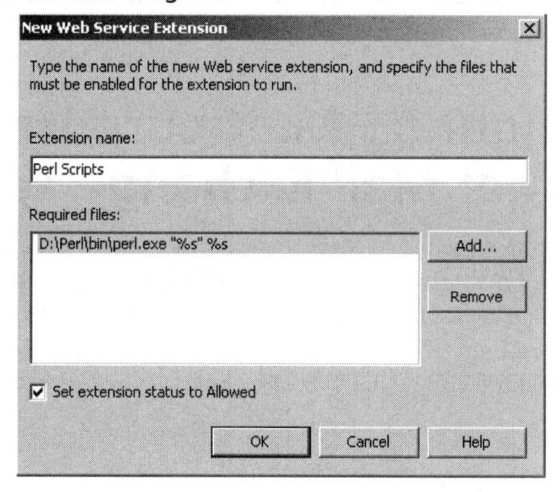

[Dialog box screenshot: New Web Service Extension with Extension name "Perl Scripts" and Required files "D:\Perl\bin\perl.exe "%s" %s", with Set extension status to Allowed checked]

4. In the **Required files** section, click **Add**, then select the path and name of the file that will handle requests for this extension.
5. Click **OK**.
6. If the extension must be enabled immediately, enable the **Set extension status to allowed** option.
7. Click **OK** to save your changes.

REALITY CHECK...

To minimize server load and help reduce malicious attacks, you should only enable *required* web service extensions. IIS returns a generic 404 response for any request that is addressed to a disabled or unknown web service extension; this prevents disclosure of IIS server information. IIS also writes the 404 error with the substatus code of 2 (404.2) in the W3C extended log files to indicate that the request was blocked due to a disabled web service extension.

If there are sudden attacks to any particular extension that you have enabled, you can temporary disable the affected extension to protect your IIS server (for example, while waiting for patches or fixes to be released). Once you confirm that there are no more security issues with the extension, you can re-enable it.

It is *not* recommended that you enable the **All Unknown ISAPI Extensions** or **All Unknown CGI Extensions** options for web service extensions, as these options may contribute to potential security risks.

Configuring Multipurpose Internet Mail Exchange Types

MIME types specify how web browsers or mail programs will handle data files received from the server. In addition to sending web pages to a client web browser, IIS also specifies the MIME type associated with the data it is sending, as well as which client applications will be able to process or display the data.

BY THE BOOK...

IIS is preconfigured to serve a default common set of global registered MIME types. These file extensions are recognized by all websites. You can also define your own MIME types and change or remove unwanted MIME types. Additional MIME types can be defined at the global, website and directory levels. Global level MIME types are applied to the entire IIS server, whereas website level MIME types are applied to directories within that website, and directory level MIME types are only applied to specific files in the specified folder.

MIME types defined at different levels are independent of one another. However, if you configure the same MIME types at different levels, the lower-level MIME type definition (for example, global) will override the MIME type at a higher level (for example, directory).

Notes from the Underground...

Unauthorized Access

In an *unauthorized access* attack, an unauthorized user attempts to access and/or download sensitive or restricted information on the server. This type of attack is typically possible when there is a weak or improper configuration of Web and NTFS permissions. Although IIS 6.0 only serves well-known file extensions registered in MIME types, the risk is that your sensitive data might be already in the registered list (such as a Microsoft Word document).

To prevent unauthorized access attacks, you must:

- Disable anonymous access to confidential files.
- Group sensitive data files in one particular folder and secure it with strong NTFS permissions.
- Configure proper IIS authentication to specifically grant access only to authorized users.
- Encrypt and password-protect sensitive data files.
- Remove unwanted MIME type mapping from files that should not be served by IIS.
- Enable only required web service extensions.

To add or remove global MIME types, perform the following procedures:

1. In IIS Manager, expand the local computer, right-click the computer to which you will add a MIME type, and click **Properties**.

2. The **Local Computer Properties** dialog box (Figure 4.3) will be displayed. Click the **MIME Types** button.

Figure 4.3 Creating New Global MIME Types – Local Computer Properties Dialog Box

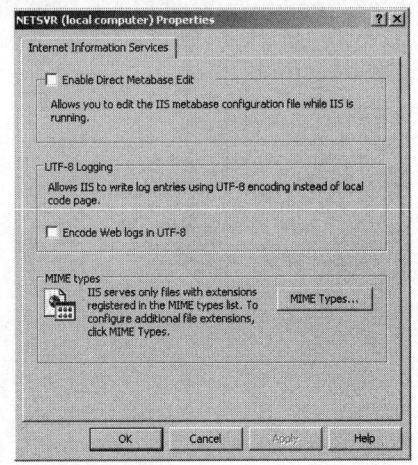

3. In the MIME Types dialog box (shown in Figure 4.4), click New to add a new MIME type.

Figure 4.4 Creating New Global MIME Types – MIME Types Dialog Box

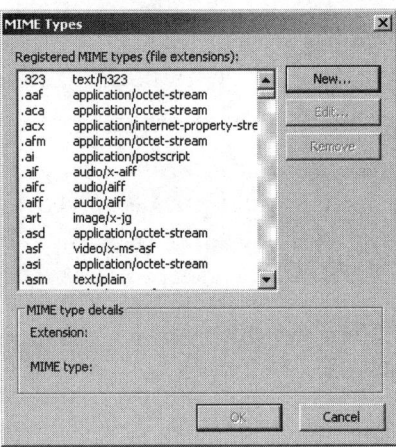

4. In the **MIME Type** dialog box (shown in Figure 4.5), enter the new file **Extension**.

Figure 4.5 Creating New Global MIME Types – MIME Type Dialog Box

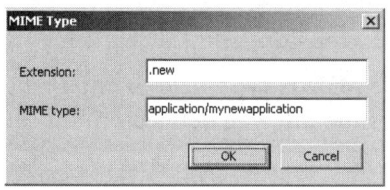

5. Use the **MIME type** field to enter a description that exactly matches the file type defined on the client computer.
6. Repeat steps #3-#5 until you have added all desired MIME types.
7. To remove a MIME type, select it from the **Registered MIME types** list and click **Remove**, then click **Yes** to confirm.
8. Once you have added the desired extensions and removed the undesired extensions, click **OK** to save your changes.

To define a new MIME type at the website or directory level, you will first need to navigate to that website or directory and perform the following steps:

1. In IIS Manager, expand the local computer, expand the **Web Sites** node, right-click the appropriate website or directory, and click **Properties**.
2. In the **Properties** dialog box, click the **HTTP Headers** tab. The **Web Site Properties** dialog box is shown in Figure 4.6.

Figure 4.6 Creating New Web Site MIME Types – HTTP Headers Tab

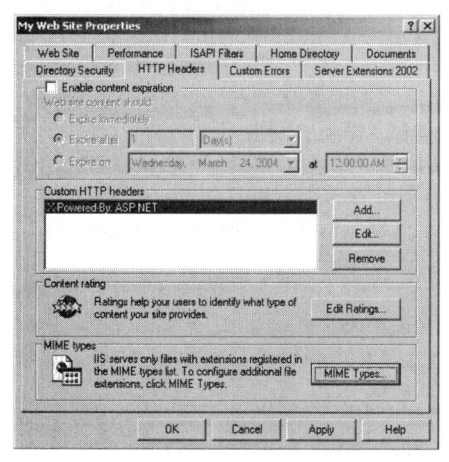

3. Click the **Mime Types** button.
4. Click **New**.
5. In the **Extension** field, enter the file name extension.
6. Use the **MIME type** field to enter a description that exactly matches the file type defined on the client computer.
7. Click **OK**.

You can change or remove unwanted MIME types where you feel necessary. To do so, perform the following steps:

1. In IIS Manager, expand the local computer, expand the **Web Sites** node, right-click the appropriate website or web directory, and click **Properties**.
2. Select the **HTTP Headers** tab and click **MIME Types**.
3. Select the desired MIME type from the **Registered MIME types** list.
4. To remove the MIME type, click **Remove** and click **Yes** to confirm. To edit the MIME type, click **Edit**, modify the details and click **Yes** to save the changes.
5. Click **OK**.

REALITY CHECK...

As well as controlling the way that your web browser handles data files, you can also use MIME types to restrict the file types that will be served by IIS. This will help prevent unauthorized access to *non-legitimate* files, such as configuration (.ini) and batch command (.bat) files, or any system-protected files that are not supposed to be processed and sent to attackers. By removing these file type extensions from the access list, you can prevent the IIS server from sending those file types.

By default, IIS 6.0 only serves registered MIME types. If an undefined MIME type file is requested, IIS returns a generic 404 response and writes a 404 error with the substatus code of 3 (404.3) in the W3C extended log file to inform you that the request was blocked because the requested MIME type was not registered.

You have the option configure IIS to serve all files regardless of file extensions by adding a wildcard (*) MIME type, however this setting is *not recommended*, as it will instruct IIS to serve all file extensions.

Configuring IP Address Restrictions

By now, you should understand how you can limit the types of applications that will be supported by IIS (by creating web service extension access lists) and how you can limit the types of files that will be served by IIS (by creating MIME type access lists). Now that you have configured the types of files that can be accessed and served, your next step should be to lay down controls that specify who can and cannot access these files and applications. One way to do this is to limit or restrict access by clients with specific IP addresses.

> **BY THE BOOK...**
>
> Configuring the IP address restriction allows you to filter or block unwanted client requests based on client IP addresses or the machine domain name.
>
> When a request is received by the IIS server, IIS will first look through the IP Address and domain name restriction list as defined for the web resource. If the client IP address or domain name is not specifically denied access on the list, IIS will continue processing the request.
>
> By default, the IP address restriction is disabled, meaning any IP address is allowed to access the server.
>
> You are recommended to limit the number of restricted entries as every request will need to go through this list when it is sent by a client. For example, if you have hundreds of entries on this restriction list, this may a create system overload as each request will need to pass this process. You are also not recommended to enable domain name restrictions as each client IP will need to be entered to its Full Qualify Domain Name (FQDN) before IIS will be able to determine whether the domain name is on the restriction list.
>
> IP address and domain name restrictions can be applied to website, virtual directory, directory and file levels. Similar to NTFS permissions, restricted permissions apply. For example if a client IP address is granted access a particular virtual directory, but denied access to a particular virtual directory's content file, the client will not be able to access the requested content

First, we'll look at how control access works in IIS so that you can gain a better understanding of where restrictions can be placed. Figure 4.7 illustrates the process that occurs when IIS receives a request.

Figure 4.7 IIS Access Control Process

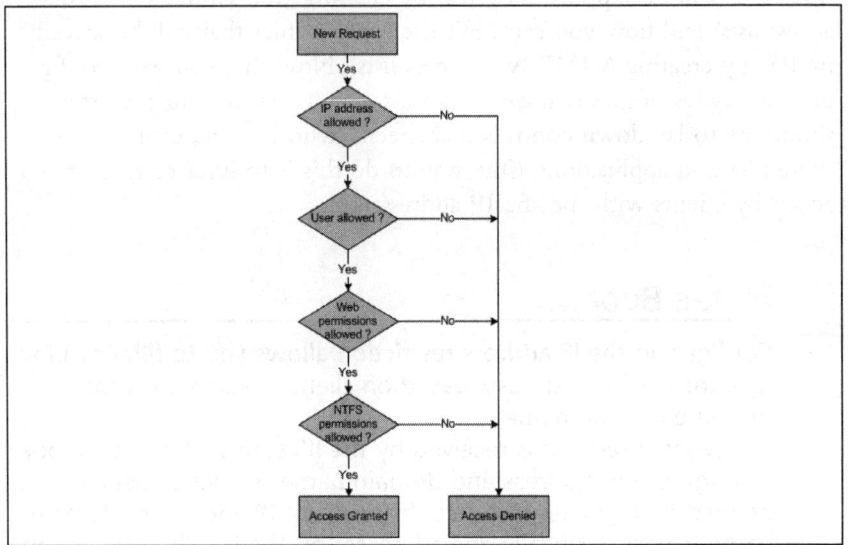

When a user sends a request to IIS, the following actions occur:

1. IIS determines if the client's IP address is on the IP address restriction list. If so, the request fails and IIS returns a 403.6 Access Forbidden - IP address rejected message to client.

2. If the request has come from a valid IP address, IIS checks the user information. If anonymous access is not allowed, IIS will request authentication information from the client, who will be prompted to enter a valid user name and password. If the user does not exist or fails to provide correct user credentials, the request fails and IIS returns a 401 Access is denied message to the client.

3. If the user is allowed access, IIS will then check to determine if the user has site permissions such as Read and Write permissions for the requested resource. If the user does not have such permissions, the request fails and IIS returns 403 Access Forbidden message to the client.

4. If there is another security module, such as Microsoft ASP.NET impersonation, the request will be forwarded to the appropriate request handler.

5. Next, IIS checks the NTFS permissions of requested resource. If the user does not have NTFS permissions for that resource, the request fails and IIS returns a 401 Access is denied message to the client.

6. If the user has sufficient NTFS permissions, the request is processed by IIS.

In configuring IP address restrictions, you can grant or deny access to a computer based on its IP address and/or domain name. For example, suppose that you have an IIS server hosting two websites; one for public access and one for private internal web applications. To allow only internal client machines or specified domain names to access the private site, you can configure the private website to accept incoming requests only from those granted IP addresses and domain names.

IP address-based access can be configured at the website, virtual directory, directory, and file levels. Perform the following steps to configure IP address restrictions for a single computer at website level:

1. In IIS Manager, expand the local computer, expand the **Web Sites** node, right-click the designated website, and select **Properties**.

2. Click the **Directory Security** tab (shown in Figure 4.8).

3. In the **IP address and domain name restrictions** section, click **Edit**.

Figure 4.8 Configuring IP Address Restrictions – Directory Security Tab

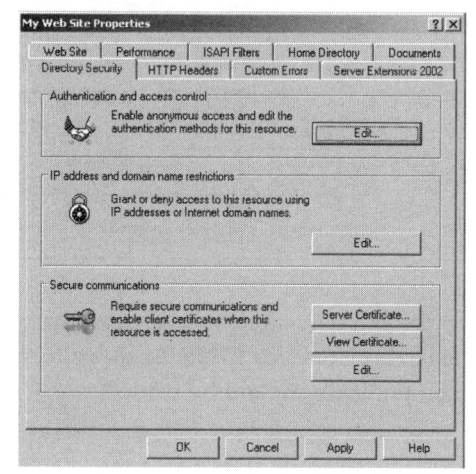

78   Chapter 4 • Configuring Basic Web Server Security

4. In the **IP Address and Domain Name Restrictions** dialog box (Figure 4.9), click **Granted access** or **Denied access**.

- When you select **Denied access**, you deny access to all computers and domains, except to those that you specify in the **Except the following** list.

- When you select Granted access, you grant access to all computers and domains, except to those that you specify in the **Except the following** list.

Figure 4.9 Configuring IP Address Restrictions – IP Address and Domain Name Restrictions Dialog Box

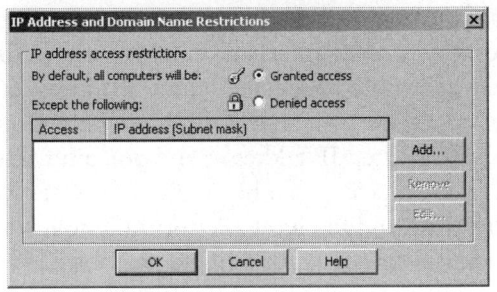

5. To add exceptions to this restriction, click **Add**.
6. Click **Single computer**. The **Deny Access** or **Grant Access** dialog box will open (Figure 4.10).

Figure 4.10 Configuring IP Address Restrictions – Single Computer Deny Access Dialog Box

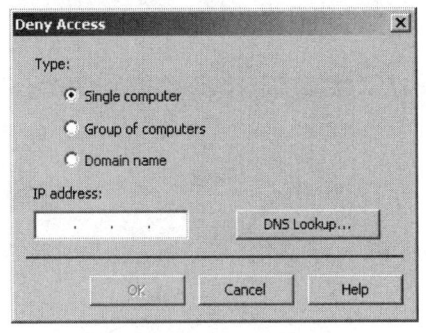

7. Enter the IP address of the computer that you wish to make the exception, or click **DNS Lookup** to search for and select the computer or domain by name

8. Click **OK** to make an exception of the desired computer.
9. Click **OK** in the **IP Address and Domain Name** dialog box.
10. Click **OK** in the **My Web Site Properties** dialog box.

The following steps will allow you to configure IP address restrictions for a group of computers:

1. In IIS Manager, expand the local computer, expand the **Web Sites** node, right-click the designated website, and select **Properties**.
2. Click the **Directory Security** tab. In the **IP address and domain name restrictions** section, click **Edit**.
3. In the **IP Address and Domain Name Restrictions** dialog box, click **Granted access** or **Denied access**.
4. To add exceptions to this restriction, click **Add**.
5. Click **Group of computers** (Figure 4.11).

Figure 4.11 Configuring IP Address Restrictions – Group of Computers Deny Access Dialog Box

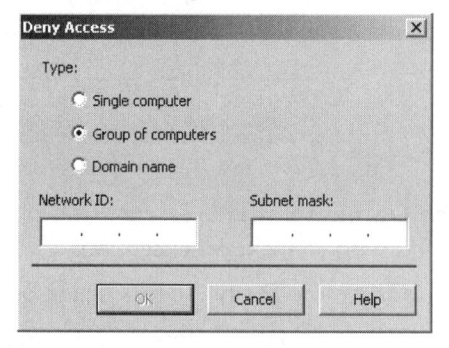

6. In the **Network ID** box, enter the IP address of the host network.
7. In the **Subnet mask** box, enter the subnet ID of the group of computers to which you will grant or deny access.
8. Clicks **OK** in the **Deny Access** dialog box.
9. Click **OK** in the **IP Address and Domain Name Restrictions** dialog box.
10. Click **OK** in the **My Web Site Properties** dialog box.

The following steps will allow you to configure IP address restrictions for a domain:

1. In IIS Manager, expand the local computer, expand the **Web Sites** node, right-click the designated website, and select **Properties**.
2. Click the **Directory Security** tab. In the **IP address and domain name restrictions** section, click **Edit**.
3. In the **IP Address and Domain Name Restrictions** dialog box, click **Granted access** or **Denied access**.
4. To add exceptions to this restriction, click **Add**.
5. Click **Domain name** (Figure 4.12).

Figure 4.12 Configuring IP Address Restrictions – Domain Name Deny Access Dialog Box

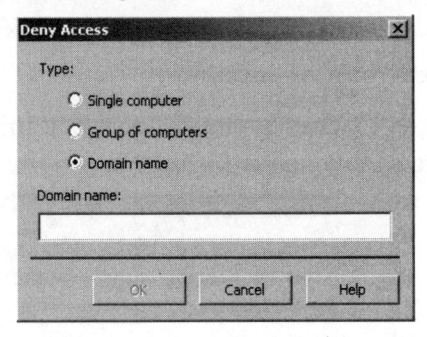

6. In the **Domain name** field, enter the name of the domain that you wish to make an exception.
7. Clicks **OK** in the **Deny Access** dialog box.
8. Click **OK** in the **IP Address and Domain Name Restrictions** dialog box.
9. Click **OK** in the **My Web Site Properties** dialog box.

The following issues are important to note when configuring IP address restriction based on domain names:

- Looking up DNS addresses can degrade the performance of the IIS server.
- Users accessing the IIS server via a proxy server will take on the IP address of the proxy server.

- When configuring restriction via domain name, you should enter the *.domainname.com syntax format rather than the domainname.com syntax. IIS may not be able to check against requests coming from the domainname.com.

When deciding to configure IP address and domain name restriction, you first need to know how many IP addresses or domain names IIS will need to verify and process. It is *recommended* that you keep the list small and limit it to a few entries. If you are allowing access to a website only for certain IP addresses or domain names, you should configure **Deny Access**, and deny all other IP addresses.

REALITY CHECK...

IP address restriction is the first level of defense when requests reach the IIS server. You can control access at this level to protect your IIS server. When you suspect that attackers are trying to gain access to your system, denying access to suspected IP addresses or domain names can help protect your IIS server.

Although you can also block access using firewall or router access lists, IP address restrictions provide you with the fastest configuration time and add an additional layer of protection.

Other useful tools, such as Internet Protocol Security (IPSec), Internet Connection Firewall (ICF), Internet Authentication Services (IAS) and TCP/IP Filtering, can be used to further protect your IIS server. For more details on these security tools and how to configure them, refer to the Windows Server 2003 help documentation

Setting Website Permissions

Once you have configured IP address restrictions, you should also consider applying restrictions to the website itself. Website permissions refer to permissions that are applied to all users accessing the website. These permissions are different from NTFS permissions, which are applied to files or folders for a specified user or groups of Windows users. When there is conflict between the website permissions and the NTFS permissions, the more restrictive permissions are applied.

By the Book...

Website permissions can be applied at website, virtual directory, directory, or file level. Website general content permissions include:

Read Enabled by default, this permission allows users to view directory and file content.

Write This permission allow users to modify directory or file content.

Script source access This permission allows users to access source files, including source code for scripts.

Directory browsing This permission allows users to view directory file listings.

Log visits Enabled by default, this records a log entry for each visit to the content.

Index this resource This type of permission is enabled by default if indexing service is installed, and allows the indexing service to index the site's content to facilitate searching.

Website executable permissions include:

None This prevents users from running programs or scripts.

Script only Enables script engine application mapping.

Scripts and Executables Allows scripting engines and Windows binaries to run in this directory.

You *should not* view website permissions as a replacement for NTFS permissions; in fact you should configure web permissions *in conjunction with* NTFS permissions. Combining the two allows you to secure web content as well as to control the way in which resources are accessed. The following is a list of best security practices when applying website and NTFS permissions.

- **Grant minimum permissions** Typically, you only need *Read* and *Log visit* permissions for general use and *Script only* permissions if the directory contains script engine applications. Do not give any extra permissions unless they are required. For example, if you have an images folder that contains image files only, set the *Execute permissions* to *None*, because static images files do not require any scripting engine to process the requests.

- **Grant special permissions on an as-needed basis** Special permissions include *Write, Script source access* and *Scripts and Executables*; use these permissions with extreme care. It is *not recommended* that you configure these permissions on a live server unless you are sure of what you are configuring. For example, and appropriate occasion for enabling Write or Script Source

Access is when allowing WebDAV authoring. See Chapter 11 for more information on WebDAV.

- *Write* This permissions provide potential security threats to the server, as users may be allowed to upload malicious scripts to attack the server. For example, if you are hosting an online accounting system and write permissions are configured incorrectly, attackers could upload illegal scripts and try to steal the sensitive accounting data.

- *Script source access* This type of access allows users to directly access script source code via IIS. Enabling this type of access grants users to download and view scripts source files remotely, revealing internal application structures, business logic, database schemas and configuration details. For example, hackers can use this type of access to retrieve Active Server Page (ASP) application configuration files (global.asa), which normal hold the database connection details of the application. Hackers can then use the login details to gain unauthorized access to the database server.

- *Scripts and Executables* This permissions allows users to invoke scripting engines and execute Windows binaries files. Binary application executable files may include CGIs such as a Perl interpreter running an executable file (exe). Granting this type of permission may allow attackers to execute other Windows binaries files, such as command shell executables (cmd.exe). In this way, attackers could use command shell access to damage your server, for example, using a command shell to delete files from the website.

- **Group executable files in separate directory** By grouping executable files together, you can more easily configure access permissions and audit special application access.

- **Deny write access for anonymous users** You should always *deny* write access for anonymous user to help protect your server from being compromised. Only grant write permission if it is absolutely required.

- **Group all anonymous users** If you have to configure different anonymous users for different websites, you can create a user group to group all anonymous user together. This allows you to *deny* resource access based on group membership.
- **Configure strong NTFS permissions on resources** Secure your web contents by assigning minimum NTFS permissions.
- **Remove unwanted application mapping** You can further control which types of application programs can be run within the website or virtual directory.

You can configure Web permissions and content at website, virtual directory, directory and file levels. You may execute permissions at all levels other than the file level. Use the following steps to configure permissions at the website level.

1. In IIS Manager, expand the local computer, expand the **Web Sites** node, right-click the appropriate website, and click **Properties**.
2. Select the **Home Directory** tab (shown in Figure 4.13).

Figure 4.13 Configuring Website Permissions – Home Directory Tab

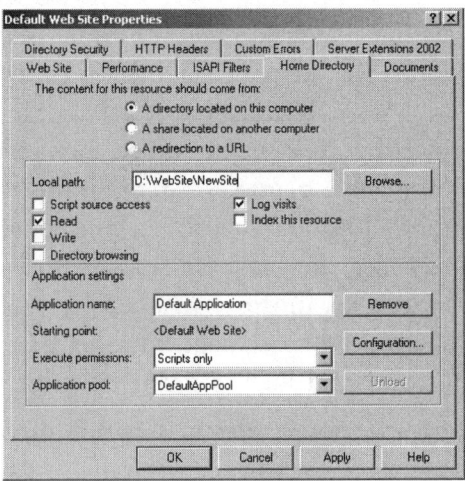

3. Select the desired web content general permissions (located in the middle section):
   - **Read** is enabled by default; and allows users to view directory or file resource.

Configuring Basic Web Server Security • Chapter 4   85

- **Write** allows users to modify directory or file resource.

- **Script Source Access** enables users to access script source files. If *Read* and *Write* are enabled, users can access and upload the script files.

- **Directory Browsing** allows users to view the directory file listing.

- **Log visits** is enabled by default. This creates a log entry in the log file..

- **Index** This Resource allows *Indexing Service* to index the content for search support

4. Select, in the **Application Settings** section, the following execution levels in the **Execute Permissions** dropdown list:

   - **None** does not support any scripts and executables.

   - **Script Only** only allows scripts engine execution.

   - **Scripts and Executables** supports script engine and windows binaries executable files.

5. Click **OK**

Perform the following steps to set permissions for file contents:

1. In IIS Manager, expand the local computer, expand the **Web Sites** node, expand the appropriate website, right-click the desired **File**, and click **Properties**.

2. Select the **File** tab (shown in Figure 4.14).

Figure 4.14 Configuring File Permissions – File Tab

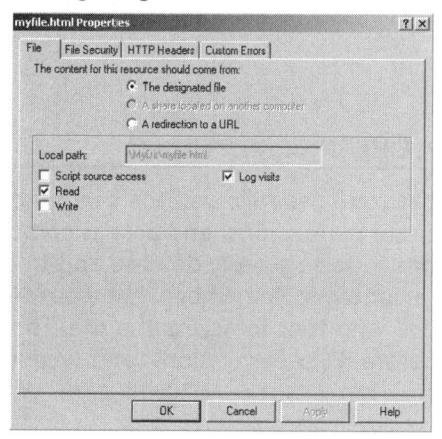

3. Select the desire web content general permissions:

To remove unwanted application mapping at website level, perform the following steps:

1. In IIS Manager, expand the local computer, expand the **Web Sites** node, right-click the appropriate website, and click **Properties**.
2. Click on the **Home Directory** tab.
3. In the **Application Settings** section, click **Configuration**.
4. In the **Application Extensions** section (Figure 4.15), select the desired application mapping and click **Remove**.

Figure 4.15 Removing Unwanted Application Mapping – Application Configuration Dialog Box

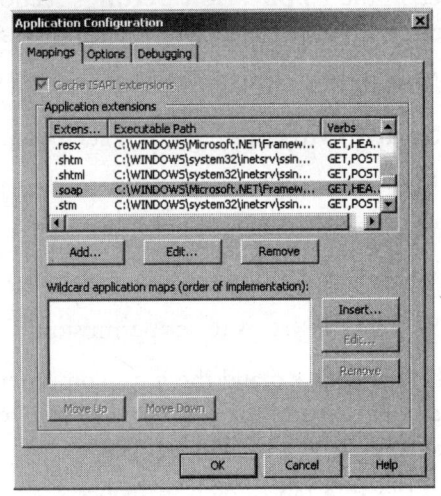

5. Click **Yes** to confirm.
6. Click **OK**.

REALITY CHECK...

Ensure that you have followed the best practices when configuring website permissions, and always combine them with NTFS permissions to form a basic defense and to control access to your site's contents. Remember that website permissions apply to everyone who tries to access the site. These permissions are applied before NTFS permissions, and whenever there is conflict between the two permissions, the *more restrictive* permissions are applied.

Take note that you should grant permissions on an as-needed basis; do not grant anything extra unless it is absolutely necessary. Ensure anonymous users always have *read* but not *write* permission unless it is absolutely required. If write access is required, always grant it at the lowest possible level, for example, to a single file or folder.

Script only is more secure than *Script and Executables*. Removing unwanted application mapping allows you to control the type of application that can be executed in the website or virtual directory. Again, this can reduce possible attacks on your system.

Securing Web Resources

Web resources refer to static and dynamic content served by IIS server, there are many security settings to help you further secure these resources together with the new security features introduced in IIS 6.0. You will focus on change default web root path, creating your own default document, configuring resource access list via NTFS permissions.

BY THE BOOK...

IIS 6.0 includes many new security features specific to web resource access, including:

1. New kernel mode driver called HTTP.SYS, which is specifically tuned to increase performance and scalability of IIS, as well as to make buffer overflow exploits more difficult. IIS parses and queues incoming HTTP requests and caches and returns web contents. This means that user code will not be executed by the kernel, thereby helping to prevent poor code from bringing down the entire IIS server.

2. Stronger support of account delegation as well as Advanced Digest and Microsoft Passport new authentication methods.

3. Worker Process Isolation mode, web applications are now in-process hosted w3wp.exe. In previous versions, applications were hosted in inetinfo.exe. format. And, medium pooled or out-of-process were hosted in dll-

host.exe. The process identity also changed from high privileges account *LocalSystem* to low-privileged *Network Service* user account when running worker process. These changes have reduced security risks as the running process identity account only has limited access rights.

4. Anonymous users *IUSR_<COMPUTERNAME)>* no longer have NTFS *write* permissions for the default web root folder.

5. Anonymous access to command line utilities that are located in system folder is prohibited in IIS 6.0. Administrative privileges are required to run command line administrative tools such as cmd.exe and Active Directory Services Interfaces (ADSI) scripts.

6. The ASP method Parent Path is disabled in IIS 6.0 by default. The Parent Path option allows you to use "..\" in ASP scripts to refer files that are relative to the current directory. It uses "..\..\format" to navigate directory structure of the web application. This poses a security risk if a web application is located in system drive and requests are being made to access system-related files.

By default, IIS creates the default web root path on your system drive during installation, typically C:\Inetpub\Wwwroot>. It is best to relocate your content files to another partition or hard drive in order to restrict access to sensitive system information located on the system drive if there is a security breach.

Moving web content to new disk volume will also protect you from directory traversal attacks, which involves an attacker sending a request to a file outside the folder structure of an IIS server. For example, a common attack request is accessing cmd.exe located in the %Windir%/system32 folder with the following method:

```
GET ..\..\Windows\system32\cmd.exe
```

If your web content is on another partition or disk, this type of attack will fail simply because cmd.exe does not exist on the same disk partition or volume, and with IIS 6.0, default access permissions to system files like cmd.exe are available to member of the *administrators* user group only.

To relocate your web content, first copy your web application files to a new hard drive or disk partition. Next, configure the website's properties to point to this new home path as detailed in the following steps:

1. In IIS Manager, expand the local computer, expand the **Web Sites** directory, right-click the appropriate website, and click **Stop**.
2. Right-click the website again, and click **Properties**.
3. Click the **Home Directory** tab, and under **The content for this resource should come from** section, select either **A directory located on this computer**, **A share located on another computer**, or **A redirection to a URL**, depending on where your home directory is located.
4. In the **Local path** box, browse to the local path name or type the share name or URL of your directory. In the example shown in Figure 4.16, we are changing the path to **Drive D** under **WebSite\NewSite** directory.

Figure 4.16 Configuring Web Site Home Directory Path – Home Directory Tab

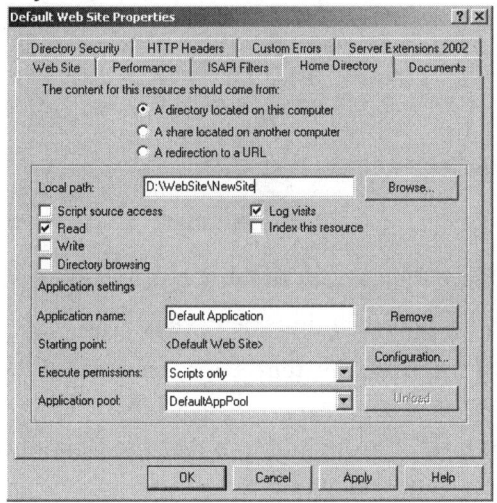

5. Click **OK**.
6. Right-click the website you just changed, and click **Start** to restart your website.

Once you have changed the home directory path, you need to define the *default document*. This document refers to a home page or index page that clients will receive when they send requests to a website without specifying a page name. This setting can be applied at both the website and web directory levels. If IIS cannot find a default document and directory browsing is not enabled, the client browser will receive a *Directory Listing Denied* error. Use the following steps to configure default documents:

1. In IIS Manager, expand the local computer, expand the **Web Sites** node, right-click the appropriate website, and select **Properties**.
2. Click the **Documents** tab (shown in Figure 4.17).

Figure 4.17 Configuring a Website Default Document – Document Tab

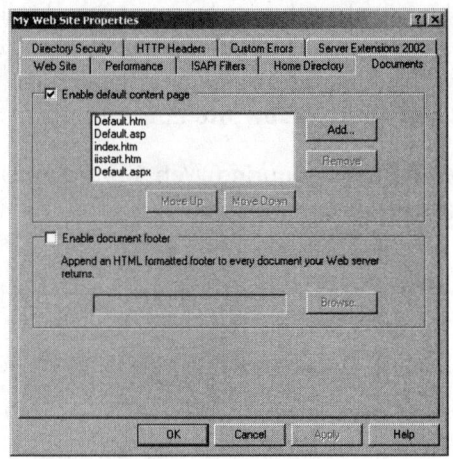

3. Ensure the **Enable default content page** option is enabled.
4. To add a default document, click **Add**.
5. On the **Add Content Page** dialog box (Figure 4.18), enter the document name and click **OK**

Figure 4.18 Configuring a Website Default Document – Add Content Page Dialog Box

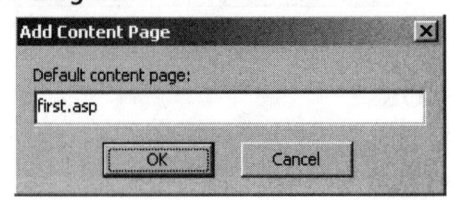

6. To remove a default document from the list, select it, then click **Remove**.
7. To change the order in which the default documents in the list will be served to clients, click a document in the list and click

the **Move Up** or **Move down** buttons until it is in the desired place in the list.

8. Click **OK**.

The first thing you should do after relocating your default home directory and configuring default documents is to deny write access for default anonymous users (IUSR_<COMPUTERNAME>). The basic rule of thumb is the fewer access permissions you grant the better security you will have. Table 4.2 shows the basic Access Control Lists (ACLs) for a common web root or content directory.

Table 4.2 Basic Access Control Lists

User Account or User Group	NTFS Permissions
Administrators	Full Control
IIS_WPG	Read & Execute, List Folder Contents, Read
IUSR_<COMPUTERNAME>	Read & Execute, List Folder Contents, Read, Write (Deny)
System	Full Control

NTFS permissions are set and managed using ACLs. The access lists specify which users and groups are able to access or modify a particular resource. An ACL consists of one or more access control entries (ACEs). You can configure NTFS permissions for files and folders using Windows Explorer or command line utilities such as Change Access Control Lists (Cacls.exe) and Extended Change Access Control List (Xcacls.exe).

Use the following steps to assign NTFS permissions using Windows Explorer:

1. Select **Windows Explorer** from the **Start** menu or press the **Windows Logo key**.

2. In **Windows Explorer**, click the content folder that contains the page or pages that you want to protect.

3. Right-click the folder, click **Properties**, and then click the **Security** tab.

4. In the top pane, select the **user** or **group** that you just added, then select the permissions that you want to grant in the bottom pane. Grant **System** accounts and **Administrator** groups **Full Control**.

5. Click **OK**.

Cacls.exe and *Xcacls.exe* are command-line utilities that allow system administrators to view and modify NTFS permissions for files or folders. You can use these tools to set all file system security access permissions just like you did in Windows Explorer. Both utilities allow you to display and modify files and folder ACLs.

Cacls.exe syntax is as follows. Refer to Table 4.3 for a description of the parameters.

```
cacls FileName [/t] [/e [/r User [...]]] [/c] [/g User:Permission]
[/p User:Permission [...]] [/d User [...]]
```

Table 4.3 Cacls.exe Parameters

FileName	Required. Displays Discretionary Access Control Lists (DACLs) for the specified file or directory.
/t	Changes DACLs of specified files in the current directory and all subdirectories.
/e	Edits a DACL instead of replacing it.
/r *User*	Revokes access rights for the specified user. Must be used in conjunction with the /e option.
/c	Continues to change DACLs, ignoring errors.
/g *User:Permission*	Grants access rights to the specified user. Permissions include **n** (none), **r** (read), **w** (write), **c** (change), and **f** (full control).
/p *User:Permission*	Replaces access rights for the specified user. Permissions include **n** (none), **r** (read), **w** (write), **c** (change), and **f** (full control).
/d *User*	Denies access for the specified user.
/?	Displays help at the command prompt.

For example, to prevent all default anonymous accounts from accessing **D:\WebSite\NewSite**, enter the following command:

```
C:\> cacls.exe D:\WebSite\NewSite /t /e /p iusr_<computername>:n
```

Xcacls.exe syntax is as follows. Refer to Table 4.4 for a description of the parameters

```
xcacls FileName [/t] [/e] [/x] [/c] [/g User:Permissions;Spec] [/r
User] [/p User:Permissions;Spec] [...]] [/d User [...]] [/y]
[/?|/h]
```

Table 4.4 Xcalcs.exe Parameters

FileName	Indicates the name of the file or directory to which the ACL or ACE is applied. All standard wildcard characters can be used.
/t	Recursively walks through the current directory and all of its subdirectories, applying the chosen access rights to the matching files or directories.
/e	Edits the ACL instead of replacing it.
/x	Edits the ACL instead of replacing it. This affects only the ACEs that the specified users already own.
/c	Causes Xcacls to continue if an "access denied" error occurs. If /c is omitted, Xcacls stops on this error.
/g *User:Permissions;Spec*	Grants the User access to the matching file or directory. *Permissions* apply the specified access right to files. Spec applies the specified access right to a directory. When this is the case, *Permissions* is used for file inheritance in this directory. Valid Permissions and Spec entries include: R (read) C (change) F (full control) P (change permissions – special access) O (take ownership – special access) X (execute – special access) E (read – special access) W (write – special access) D (delete – special access) T (ACE not specified. Sets an ACE for the directory itself without specifying an ACE that is applied to new files created in that directory. At least one access right must follow. *Spec* entries that precede **T** are ignored. This option is used only by Spec.
/r User	Revokes all access rights for the specified user.
/p *User:Permissions;Spec*	Replaces access rights for the specified user. *Permissions* applies the specified access right to files. *Spec* applies the specified access right to a directory. When this is the case, *Permissions* is used for file inheritance in this directory.

Continued

Table 4.4 Xcalcs.exe Parameters

	Valid Permissions and Spec entries include: **R** (read) **C** (change) **F** (full control) **P** (change permissions – special access) **O** (take ownership – special access) **X** (execute – special access) **E** (read – special access) **W** (write – special access) **D** (delete – special access) **T** (ACE not specified. Sets an ACE for the directory itself without specifying an ACE that is applied to new files created in that directory. At least one access right must follow. *Spec* entries that precede T are ignored. This option is used only by *Spec*.
/d User	Denies the specified user access to the file or directory.
/y	Disables the confirmation when replacing user access rights. By default, Xcacls asks for confirmation. Therefore, when Xcacls is used in a batch routine, the routine stops responding until an answer is received. Use the /y parameter when you use Xcacls in batch mode.
/?	Displays help at the command prompt.

For example, to grant the default anonymous account read-only access to D:\WebSite\NewSite, enter the following command:

```
C:\>xcacls.exe D:\WebSite\NewSite /g iusr_<computername>:r /e
```

For more details about *Cacls.exe* and *Xcacls.exe*, please refer to the Windows Server 2003 help documentation.

It is important to note that the **Deny write** permission is configured for anonymous accounts to ensure anonymous users will not be able to write or modify web contents, thus minimizing the risk of anonymous uploading of malicious attack scripts against IIS server. However, there are times when you want anonymous users to have write access to content files or folders, for example in an application that writes detail into a text file or application such as a Microsoft Access database (mdb) file. For special requirements like this, you should only grant access specifically to the desired files or folders, and you should not grant the **Everyone** group Full control permissions to any content directory.

Table 4.5 shows the recommended NTFS permissions that should be applied according to different file contents. You should always group different file types in separate folders to simplify administrative tasks when applying NTFS permissions.

Table 4.5 NTFS Permissions

Content Types	User / Group	NTFS Permissions
CGI files (.exe, .dll, .cmd)	Administrators Anonymous User System	Full Control Execute Full Control
Include files (.inc, .shtm, .shtml)	Administrators Anonymous User System	Full Control Read Full Control
Script files (.asp, .aspx, .vbs)	Administrators Anonymous User System	Full Control Read Full Control
Static files (.txt, .gif, .jpg, htm, .html)	Administrators Anonymous User System	Full Control Read Full Control

Table 4.6 outlines the user and user group default NTFS permissions upon IIS 6.0 installation.. These apply to the World Wide Web Service component (W3SVC) and Microsoft ASP.NET, but not File Transfer Protocol (FTP), Simple Mail Transfer Protocol (SMTP), Network News Transfer Protocol (NNTP) and Microsoft FrontPage Server Extensions (FPSE).

If you decide to create your own anonymous access account, you must ensure that the user has all the required users rights and permissions outlined here. For example, suppose you are hosting many different websites on the IIS server, one of which requires write access to its web contents directory. By default, the anonymous access user account is IUSR_<COMPUTERNAME>. Instead of having all websites running under this account with write access, you can create a new anonymous account for that particular website. This will prevent other anonymous users from having the same *write* permissions, as they are not needed by those websites.

Table 4.6 Default NTFS Permissions

Directory	Users/Groups	Permissions
%windir%\help\iishelp\common	Administrators	Full Control
	System	Full Control
	IIS_WPG	Read
	Users	Read, Execute
%windir%\IIS Temporary Compressed Files	Administrators	Full Control
	System	Full Control
	IIS_WPG	List, Read, Write
	Creator Owner	Full Control
%windir%\system32\inetsrv	Administrators	Full Control
	System	Full Control
	Users	Read, Execute
%windir%\system32\inetsrv*.vbs	Administrators	Full Control
%windir%\system32\inetsrv\ASP Compiled Templates	Administrators	Full Control
	IIS_WPG	Read
%windir%\system32\inetsrv\History	Administrators	Full Control
	System	Full Control
%windir%\system32\Logfiles	Administrators	Full Control
	System	Full Control
	Users	Read, Execute
%windir%\system32\inetsrv\metaback	Administrators	Full Control
	System	Full Control
Inetpub\Adminscripts	Administrators	Full Control
Inetpub\wwwroot	Administrators	Full Control
	System	Full Control
	IIS_WPG	Read, Execute
	IUSR_<COMPUTERNAME>	Read, Execute
	ASPNET	Read, Execute

Table 4.7 lists the registry access permissions for IIS-related users and user groups. Hkey_Local_Machine (HKLM) refers to the main registry key path configuring the local machine. It is important to note that the

system registry holds the configuration settings of the operating system, and an invalid configuration can damage the system or cause the operating system to malfunction. It is recommended that you back up the registry file before you start configuring registry settings.

Table 4.7 Default Registry Permissions

Path	Users/Groups	Permissions
HKLM\System\ CurrentControlSet\Service\ASP	Administrators System IIS_WPG	Full Control Full Control Read
HKLM\System\ CurrentControlSet\Service\ HTTP	Administrators System IIS_WPG	Full Control Full Control Read
HKLM\System\ CurrentControlSet\Service\ IISAdmin	Administrators System IIS_WPG	Full Control Full Control Read
HKLM\System\ CurrentControlSet\Service\ w3svc	Administrators System IIS_WPG	Full Control Full Control Read

Table 4.8 outlines IIS's built-in user accounts rights. For more details about each user's privileges, you can refer to the Windows Server 2003 help documentation.

Table 4.8 Default User Rights

Users/Groups	Users Rights
LocalSystem Network Service	Full Access to entire system Access this computer from a network Adjust memory quotas for a process Allow log on locally Bypass traverse checking Generate security audits Log on as a batch job Log on as a service Replace a process-level token
Local Service	Access this computer from a network Adjust memory quotas for a process Bypass traverse checking Generate security audits Log on as a batch job Replace a process-level token

Continued

Table 4.8 Default User Rights

Users/Groups	Users Rights
IIS_WPG	Access this computer from a network Bypass traverse checking Log on as a batch job
IUSR_<COMPUTERNAME>	Access this computer from a network Allow log on locally Bypass traverse checking Log on as a batch job
IWAM_<COMPUTERNAME>	Access this computer from a network Adjust memory quotas for a process Bypass traverse checking Log on as a batch job Replace a process-level token
ASPNET	Access this computer from a network Log on as a batch job Log on as a service

REALITY CHECK...

The more restrictions you apply to web contents, the smaller your chances are of falling prey to successful attacks on your system. You should always grant *minimum* permissions and *never* grant anonymous user rights unless it is absolutely necessary.

The IIS web access log file can be an invaluable tool because it can tell you if something suspicious is taking place on your IIS server. IIS writes a 401.3 *Unauthorized: Access is denied due to an ACL set on the requested resource* whenever users request content for which they do not have read permissions.

To read more about Default Permissions and User Rights for IIS 6.0, you can refer to a Microsoft Knowledge Base article *http://support.microsoft.com/?id=812614*.

Enabling and Securing Web Access Log Files

The IIS web access log file records every web content request and provides extensive information regarding the server and user activity. This enables you to understand how content are being accessed, from where they were accessed, and by what kind of browser, to name a few. By providing you with information about potential access trends and intrusion detection, the log file can provide you with additional clues for troubleshooting. Therefore, it is vital for you to understand the site logging activity process, the available formats, and the types of information logged.

BY THE BOOK...

IIS 6.0 allows you to collect user access activity information by enabling the logging feature. Information can be logged using the following formats:

W3C Extended A customizable format that allows you to configure the types of information to be collect when IIS writes the log entry. This format follows the W3C working draft specification. You can visit www.w3.org/TR/WD-logfile for information about the working draft.

NCSA Common National Center for Supercomputing Applications (NCSA) common format is an old specification of log file. Details that are logged are fixed and not customizable. Data captured includes: remote host name, data, time, request type, HTTP status and the number of bytes sent by the server.

IIS Log A fixed format that records more information than NCSA common format. These extra details include the time taken to process the request, bytes received by the server, and Win32 status.

ODCB Logging A fixed set of data that can be recorded in a database source.

New log file features introduced in IIS 6.0 include:

UTF-8 logging In earlier IIS versions, log files are logged in ASCII text or local codepage mode. In IIS 6.0 you can configure the logging in Universal Transformation Format (UTF) 8 mode. Logging in UTF-8 mode allows logging of requests that contain extended characters not supoorted in standard ASCII format. For example, with UTF-8 logging, you can request log entries that are in Unicode text such as Japanese content and filenames.

Remote logging In IIS 6.0, you can redirect log files on a remote share network path using the Universal Naming Convention (UNC) method. This allows you to configure a different log path to centralize log storage for backup and analysis purposes.

Centralized Binary logging This format allows multiple websites to write unformatted binary log data to a single file.

Http Error logging This log file format captures HTTP API errors record by the HTTP.SYS driver.

Protocol substatus This is only available in W3C extended format, and provides further detail in addition to standard protocol status to help you further understand request statuses.

This section will discuss how to configure W3C extended format access logging and ODBC logging, as well as how to secure your log files. IIS Log and NCSA Common log file formats are *not recommended* simply because they do not provide enough detail for today's complicated web server requests.

Site activity logging can be enabled and disabled at website, virtual directory, directory and file levels. To enable W3C extended format logging on a website, perform the following steps:

1. In IIS Manager, expand the local computer, expand the **Web sites** node, right-click the website you wish to configure and click **Properties**.

2. On the **Web Site** tab (shown in Figure 4.19), enable the **Enable logging** option.

Figure 4.19 Enabling W3C Extended Format Logging – Web Site Tab

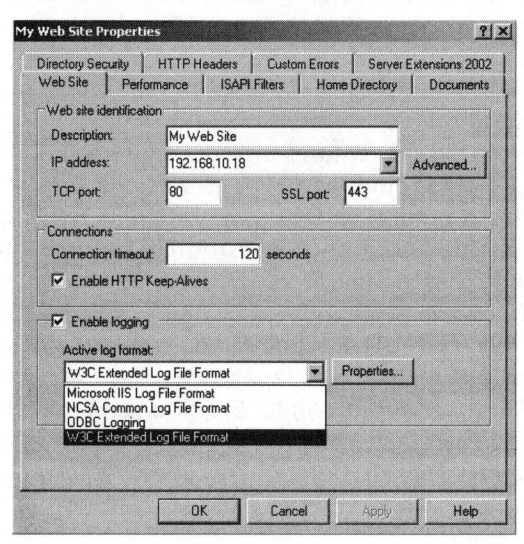

3. Select **W3C Extended Log File Format** from the **Active log format** drop-down list.

4. Click **OK**.

It is recommended that you log every single request to your Web server. However there may be times when you want to disable logging for certain resource contents to reduce the size of logfiles. For example, you might want to instruct IIS not to write log entries if the requested content is a static image file. You can do this by grouping all image files to a separate folder and disabling logging for that folder. On the other hand, if you analyze the log files using third party log analyzer tools, you can configure the analyzer to exclude certain type requests when generating web usage reports. Once logging is enabled on a website, you can disable logging on any virtual directory, directory or file that you wish. Use the following steps to disable logging for a directory or virtual directory:

1. In IIS Manager, expand the local computer, expand the **Web sites** node, expand the desired website.
2. Right-click the desired directory or virtual directory, and select **Properties**.
3. On the **Directory** or **Virtual Directory** tab (Figure 4.20), disable the **Log visits** option.

Figure 4.20 Disabling Virtual Directory Logging – Virtual Directory Tab

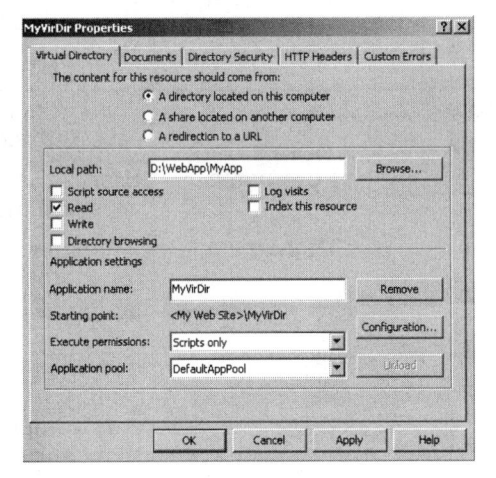

4. Click **OK**.

It is recommended that you use W3C Extended format whenever possible because it allows you to customize which data properties will be logged and allows you to limit unnecessary data in order to reduce the size of the log file. The following code is an example of log file that logs the time, client IP address, method, Uniform Resource Identifier (URI) stem, protocol status, and protocol version properties.

```
#Software: Internet Information Services 6.0
#Version: 1.0
#Date: 2004-2-14 14:14:18
#Fields: time c-ip cs-method cs-uri-stem sc-status sc-substatus
cs-version
14:14:19 192.168.10.18 GET /index.asp 200 0 HTTP/1.1
```

This entry indicates that on *Feb 14, 2004*, at *2:14P.M*, a user with IP address *192.168.10.18* sent a *GET* request for the */index.asp* file with *HTTP version 1.1* and response was returned without error. Note that different log formats use different time zone stamps in the log file. W3C extended format uses Greenwich Mean Time (GMT). Also note that the log entry includes the time *14:14:19* at the bottom. This indicates that the server took 1 second to respond; this time does not include the network travel time of the request and response.

Table 4.9 describes each property available in W3C extended version logs. The key to quickly identifying whether a request is successful or not is to look at the protocol status field. An HTTP 200 entry indicates a server response with zero error, but a 404 response informs client browser that specific request for the content was not found.

Table 4.9 W3C Extended Logging Fields

Property	Field	Description
Client IP Address	c-ip	IP address of the client that accessed the IIS server.
User Name	cs-username	User name of the client that accessed the IIS server.
Service Name	s-sitename	Sitename serving the request, for example, W3Svc1.
Server name	s-computername	IIS server name.
Server IP Address	s-ip	IP address of the server serving the request.
Server Port	s-port	Port number of the IIS server that served the request.
Method	cs-method	Client action request, for example GET or POST.
URI Stem	cs-uri-stem	Request content name, such as HTML or ASP page.
URI Query	cs-uri-query	Query action along with client request.
Protocol Status	sc-status	Status code of the request.

Continued

Table 4.9 W3C Extended Logging Fields

Property	Field	Description
Protocol Substatus	sc-substatus	Substatus code of the request.
Win32 Status	sc-win32-status	Status code in Windows terms.
Bytes Sent	sc-bytes	Number of bytes sent by the server.
Bytes Received	cs-bytes	Number of bytes received by the server.
Time Taken	time-taken	Amount of time to process the request.
Protocol Version	cs-version	Client protocol version, such as HTTP or FTP.
Host	cs-host	Client computer name.
User Agent	cs(User-Agent)	Application used by client, for example, browser.
Cookie	cs(Cookie)	Content of cookies sent or received.
Referrer	cs(Referrer)	URL of the site that directed the client to the current site.

In IIS 6.0, Protocol Substatus is a new property that gives you additional details. As mentioned earlier, requests to a disabled web service extension will return general 404 pages not found error to the client browser and a .2 substatus code is written in the log entry. This status code can help you in troubleshooting and identifying potential attacks against the server.

Table 4.10 lists the IIS HTTP status codes. Status codes can help you identify whether or not a request is successful. This information can help you in troubleshooting and give you clues about why a request failed. For example, a 403.6 reply indicates that the request was denied because the client IP address was rejected by IIS, and a 401.3 response indicates that a request was denied due to insufficient NTFS access permissions.

Table 4.10 IIS HTTP Status Codes

HTTP Status Code	Description
1xx Informational	Provisional response before regular responses
100	Continue
101	Switching protocols
2xx Success	Client requests successfully accepted
200	Succeeded
201	Created
202	Accepted
203	Non-authoritative information
204	No content
205	Reset content
206	Partial content
3xx Redirection	Client browser needs one more action to complete the request
302	Object moved
304	Not modified
307	Temporary redirected
4xx Client error	Client side requests error
400	Bad request
401.1	Logon failed
401.2	Logon failed due to server configuration
401.3	Unauthorized due to ACL on resource
401.4	Authorization failed by filter
401.5	Authorization failed by ISAPI/CGI application
401.7	Access denied by URL authorization policy on the Web server
403.1	Execute access forbidden
403.2	Read access forbidden
403.3	Write access forbidden
403.4	SSL required
403.5	SSL 128 required
403.6	IP address rejected
403.7	Client certificate required

Continued

Table 4.10 IIS HTTP Status Codes

HTTP Status Code	Description
403.8	Site access denied
403.9	Too many users
403.10	Invalid configuration
403.11	Password change
403.12	Mapper denied access
403.13	Client certificate revoked
403.14	Directory listing denied
403.15	Client Access Licenses exceeded
403.16	Client certificate is untrusted or invalid
403.17	Client certificate has expired or is not yet valid
403.18	Cannot execute requested URL in the current application pool
403.19	Cannot execute CGIs for the client in this application pool
403.20	Passport logon failed
404.0	File or directory not found
404.1	Website not accessible on the requested port
404.2	Web service extension lockdown policy prevents this request
404.3	MIME map policy prevents this request
405	HTTP verb used to access this page is not allowed (method not allowed)
406	Client browser does not accept the MIME type of the requested page
407	Proxy authentication required
412	Precondition failed
413	Request entity too large
414	Request-URI too long
415	Unsupported media type
416	Requested range not satisfy
417	Execution failed
423	Locked error
5xx Server error	Server side process error

Continued

Table 4.10 IIS HTTP Status Codes

HTTP Status Code	Description
500.11	Application is shutting down on the Web server
500.12	Application is busy restarting on the Web server
500.13	Web server is too busy
500.14	Invalid application configuration on the server
500.15	Direct requests for Global.asa are not allowed
500.16	UNC authorization credentials incorrect
500.18	URL authorization store cannot be opened
500.100	Internal ASP error
501	Header values specify a configuration that is not implemented
502.1	CGI application timeout
502.2	Error in CGI application
503	Service unavailable
504	Gateway timeout
505	HTTP version not supported

For more details about HTTP status code definitions, refer to www.w3.org/Protocols/rfc2616/rfc2616-sec10.html#sec10.

To customize the W3C extended logging fields, perform the following steps:

1. In IIS Manager, expand the local computer, expand the **Web sites** node, right-click the website you wish to configure and click **Properties**.

2. Enable the **Enable logging** option.

3. Ensure **W3C Extended Log File Format** is selected from the **Active log format** drop-down list.

4. Click **Properties**.

5. In the **Logging Properties** dialog box, click the **Advanced** tab (Figure 4.21).

Figure 4.21 Customizing W3C Extended Logging Fields – Advanced Tab

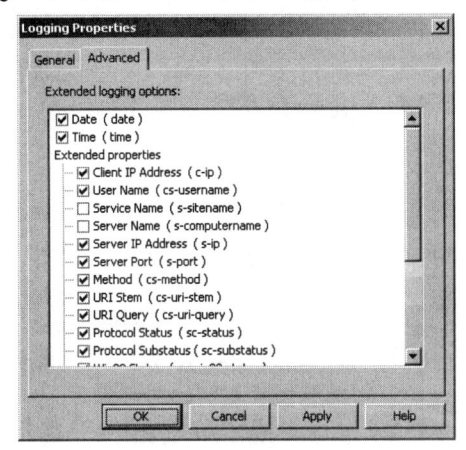

6. Enable the desired logging fields by placing a check in the checkbox of each field you want to want to use and removing the check from the checkbox of all fields you don't want to use.
7. Click **OK**.

You can also log site activity to Open Database Connectivity (ODBC) application, such as Microsoft Access or Microsoft SQL server. This allows you to query the log files in the database so that you can produce useful reports for further access analysis. When ODBC logging is enabled, IIS disables the kernel-mode cache, so implementing ODBC logging can actually degrade overall server performance.

Compared with W3C extended format logging, ODBC logging supports fewer properties (Table 4.11).

Table 4.11 ODBC Logging Properties

Property Name	Description	Property Type
ClientHost	Client IP address	varchar(255)
Username	Authenticated user name	varchar(255)
LogTime	Local date and time	datetime
Service	Name of service, such as WWW or FTP	varchar(255)
Machine	Server name	varchar(255)
ServerIP	Server IP address	varchar(50)

Continued

Table 4.11 ODBC Logging Properties

Property Name	Description	Property Type
ProcessingTime	Request processing time in milliseconds	int
BytesRecvd	Number of bytes received	int
BytesSent	Number of bytes sent	int
ServiceStatus	IIS status code, for example, 200	int
Win32Status	Windows status code	int
Operation	Request action, for example, GET or POST	varchar(255)
Target	Requested content or resource	varchar(255)
Parameters	Operation parameters, for example, user name	varchar(255)

When configuring ODBC logging on a Microsoft SQL server, you must first create the new database and table structure. Next, you must configure the system data source name (DSN) for the SQL server connection. Finally, you must configure IIS ODBC logging. The following steps will allow you to create the database and table structure for ODBC logging:

1. Log on to the server with a user account that has administrative access on the computer that is running SQL Server.
2. Open the **SQL Server Query Analyzer**.
3. Select **File | Open**.
4. Browse the **%Windir%\System32\Inetsrv** folder.
5. Double-click **Logtemp.sql**.
6. In the first line of the **Logtemp.sql** script, replace **inetlog** with **InternetLog**.
7. Select the database in which you will create the **InternetLog** table. By default, the database is **Master**, but it is not recommended that you use this database.
8. Click **Execute**.
9. Close the SQL Server Query Analyzer.

Use the following steps to configure the DSN source:

1. On the IIS computer, select **Start | Administrative Tools | Data Source (ODBC),** and then click the **System DSN** tab.
2. In the **ODBC Data Source Administrator** dialog box (Figure 4.22), click **Add**.

Figure 4.22 Configuring System DSN - ODBC Data Source Administrator Dialog Box

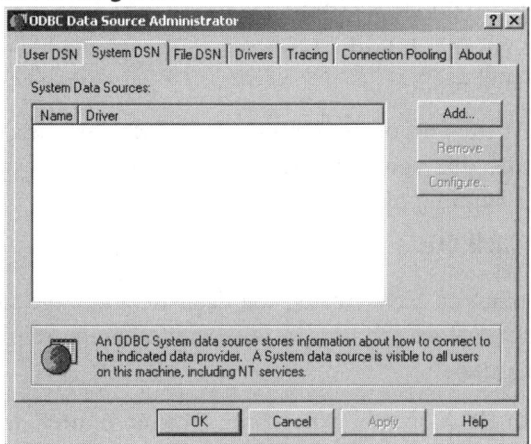

3. When the **Create New Data Source** dialog box appears, select **SQL Server**, then click **Finish**.
4. In the **Create a New Data Source to SQL Server** dialog box (Figure 4.23), enter **HTTPLOG** in the **Name** field.
5. Enter a **Description** and select the SQL **Server** that you want to connect to.
6. Click **Next**.

Figure 4.23 Configuring System DSN – Create a New Data Source to SQL Server Dialog Box

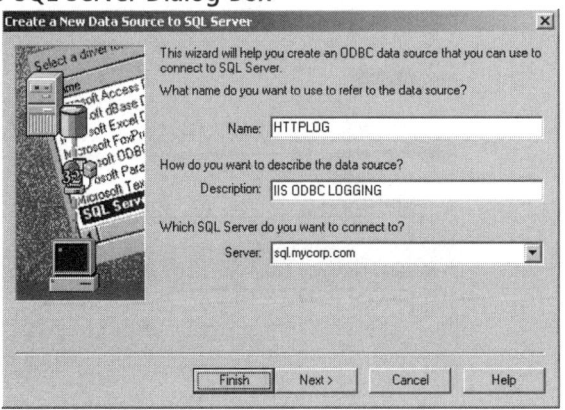

7. Select **With Windows NT authentication using the network login ID** for the computer that is running SQL Server.
8. Ensure the Windows user has access to the SQL server, and click **Next** to continue.
9. Check the client configuration and use the default **Named Pipe** setting. Make sure that the SQL server name is correct, and then click **Next**.
10. Map the **default database** to the database where the template table resides.
11. At the end of the wizard, click **Test the data source**. Make sure that you have successfully connected to the computer that is running SQL Server.
12. Click **OK**.

Now that you have created the database and table structure and configured the DSN source, you can use the following steps to configure IIS ODBC logging:

1. In IIS Manager, expand the local computer, expand the **Web sites** node, right-click the website you wish to configure and click **Properties**.
2. Enable the **Enable logging** option.
3. Ensure **ODBC Logging** is selected in the **Active log format** drop-down list and click **Properties**.
4. In the **Logging Properties** dialog box, click the **Advanced** tab (Figure 4.24).

Figure 4.24 ODBC Logging Properties Dialog Box

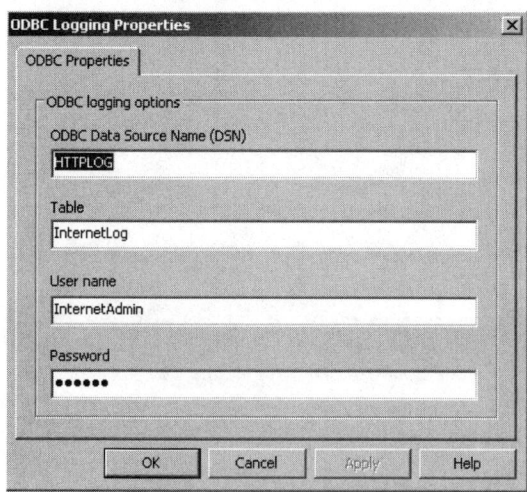

5. Enter a **User name** and **Password** in the available fields.
6. Click **OK**.

You *should not* use ODBC logging if your IIS server is a busy server, since ODBC logging consumes a lot of system resources. Instead, you may want to import IIS log files to the SQL server rather than perform real-time remote logging to the Microsoft SQL server. It is also advised that you do not use SQL SA accounts for ODBC logging, because if malicious users gained access to the server, they could use the SA account to access the entire SQL server.

In IIS 6.0, you can use *centralized binary logging* to increase performance if you are hosting hundreds or thousands of high-volume web-sites. Once enabled, all websites begin writing binary, unformatted log data to the centralized log file and you will not have the option to log to a specific site in a different log format. The default website log file path is located in the %Windir/system32/Logfiles/W3Svc folder,, and the file extension is .ibl, which stands for Internet Binary Log. You cannot read the binary log file using normal text utilities, but you can extract the data from the binary log file by doing one of the following:

- Create your own tool to read the raw data and convert it to meaningful text. You can get more detail about the file headers and descriptions at msdn.microsoft.com.
- Use the log parser tool that ships with the IIS 6.0 resource kit.

To enable centralized binary logging for IIS server, perform the following steps:

1. At the command prompt, access the **AdminScripts** folder (the default path is C:\Inetpub\Adminscripts>).
2. Type **cscript.exe adsutil.vbs SET W3SVC/CentralBinaryLoggingEnabled true**, and press the **Enter** key.
3. Restart the WWW service by entering **net stop w3svc**, then **net start w3svc** at command prompt.

Now that you know how to configure different types of logging formats, it is time to secure the log files. It is important that these log files remain unchanged so that intruders who gain access to your IIS server cannot hide their tracks. The default log path is located at %Windir/system32/Logfiles/W3svcX, where X indicates the site ID that the log file belongs to. This site ID is the identification number generated by IIS when you create the website. In previous versions of IIS, identification numbers are incremental, but in IIS 6.0, the site ID is randomly created by IIS. It is recommended that you relocate this default log path to a dedicated disk volume and secure it with the following NTFS permissions:

- **Administrators** Full Control
- **System** Full Control
- **Backup Operator** Read

If you need to grant log file access to a user or application, you should only grant *read* permissions, as the log file should not be modified at all. When relocating the default log path, you can either place it on a dedicated disk partition or you can configure remote logging, which is another way to help you secure the log file from being modified by attackers. To configure remote logging, perform the following steps.

1. Create and share a log file directory on a remote server in the same domain as the Web server running IIS.

2. Ensure that your IIS server has **Full Control** access permission on the remote share and read and write permissions on the remote log file directory.

3. In IIS Manager, expand the local computer, right-click the **Web Sites** folder, and click **Properties**.

4. On the **Web Site** tab, ensure that the **Enable logging** option is enabled.

5. Select the desired log format from the **Active log format** drop-down list and click **Properties**.

6. In the **Logging Properties** dialog box, click the **General** tab (Figure 4.25)

7. Enter the full UNC path in the **Log file directory** field, for example, **\\servername\W3clogs**, where *servername* represents the name of the remote server, and *W3clogs* represents the remote share name.

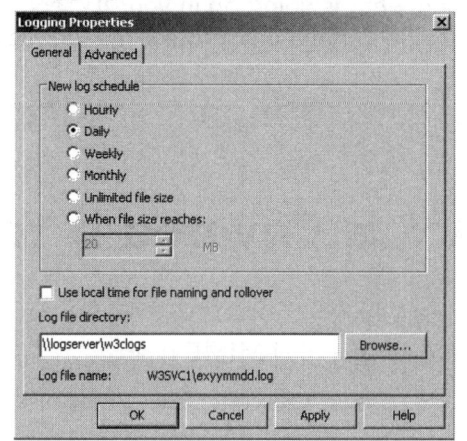

Figure 4.25 Logging Properties – General Tab

8. Click **OK**.

It is highly recommended that you enable IPSec between your web servers and remote logging shared server, as it can prevent data from being intercepted by malicious individuals or network sniffing applications. For more details on IPSec configuration, refer to the Windows Server 2003 help documentation. The following list displays the basic security guidelines that you should follow when enabling and securing an IIS log file:

- Log every single request.
- Always choose W3C extended format and customize the required extended fields.
- Relocate the default log path to a different disk partition or drive.
- Use remote logging whenever possible.
- Grant access to Administrators and System accounts only.
- Archive and backup log files periodically for future tracking.

REALITY CHECK...

Web access log files can provide you with every detail about each request to your IIS server. It is important to know what information can be obtained from the log file to help you identify potential security risks, as well as to troubleshoot request error issues.

The log file is a basic starting point for you to trace and understand what is going on in your IIS server; you should always enable logging and protect the log file using NTFS permissions.

Your A** is Covered if You...

- ☑ Enabled only required web service extensions.
- ☑ Removed unneeded MIME types.
- ☑ Relocated your web content to a new disk volume.
- ☑ Configured a default document for websites.
- ☑ Secured your web content with proper NTFS permissions.
- ☑ Secured your web content with proper website permissions.
- ☑ Configured IP Address and Domain name restrictions
- ☑ Removed unwanted application mappings
- ☑ Denied anonymous user write access to web contents
- ☑ Enabled website request logging.
- ☑ Secured your IIS log files.

Chapter 5
Advanced Web Server Security Configuration

In this Chapter

Now that you are familiar with core web security features in IIS 6.0 such as web service extensions and MIME map settings, we will examine other security options in IIS. We will take an in-depth look at the authentication mechanisms and how IIS user accounts are used. Additionally, we will look at some not-so-often-discussed configuration options that can protect your web applications.

- Configuring Authentication
- Configuring IIS User Accounts
- Configuring URLScan
- Configuring Your Server to Use SSL
- Configuring URL Authorization with the Authorization Manager
- Configuring Custom Error Messages
- Securing Include Files
- Disabling Parent Paths
- Configuring IP Address, TCP Port and Host-Header Combinations

By the end of this chapter you should be familiar with all aspects of the IIS request processing cycle and how settings in IIS can be used to secure your application against various forms of attack. Additional material on the configuration options and their relationship to one another can be found online at www.syngress.com/solutions.

Configuring Authentication

When IIS 6.0 attempts to read a resource from the server's disk, for example, a Hypertext Markup Language (HTML) page, an image, or an active server pages (ASP)/ASP.NET page, it impersonates a Windows user account. That user account's permissions are checked against the NT file system (NTFS) Access Control List (ACL) for the file in question to determine whether the requested action is permitted. In the special case where the end user is not required to supply credentials, IIS 6.0 impersonates the preconfigured "Anonymous User" account.

BY THE BOOK...

IIS provides 7 different authentication mechanisms:

- **Anonymous Authentication** Users do not have to supply credentials and a fixed user account is impersonated.
- **Basic Authentication** Users are prompted to supply a username and password, which are sent unencrypted across the network. Basic authentication is supported by almost all browsers.
- **Digest Authentication** A hash of the user's password is sent across the network. Digest authentication requires domain controllers to be running Windows 2000 or Windows 2003. Digest authentication requires user passwords to be stored using reversible encryption in Active Directory (AD).
- **Advanced Digest Authentication** This is similar to digest authentication in that the same hash process is used for sending the user's password from client to server. With advanced digest authentication however, the user's password is already stored as a Message Digest (MD)5 hash in Active Directory, obviating the need to store the password using reversible encryption. Advanced digest authentication requires a Windows 2003 functional level domain.
- **Integrated Windows Authentication (IWA)** Uses hashing technology to send the user's credentials across the network. IWA offers two authentication systems; NTLM v2 for legacy clients, and Kerberos for Internet Explorer v5 and later. IIS 6.0 supports both NTLM v2 and Kerberos. IWA is the default authentication mechanism in IIS 6.0.

- **UNC (Universal Naming Convention) Authentication** Allows IIS 6.0 to access resources stored on a remote computer using a preconfigured user account specified by the administrator, who has permissions to the remote resource.
- **Microsoft Passport Authentication** A single sign-on technology in which the user's identity is verified by Microsoft's Passport system and authorization to resources is determined by the application.

Any of the above authentication mechanisms can be applied to all websites, an individual website, an individual folder, or a file within a folder. For example, a website can be configured to allow anonymous access, while a single folder within that website can be secured using one of the other authentication mechanisms so that only users with a valid Windows account can get access to the resources in that folder.

Additionally, each resource can have multiple authentication mechanisms enabled. The server and browser will negotiate and choose the most secure method support by both.

The Authentication Process

Regardless of which combination of authentication mechanisms you configure for your website's resources, a browser making an initial request will not send user credentials. That is, the initial request will be made using an anonymous request. If anonymous authentication is configured for the requested resource, then IIS will impersonate the configured anonymous user account (see "Configuring Anonymous Authentication" later in this section).

If anonymous authentication is not enabled, but one of the other authentication mechanisms is enabled, the server and browser will negotiate to select the most secure authentication mechanism enabled on the server and supported by the browser, starting with Integrated Windows Authentication, then Digest/Advanced Digest, and finally Basic Authentication. Passport authentication is not included in this process, as it is a special case. Enabling passport authentication disables all other types of authentication.

Note: If no authentication mechanism is configured, the server will return a Hypertext Transfer Protocol (HTTP) 401.2 "Unauthorized: Logon failed due to server configuration" error.

For subsequent requests to the server, the browser will continue to use the credentials of the previous requests for the new request. For example, if the previous request was anonymous, then the new request will also be anonymous, and if the user supplies a valid Windows username/password using basic authentication, the browser will continue to send that username/password combination for subsequent requests. This behavior will only change if:

- The user closes the browser, in which case the next request to the website will revert to an anonymous request.

- The Web server indicates that the credentials or authentication mechanism are not valid for this new request. In this case, the browser will attempt to negotiate a different authentication mechanism and/or prompt the user for alternate credentials that are valid for the new request.

This has important implications for authentication mechanisms like basic authentication, which does not encrypt user credentials, since all subsequent requests will include the user's credentials, even if the user is not required to authenticate (that is, if anonymous authentication is allowed).

Recall from the request processing flow introduced in Chapter 4 that the authentication and authorization phases of the request processing cycle are separate. At the authentication stage, the user has to supply valid user credentials. Whether the authenticated user has appropriate NTFS file permissions to perform the requested action is determined at a subsequent point in the request processing cycle.

Configuring Anonymous Authentication

When anonymous authentication is permitted, users do not have to supply a Windows username or password to access the resource. In order to access the resource, IIS 6.0 impersonates a configured anonymous user account. In this process, IIS logs on to the server as a particular user on your behalf. If NTFS permissions allow the anonymous user account appropriate access (for example, to read a resource, or write to a file), then the action is performed.

If the configured anonymous user account does not have permissions to access the resource, and an alternate authentication mechanism is enabled, and the browser supports that alternate authentication mechanism, then the user will be prompted to provide a valid Windows username and password. If no alternate mechanism is specified, IIS will return a "401.3 Access Denied Due to ACL on Resource" error.

By default, the anonymous user account is IUSR_<webservername>. This account is created when IIS 6.0 is installed, and IIS keeps a record of the password for this account. You can change the account that is used for anonymous access, and you can enable or disable anonymous access for all websites, or for specific websites, folders, or files. Use the following steps to disable anonymous access:

1. Open the IIS Manager. Right-click the website, folder or file you wish to edit and select **Properties**. To change the settings for all websites, right-click the **Websites** node instead.

2. On the **Directory Security** or **File Security** tab, click **Edit** (shown in Figure 5.1).

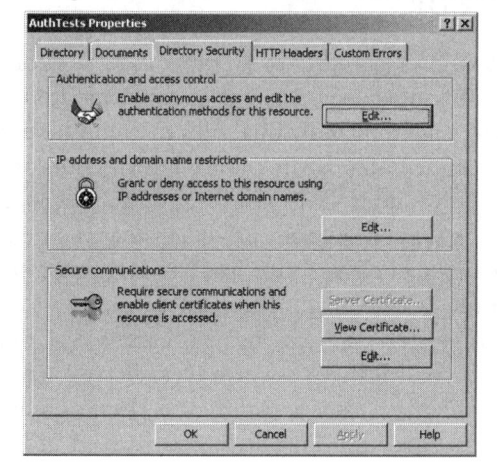

Figure 5.1 Editing Authentication and Access Control

3. To disable anonymous access for the selected resource, disable the **Enable Anonymous Access** option.

4. To change the user account that is impersonated when anonymous access is enabled, enter the desired **User name** or click **Browse** to search for and select the desired username. Enter a **Password** for the user account (Figure 5.2).

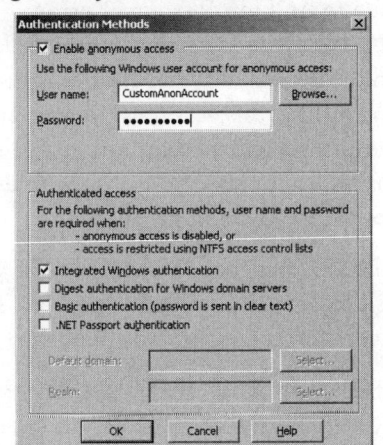

Figure 5.2 Editing Anonymous Access

5. Click **OK**.

Using Windows Explorer or a command line tool, ensure that the configured anonymous user account has appropriate NTFS permissions to the website, folder, or individual files that you have just changed the anonymous user account for (for more information on setting NTFS permissions, see Chapter 4). If you use a custom account, ensure that this account has the same minimum privileges that the default IUSR_<machinename> account has. You can find information on these privileges in the "Configuring IIS User Accounts" section of this chapter.

Note that in previous versions of IIS, there was an additional option to allow IIS to control the password. This allowed IIS to impersonate the configured anonymous user account even IIS didn't have the current password for that account. This feature is disabled in IIS 6.0 by default. See "Configuring SubAuthentication" in this section for more information on this password synchronization feature, and how to enable it.

Configuring Basic Authentication

When basic authentication is configured, users are prompted to supply a valid Windows username and password in order to access resources. The username and password are base64 encoded and passed to the server.

Be aware that base64 encoding is not encryption, and can easily be decoded using readily available tools. To secure the transmission of user credentials between client and server, it is recommended that the connection be secured using Secure Sockets Layer (SSL).

After the initial request in which the user supplies access credentials, the browser will automatically continue to send the same user credentials for all subsequent requests for resources on this server (until the browser is closed). Therefore, all subsequent requests for resources should also be secured using SSL.

Basic authentication is part of the HTTP 1.0 specification, and is thus supported by all major browsers. Because of its simplicity, it can be used safely through proxy servers and firewalls. While using Basic Authentication, IIS 6.0 can access network resources (for example, if it has to log in to a remote SQL server) using the authenticated user's credentials

Note that users will not be prompted for a username and password if anonymous authentication is also enabled. When a browser makes a request for a resource, it does not send user credentials (the request is "anonymous"). If anonymous authentication is enabled, IIS 6.0 will impersonate the configured anonymous user account and process the request. To force the browser to prompt the user for credentials, anonymous authentication must be disabled.

Basic authentication can be configured for all websites, or for individual websites, folders, or files. To configure basic authentication, perform the following steps:

1. Open the IIS Manager. Right-click the desired website, folder or file and select **Properties**. To change settings for all websites, right-click the **Websites** node instead.
2. On the **Directory Security** or **File Security** tab, click **Edit**.
3. Enable the **Basic Authentication (password is sent in clear text)** option (Figure 5.3).

Figure 5.3 Enabling Basic Authentication

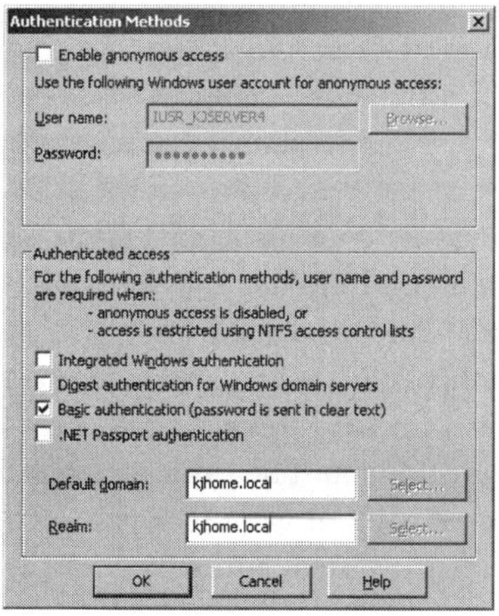

4. IIS will provide a warning concerning the vulnerability of clear text passwords and you will be prompted to confirm your selection. Select **Yes** to enable Basic Authentication.

5. If desired, enter a Windows domain in the **Default domain** field to specify the domain against which the user's credentials will be checked if the user does not supply a domain name when prompted by his or her browser. If you do not supply a name, IIS 6.0 will use the name of the local machine.

6. If desired, enter a Windows domain in the **Realm** field. This entry will be displayed as part of the dialogue box prompting for user credentials in the user's browser. It is recommended that you make this the same as the **Default domain** field.

Configuring Digest Authentication

When digest authentication is configured, users are prompted to supply a Windows username and password. The username is passed in clear text, but the password is hashed by the client. Hashing relies on the use of mathematical algorithms that cannot be reversed. Given a "hashed" value, the original value is impossible to determine from the hash alone. Simple examples of hashing functions include trigonometric functions like Sin() and Cos(). The sine of any value yields a distinct result, however given the result, it is impossible to determine the original value, since the inverse sine of the result yields an infinite number of possible original values.

Digest authentication is defined in RFC 2617, and is an open standard. A number of browsers support digest authentication, including Microsoft Internet Explorer v5 and later, Mozilla v1.4 and later, and Opera v6 and later. Because older browsers do not support digest authentication, you may need to enable basic authentication if you want your website to support these older browsers. Digest authentication is safe to use through proxies and firewalls.

When a browser requests a resource secured with digest authentication, IIS 6.0 will send back a random piece of data called a *nonce*. The browser will generate its own piece of random data (the client nonce, or cnonce). It will then combine the cnonce with the server's nonce, the user's password, and some other data about the request, and generate a hash. The client returns this hash, plus its cnonce, to IIS 6.0. This is called *the digest*. IIS 6.0 will forward this result to the domain controller responsible for the relevant domain. The domain controller will perform the same operation on its copy of the user's password, and if the hashes match, then the user is deemed authenticated.

Because only the cnonce and hash are required to access a resource, digest authentication is susceptible to replay attacks if someone is able to capture packets between the client and the server. This replay window is limited because the server will eventually expire the nonce originally sent to the client, meaning that the hash value is no longer valid to access the resource.

Note that the user will not be prompted to supply a username and password if anonymous authentication is also enabled. When a browser makes a request for a resource, it does not send user credentials (the request is "anonymous"). If anonymous authentication is enabled, IIS 6.0 will impersonate the configured anonymous user account and process the request. To force the browser to prompt the user for credentials, anonymous authentication must be disabled.

The following are required in order to use digest authentication:

- A browser that supports digest authentication (for example, Internet Explorer 5 or later, Mozilla 1.4 or later, or Opera v6 or later).

- The IIS 6.0 server and the user account being used must both reside in the same Windows domain (or trusted domains).

- The user password must be stored using reversible encryption in Active Directory. Digest authentication is not supported for accounts that are local to the IIS 6.0 server. The user account must be a domain account.

- The domain controllers must be running Windows 2000 Server or Windows Server 2003.

- SubAuthentication must be enabled (see "Configuring SubAuthentication" later in this section).

- The process identity of the web application pool that the request is being served from must be running as LocalSystem, not as the default Network Service. See "Configuring IIS User Accounts" in this chapter for information on changing the process identity of a web application pool. Note that setting the process identity to LocalSystem could pose a security risk, as this identity has full access to the entire system.

- The UseDigestSSP metabase key must be set to 0 (false) in the IIS metabase. If this key is not present, then IIS 6.0 will assume that it is 0. This key can be set for all websites, individual websites, folders, or files. If the key is set to 1 (true), IIS 6.0 will attempt to use advanced digest authentication instead, which may fail if the requirements for advanced digest authentication are not met.

To set this key, you can use the graphical Metabase Explorer tool supplied with the IIS 6.0 Resource Kit. You can download the IIS 6.0 Resource Kit tools from www.microsoft.com/downloads/details.aspx?FamilyID=56fc92ee-a71a-4c73-b628-ade629c89499&DisplayLang=en. Alternatively, you can use the following command line script, ensuring that you have administrative privileges on the IIS 6.0 server:

```
adsutil.vbs set w3svc/UseDigestSSP 0
```

See the IIS online help (accessible from the IIS Manager) for examples on using this script to manipulate the IIS Metabase, and visit www.syngress.com/solutions to view the appendix for additional information.

Digest authentication can be configured for all websites, or for individual websites, folders, or files. To configure digest authentication:

1. Open the IIS Manager. Right-click the website, folder, or file you wish to edit and select **Properties**. To change settings for all websites, right-click the **Websites** node instead.
2. On the **Directory Security** or **File Security** tab, click **Edit**.
3. Enable the **Digest authentication for Windows domain servers** option (shown in Figure 5.4).
4. IIS will display a warning stating that digest authentication only works with domain accounts. Click **Yes** to enable digest authentication.

Figure 5.4 Configuring Digest Authentication

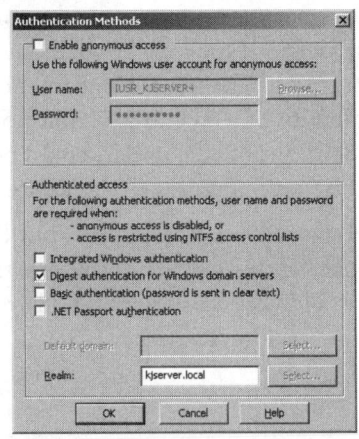

5. If desired, enter a Windows domain in the **Realm** field. This is the Windows domain that will be used to authenticate the user if the user does not supply a domain as part of his or her credentials. It will also be displayed to user as part of the password prompt.

IIS versions prior to IIS 6.0 contain a bug that results in basic authentication being listed prior to digest authentication if both are enabled for a resource. This results in some browsers (including Internet Explorer) choosing basic authentication instead of digest authentication. In IIS 6.0, this bug has been fixed and digest authentication is listed before basic authentication when a list of supported authentication mechanisms is sent to the client.

Configuring Advanced Digest Authentication

Advanced digest authentication is similar to digest authentication in its communication between client and server. However, advanced digest authentication differs from digest authentication in the following ways:

- In advanced digest authentication, the domain controllers (DCs) must be running Windows Server 2003, and the domain functional level must be raised to Windows 2003. Windows 2003 domain controllers store a number of hashes of a user's password when the user password is set. This includes an MD5 hash of the password. These pre-calculated hashes are stored as fields in the AltSecId field of the user object in Active Directory.

- In advanced digest authentication, the user's password does not have to be stored using reversible encryption in Active Directory. This is because the hash sent by the IIS 6.0 server to the domain controller can be compared directly with the pre-calculated MD5 password hash stored in Active Directory.

- IIS 6.0 does not require SubAuthentication, so the process identity web application pool servicing the request for the resource does not have to be LocalSystem.

- The UseDigestSSP metabase property must be set to 1 (true). If this property is set to 0, or not set at all, digest authentication will be used. Digest authentication may fail if the other requirements for digest authentication are not met.

To set the UseDigestSSP key, you can use the graphical Metabase Explorer tool supplied with the IIS 6.0 Resource Kit. You can download the IIS 6.0 Resource Kit tools from: www.microsoft.com/downloads/details.aspx?FamilyID=56fc92ee-a71a-4c73-b628-ade629c89499&DisplayLang=en.

Alternatively, you can use the following command line script, ensuring that you have administrative privileges on the IIS 6.0 server:

```
adsutil.vbs set w3svc/UseDigestSSP 1
```

See the online help system (accessible from the IIS Manager) for examples on using this script to manipulate the IIS Metabase.

Advanced digest authentication can be configured for all websites, or for individual websites, folders, or files. Use the following steps to configure advanced digest authentication:

1. Open the IIS Manager. Right-click the website, folder, or file you wish to edit and select **Properties**. To change settings for all websites, right-click the **Websites** node instead.
2. On the **Directory Security** or **File Security** tab, click **Edit**.
3. Enable the **Digest authentication for Windows domain servers** option.
4. IIS will provide a warning stating that digest authentication only works with domain accounts. Click **Yes** to enable advanced digest authentication.

Configuring Integrated Windows Authentication

Integrated windows authentication is deemed by IIS 6.0 to be the most secure method of authenticating clients. When a server is configured to use IWA, the user is prompted to supply credentials; however, credentials are not passed across the network in clear text. Additionally, Internet Explorer can be configured to automatically supply the user credentials of the current user (by default, this is enabled for sites in the *intranet security zone*. For more information on the IE intranet security zone, see http://support.microsoft.com/?id=258063). If the automatically supplied user credentials are not acceptable to the IIS 6.0 server, then the user is prompted to supply alternate credentials.

IWA encompasses two authentication mechanisms:

- NTLM v2, for older clients. NTLM v2 authentication is supported by Internet Explorer v3 and later, as well as some third-party browsers, such as Mozilla v1.4.

- Kerberos v5 authentication, which is supported by Internet Explorer v5 and later.

When a browser requests a resource secured using IWA, the IIS 6.0 server returns two HTTP WWW-authenticate headers; one for Kerberos authentication and one for NTLM v2. The browser then selects the more secure of the two that it supports.

NTLM v2 authentication is similar to digest authentication. When a browser wishes to use NTLM authentication:

- The server sends a nonce to be used in creating a digest of the user's password.

- The browser hashes the user's password using the NTLM v2 algorithm. It then adds the server-supplied nonce to the result of this first hash and creates a digest by hashing this combined string. This is returned to the server.

- The server (or domain controller) already has the user's password stored as an NTLM v2 hash. It merely adds the nonce and performs the same secondary hash the client performed. If the two hashes match, the user is deemed authenticated. The benefit of this mechanism over digest authentication is that it obviates the need to store user passwords using reversible encryption.

One drawback to NTLM v2 authentication is that it requires a number of requests and responses to go back and forth between the client and server. This must be done over a continuously open HTTP connection. Because of this requirement, NTLM v2 authentication does not work through most HTTP proxies.

Kerberos v5 authentication is an open, industry-standard, ticket-based authentication method first developed at the Massachusetts Institute of Technology (MIT). It uses challenge/response technologies, timestamps for nonces, and a ticket granting service to facilitate a single sign-on. Kerberos v5 is a much more complex authentication mechanism than NTLM v2.

When a client wishes to access a resource secured with Kerberos authentication:

- It first contacts the Kerberos authentication server (AS). The AS, using a secret known to both the AS and client (namely a hash of the user's password) transmits a temporary *ticket granting ticket* (TGT) to the client. The TGT can then be used instead of a hash of the user's password for subsequent accesses to network resources. This obviates the need to cache the hash of the user's password (which increases security by not requiring the user to enter his or her password for each network access, and increases performance by allowing the application to cache the TGT). The TGT is valid only for a limited time, thereby reducing its usefulness to attackers in case it is stolen.

- The client then contacts the ticket granting services (TGS), to get a ticket to access the service hosting the secured resource (that is, the website hosted by IIS 6.0). The TGS transmits a ticket to the browser again using a shared secret (the TGT). Additionally, the TGS transmits a session key to the browser.

- The AS and TGS are together known as the Kerberos Distribution Center (KDC). In a Windows domain, domain controllers host the KDC.

- The browser then contacts IIS 6.0 with the ticket received from the TGS. The ticket is encrypted with a key known to IIS6, and contains a session key. The browser also transmits a timestamp encoded with the session key. The server uses the extracted session key to decode the timestamp and ensure that the time matches the web server's time (a slight discrepancy is allowed). This prevents replay attacks, since an attacker cannot generate an updated encrypted timestamp.

The Kerberos authentication method is depicted in Figure 5.5.

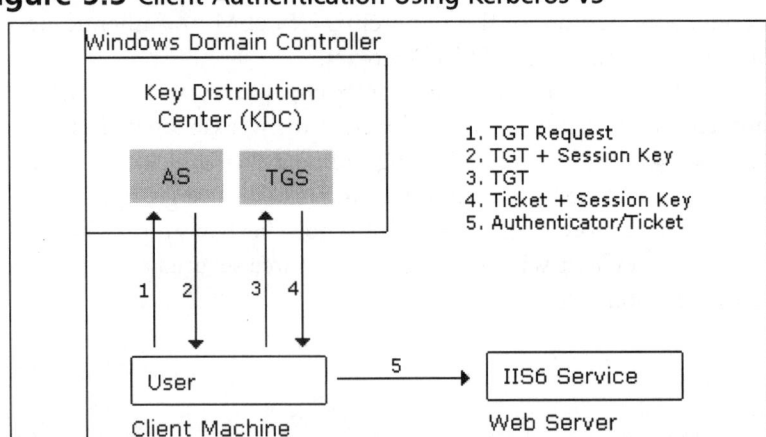

Figure 5.5 Client Authentication Using Kerberos v5

For more information on Kerberos authentication, the following URLs may be useful:

- **Kerberos Explained** www.microsoft.com/msj/0899/kerberos/kerberos.aspx
- **Windows 2000 Kerberos Authentication** www.microsoft.com/technet/prodtechnol/windows2000serv/deploy/confeat/kerberos.mspx
- **JSCI Kerberos FAQ** www.wedgetail.com/jcsi/kerberos/FAQ.html

Note that the user will not be prompted to supply a username and password if anonymous authentication is also enabled. When a browser makes a request for a resource, it does not send user credentials (the request is "anonymous"). If anonymous authentication is enabled, IIS 6.0 will impersonate the configured anonymous user account and process the request. To force the browser to prompt the user for credentials, anonymous authentication must be disabled. Additionally, as mentioned previously, Internet Explorer can be configured to automatically send the credentials of the current user. In this instance, the user is not prompted for credentials, but the browser does send them to the server.

When using Kerberos authentication, IIS 6.0 can access a remote resource (for example, to log in to a remote SQL server) using the authenticated user's credentials when delegation is configured. This is not possible when using NTLM v2 authentication unless IIS 6.0 resides in a Windows 2003 domain.

To use Kerberos authentication, the following requirements must be met:

- Clients must support Kerberos authentication. This requires Internet Explorer v5 or later. Additionally, the client operating system must be Windows 2000 or Windows XP or Windows Server 2003. Windows NT 4 and earlier, and Windows 9x do not natively support Kerberos authentication.

- In Internet Explorer, the **Use Integrated Windows Authentication (requires a restart)** option must be enabled. This option is not enabled by default when using Internet Explorer v5 on Windows 2000. For more information see http://support.microsoft.com/?id=299838.

- Client machines must be able to contact the KDC or Windows domain controllers to get their Kerberos tickets. For this reason, Kerberos authentication is often described as being stopped by firewalls, since firewalls typically do not allow computers on the unsecured side to communicate with DCs located on the secured side.

- The Service Principal Name (SPN) must be registered with Active Directory. By default, the NetBIOS name (http://servername) of the IIS 6.0 server is registered under the default application pool identity (network service) that it runs under. To make alterations or add new SPNs you use the Setspn.exe tool. If you change the account that is used as the process identity of the application pool servicing http://servername you need to reregister the SPN: Setspn.exe –A http/<servername> Domain\NewUserAccount.

If the website is accessed using a Domain Name System (DNS) or Windows Internet Name Service (WINS) name that differs from the NetBIOS name, then this must also be registered manually using the setSPN tool. Replace the server name with the DNS or WINS name that the website is being accessed with. For more information on using the Setspn.exe tool, see: http://support.microsoft.com/?id=294382.

Setspn.exe is part of the Windows 2000 Resource Kit, and is available for download from www.microsoft.com/windows2000/techinfo/reskit/tools/existing/setspn-o.asp.

Note that if you have multiple web applications within a website, and you assign them to web application pools that have differing process identities, Kerberos delegation will not work. Kerberos delegation requires a given SPN, being the website's host name (for example, www.myCompany.com) to be associated with a single user account. Web applications allocated to web application pools running under differing process identities share the same SPN, but do not run under the same user account, and Kerberos delegation will fail.

Integrated Windows authentication can be configured for all websites, or for individual websites, folders, or files. Use the following steps to configure IWA:

1. Open the IIS Manager. Right-click the website, folder, or file you wish to edit and select **Properties**. To change settings for all websites, right-click the **Websites** node instead.

2. On the **Directory Security** or **File Security** tab, click **Edit**.

3. To enable IWA, enable the **Integrated Windows Authentication** option.

Configuring UNC Authentication

UNC authentication (also known as UNC passthrough authentication) allows you to configure IIS to use a specified user account for accessing resources on a remote share. When you create a virtual directory or a website that obtains its content from a remote share, IIS prompts you to supply a username and password for the remote share. This will be used when a user requests a resource from your website. To configure UNC authentication:

1. Open the IIS Manager, and locate the folder under which you will create a new virtual directory.
2. Right-click the folder and select **New | Virtual Directory**.
3. Enter an **Alias** for the virtual directory. This will be the folder name used by visitors to your site. For example, if you enter **UNCTest**, users will access this folder as http://yourserver/UNCTest/.
4. Click **Next**.
5. Use the **Path** field to enter a UNC path to a remote server, for example, **\\remoteServer\shareName**.
6. Click **Next**.
7. Disable the **Always use authenticated user's credentials when validating access to the network directory** option.
8. Enter the **User name** and **Password** that will be used to access the remote share (shown in Figure 5.6). Note that if the username and password you supply are not valid for the remote share, users will receive an "HTTP 500 Internal Server Error: Invalid Username or Password" error message.

Figure 5.6 Configuring UNC Authentication

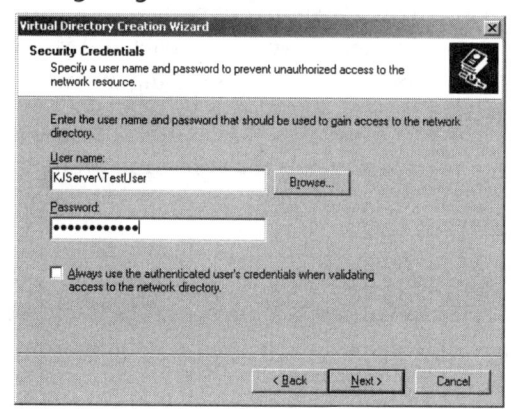

9. Re-enter the password when prompted, then click **Next**.
10. Choose the web permissions that should be allowed for the virtual directory. The default is to allow **Read** (for static files) and **Scripts** (for dynamic content).

Passport Authentication

Passport authentication is a single sign-on authentication mechanism that is a proprietary Microsoft technology. When passport authentication is enabled on a resource, all other methods are disabled. When users access the resource, IIS checks for a passport authentication ticket cookie. If the cookie is not present, or if the credentials are not valid for the resource, the user is redirect to a Microsoft passport logon server. After authenticating, the user is redirected back to the original URL.

Enabling passport authentication requires that you sign up with the Microsoft passport service. For more information on Microsoft passport authentication, see: www.microsoft.com/net/services/passport/business.asp. For more information on enabling passport authentication on an IIS server, see: www.microsoft.com/resources/documentation/IIS/6/all/proddocs/en-us/sec_auth_passport.asp.

Configuring SubAuthentication

SubAuthentication is the mechanism by which IIS can synchronize the passwords it uses with passwords stored in Active Directory or the local security accounts database. SubAuthentication was installed by default in earlier versions of IIS, but it is not installed by default with IIS 6.0 because it constitutes a potential security vulnerability. A user with privileges to administer a website can set the anonymous user to an account with elevated privileges (for example, a domain administrator account) without supplying a corresponding password, by enabling the **Allow IIS to Control Password** option.

SubAuthentication may have to be enabled if you want IIS to synchronize passwords, or if you want to use digest authentication. To enable SubAuthentication:

1. Enter the following at the command prompt and press **Enter**:

    ```
    rundll %windir%\system32\iissuba.dll,RegisterIISSUBA
    ```

2. Set the process identity for the application pool in question to **LocalSystem** (see "Configuring IIS User Accounts" in this chapter for more information on configuring web application

pool identities). Note that setting the process identity to LocalSystem could pose a security risk, as this identity has full access to the entire system.

3. Set the **AnonymousPasswordSync** metabase property to **1** (true). To set this key, you can use the graphical Metabase Explorer tool supplied with the IIS 6.0 Resource Kit. You can download the IIS 6.0 Resource Kit tools from www.microsoft.com/downloads/details.aspx?FamilyID=56fc92e e-a71a-4c73-b628-ade629c89499&DisplayLang=en.

    Alternatively, you can use the following command line script to set this property, ensuring that you have administrative privileges on the IIS 6.0 server:

    ```
    adsutil.vbs set w3svc/AnonymousPasswordSync 1
    ```

    See the IIS online help (accessible from the IIS Manager) for examples on using this script to manipulate the IIS Metabase.

To disable SubAuthentication, enter the following at a command prompt and press **Enter**:

```
rundll %windir%\system32\iissuba.dll,UnregisterIISSUBA
```

Configuring Delegation

Delegation is the process by which a service may impersonate a user account and log on to network resources on behalf of that user. Kerberos supports this process if both the computer impersonating, and the user account being impersonated are configured to be *trusted for delegation*.

In a Windows 2003 domain, delegation can be limited to specific services. So, if you enable IIS 6.0 to be able to impersonate specific users, you can limit the services that IIS 6.0 can connect to when it impersonates. In a Windows 2000 domain, this restriction cannot be set.

Perform the following steps to enable delegation in a Windows 2003 domain:

1. Open the **Active Directory Users and Computers** Administrative tool on a Domain Controller, or any machine where this tool has been installed.

2. Locate the computer account for the server that IIS 6.0 is running on. Right-click it and select **Properties**.

3. On the Delegation tab choose either **Trust this computer for delegation to any service (Kerberos Only)** or **Trust this computer for delegation to specified services only**. If you choose the latter, enable either **Use Kerberos Only** or **Use any authentication protocol**.

4. If you have chosen to allow delegation for specific services only, click the **Add** button. In **Add Services**, select **Users or Computers**. Enter the target computer name in the **Enter the object names to select** field. In the **Add Services** section, add the service(s) that IIS 6.0 can connect to.

5. Locate the user account(s) that will be trusted for delegation. Right-click and select **Properties**.

6. On the Delegation tab, enable the **Trust this user for delegation to any service (Kerberos only)** or **Trust this user for delegation to specified services only** option. If you choose the latter, enable either **Use Kerberos Only** or **Use any authentication protocol**. If you choose Use any authentication protocol, IIS 6.0 can use a Kerberos token to access a remote resource on the user's behalf even if the initial authentication to IIS by the browser was via NTLM or digest authentication. More information on Windows 2003 protocol transition can be found on the Microsoft website: www.microsoft.com/technet/prodtechnol/windowsserver2003/technologies/security/constdel.mspx.

7. If you have chosen to allow delegation for specific services only, click the **Add** button and select **Users and Computers**. Enter the name of the computer that the user will be trusted to delegate for.

8. In **Add Services**, select the service or services that will be trusted for delegation, then click **OK**.

REALITY CHECK...

IIS 6.0 offers a wide variety of standard and proprietary authentication mechanisms. The following may be used as a useful summary of benefits and drawbacks:

- Basic authentication is the most widely supported, as it is part of the HTTP 1.0 specification. It works safely through HTTP proxies and firewalls. However, user credentials are

not encrypted, and so alternate methods (such as SSL) should be used to ensure that user credentials cannot be intercepted. If IIS 6.0 has to access a network resource using the authenticated user's credentials, then this can be done when using basic authentication.
- Digest/advanced digest authentication is an improvement over basic authentication, and is an open standard defined in RFC 2617. It relies on the client supporting HTTP v1.1. The user password is hashed, and thus cannot be decrypted. However, it is vulnerable, in a time-limited sense, to replay attacks. Digest/advanced digest authentication works safely through HTTP proxies and firewalls. However there are additional server requirements above basic authentication.
- Integrated Windows authentication is deemed by IIS 6.0 to be the most secure method of authenticating clients. It comprises two authentication systems; NTLM v2, which is supported by IE v3 and later (and Mozilla v1.4 and later), and Kerberos, which is supported by IE v5 and later running on Windows 2000, Windows XP or Windows Server 2003. Depending on how delegation is configured, it may be possible for IIS 6.0 to connect to remote resources on the user's behalf.

Configuring IIS User Accounts

IIS 6.0 uses a number of built-in Windows accounts, as well as a number of IIS-specific user accounts. The user accounts that are actively used depend on whether IIS 6.0 is running in IIS5 isolation mode or in IIS 6.0 worker process mode (see Chapter 1 for more information on these modes).

BY THE BOOK...

IIS 6.0 provides two major application processing modes: IIS 6.0 worker process isolation mode and IIS 5.0 isolation mode (for backward compatibility with IIS 5.0 applications).

In IIS 6.0 worker process isolation mode web applications are assigned to web application pools, which can each be configured to use a separate process identity. The core IIS 6.0 services run under LocalSystem.

In IIS 5.0 isolation mode, web applications can either run inside the core IIS processes (running as LocalSystem), or out of process in a separate dllhost.exe process. These processes can be assigned separate process identities.

The default accounts used by IIS 6.0 in worker process isolation mode for running any process that executes user-supplied code are low privilege accounts, which helps reduce the possible damage that a malicious attacker can inflict should an application be compromised.

IIS 6.0 Running in Worker Process Mode

When IIS 6.0 is running in worker process mode, websites and web applications (by default, a website is always configured as a web application) run inside web application pools. Each web application pool is represented by a w3wp.exe process, which is visible in Task Manager. Each w3wp.exe process has a process identity. This is the user context that the worker process runs under. This identity is required because a w3wp.exe process can be running even if there are no requests coming in from browsers.

IIS 6.0 provides the following three preconfigured user accounts that can be used as the process identity for a web application pool. You can also provide your own user account, which we will examine shortly.

- **LocalSystem** The built-in LocalSystem account has a high level of access rights. It is part of the Administrators group and can access the entire system. Running a worker process as LocalSystem can be a security risk; if the worker process or an application running inside that worker process is compromised, attackers may have full access to the system. Some IIS configurations (for example, enabling digest authentication or enabling SubAuthentication) require the relevant worker process to run as LocalSystem.

- **Network Service** The built-in Network Service account has far fewer access rights to the system than LocalSystem. This is the default process identity when creating new web application pools. The Network Service user account is able to access the same network resources as the computer it is running on.

- **Local Service** The built-in Local Service account has the same privileges as Network Service on the local machine, but is unable to access the network. Use this account if the worker process does not need access to resources outside the local computer

- **IIS_WPG Group** The accounts mentioned are all members of the IIS_WPG group. This group is assigned the minimum permissions required for a worker process to start. If you manually create a separate user account to use as a worker process identity, ensure that it is added to this group, otherwise the worker process may fail to start.

These accounts have the following user rights (as shown with an "x" in Table 5.1). This table also lists the IUSR_<machinename> account, which will be discussed shortly.

Table 5.1 User Rights for Common IIS 6.0 User Accounts

User Right	Local System	Network Service	Local Service	IIS_WPG Group	IUSR_<machinename>
Full Access	x				
Replace a Process Level Token (SeAssignPrimaryTokenPrivilege)		x	x		
Adjust Memory Quotas for a process (SeIncreaseQuota-Privilege)		x	x		
Generate Security Audits (sseAuditPrivilege)		x	x		
Bypass Traverse Checking (SeChangeNotifyPrivilege)		x	x	x	x
Access this computer from a network (SeNetworkLogonRight)		x	x	x	x
Logon as a Batch Job (SeBatchLogonRight)		x	x	x	x

Continued

Table 5.1 User Rights for Common IIS 6.0 User Accounts

User Right	Local System	Network Service	Local Service	IIS_WPG Group	IUSR_<machinename>
Logon as a Service (SeInteractiveLogonRight)	x				
Allow Logon Locally (SeInteractiveLogonRight)		x			x

Changing the Process Identity of a Web Application Pool

Perform the following steps to change the process identity of a web application pool:

1. Open the IIS Manager and expand the **Application Pools** node. Right-click the web application pool that you wish to change the identity of and select **Properties**.

2. On the **Identity** tab, select one of the three preconfigured accounts from the drop-down list (shown in Figure 5.7) or specify a custom account by selecting the **Configurable** option.

Figure 5.7 Configuring a Web Application Pool Identity

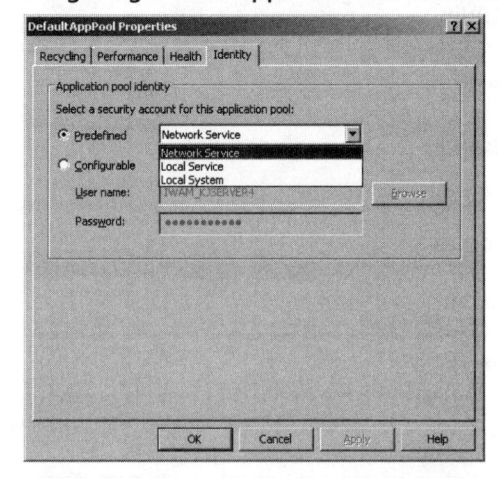

3. Click **OK**.

Other User Accounts – IUSR_<machinename>

The IUSR_<machinename> account is also important when running IIS 6.0 in worker process isolation mode. When anonymous authentication is configured, the user requesting the resource from IIS does not have to provide Windows user credentials. Instead, IIS impersonates the configured anonymous user account, which is IUSR_<machinename> by default.

Note that by default, ASP.NET applications do not use IUSR_<machinename> for anonymous requests. ASP.NET applications use the process identity of web application pool they are in. This can be changed to the IIS anonymous user account in the web.config file by adding:

```
<identity impersonate="true">
```

All other requests (for static files, or ASP applications) use IUSR_<machinename>. Table 5.1 lists the user rights held by IUSR_<machinename>.

You can change the account that is used for anonymous access for all websites, or for individual websites, folders, or files. To do so, perform the following steps:

1. Open the IIS Manager. Right-click the website, folder, or file you wish to edit and select **Properties**. To change settings for all website, right-click the **Websites** node instead.
2. On the **Directory Security** or **File Security** tab, click **Edit**.
3. To disable anonymous access for the resource, disable the **Enable Anonymous Access** option. To change the user account that is impersonated when anonymous access is enabled, enter the **User name** of the user account, or click the **Browse** button to search for and select the account. Enter the **Password** for the user account and click **OK**.

IIS 6.0 Running in IIS5 Isolation Mode

When running in IIS 5.0 isolation mode, web application pools are not used to host websites or web applications. Instead, each website or web application can be set to one of three isolation levels:

- **Low Isolation** When set to low isolation, the web application runs inside the InetInfo.exe process. This process runs as the built-in LocalSystem.

- **Medium Isolation** When set to medium isolation, the web application runs inside dllhost.exe. A single dllhost.exe process hosts all web applications set to medium isolation. By default, the process identity of dllhost.exe is IWAM_<computername>.

- **High Isolation** When set to high isolation, the web application runs inside a dedicated dllhost.exe. There will be one dllhost.exe process for each web application configured to use high isolation. As with medium isolation, the process identity for the dllhost.exe process is IWAM_<computername>.

Note that these descriptions do not apply to ASP.NET applications. All ASP.NET applications run inside a single, separate process called aspnet_wp.exe. This uses the local ASPNET account as its process identity. Table 5.2 lists the user rights held by these accounts. A user right held by an account is indincated with an "x." If a particular user is explicitly denied a right, it is indicated with a "denied."

Table 5.2 User Rights Held by Common IIS 5.0 Isolation Mode User Accounts

User Right	IUSR_<machinename>	IWAM_<machinename>	ASPNET
Replace a Process Level Token (SeAssignPrimaryTokenPrivilege)		x	
Adjust Memory Quotas for a process (SeIncreaseQuotaPrivilege)		x	
Bypass Traverse Checking (SeChangeNotifyPrivilege)	x	x	

Continued

Table 5.2 User Rights Held by Common IIS 5.0 Isolation Mode User Accounts

User Right	IUSR_ <machinename>	IWAM_ <machinename>	ASPNET
Access this computer from a network (SeNetworkLogon-Right)	x	x	x
Logon as a Batch Job (SeBatchLogon-Right)	x	x	x
Logon as a Service (SeInteractiveLogon-Right)			x
Allow Logon Locally (SeInteractiveLogon-Right)	x		Denied
Logon through Terminal Services (SeDenyRemoteInteractiveLogonRight)			Denied

IWAM_<computername> Account

IWAM_<computername> is the default process identity for *out of process* web applications. Out of process refers to being outside the code InetInfo.exe process, and thus refers to medium and high isolation applications.

Use the following steps to change the user account used for an out of process application:

1. Open the **Component Services** MMC snap-in, located in the **Administrative Tools** folder.

2. Expand the **Computer** node, then expand the **COM+ Applications** node.

3. Right-click **IIS Out-Of-Process Pooled Applications** and select **Properties**.

4. On the **Identity** tab, select one of the preconfigured accounts or enter your own custom account and corresponding password.

5. Click **OK**.

ASPNET Account

The ASPNET account is used as the process identity for the aspnet_wp.exe process. This process is used to host all ASP.NET applications running on the server.

To change this process identity you need to edit the **<ProcessModel>** section of the machine.config file located in %windir%\Microsoft.Net\Framework\<framework_version>\config\. The machine.config file is an XML file, and can be edited in any text editor.

IUSR_<machinename>

The IUSR_<machinename> account is used for the same purposes in IIS5 isolation mode as in IIS 6.0 worker process isolation mode.

> **REALITY CHECK...**
>
> IIS 6.0 ships in a locked-down configuration, and this extends to the user rights granted to the accounts that are used in a default IIS configuration. Unless you have a good reason to do so, it is generally unwise to change the default configuration.
>
> You may wish to change the anonymous user account to a domain account if your web application requires the privileges that a domain user has. Or, if you are a hosting company that needs to strictly isolate each client's website, you will also need to have a custom configuration. In other circumstances however, the default configuration is a good compromise between safety and flexibility.

Configuring URLScan

Microsoft provides an Internet Server Application Programming Interface (ISAPI) filter called URLScan, which is designed to examine incoming requests very early in the processing cycle, and to reject requests that are not deemed to be acceptable. URLScan was initially released with the

IISLockDown tool. The IISLockDown tool, when run on Windows 2000 machines, disables a number of IIS features that were enabled by default, thus reducing the attack surface of IIS 5.0. There is no IISLockDown tool for IIS 6.0, as IIS 6.0 ships in a locked-down state.

> ### BY THE BOOK…
>
> URLScan is a security tool that restricts the types of HTTP requests that IIS will process. By blocking specific HTTP requests, the URLScan security tool helps prevent potentially harmful requests from reaching the server. URLScan v2.5 has been updated to work with IIS 6.0, and installs on servers running IIS 4.0 and later.
>
> Many of the features of URLScan were absorbed into IIS 6.0. However, URLScan does offer a number of features that are not available with IIS 6.0, and also offers additional flexibility that is not available with IIS 6.0.
>
> Microsoft provides information about URLScan capabilities at www.microsoft.com/technet/security/tools/urlscan.mspx. Included is a comparison between URLScan's capabilities and IIS 6.0 native capabilities to help evaluate whether URLScan is appropriate for your server.

URLScan can be downloaded from www.microsoft.com/technet/security/tools/urlscan.mspx. To install URLScan, run the setup.exe file. To uninstall it at any time, use the **Add/Remove Programs Control Panel**. Once URLScan is installed, you can configure its settings by navigating to %windir%\system32\inetsrv\urlscan, which contains the URLScan.ini file. Open this file in Notepad.exe (or a similar text editor) to edit the settings. URLScan.ini settings are read in by the URLScan filter when IIS is started. For changes to the settings to take effect, you will have to restart the IISAdmin service. You can do that within the IIS Manager by right-clicking on your server and selecting **All Tasks | Restart IIS**. You can also restart IIS from the command line by typing **iisreset.exe**.

Configuring URLScan.ini

The URLScan.ini file is divided into sections. The first section, **[Options]**, contains most of the major settings (listed in Table 5.3). Other sections contain supplemental information pertinent to the selections made in the **[Options]** section. To comment out any particular setting, begin the line with a semicolon.

Table 5.3 The [Options] section of URLScan.ini

Parameter	Explanation
UseAllowVerbs = 0 | 1	If UseAllowVerbs is set to 1, the HTTP verbs (for example, GET and POST) listed in the [AllowVerbs] section will be used. Requests using other verbs will be rejected. If set to 0, requests using the HTTP verbs listed in the [DenyVerbs] section will be denied, and all other requests allowed. The default is 1.
UseAllowExtensions = 0 | 1	If UseAllowExtensions is set to 1, requests for files ending in the extensions listed in the [AllowExtensions] section will be allowed, and all others denied. If set to 0, requests for files ending in the extensions listed in the [DenyExtensions] section will be denied, and all others allowed.
NormalizeUrlBeforeScan = 0 | 1	Requests can be encoded. Here a value in the URL is replaced with a % sign followed by the numerical ASCII value. For example, the "." character can be encoded as %2E, the letter "a" as %61, and so forth. Setting NormalizeUrlBeforeScan to 1 un-encodes the URL before attempting to match any of the rules specified in URLScan.ini. This prevents attackers from attempting to bypass URL restrictions (for example, by encoding extension). The NIMDA worm was able to spread from IIS server to IIS server by exploiting an un-encoding bug in IIS. The default is 1.

Continued

Table 5.3 The [Options] section of URLScan.ini

Parameter	Explanation
VerifyNormalization = 0 | 1	An encoded request can be encoded again. For example the character "." can be encoded as %2E. The % can be encoded as %25, resulting in %252E. Previous versions of IIS were found to be vulnerable to attacks involving multiple levels of encoding. By setting VerifyNomalization to 1 in conjunction with NormalizeUrlBeforeScan), URLScan will canonicalize the URL, then repeat the process on the un-encoded URL and compare the results. If they are different, the URL has been encoded more than once, and the request will be rejected. The default is 1.
AllowHighBitCharacters = 0 | 1	AllowHighBitCharacters = 1 allows requests to contain UTF8 characters in the URL. High bit characters may be required for languages that contain extended character sets. If your files are named using only ASCII characters, this should be set to 0. The default is 0.
AllowDotInPath = 0 | 1	AllowDotInPath determines whether URLs that contain a "." character that is not part of the file extension should be allowed. A setting of 0 denies requests with the "." character if it's not part of the file extension. The presence of a "." character may indicate a *directory traversal* attack, where the attacker attempts to navigate outside the web root using a URL that contains "../" to move up a directory from the current directory. It may also indicate an attack that attempts to call a denied file, but attempts to hide the attack by including the name of safe file in the URL, for example, `/someExecutable.exe?someSafeFile.html`

Continued

Table 5.3 The [Options] section of URLScan.ini

Parameter	Explanation
	However, some web applications (such as Outlook Web Access) may require you to set this to 1, because filenames for individual messages are based on the subject of the message, and the subject may contain the "." character.
RemoveServerHeader = 0 | 1	As part of an HTTP response, the server normally returns an HTTP server header indicating the type of server responding. IIS 6.0 returns "Server: Microsoft-IIS/6.0". By setting this to 1, this behavior is suppressed. Some corporate policies require this setting to obscure the brand and version of the server. However, this does not provide protection against automated attacks that systematically attempt to exploit vulnerabilities from a wide variety of platforms, nor will it prevent OS fingerprinting via other means. By default, this is set to 0.
AlternateServerName = <name>	If RemoveServerHeader is set to 1, you can supply an alternate HTTP Server: header by supplying a value for AlternateServerName.
EnableLogging = 0 | 1	If set to 1, URLScan will log rejected requests to a URLScan logfile. If set to 0, logging is not enabled.
PerProcessLogging = 0 | 1	If set to 1, URLScan will create separate log files for each w3wp.exe worker process. The log file name includes the process ID (PID) of each worker process. If set to 0, all rejected requests are logged to the same file.
PerDayLogging = 0 | 1	If set to 1, URLScan will create separate log files each day. The log file name will contain (in MMDDYY format) the day pertaining to the log file. If this setting is used in conjunction with PerProcessLogging, the file name will contain both the date and the PID in the format, for example, Urlscan.DDMMYY.<processID>.log.

Continued

Table 5.3 The [Options] section of URLScan.ini

Parameter	Explanation
LoggingDirectory = <path>	A full path that indicates where URLScan logs should be stored. By default, this is %windir%\system32\inetsrv\urlscan\logs\.
AllowLateScanning = 0 | 1	This setting determines whether the URLScan filter is a high priority filter (it applies before other ISAPI filters) or a low priority filter (it applies after high priority filters). AllowLateScanning = 0 loads URLScan as a high priority filter, and is the default. If you wish to use Frontpage Server Extensions, you will need to set this to 1.
UseFastPathReject = 0 | 1	This setting is used to determine the user experience and IIS logging of rejected requests. Setting UseFastPathReject = 1 will cause URLScan to send a plain "404 File Not Found" error message to the client, and URLScan will not log the rejection in the IIS logs.
RejectResponseURL = <URL>	If UseFastPathReject is set to 0, you can deliver a customized "404 File Not Found" page by supplying a valid virtual path for this parameter. For example, /someDirectory/someErrorPage.htm. This means that you can deliver the same rich user experience as with legitimate requests (that is, non-blocked) requests for non-existent resources. Additionally, the following variables are available as part of the request context, which can be accessed from an ASP page or ASP.NET page (in the Request.ServerVariables() collection): ■ HTTP_URLScan_Status_Header = why the request had been blocked. ■ HTTP_URLScan_Original_Verb = the request's HTTP verb.

Continued

Table 5.3 The [Options] section of URLScan.ini

Parameter	Explanation
	■ HTTP_URLScan_Original_URL = the original URL requested. If RejectResponseURL is set to /~*, URLScan enters a special logging mode where requests are not rejected, but requests that would be rejected are still logged in the URLScan log. This is useful for testing your URLScan.ini settings.
LogLongURLs = 0 | 1	Setting LogLongURLs allows URLScan to log rejected URLs up to 128KB. If set to 0, only the first 1KB of a rejected URL will be logged.

The URLScan.ini file contains a number of additional sections, which we'll examine briefly here.

Other Sections

The [AllowVerbs] and [DenyVerbs] sections define the HTTP verbs (also known as methods) that URLScan permits. URLScan decides which section to use based on the value of the UseAllowVerbs parameter examined in the [Options] section. Common HTTP verbs include GET, POST and HEAD. Other verbs are used by applications, such as FPSE and Web Distributed Authoring and Versioning (WebDAV).

Both the [AllowVerbs] and the [DenyVerbs] sections have the same syntax. They are made up of a list of HTTP verbs, and each verb appears on its own line. URLScan.ini comes with some predefined default lists.

The [DenyHeaders] section allows you to deny requests that contain any of the specified HTTP headers in the request. When a client makes a request to the server, it sends a set of HTTP headers. These commonly include the *User-Agent* (a string that describes the browser), *Referer* (the page the browser came from) and *Accept* (which types of files the browser can accept). To block a request based on the presence of a HTTP header, add the header name followed by a colon. URLScan.ini contains a default list of HTTP headers that block WebDAV requests.

The [AllowExtensions] and [DenyExtensions] sections permit you to define requests for files with extensions that URLScan will block. For example, you can configure URLScan to reject requests for .exe files to prevent Web users from executing applications on your system. URLScan decides which section to use based on the value of UseAllowExtensions discussed in the [Options] section.

Both the [AllowExtensions] and the [DenyExtensions] sections have the same syntax. They are made up of a list of filename extensions, and each extension appears on its own line. The extension starts with a period (.) (for example, **.ext**). You can configure URLScan to block requests that contain certain sequences of characters in the URL using the [DenyUrlSequences] section. For example, you can block requests that contain two consecutive periods (..), which are frequently used with exploits that take advantage of directory traversal vulnerabilities. To specify a character sequence to block, put the sequence on a line by itself in the [DenyUrlSequences] section.

Note that adding character sequences may adversely affect Outlook Web Access (OWA) for Microsoft Exchange. When you open a message from OWA, the subject line of the message is contained in the URL that is requested from the server. Subject lines that contain characters or sequences listed in the [DenyURLSequences] cannot be previewed, opened, or moved by OWA users.

The [RequestLimits] section allows you to limit the size of any part of the incoming request, including limits on the length of individual HTTP headers. To limit the length of any HTTP header, propend Max- followed by the HTTP header name, for example:

```
Max-User-Agent: 1000        ; limit user-agent header to 1000 bytes
```

URLScan.ini comes with default settings for overall content-length (30,000,000 bytes), maximum URL length (260 bytes) and maximum querystring length (2048 bytes).

REALITY CHECK...

Most of the functionality of URLScan is already included in IIS 6.0. Additionally, the built-in security features in IIS 6.0 provide a simpler way of maintaining your security policy. For example, disabling the ASP web services extension in the IIS Manager automatically disables all extensions that are mapped to asp.dll. To do the same thing in URLScan would require manually adding each extension (including any custom file extensions you have mapped to asp.dll).

However, URLScan does provide some advantages. It offers greater granularity that IIS 6.0 in rejecting requests. If you require the granularity provided by URLScan, it cannot easily be replicated in IIS 6.0's native features. URLScan also intercepts requests very early in the request processing cycle, leading to faster rejection of disallowed requests. By contrast, rejection of a request for a disabled web service extension occurs very late in the request processing cycle. Finally, as a defense-in-depth measure, running both IIS 6.0 and URLScan diversifies risk. A bug in either product that may make your server vulnerable may be prevented by the other, helping to keep your server uncompromised.

Configuring Your Server to Use SSL

Secure Sockets Layer is an industry standard method of encrypting traffic. While it is typically used for securing HTTP traffic, the technology can also be used for securing other types of traffic such as Simple Mail Transfer Protocol (SMTP). SSL should be used whenever you need to send sensitive information between client and server (for example, authentication credentials or user-supplied information such as credit card numbers). This is particularly important when using basic authentication, as user credentials are passed in an unencrypted format (see Configuring Authentication in this chapter for more information on basic authentication). The technologies that SSL uses can also be used to certify the identity of a server (or client), so you should use SSL whenever you need to certify the identity of your server or clients.

> **BY THE BOOK...**
>
> Secure Sockets Layer is a public key-based security protocol that is used by Internet services and clients to authenticate each other and to ensure message integrity and confidentiality. Certificates are used to authenticate the server (and optionally the client), and cryptography is used to ensure message confidentiality and prevent tampering.
>
> SSL should be used to secure the transmission of any sensitive data, including user credentials and user supplied data (such as credit card numbers). Use of SSL however, does place an additional resource burden on the server, as there is an overhead involved in encrypting and decrypting packets.

SSL uses certificates and public key cryptography to establish the identity of the server or client, and to create secure, encrypted traffic between server and client.

First, the identity of the server or client and the validity of its SSL certificate are checked. When a client requests a resource using the https:// protocol (and the server is configured to allow https:// traffic), the server will return its SSL certificate. The client will perform a number of checks on this certificate:

- It will check to ensure that the certificate hasn't expired.

- It will ensure that the name of the server that it is connecting to is the same as the name of the server in the certificate (for example, this can stop a malicious attacker from setting up a site pretending to be syngress.com since only syngress.com has a certificate containing "www.syngress.com" as the site to be secured. This works in conjunction with the next check).

- It will ensure that the certificate was originally issued by a trusted Certificate Authority (CA). Browsers have built-in trust for a number of major commercial CAs such as Verisign or Thawte. You can check the trusted CAs in Internet Explorer by accessing **Tools | Internet Options | Content | Certificates | Trusted Root Certificate Authorities** in Internet Explorer. Because the browser trusts those CAs, it trusts certificates issued by those CAs. These CAs are expected to perform due diligence on applicants for certificates to ensure that only legitimate applicants are issued with certificates. This prevents a malicious user from setting up their own CA, and issuing themselves a certificate for syngress.com. The browser will not trust a certificate issued by a non-trusted CA.

Your organization (or partner organizations) can setup a CA and configure browsers within the organization to trust certificates issued by it. This is useful if you have non-public websites that have to be secured with SSL, as it avoids the expense of purchasing a certificate from a commercial CA. Optionally, a browser may also check the CA's certificate revocation list (CRL) to ensure that a legitimately issued certificate (one that meets the checks) has not been subsequently revoked by the issuing CA.

If the certificate meets all these requirements, then the client and server can proceed to the next step: configuring a secure channel to encrypt traffic. If the certificate does not meet these requirements, the user will be warned about potential problems with the certificate and must manually decide whether to proceed or not (as shown in Figure 5.8 and Figure 5.9).

Figure 5.8 The Hostname Requested does not Match the Hostname in the Certificate

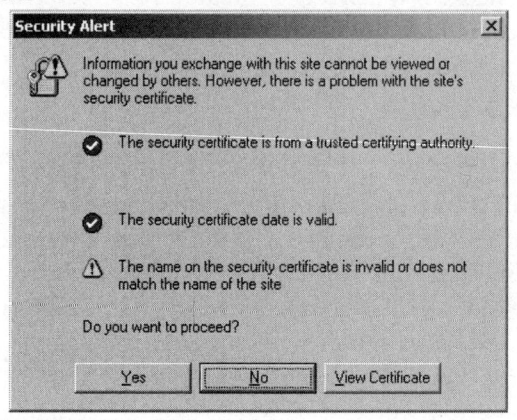

Figure 5.9 The Certificate is Issued by an Untrusted Certificate Authority

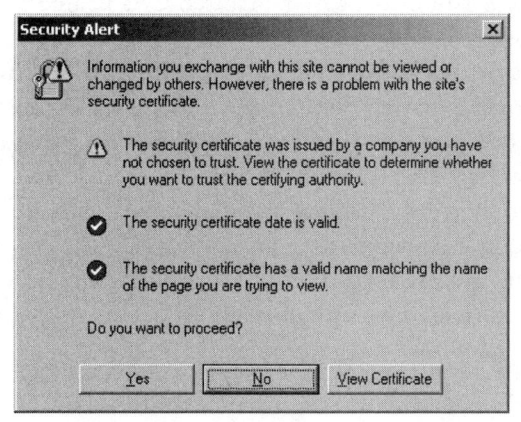

To set up the encryption to be used for traffic, the browser will extract the server's public key from the server's SSL certificate. The client will generate a random session key and encrypt this with the server's public key and return it to the server. The server will use its private key to decrypt the transmission and extract the session key. Future communication between the browser and server will be based on this session key using symmetric encryption (which is faster than public/private key encryption). More information on public key encryption, certificates, and certificate trust hierarchies is available in Chapter 11, which covers

Microsoft Certificate Services. Microsoft Certificate Services can acts as a CA for your organization.

In the next section we will look at the options available in IIS 6.0 has for configuring SSL. When securing SSL websites, be aware that you cannot use host headers to run multiple SSL-secured websites on a single IP address. For more information on host headers, see "Configuring IP Address, TCP Port and Host-Header Combinations" in this chapter.

Generating a Certificate Request

The first step in configuring IIS 6.0 to allow https:// requests is to generate a certificate request. This request for an SSL certificate will be sent to a CA for processing. This can be a commercial CA (in the event that your Web server will be available to the general public), or an internal, organizational CA (in the event that the site will be accessed by internal users only). To generate a CA request:

1. Open the IIS Manager. Right-click the website for which you will generate a certificate request, then click **Properties**.

2. Select the **Directory Security** tab. At this stage, your Web server does not have an SSL certificate, so the **View Certificate** option should be unavailable.

3. Click the **Server Certificate** button to begin the Web Server Certificate wizard.

4. Click **Next** on the initial Welcome screen.

5. The Web Server Certificate wizard allows you to generate a new certificate request, or to manage existing certificates. For example, if you have moved an existing website to this server, you could import the existing certificate for use with this website. In this case, we do not already have a certificate, so choose **Create a new certificate** and click **Next** (shown in Figure 5.10).

Figure 5.10 Create a New Certificate Request

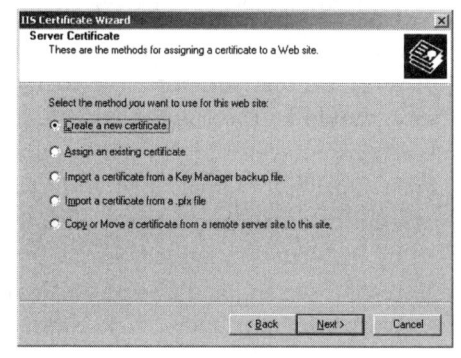

6. You can now choose to either create a request and submit it manually to a CA, or submit the request automatically to an online CA. The latter option is available if you have an Active Directory Integrated Enterprise Root CA (see Chapter 11 for more information). In this case, we will create the request, and submit it manually. Choose **Prepare the Request now, but send it later** and click **Next**.

7. On the next screen, enter a "friendly" **Name** for the certificate (Figure 5.11). Additionally, choose a **Bit length** to be used for the public key encryption. **1024** bits is the standard length. Higher values are stronger, but place an increased computational burden on your server.

Figure 5.11 Entering a Friendly Name and Configuring Key Bit Length

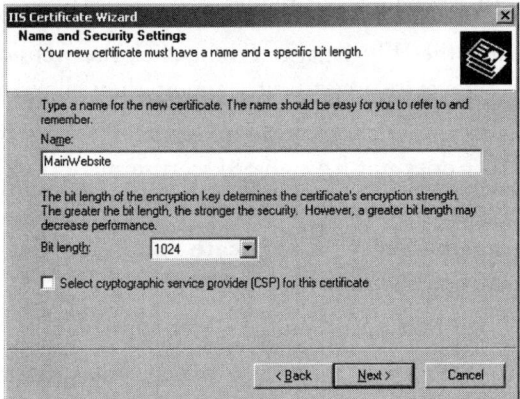

8. Click **Next**.

9. Next, enter your **Organization**, and **Organizational unit**. These do not affect the security of your certificate, but are visible to end users if they examine the details of your certificate. After entering these details, click **Next**.

10. The next screen asks for your server's common name (Figure 5.12). It is critical that you enter the correct name at this step. The name should be the same as what users will enter in their browsers to access your site. If this is a public site, you should use a Fully Qualified Domain Name (FQDN) such as **www.myCompany.com**. If this is an internal site that will be accessed by its NetBIOS name, you can enter the NetBIOS name instead, for example, **ITSupportIntranet**. Enter your server's **Common name** and click **Next**.

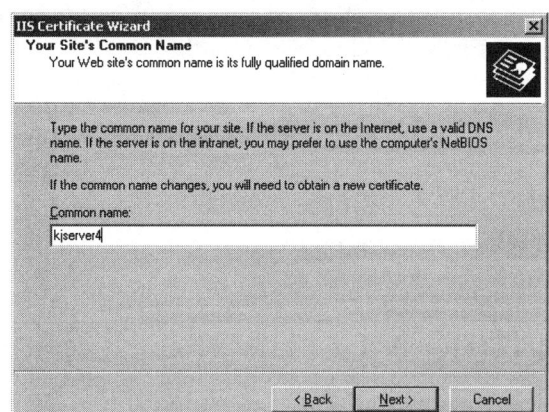

Figure 5.12 Enter Your Site's Common Name

11. In the next step, you are required to select your **Country** and enter your **State/Province** and **City/Locality**. These do not affect the security of your certificate, but are visible to end users who choose to view the details of your certificate. After entering the proper information, click **Next**.

12. In the next step, you save the request to a file. This file will be submitted to your CA as a request for an SSL certificate. Choose a location and click **Next** (Figure 5.13).

Figure 5.13 Choosing a Filename for the Certificate Request

13. You will be asked to confirm all the details you have entered. If you need to change any details, click the **Back** button to

return to the appropriate previous screen. When the details are all correct, press **Next** to create your certificate request, then click **Finish** to close the wizard.

IIS 6.0 remembers that you have generated a certificate request for the website in question. The next time you start the Web Server Certificate wizard, you will have the option to process the pending request (that is, install a certificate) or delete the pending request. Choose the second option if you want to remove the existing pending request and generate a new certificate request.

Submitting a Certificate Request

The certificate request must now be submitted to a Certificate Authority. You can submit the request to a commercial CA (such as Versign, Thawte or GeoTrust), or to an internal CA. In this case we will submit the request to a Microsoft Certificate Services server. Use the following steps to submit your request:

1. Obtain the name of your Microsoft Certificate Service server.
2. Browse to **http://<certificate server name>/certsrv/** (shown in Figure 5.14).

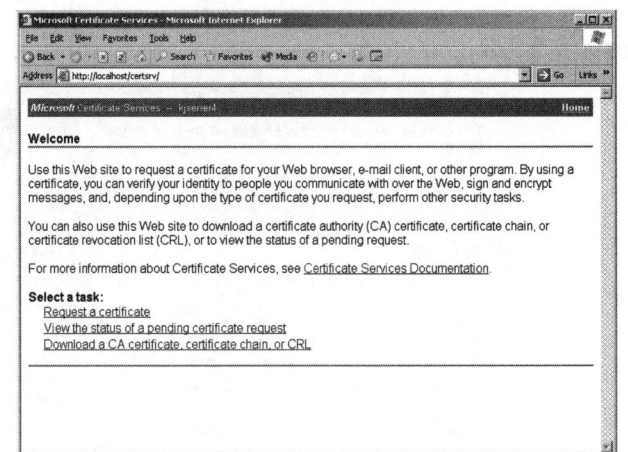

Figure 5.14 Certificate Services Website

3. Select **Request a Certificate** and then choose **Submit an Advanced Certificate Request**.

4. On the Advanced Certificate Request page, select **Submit a certificate request by using a base-64-encoded CMC or PKCS #10 file**.

5. Using Notepad, open the certificate request file you saved in the previous section (located in c:\certreq.txt by default), and paste the entire contents into the textbox (shown in Figure 5.15). By default, the **Browse for a File** option will not work if you a browsing from a Windows Server 2003 machine due to default IE security restrictions, though it will work if you are browsing from a different OS.

Figure 5.15 Entering the Certificate Request

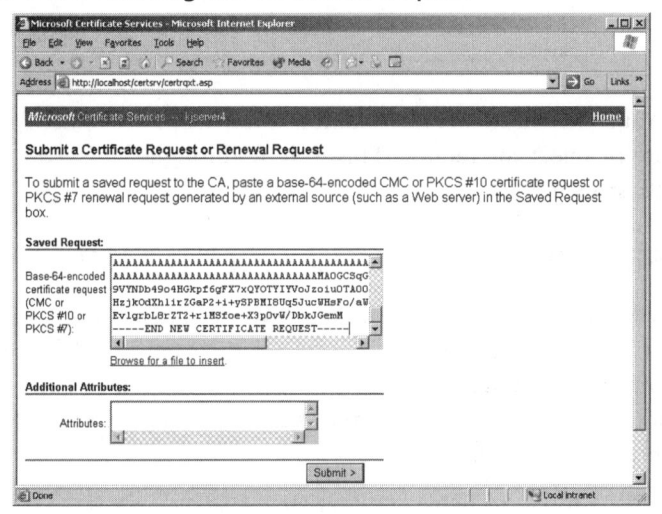

6. Click the **Submit** button to submit your request. If the data in the certificate request file is valid, the Certificate Service website will present an acknowledgement page (Figure 5.16).

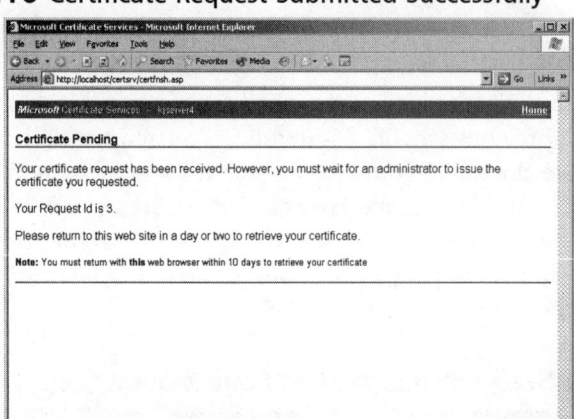

Figure 5.16 Certificate Request Submitted Successfully

[screenshot: Microsoft Certificate Services - Certificate Pending page showing "Your certificate request has been received. However, you must wait for an administrator to issue the certificate you requested. Your Request Id is 3. Please return to this web site in a day or two to retrieve your certificate."]

Your Certificate Services administrator will now either issue a certificate or reject the request. This is done through the Certificate Services MMC snap-in.

Installing an Issued Certificate

Once your certificate has been issued, you can install it on your Web server. In this section, we will download and install the SSL certificate generated by Microsoft Certificate Services. If you have submitted your request to a commercial CA, they will have procedures for you to follow to obtain your certificate.

1. Browse to **http://<certificate server name>/certsrv**, and select **View the status of a pending certificate request**".

2. Select the certificate request you submitted earlier.

3. Download the certificate using either of the encoding methods (shown in Figure 5.17) and save the file onto your hard disk.
   Note that the server running Microsoft Certificate Services has URLScan installed, .cer files are blocked in the default configuration. You will need to edit the URLScan.ini file to allow requests for files with the .cer extension. This applies only to the Web server running on the Microsoft Certificate Services server, not the Web server you are installing the certificate onto.

Figure 5.17 Download the Issued Certificate

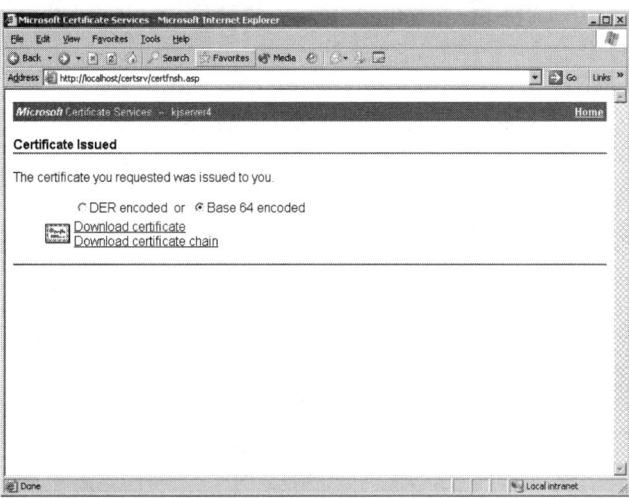

4. Open IIS Manager, right-click the website on which you will be installing the certificate and click **Properties**.
5. On the **Directory Security** tab, click the **Server Certificate** button to start the Web Server Certificate wizard.
6. Click **Next** on the initial Welcome screen.
7. Select the **Process the pending request and install the certificate** option (Figure 5.18) and click **Next**.

Figure 5.18 Installing the Issued Certificate

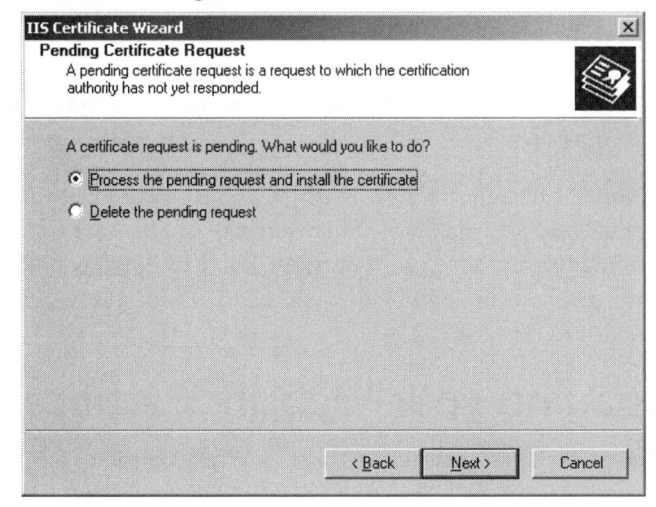

8. Enter the path of the certificate you downloaded and saved earlier in this section and click **Next** (Figure 5.19).

Figure 5.19 Enter the Path to the Certificate

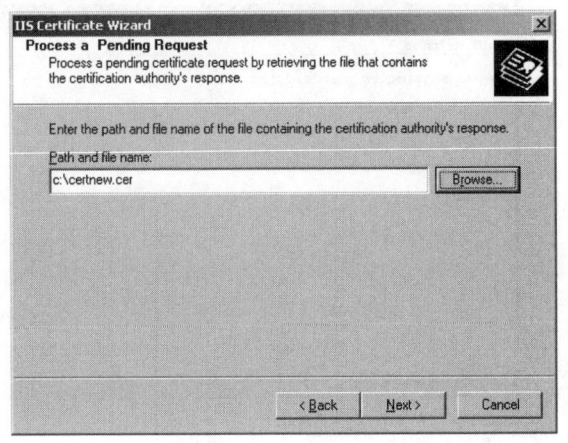

9. Enter the SSL port that this website should use. By default, this is port **443**. Note that only one website per IP address can listen on port 443 (you cannot use host headers with SSL-secured sites). Click **Next**.
10. A screen detailing your choices will be presented. Confirm that the information is correct. If anything needs to be altered, click the **Back** button to return to the appropriate screen. If everything is correct, click **Next** to install the certificate.
11. Click **Finish** to close the wizard.
12. To verify that your SSL certificate is installed correctly, open your web browser and navigate to **https://<your server name>/**.

If you are having problems with your SSL-secured site after you finish installing the certificate, Microsoft has an SSL diagnostics tool you can run that checks for common issues. You can download SSLDiag from www.microsoft.com/downloads/details.aspx?FamilyID=cabea1d0-5a10-41bc-83d4-06c814265282&.

Managing your Website Certificates

To manage certificates issues to your websites, use the "Web Server Certificate" wizard. This wizard allows you to export certificates (for example, if you wish to move the website to a new server), create new requests, and remove the currently installed certificate.

Configuring IIS SSL Options

To configure the website's SSL settings:

1. Open the IIS Manager, right-click the desired website, folder, or file, and select **Properties**.
2. On the **Directory Security** or **File Security** tab, select **Edit**.
3. To require an SSL connection to access the resource, enable the **Require secure channel (SSL)** option (shown in Figure 5.20).

Figure 5.20 Require a Secure Connection for the Resource

4. To require 128-bit encryption, enable the **Require 128-bit encryption** option. Older browsers, and browsers distributed in countries where US export restrictions still apply, may not support 128-bit encryption, and will not be able to negotiate a connection if this option is enabled. However, if this option is not enabled, these browsers will fall back to lower levels (for example, 40-bit encryption). These levels are no longer deemed secure because modern computers can break the encryption relatively quickly.

5. Client certificates can be used to identify clients in the same way that a server's SSL certificate identifies the server. By default, client certificates are ignored, but you can choose to **Accept client certificates** or **Require client certificates** (the former

allows client certificates as an option, and the latter requires the client to present a certificate to allow the connection).

6. To map client certificates to Windows user accounts, enable the **Enable client certificate mapping** option and click **Edit** to map certificates to user accounts. See Chapter 11 for more information on issuing certificates to clients.

7. If you are using client certificates to identify users and wish to restrict the CAs whose certificates you will accept, enable the **Enable certificate trust list** option and click **Add** to add the desired CAs. Certificates from CAs not defined here will not be accepted. This may be useful in an intranet scenario where you want only certificates issued by your own internal CAs to be used for identifying clients.

8. Click **OK**.

REALITY CHECK...

SSL provides a secure and trusted method of verifying the identity of servers and clients, and for encrypting traffic between server and client. It is designed to prevent identity hijacking threats (where a server or client is not who it claims to be), man-in-the-middle attacks (where an attacker attempts to intercept and modify traffic in transit), and snooping attacks (where an attacker tries to intercept and read traffic in transit).

Despite these benefits, there are some limitations to SSL. First, any information transmitted as part of the requested URL (for example, as part of the query string) is not encrypted. If you pass sensitive information in the URL request, it can be read by anyone intercepting traffic. The following URLs, for example, would be vulnerable:

- https://user:password@www.myCompany.com and
- www.myCompany.com?user=user&password=password

Second, information that is transmitted in an encrypted format is decrypted at both the client and server sides. An attacker who was able to compromise a client or server would be able to read the decrypted information in clear text. This could be done on-the-fly, or it could be done by retrieving information stored in databases or in IIS log files.

Another limitation of SSL is the inability to use host headers to run multiple SSL-secured websites on a single IP address. A normal, unsecured HTTP v1.1 request includes a host: HTTP header:

```
Get /default.aspx HTTP/1.1
Host: www.myCompany.com
Accept: */*
Connection: Keep-Alive
User-Agent: Mozilla/4.0 (compatible; MSIE 6.0; Windows NT 5.1; .NET CLR 1.1.4322)
Accept-Encoding: gzip, deflate
```

When an SSL-secured connection is used, everything except the first line (the GET request) is encrypted. Because of this, the Web server does not know to which website the request should be routed. As a result, the Host: HTTP header cannot be used to identify which server the browser is seeking the resource from. Each SSL-secured website must by run on its own IP address or TCP port (if using a single IP address and multiple websites).

For more information on host headers see "Configuring IP Address, TCP Port and Host-Header combinations" in this chapter.

Configuring URL Authorization with the Authorization Manager

Windows Server 2003 introduces a new *role-based* authorization manager. While traditional authorization has revolved around creating Access Control Entries (ACEs) on predefined resources such as files or registry keys, the Authorization Manager is designed to provide access control to tasks that comprise an application.

The Authorization Manager can be managed using an MMC snap-in. To access the Authorization Manager, select **Start | Run** and enter **azman.msc**. An authorization application programming interface (API) is also exposed that applications (including ASP and ASP.NET web-based applications) can utilize to access the services provided by the Authorization Manager.

BY THE BOOK...

In the Windows Server 2003 family, Authorization Manager introduces a new role-based authorization mechanism. Rather than base access on static Access Control Entries (ACEs), access can be granted or denied based on the type of work the user is performing.

Authorization Manager allows you to define tasks and roles. Only those users who are in configured roles are allowed to execute the defined tasks. The rules governing role membership can be programmed using a scripting language, offering the ability to dynamically decide what tasks can be executed.

For example, a role called "Expense Authorizers" may allow users in the role to authorize expenses via a web-based application, but only if the expense amount is less than a specified level (which in turn may be dynamically determined, by being retrieved from a database). Users who are not in the role cannot authorize expenses at all.

A detailed analysis of the full scope of Authorization Manager is beyond the scope of this book. Authorization Manager provides a set of APIs that can be programmed against in ASP or ASP.NET applications. An example is the "Authorization and Profile Application Block" produced by the Microsoft Patterns and Practices group, which can use an Authorization Manager datastore. The Authorization and Profile Application Block can be downloaded from: http://msdn.microsoft.com/library/default.asp?url=/library/en-us/dnpag/html/authpro.asp?frame=true.

In addition to the APIs, a URL Authorization feature is available, which allows administrators to determine who can access a given URL without setting ACEs on the physical file. Instead, rules determining who can access the URL can be managed via Authorization Manager. In this section we will examine the concepts used in Authorization Manager by building and configuring a simple, dynamic, authorization rule.

After you create the authorization store itself, you will be required to configure access to it, and to create applications, operations, scopes, and roles. Finally, you will associate resources with the applications.

Creating the Authorization Store

To begin, use the following steps to create an authorization store that will hold the application's rules:

1. To open the Authorization Manager MMC snap-in, select **Start** | **Run** and enter **azman.msc**.

2. By default, the application will open in admin mode. This mode does not allow the creation of new authorization stores, only the administration of previously created stores. To create a new store, you must first switch to developer mode. To do so, right-click **Authorization Manager** and select **Options**. Select **Developer Mode** (Figure 5.21) and click **OK**.

Figure 5.21 Switching from Administrator to Developer Mode

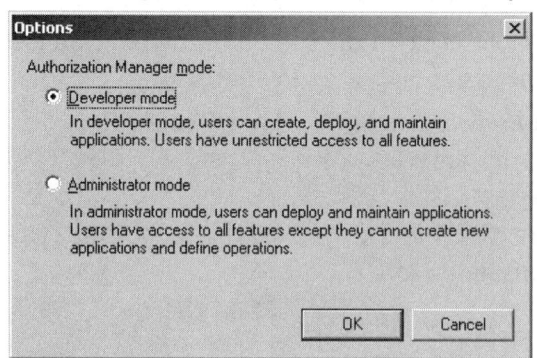

3. Right-click **Authorization Manager**, and select **New Authorization Store**.
4. Select to either store the authorization store in **Active Directory** or in a local **XML file**. For this example, we will use an XML file. Enter the name and location in the **Store name** field or click the **Locations** button to search for and select the store (Figure 5.22). Enter a **Description** and click **OK**.

Figure 5.22 Create a new XML Authorization Store

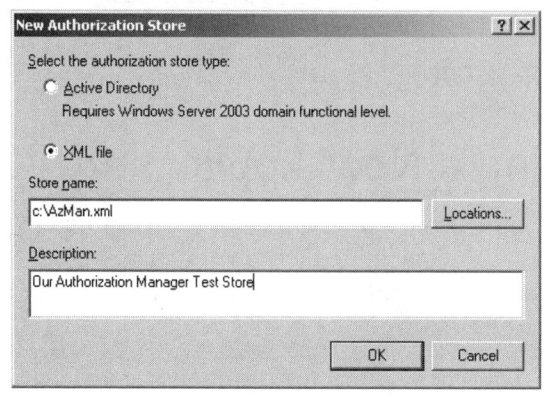

Configuring Access to the Authorization Store

Now that the authorization store has been created, you must give the IIS worker process access to read it. The default IIS worker process identity is **Network Service**. However, if you have a web application that you'd like to secure running under a different process identity, you give that account permission to read the store instead.

1. Right-click on the authorization store you created in the previous step and select **Properties**.

2. On the **Security** tab, select **Reader** from the **User Roles** drop-down list. Click **Add** and select **Network Service** (Figure 5.23).

Figure 5.23 Allow the Network Service user to access the Authorization Store

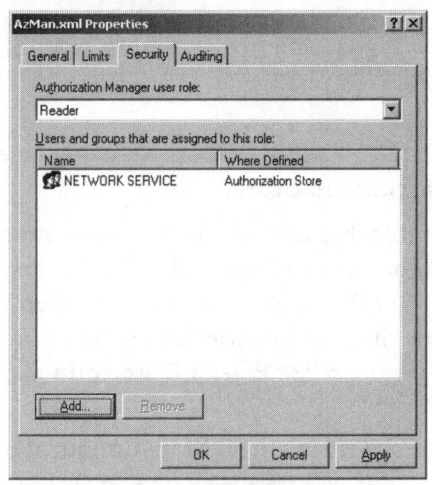

3. Click **OK**.

Creating a New Application

Next, you must create a new application. Each store can host multiple applications, each containing their own roles, tasks, and rules. For URL authorization, the application must be called **IIS 6.0 URL Authorization**.

1. Right-click on the authorization store you created previously and select **New Application**.

2. Enter **IIS 6.0 URL Authorization** as the application name, and enter a **Description** and **Version information** (Figure 5.24).

Figure 5.24 Creating the IIS 6.0 URL Authorization Application

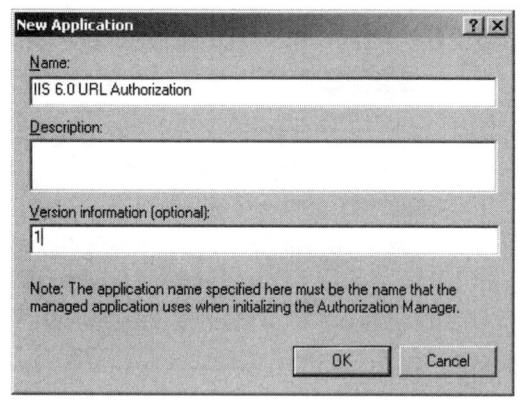

3. Click **OK**.

Creating an Operation

Operations are used to determine whether access should be granted to a specified URL. In the following steps, you will create an operation called **AccessURL**.

1. Expand the **IIS 6.0 URL Authorization** application that you created earlier, then expand the **Definitions** node (Figure 5.25).

Figure 5.25 Operation Definitions Node

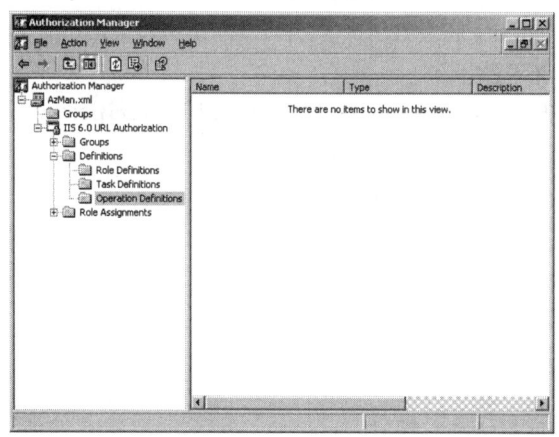

2. Right-click **Operations Definitions** and select **New Operation**.

3. Enter **AccessURL** as the operation **Name**, and enter **1** as the **Operation Number** (Figure 5.26).

Figure 5.26 Creating the AccessURL Operation

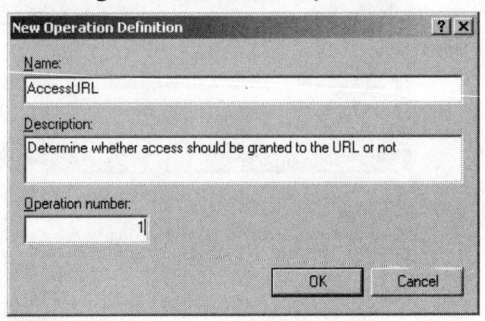

```
New Operation Definition                          ? X
Name:
AccessURL
Description:
Determine whether access should be granted to the URL or not

Operation number:
        1

                              OK        Cancel
```

4. Click **OK**.

Note that in Authorization Manager, tasks are the smallest work unit. They can be combined (or grouped) into operations. Typical tasks might be "read a file", or "open a database connection". Operations combine various tasks into a logical work unit (for example, "authorize a payment").

Creating a Scope

Each web application that uses URL authentication requires a scope. Multiple web applications can share a scope, or they can each have their own scope.

1. Right-click **IIS 6.0 URL Authorization** and select **New Scope**.

2. Enter a meaningful **Name** and **Description** for the scope, then click **OK** (Figure 5.27).

Figure 5.27 Creating a Web Application Scope

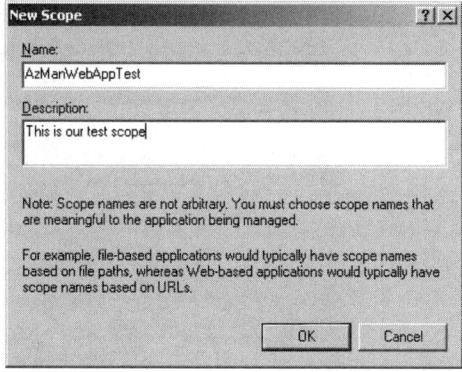

Creating a Role

Next, configure a *viewer* role for the scope. Users in this role will be able to execute the AccessURL operation that we defined earlier.

1. Expand the scope you created earlier, then expand the **Definitions** node (Figure 5.28).

Figure 5.28 Creating the Viewer Role

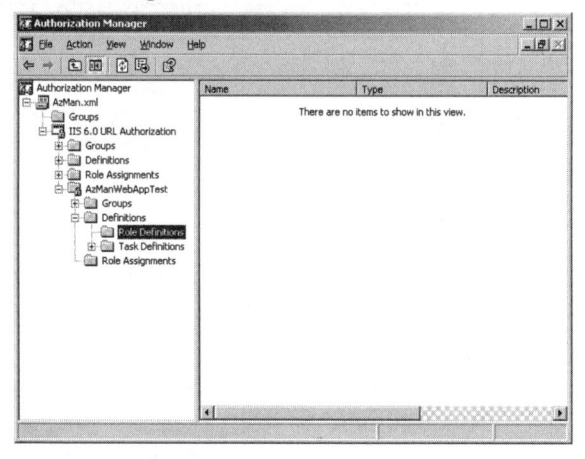

2. Right-click **Role Definitions** and select **New Role Definition**.
3. Set the **Name** to **Viewer** and, if desired, enter a **Description** (Figure 5.29).

Figure 5.29 New Role Definition

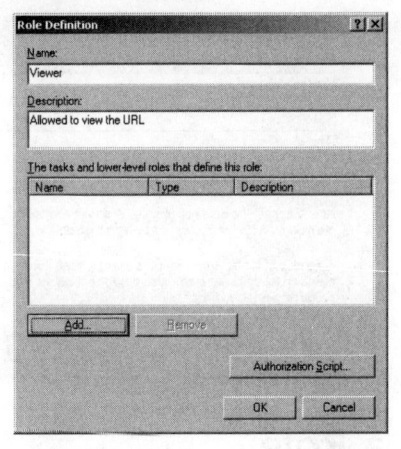

4. Click **Add** and select the **Operations** tab. Enable the **AccessURL** checkbox (shown in Figure 5.30) and click **OK**.

Figure 5.30 Adding the "AccessURL" Operation

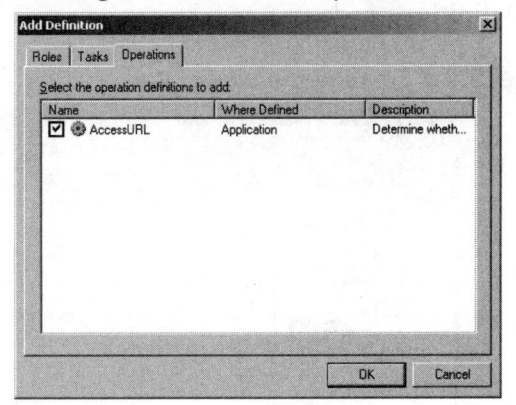

5. Next, add a business rule to dynamically determine whether the AccessURL option can be executed. Enter the following code in Notepad, and save it as **AzManTest.vbs** on your hard disk:

```
AzBizRuleContext.BusinessRuleResult = False
If Hour(Time()) < 12 then
    AzBizRuleContext.BusinessRuleResult = True
Else
    AzBizRuleContext.BusinessRuleResult = False
End If
```

Advanced Web Server Security Configuration • Chapter 5 171

6. In Authorization Manager, click the **Authorization Script** button and use the **Browse** button to load the script into the window (Figure 5.31).

    The code allows access to the URL if the current system time is before midday, and denies access if the time is after midday. Click **OK** twice to exit and return to Authorization Manager. If your current system time is greater than 12, swap the < sign for a > sign.

Figure 5.31 Adding a Business Rule

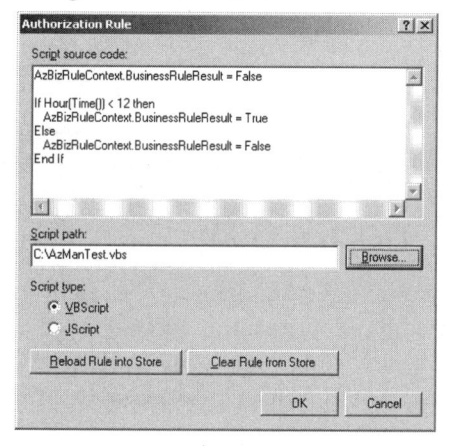

![Authorization Rule dialog showing script source code:
AzBizRuleContext.BusinessRuleResult = False
If Hour(Time()) < 12 then
    AzBizRuleContext.BusinessRuleResult = True
Else
    AzBizRuleContext.BusinessRuleResult = False
End If
Script path: C:\AzManTest.vbs
Script type: VBScript selected, JScript]

7. Next, assign Windows users to the application role. Right-click the **Role Assignments** node and select **Assign Roles**. Enable the **Viewer** checkbox and click **OK**. Viewer should now be added as an icon under Role Assignments.

8. Right-click **Viewer** and select **Assign Windows Users and Groups**. Add the desired user account and click **OK**. The Authorization Manager should look similar to Figure 5.32.

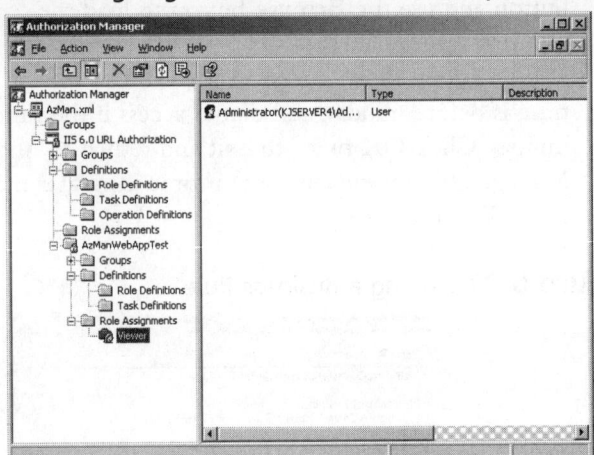

Figure 5.32 Assigning Windows Users and Groups to a Role

Configuring IIS 6.0

Now that we have completing defining the application in Authorization manager, we need to associate an resource (e.g. a webpage) with this application. We also need to make some configuration changes to IIS, to link IIS to Authorization Manager. To associate an IIS resource with this application:

1. Create a new folder under the default website root, and name the folder **AzManTest**. Place a simple HTML page within that folder, containing the desired text. Your entry should look like the following:

   ```
   <html>
   <body>Hello World</body>
   </html>
   ```

2. Open the IIS Manager, right-click the **AzManTest** folder and select **Properties**. On the **Directory** tab, click **Create** to create a new web application.

3. Click the **Configuration** button (Figure 5.33).

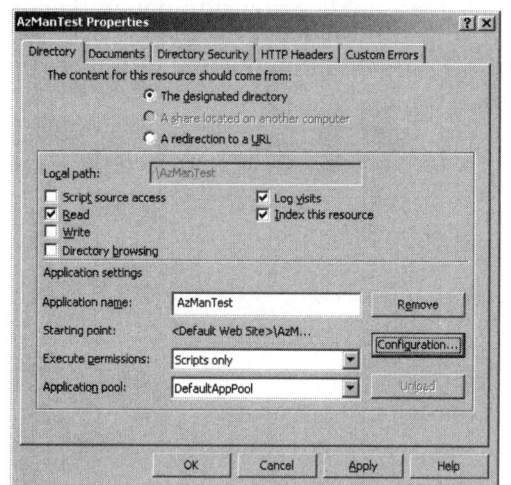

Figure 5.33 Configuring the IIS Web Application

[Screenshot: AzManTest Properties dialog, Directory tab]

4. On the **Mappings** tab, click the **Insert** button.
5. In the **Add/Edit Application Extension Mapping** window (Figure 5.34), click **Browse** and navigate to **%windir%\system32\inetsrv**. Select **urlauth.dll** and click **Open**. Click **OK** twice.

Figure 5.34 Add the URLAuth ISAPI Interceptor

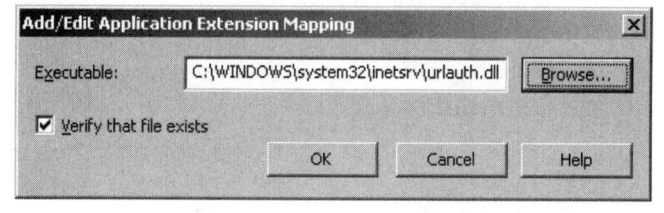

[Screenshot: Add/Edit Application Extension Mapping dialog showing Executable: C:\WINDOWS\system32\inetsrv\urlauth.dll]

6. Click the **Directory Security** tab and click the **Edit** button.
7. Disable the **Allow Anonymous Access** option. Ensure that at least one of the other options is checked.
8. In the IIS Manager, access the **Web Service Extension** node and click **Add a New web Service Extension**.
9. Click the **Add** button. Click **Browse** and navigate to **%windir%\system32\inetsrv**, then select **urlauth.dll**. Click **OK**.

10. Enter **URL Authorization** in the **Extension Name** field and enable the **Enable Extension** option (Figure 5.35).

Figure 5.35 Adding the URL Authorization Web Service Extension

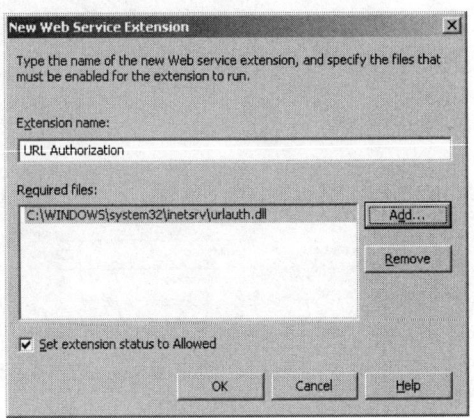

11. Click **OK** and close the IIS Manager.

We will now associate the AzManTest folder with the scope we defined in Authorization Manager.

1. Use Notepad to enter the following code into a text file, and save it as **SetURLAuth.js**:

   ```
   var objVDir =
   GetObject("IIS://localhost/w3svc/1/root/AzManTest");
   objVDir.AzEnable = true;
   objVDir.AZStoreName = "MSXML://c:\AZMan.xml";
   objVDir.AzScopeName = "AzManWebAppTest";
   objVDir.AZImpersonationLevel = 1;
   objVDir.SetInfo();
   ```

2. Replace **c:\AzMan.xml** with the path to the XML authorization store you created, and replace **AzManWebAppTest** with the name of the scope you defined under IIS 6.0 URL Authorization in Authorization Manager.

3. Double-click the JS file to run it.

Testing the Authorization Store

The final step is to test the URL authorization. To begin, open a web-browser and navigate to **http://<yourserver>/AzManTest/default.htm**. Note that if you are using Internet Explorer and **Integrated Windows Authentication** is enabled, IE will automatically log you on. Since we explicitly added our account to the **Viewer** role, we will be permitted to view the page. To prevent an auto-logon, use the IP address or the FQDN of the server instead.

According to the business rules we set up in the above exercise, if you open a new browser window and enter **http://<IPAddress>/AzManTest/default.htm**, and supply a username/password that is not associated with our usual account, we should be denied access. This is because we did not add any other users to the Viewer role in our authorization store.

To test the business rule, edit the AzManTest.vbs file you created earlier, and swap the < for a > symbol (or visa versa), so that the code should deny access based on your current time. In the Authorization Manager, navigate to the **Role Definitions** node, and double-click the **Viewer** icon. On the **Definition** tab, click **Authorization Script**, and choose **Reload Rule Into Store**. The Script Source window should reflect your change. If you now attempt to reload the page you successfully loaded before, you will be denied access with a HTTP 401.1 "Unauthorized: Access is denied due to invalid credentials" error.

Configuring Custom Error Messages

IIS provides you with the ability to return a customized URL to users when a HTTP error is generated. These are commonly used to produce a nicer user experience, especially in the case of "404 File Not Found" situations. However, using custom error messages can also provide a security benefit. In the event of an application error, a custom error message can prevent information disclosure (by preventing the user from seeing the error's source and stack trace), and by allowing the server to log the error or alert the administrator.

By the Book...

IIS 6.0 provides two methods for configuring custom error messages for ASP based applications. Either of these methods can be used when an *unhandled exception* is raised. An unhandled exception is an error that is not taken care of (handled) within the code itself. A simple generic error page can be sent back for any unhandled ASP error, or a custom page can be sent back. IIS does not handle ASP.NET errors natively in IIS 6.0. Instead, to configure a custom page for unhandled ASP.NET exceptions you must edit the ASP.NET web.config file.

By using custom error pages for unhandled application errors, you can reduce the risk of disclosing sensitive information about the structure of the application that can aid an attacker. Some examples of information disclosure are provided later in this section.

Additionally, you can provide a better monitoring environment for administrators by having a page generate an alert (for example, via e-mail), or log an event (for example, to a database). The alert can include information about the requested URL, querystring, remote IP address, and the error type.

The Default ASP Error Message

Before customizing the error message, we will look at what the default ASP error message looks like (Figure 5.36).

Figure 5.36 Default ASP Error Message Disclosing a Connection String

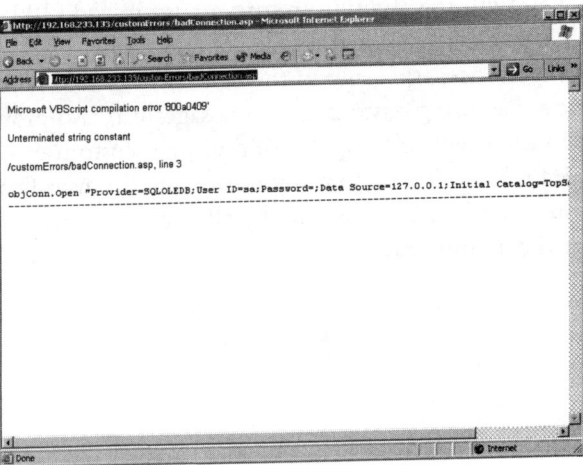

This piece of programming contains a simple VBScript error on the same line that holds the connection string to an SQL server. Also visible in the connection string is the User ID being used to login to the server, the Password (a blank one), and the IP address of the SQL server (the same as the Web server). While not all coding errors might so easily result in information that could be of use to attackers, the possibility of disclosing some information that would be useful to attackers is real.

Notes from the Underground...

The Risks of Information Disclosure

Many poorly programmed web applications share a common characteristic – they fail to rigorously filter input supplied by the user. This allows a malicious attacker to mount SQL injection attacks, cross-site-scripting attacks, or replay attacks.

SQL injection vulnerabilities occur when a web application takes user input, concatenates it with an existing, predefined SQL string, and submits it to the database for processing. If the user input is not adequately screened, then it may be possible to "inject" malicious SQL code.

For example, a typical login form on a webpage might solicit a username and password from a visiting user, and concatenate that with the following string:

```
SELECT * FROM Users WHERE Username = '<supplied
username>' AND UserPassword = '<supplied password>'
```

If the attacker could enter the following as a username: ' OR 1=1 —, then the SQL statement becomes:

```
SELECT * FROM Users WHERE Username = '' OR 1=1 -- AND
UserPassword = ''
```

For an SQL server database, the double dashes (—) indicate that the rest of the line is a comment, and since 1=1 is always true, all user records will be returned from the database, allowing the user to log in. In a more malicious example, assume a form that allows a user to submit an OrderID, and the form returns all items that were purchased as part of that order:

```
SELECT ItemName, ItemDescription, Quantity FROM Items
INNER JOIN OrderItems WHERE OrderID = <user supplied
OrderID>
```

Continued

> If a malicious user could enter the following as a OrderID:
> 1 UNION SELECT Username, UserPassword, 1 FROM Users, the
> final SQL statement would be:
>
> ```
> SELECT ItemName, ItemDescription, Quantity FROM Items
> INNER JOIN OrderItems WHERE OrderID = 1 UNION SELECT
> UserName, UserPassword, 1 FROM Users
> ```
>
> This would allow the attacker to see all users and their passwords in the database.
>
> SQL injection attacks usually require the attacker to know something about the schema of the database so that they can appropriately name the tables and fields in their malicious SQL code. By failing to suppress the default error messages ASP generates, an attacker can easily map the tables and fields that do exist. An example of this is beyond the scope of this book, however the following two papers from security firm NGSSoftware demonstrate how this can be done: www.nextgenss.com/papers/advanced_sql_injection.pdf and www.nextgenss.com/papers/more_advanced_sql_injection.pdf.

Configuring a Basic ASP Error Message

IIS 6.0 provides the ability to replace the default error messages generated by ASP applications with a generic error message that masks the underlying error cause. Configuring this option is straightforward; however it provides no alerting capabilities, and does not provide a rich user experience. This setting can only be configured on a website or web application root, but not on individual folders or files.

1. Open the IIS Manager and navigate to the website or web application that you would like to configure the error for. Web applications are represented with a small cog icon. Right-click and select **Properties**.

2. On the **Home Directory** tab (for websites) or **Virtual Directory** tab (for web applications), click the **Configuration** button.

3. On the **Debugging** tab, select **Send the following text error message to the client** (shown in Figure 5.37) and edit the text if desired.

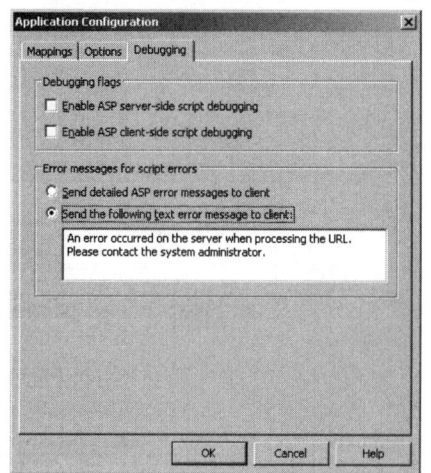

Figure 5.37 Configure a simple ASP Error Message

4. Click **OK** twice.

Configuring a Custom ASP Error Message

IIS 6.0 provides a more feature-rich capability that allows you to return a completely customized error page (which could be themed with your corporate style). In addition, since this page can be an ASP page itself, you can use the intrinsic ASPError object to get information about the page that generated the error, the error's source (including line number), and information posted to the server by the user that may have resulted in the error.

This custom error page can be configured for a website, a folder, or any individual ASP page within the site, providing greater flexibility for you as an administrator. To configure this option:

1. Open the IIS Manager, and right-click the desired website, folder, or individual ASP file. Select **Properties**.

2. On the **Custom Errors** tab, scroll down to **500:100 Internal Server Error – ASP Error** (Figure 5.38) and click **Edit**.

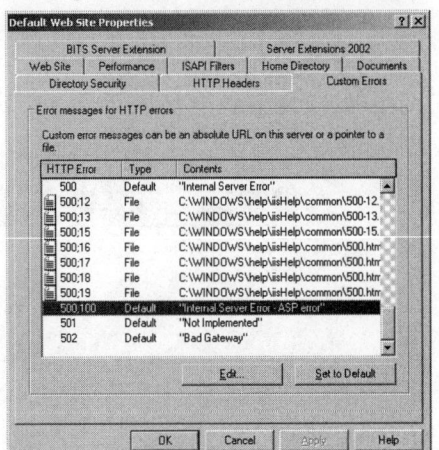

Chapter 5 • Advanced Web Server Security Configuration

Figure 5.38 Locating the ASP 500:100 Error Page

3. Select a **Message type** option (Figure 5.39) and click **OK**.

Figure 5.39 Choices for Custom Error Page

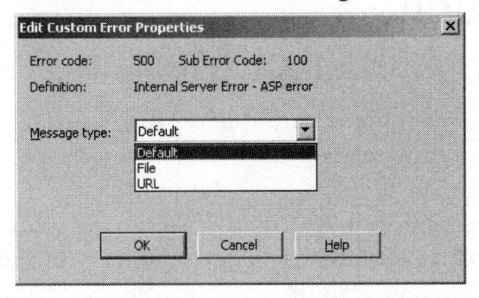

4. The **File** option serves any file off your server's hard disk without any server-side processing (as shown in Figure 5.40). This is useful only if you are serving an HTML page to the client. The HTML page could contain your corporate branding, and a message indicating that an error has occurred. If you choose this option, enter the name of the **File** that contains the error message, or click the **Browse** button to search for and select the desired file.

5. Click **OK**.

Figure 5.40 File Message Type

[Dialog: Edit Custom Error Properties — Error code: 500, Sub Error Code: 100, Definition: Internal Server Error - ASP error, Message type: File, File: c:\errorpages\500.htm]

6. The **URL** option allows you to specify a virtual path that points to another page on the server. This is useful if the custom error page will do some server-side processing itself (for example, generating an e-mail and sending it to the administrator). If you choose this option, enter the **URL** (which can be an ASP page itself) and click **OK** (Figure 5.41).

Figure 5.41 Configuring the URL Option

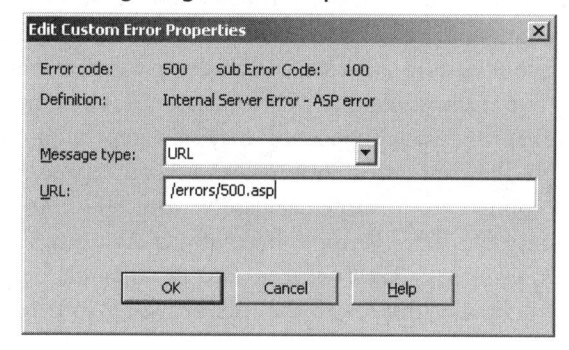

[Dialog: Edit Custom Error Properties — Error code: 500, Sub Error Code: 100, Definition: Internal Server Error - ASP error, Message type: URL, URL: /errors/500.asp]

If the custom 500-100.asp page is configured to be an ASP page, you can use the intrinsic ASPError object to return details of the unhandled exception. The following code demonstrates how to retrieve information that may be useful for debugging errors in your applications:

```
<%
Set objASPError = Server.GetLastError()
strErrorCode = objASPError.ASPCode
strErrorNumber = objASPError.Number
strErrorSource = objASPError.Source
strErrorFile = objASPError.File
```

```
strErrorLine = objASPError.Line
strErrorDescription = objASPError.Description
strASPDescription = objASPError.ASPDescription
strRemoteIP = Request.ServerVariables("Remote_Addr")
strHTTPReferer = Request.ServerVariables("HTTP_Referer")
strHTTPMethod = Request.ServerVariables("Request_Method")


' The following two lines get the information sent
' by the browser as a form POST or via the querystring
' If you are placing this into a database you may
' wish to truncate this in case it is larger than your
' field definition
strPostData = Request.Form
strGetData = Request.QueryString
%>
```

The information can be set up to be e-mailed to you, or logged to a database.

It should be noted that errors in the custom error page itself are not handled by serving another copy of the custom error page (that would lead to an infinite loop). Instead, you will need to use VBScript's (On Error Resume Next) or Jscript's (Try...Catch) error handling options to ensure that your custom error page itself doesn't generate an unhandled exception. For example, if your web application loses connectivity to your database server then your application may start generating exceptions. IIS 6.0 will serve the configured custom 500-100 error page. However if you attempt to connect to the same database in your 500-100 error page (without using On Error Resume Next if you are using VBScript), then the 500-100 error page itself will generate an unhandled exception, and this error will be sent directly to the user browsing your page.

Configuring a Custom ASP.NET Error Message

ASP.NET does not use the settings in IIS 6.0 to determine which error pages to supply when an unhandled exception occurs. Instead, it uses its own configuration files (typically a web.config file) to determine what should happen. Since ASP.NET does not use IIS 6.0 settings, a detailed discussion on how to configure error messages for ASP.NET is beyond the scope of this book. To set custom error pages, edit the <customErrors> node of the web.config file as follows:

```xml
<customErrors mode="RemoteOnly"
defaultRedirect="GenericErrorPage.htm">
    <error statusCode="403" redirect="NoAccess.htm"/>
    <error statusCode="404" redirect="FileNotFound.htm"/>
    <error statusCode="500"
redirect="InternalServerError.htm"/>
<customErrors>
```

The **mode** attribute is used to determine whether the custom errors should be displayed for all clients, or only for clients that are not browsing from the local machine. The **defaultRedirect** attribute is used for all errors that do not have a specific error message listed. For each error code that you wish to handle, add an <error> node that contains the HTTP status that the page should be served for, and a virtual path provided to, the page in question.

To handle 500 errors resulting from ASP.NET pages, you can use create an Application_Error routine in the global.asax file serving your web application. This routine will handle all exceptions not handled on a page basis.

When creating custom error messages, be aware that the error message itself must be served from the same web application pool as the page where the error was generated. Attempting to serve a custom error page from a folder that is being served by a different web application pool will generate an error.

If your custom error page is too short, Internet Explorer 5 and later will substitute its own, more detailed, error page in place of yours, unless the user chooses to disable this behavior. The user can do this by disabling the **Show Friendly HTTP Errors** option (to access this option, select **Tools | Internet Options | Advanced.** For more information, see the Microsoft KB article: http://support.microsoft.com/?id=218155.

REALITY CHECK...

Custom error pages allow you to present a rich page to your users when an error condition occurs. Additionally, error pages that handle application errors help to alert you to bugs in your application, while keeping information disclosure to attackers to a minimum (they will be aware that they have located a bug in your application, but may have some difficulty determining the nature and extent of the bug).

Regardless of whether you log the error information to a database or have the details sent via an e-mail alert, consider the use of a governor of some kind. Otherwise you run the risk on a busy site of being flooded with alerts.

Securing Include Files

Include files are a convenient way of storing commonly used HTML or code. The code or HTML is placed into a central file, and then "included" with every file that requires it. This improves the maintainability of your web applications because changes to the contents of the include file are reflected immediately in every page that includes this central file.

> **BY THE BOOK...**
>
> Include files use *directives* (pieces of code) included in web pages. IIS 6.0 provides three technologies that support server side include (SSI) directives. Files with .stm, .shtm, and .shtml extensions are processed by the SSI web service extension. ASP files (.asp) can also contain include directives. Finally, ASP.NET pages can also contain include directives. However, there are alternate ways to include content in ASP.NET pages (for example, user controls) that are superior to using include directives.
>
> Since include files are now often used to centralize web application data and settings (such as database connection strings), it is important that any include files you do have are secured against malicious attackers.

If an attacker was able to determine the name of your include files, he or she may be able to directly request the include file. A common way of finding the name of an include file is by attempting to generate an unhandled exception (error) in your code. If the error occurs in an include page, then the default ASP error page that is generated includes the name of the include file (as shown in Figure 5.42) If you are using a customized ASP error page, you can prevent this type of information disclosure.

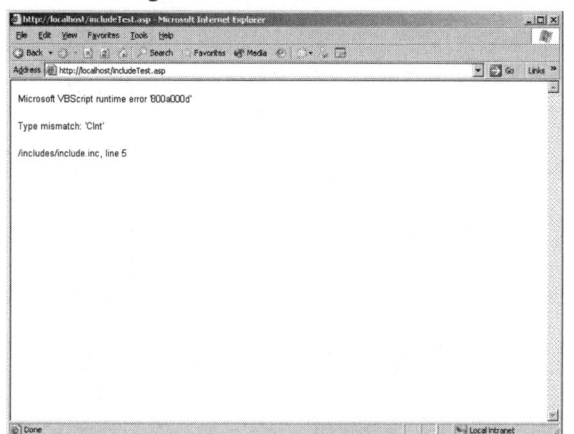

Figure 5.42 Disclosing the Name of an Include File

[Screenshot of Internet Explorer showing:
Microsoft VBScript runtime error '800a000d'
Type mismatch: 'Clnt'
/includes/include.inc, line 5]

To prevent attackers from gaining access to possible script source code in your include pages, the following configuration steps are recommended:

- If your include files contain an extension that is not used for any other purpose in your web application (for example, .inc) and you're running URLScan, add that extension to the [DenyExtension] list.

- If your include files are named with a static file extension (that is, a file extension that's not mapped to a web service extension), such .htm or .inc, remove IIS *Read* web permissions for the folder that contains your include files (ensure that there are no static files in that folder that are required to be served directly). To do this, open the IIS Manager, and expand the folder that contains your includes files. Right-click and choose **Properties**. On the **Directory** tab, disable the **Read** option (shown in Figure 5.43). This prevents static files from being served from this directory.

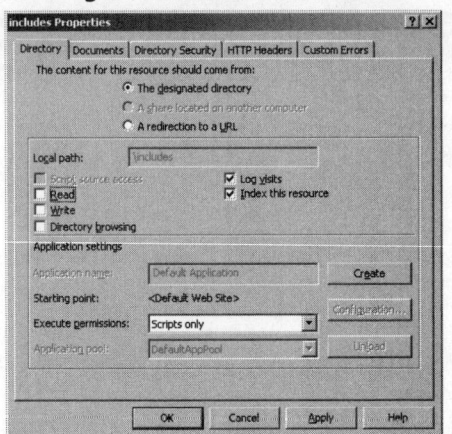

Figure 5.43 Removing IIS Web Read Permissions

[Screenshot of Includes Properties dialog showing Directory tab with Read checkbox unchecked and Execute permissions set to Scripts only]

- If your include files are named with a dynamic file extension (that is, a file extension that is mapped to a web service extension), such as .asp, remove the IIS script web permissions for the folder that contains your include files (ensure that there are no dynamic files in that folder that are required to be served directly). To do this, open the IIS Manager, and expand the folder that contains your includes files. Right-click and choose **Properties**. On the **Directory** tab, change the **Execute** permissions from **Scripts Only** to **None**. This prevents dynamic files from being served from this directory.

ASP.NET introduces the concept of *user controls* (with an .ascx extension). User controls are a superior way of storing commonly used content to include files. The default ASP.NET configuration prevents ASP.NET user controls from being requested by a user directly. This is set in the machine.Config file located in %windir%\Microsoft.NET\Framework\v1.1.4322\config, where the .ascx extension is mapped to the System.Web.HttpForbiddenHandler, which denies requests (as shown in Figure 5.44).

Figure 5.44 ASP.NET User Control Files are not Served by Default

> ### Reality Check...
>
> Some security guides recommend using the .asp extension for any include file. If the include file is requested directly, it will be processed by the ASP engine, and the source will not be sent to the user (only the results of the processing).
>
> While this may work in some cases (where the source code consists of routines, or classes), it may present problems if the included code opens database connections, generates e-mails, or instantiates other objects, since an attacker who repeatedly calls the page may start to consume an excessive amount of resources on your server (unless the include file also contains code to clean up and dispose of the objects used).

Disabling Parent Paths

Parent paths are paths that access folders located above the current folder. Enabling parent paths allows application code to access folders above the current folder.

> ### By the Book...
>
> When you enable parent paths, you specify that an ASP page should allows paths relative to the current directory (using the ../ notation). Parent paths are no longer enabled by default. This

affects your application if it has a web page that contains the *#include* server-side include directive and uses ".." notation to refer to a parent directory. Enabling parent paths corresponds to the metabase setting AspEnableParentPaths.

Enabling parent paths becomes a problem if the application navigates so far up the folder hierarchy that it is now outside the web root. For example, assume you have two web applications maintained by two different users, located in c:\inetpub\application1\ and c:\inetpub\application2\.

If parent paths are allowed, then a malicious coder could enter the following:

```
Response.Write(Server.MapPath("../application2/default.asp"))
```

in order to get the physical path to the default.asp page located in application2 (the ../ syntax tells the code to move up one folder). This physical path could then be used by the file system object to open the default.asp page and stream the source code back to the malicious user.

By default, parent paths are disabled in IIS 6.0. This prevents ASP code and include directives from using the "../" syntax to move up a folder from the current folder. If an application requires parent paths to be enabled, perform the following steps:

1. Open the IIS Manager and locate the website or web application root where the files that require parent path access are located. Right-click and choose **Properties**.

2. On the **Home Directory** or **Directory** tab click the **Configuration** button.

3. On the **Options** tab, enable the **Enable parent paths** option (shown in Figure 5.45).

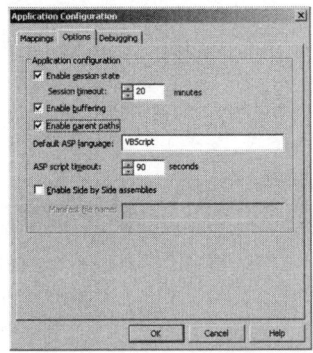

Figure 5.45 Enabling Parent Paths

Note that enabling parent paths poses a security risk. Before enabling parent paths, ensure that the application in question does not attempt to access unauthorized resources. Microsoft recommends disabling parent paths on your web servers: http://support.microsoft.com/?kbid=184717.

Configuring IP Address, TCP Port and Host-Header combinations

Introduced as part of HTTP v1.1, the *host* HTTP header allows multiple websites to be run on a single IP address using TCP port 80 only. Prior to this, each website required its own unique IP address, or had to be run on a non-standard (not port 80) TCP port.

BY THE BOOK...

When an HTTP v1.1-compatible client makes a request to a Web server for a resource (for example, a web page, image or document), it includes the DNS or NetBIOS name (the host) of the website that it's requesting the resource from. The Web server (in this case IIS) examines the supplied host header to see if it matches any of those configured on the server. If there's a match, the normal request processing process occurs. If there's no match, IIS returns an "HTTP 400 Bad Request" error to the client browser.

When configuring websites, each website can have one or more combinations of IP address plus TCP port (this is typically port 80) plus host-header name. Each combination of IP address plus TCP port plus host header name is known as a *website identity*. Each website has at least 1 website identity, but can have more.

However, on a given Web server, each such identity must be unique. If they are not unique, when an HTTP request comes in, IIS will not know which website the request should be routed to.

Requests for a website identity that doesn't match any configured on the server will be rejected with an "HTTP 400 Bad Request" error.

When configuring a website identity, the host-header name is optional. Additionally, the IP address can be a specific IP address assigned to the machine, or you can choose **All unassigned**, in which case the website identity will include all IP addresses not already assigned to other websites.

When IIS matches incoming requests to website identities, it assigns the requests in order of specificity.

- If there is a website that has an exact match of IP address plus TCP port plus host header name, the request is routed to that website.

- If there is a website that has an IP address plus TCP port match (and no host-header name), the request is routed that that website.

- If the request does not match any of the these two, but there is a website that has all unassigned addresses for the IP address, plus a TCP port match (and no host-header name), the request is routed to this website.

Otherwise, the request is rejected.

Suppose a corporation has the following four DNS names configured as shown in Table 5.4:

Table 5.4 Sample DNS Name Configuration

DNS Name	IP Address
www.myCompany.com	192.168.0.100
mail.myCompany.com	192.168.0.100
support.myCompany.com	192.168.0.100
intranet.myCompany.com	192.168.0.200

Both 192.168.0.100 and 192.168.0.200 are assigned to the same IIS server. In the IIS MMC snap-in, the website identities shown in Table 5.5 are configured:

Table 5.5 Configured Website Identities

Website Number	IP Address	Port	Host Header Name
1	192.168.0.100	80	www.myCompany.com
	192.168.0.100	80	mail.myCompany.com
2	192.168.0.100	80	<blank>
3	<All Unassigned>	80	<blank>

Requests for both www.myCompany.com and http://mail.myCompany.com will be answered by website 1, since there is an exact match. Requests for http://support.myCompany.com and http://192.168.0.100 will be answered by Website 2. Website 1 will not answer requests for http://192.168.0.100 because that doesn't match any of the configured identities for that website. Website 3 will not answer requests for http://192.168.0.100 because that's been allocated to website 2. Website 3 will only answer request on otherwise unallocated IP addresses.

Lastly, requests for http://intranet.myCompany.com and http://192.168.0.200 will be answered by Website 3. Website 3 will answer requests for http://192.168.0.200 because that IP address hasn't been allocated to any other website.

When IIS 6.0 is installed, the default website is configured to listen on "All Unassigned" IP addresses (which equates to all addresses assigned to the machine, since there are no other sites configured). To change this behavior, and have the default site listen on for requests for a specific DNS name perform the following steps:

1. Open the IIS Manager from the Administration Tools Folder.
2. Expand the **Websites** node.
3. Right-click the **default website** and select **Properties**. Note that unlike many properties, website identities can only be configured at the website level (not the folder, or file level).
4. On the **Website** tab, click the **Advanced** button.
5. Select the pre-existing website identity and click the **Edit** button.
6. Enter the DNS name that you wish the site to answer requests for (see Figure 5.46), and click the **OK** button.

Figure 5.46 Adding/Editing a Website Identity

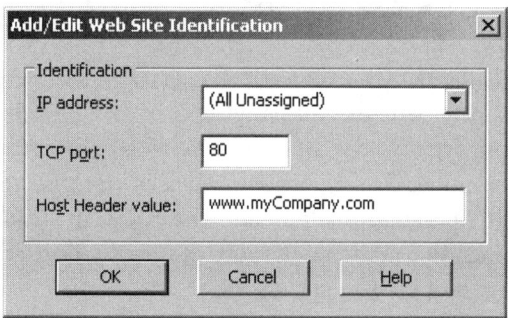

7. If the site should answer requests for more than one DNS name (like website 1 in the example above), click the Add button to add another website identity.

8. Click **OK** twice to return to the IIS Manager.

> **REALITY CHECK...**
>
> Configuring host header names for all your websites isn't strictly a security measure. Host header names were designed to allow multiple websites to be hosted on a single IP address.
>
> However, many automated worms that attack IIS, including Code Red and NIMDA are incapable of interrogating the DNS. Instead, they send HTTP requests to an IP address only, omitting a host name. If no website on your Web server is configured to listen on an IP address only, then the worm will never be able to have its payload examined by IIS. Additionally, your website's log files do not record numerous worm-inspired requests such as the following, which is a typical Code Red request from an infected machine to your server:
>
> GET/default.ida?XXXXXXXXXXXXXXXXXXXXXXXXXXXXXX
> XXXXXXXXXXXXXXXXXXXXXXXXXXXXXXXXXXXXXXXXXXXXXX
> XXXXXXXXXXXXXXXXXXXXXXXXXXXXXXXXXXXXXXXXXXXXXX
> XXXXXXXXXXXXXXXXXXXXXXXXXXXXXXXXXXXXXXXXXXXXXX
> XXXXXXXXXXXXXXXXXXXXXXXXXXXXXXXXXXXXXXXXXXXXXX
> XXXX%u9090%u6858%ucbd3%u7801%u9090%u6858%ucbd3%
> u7801%u9090%u6858%ucbd3%u7801%u9090%u9090%u8190
> %u00c3%u0003%u8b00%u531b%u53ff%u0078%u0000%u00=a
>
> Configuring host header names for all your websites will not stop a dedicated attacker, but it may make your server more resistant to automated worm-based attacks.

Your A** is Covered if You...

- ☑ Familiarize yourself with the available authentication methods, and the benefits and drawbacks of each. For basic authentication, evaluate the need for SSL to secure transmission of user credentials. For digest and IWA, ensure that your client browsers support these authentication mechanisms, and your server and network support the prerequisites for using these authentication mechanisms.

- ☑ Configure user accounts with the minimum privileges required for IIS web functionality.

- ☑ Are aware of which user account settings must to be configured so that you can isolate web applications from each other if required.

- ☑ Are familiar with the URLScan tool from Microsoft, and how it can help secure your Web server by providing an additional defensive layer.

- ☑ Configure appropriate application settings to protect your web applications from information disclosure attacks. You should develop custom application error pages that inform your developers of errors while hiding configuration information from malicious attackers. You should secure include files that may contain sensitive configuration information about your application.

- ☑ Be aware of the new Authorization Manager functionality included with Windows 2003, and how it allows for role-based authorization, as compared with the traditional ACE authorization method traditionally used to secure access to resources.

Chapter 6
Securing Application Pools

In this Chapter

To get the best out of Internet Information Server (IIS) 6.0, it is recommended that you run IIS 6.0 in worker process isolation mode. This mode allows you to isolate applications from one another so that they can be secured independently and will not affect the performance of other applications. This will increase the security and availability of applications and will improve the overall performance of the IIS server.

- Application Pools
- Isolating Web Applications
- Understanding User Impersonation

By the end of this chapter, you should have a good understanding of the benefits of using IIS 6.0 in worker process isolation mode, as well as how to implement this mode through the creation and configuration of application pools.

Application Pools

Worker process isolation mode works by allowing you to create *application pools*. An application pool is simply a group of one or more Uniform Resource Locators (URLs) or websites applications served by one or more worker processes. Because each pool uses a separate worker process, errors in one pool will not cause errors in another pool.

> **BY THE BOOK...**
>
> In worker process isolation mode, application pools provide you with the ability to configure web application boundaries, and allow you to isolate applications based on your needs. This feature not only provides more reliability in terms of application uptime, it also protects applications from each other while allowing you to have better security options when configuring different types of applications. Additionally, because requests are routed directly from the kernel, you will notice a marked performance improvement.

To create and configure application pools, you must first ensure that the server is running in worker process isolation mode. When you perform a clean installation of Windows Server 2003, worker process isolation mode will be enabled by default. However, if you are upgrading from a previous version of IIS (the Released Candidate version of Windows Server 2003), the isolation mode will be set to IIS 5.0 isolation mode to provide backward compatibility. Table 6.1 shows the default isolation mode when installing or upgrading from pervious versions.

Table 6.1 Default Application Isolation Modes of IIS Installation

Installation	Isolation Mode
New Installation	Worker process isolation mode
Upgrade from earlier version IIS 6.0	No change in isolation mode
Upgrade from IIS 5.0	IIS 5.0 isolation mode
Upgrade from IIS 4.0	IIS 5.0 isolation mode

To determine the currently selected mode, open the IIS Manager console and expand the local computer. If **Application Pools** is present in the left-hand pane, it means that worker process isolation mode is enabled (see Figure 6.1).

Figure 6.1 Checking IIS 6.0 Isolation Mode – Application Pools

If worker process isolation mode is not enabled, you must follow the steps below to enable it:

1. In the IIS MMC console, expand the local computer, right-click **Web Sites**, and click **Properties**.
2. Click the **Service** tab (Figure 6.2) and disable the **Run WWW service in IIS 5.0 isolation mode** checkbox.
3. Click **OK**.
4. Click **Yes** to restart the WWW service.

Figure 6.2 Configuring Worker Process Isolation Mode – Service Tab

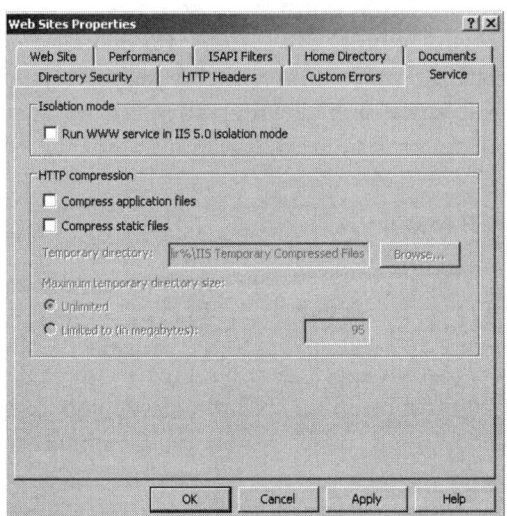

Creating Application Pools

In Worker Process Isolation, a default application pool (called DefaultAppPool) will be created. You can customize this pool to suit your needs or you can create a new application pool using the following steps:

1. In the IIS MMC console, expand the local computer, right-click **Application Pools** and select **New | Application Pool**.
2. The **Add New Application Pool** dialog box will be displayed (Figure 6.3). Enter the name of the new application pool in the **Application pool ID** field.

Figure 6.3 Creating an Application Pool – Add New Application Pool Dialog Box

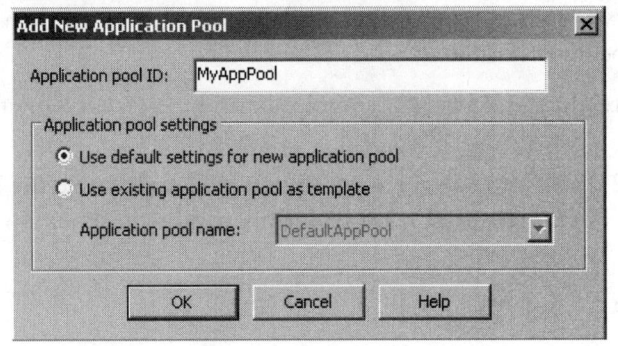

3. Use the **Application pool settings** options to specify where the application pool's settings will come from. If you select **Use existing application pool as template**, use the **Application pool name** drop-down list to select the existing application pool that will be used as a template for the new application pool.
4. Click **OK**.

Configuring Application Pools

Now that you have an application pool (either the default or one that you created), it must be configured to provide you with the desired features. Application pools can be configured to support the following:

- **Process Recycling** In earlier version of IIS, memory leaks, faulty coding and other traits can cause web applications to fail. When this happens, you may need to restart the IIS service or reboot the server itself. To help prevent this type of problem, IIS 6.0 includes a recycling feature that will automatically restart worker processes based on the amount of requests processed, memory usage, or running time. By default, the process recycling feature is enabled and is set to refresh worker processes every **29** hours.

- **Idle Timeout** This option will automatically shut down processes that have been idle for a specified amount of time. This can help you to return unused processes back to system for other application usage. Worker processes are started automatically when there is new request for the application pool. By default, this feature is enabled and is set to **20** minutes.

- **Request queue limit** This option specifies the maximum number of requests that an application will hold in its processing queue. Once the limit has been reached, IIS will reject new requests and send a 503 error message to the client. Limiting the queue length can help you to prevent overloading the server. The default request queue length is **4000** requests.

- **CPU Monitoring** This feature allows you to keep track of CPU usage and terminate worker processes that consume large amounts of CPU time. By default, CPU monitoring is not enabled.

- **Web Garden** A web garden is an application pool that consists of more than one worker process. By creating a web garden, you can improve the server's performance because even if one process is busy, incoming requests can be picked up and processed immediately by the other worker processes.

- **Health Monitoring** This feature will periodically check the health of the worker processes. If a worker process fails to respond to the check (a ping that occurs on a specified schedule), IIS will terminate the worker process and start a new one. By default, health monitoring is enabled and is set to perform a check every **30** seconds.

- **Rapid-Fail Protection** This feature allows you to prevent unhealthy applications from bringing the entire server down. When an application pool detects too many unhealthy worker processes in a given time, IIS will disable the application pool and write a warning entry in the event log. IIS will then try to invoke the application pool and start new worker processes. In the meantime, the HTTP.sys kernel driver will queue incoming requests before it forwards them to the application pool processing queue, allowing the application to run without interruption despite the problems. By default, the rapid-fail protection feature is enabled, and application pools will be disabled if the application fails more than **5** times within **5** minutes.

- **Application Pool Identity** This option allows you to specify which application identities can run particular worker processes. By specifying particular identities, you can avoid having to grant blanket access for the entire application. By default, Worker processes run under the **Network Service** identity, which is predefined and has fewer privileges that **LocalSystem** (which is the default process identity in IIS 5.0).

Configuring Application Pool Identities

By configuring an application pool identity, you can secure web applications in more effective ways. For example, if you are running a web portal solution for many customers, instead of running all applications with one application pool, you can configure one application pool for each web application, and you can configure different application identities for each application pool. Because each application is running under different identity, when one customer application is compromised, attackers cannot use the affected application pool identity to access other customer data.

Alternatively, configuring application pool identities allows you to control the application's access permissions. Suppose, for example, that you are running a web application that has a single feature that requires system registry access. If you host the application with one application pool using one identity, you will have to grant system registry access to the entire application. To limit access to the system registry, you can create additional application pools with different process identities, relocate the related script files to a new virtual directory and run the virtual directory in different application pool with access to the system registry (or other desired resource).

When configuring an application pool identity, you can select a predefined built-in account or you can customize an account. It is recommended that you choose from the predefined accounts unless you are well-versed in application pool identity configuration. The predefined accounts are:

- LocalSystem
- Network Service
- LocalService

The *Network Service* account is recommended because it provides more restrictions than *LocalSystem*, which basically grants full access to the entire system. Because of the potential high security risk it presents, it is *not* recommended that you use LocalSystem unless all access rights are absolutely required. The *LocalService* account grants even fewer rights than the Network Service, and you can choose LocalService if the application pool does not require access to network resources.

All three of these predefined accounts are located in an *IIS_WPG* built-in user group. Group membership provides the minimum permissions and user rights required to run an application. If you are configuring an application pool identity using an account other than the predefined accounts, you will need to add your Windows user to this group, or the application will fail to start.

The Network Service identity has the following user rights:

- Replace a process-level token (SeAssignPrimaryTokenPrivilege)
- Adjust memory quotas for a process (SeIncreaseQuotaPrivilege)
- Generate security audits (SeAuditPrivilege)
- Bypass traverse checking (SeChangeNotifyPrivilege)
- Access the current computer from a network (SeNetworkLogonRight)
- Log on as a batch job (SeBatchLogonRight)
- Log on as a service (SeInteractiveLogonRight)
- Allow log on locally (SeInteractiveLogonRight)

Now that you understand application pool identities, you can follow the procedures below to select the appropriate type:

1. In the IIS MMC console, expand the local computer, expand the **Application Pools** folder, right-click the application pool you would like to configure, and click **Properties**.
2. Click the **Identity** tab (Figure 6.4).

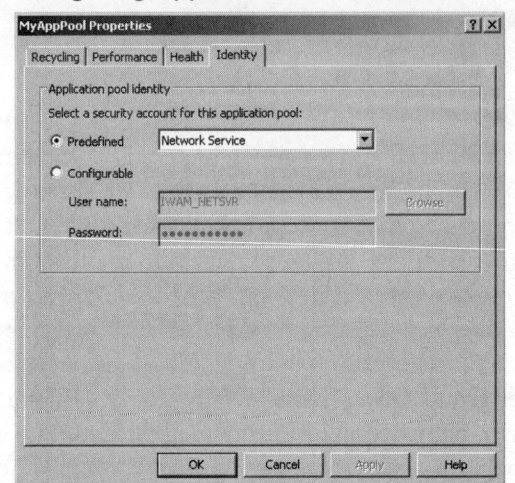

Figure 6.4 Configuring Application Pool Identities – Identity Tab

3. To use a predefined account, select the **Predefined** option select **Network Service**, **Local Service**, or **Local System** from the drop-down list. To use a configurable account, select the **Configurable** option and enter a **User name** and **Password**.
4. Click **OK**.

Reality Check...

Configure IIS 6.0 to run in worker process mode in order to take full advantage of the features that the new architecture can offer you in terms of better security, reliability, scalability, and performance improvements.

You are safest if you stick with the default Network Service application pool identity. You *should not* change the worker process identity to LocalSystem unless your application requires it to function correctly.

You should grant minimum user rights to user accounts when you are configuring application pool identities, since minimized permissions will lead to fewer potential damages and risks if a worker process has been compromised.

Isolating Web Applications

By using application pools, you can define the boundary for each application, and you can create a separate application space for each application so that when an application fails, it will not affect other applications running on the same server. Isolating web applications with application pools gives you both reliability and security. This section will discuss how to isolate applications and control how each application should run.

> **BY THE BOOK...**
>
> You can create as many applications as you wish. Websites are root-level applications by default, and when you create new website, a default application is created at the same time. You can use this default application, or you can remove it and create a new one. Applications can be defined at a website, virtual directory or directory level.
>
> When you create an application, you need a starting point or application root. You can have more than one application per website and you can have applications within applications, meaning you can have one web application consisting of many application pools and served by different worker processes. Each application space belongs to the application defined as its root, and until another application starting point is created, all files and folders will belong to that application.

One of the best features in IIS 6.0 is application isolation, where you have full isolation control of your entire application. You can completely isolate each application in its own application pool, and there is no performance penalty when compared with previous versions of IIS.

Before you can isolate applications, you must first determine where you intend to have an application and remember that you can configure the application at the website, virtual directory or directory level. Essentially the steps of creating applications at these different levels are the same. You will configure a website, virtual directory, or directory property page. The steps below demonstrate how to create a virtual directory application, and can be applied to create applications for a website or directory level as well:

1. In IIS Manager, expand the local computer, navigate and expand the appropriate website, right-click the Virtual Directory for which you wish to create the application, and click **Properties**.
2. In the **Virtual Directory** tab (shown in Figure 6.5), **Application settings** area, click **Create**.

Figure 6.5 Creating Virtual Direction Applications – Identity Tab

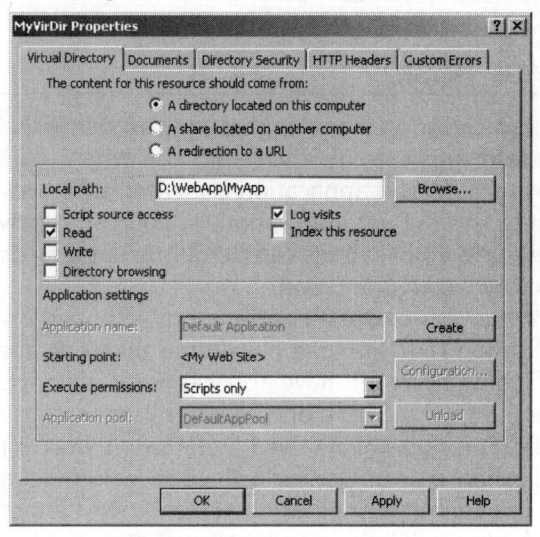

3. Enter the **Application name**.
4. Use the **Execute Permissions** drop-down list to select the desired permission execution. Select **None** to prevent any programs or scripts from running, select **Scripts only** to enable applications mapped to a script engine, or select **Scripts and Executables** to allow any application to run in this directory.
5. Click **OK**.
6. To remove the application, click **Remove**.

Application isolation is about reliability, performance and security. *Reliability* refers to each application being run by dedicated worker processes that are independent from other worker processes; when one fails, it will not affect other worker processes. *Performance* refers to the ability of the server to continue running in the face of application problems, such as memory leaks or poor coding. *Security* refers to the prevention of access to your remaining websites if a single website is breached.

To put security into perspective, consider the following scenarios:

- **Websites** Imagine you are working in an enterprise corporate environment in which each business unit hosts its own web application for day-to-day operations, but does not have access to the data in the other business units' applications. By using application isolation, you can configure each site to run under a different application pool identity, and secure the content with proper NTFS permissions to prevent unauthorized data access.

- **Components** Suppose that you just received a new component developed by a third-party vendor or some other source, and you suspect that it might contain malicious or illegal coding, and you have no time to do a code review. To prevent the potentially faulty component from bringing down your entire application or trying to sabotage your system, you can isolate the component to run in its own application pool with by default *Network Service* identity or lower privilege account.

- **Customer** Suppose that you are working for an ISP hosting company and you have several hundred customers hosting their applications on your IIS server. Again, you can configure each customer application to run in a different application pool to protect you and other customers if one of the applications tries to access confidential data, or if one of the customer applications has been compromised by hackers and the attacker is trying to cause further damage to your server.

Once you have configured an application pool identity using a configurable user account, you will have to configure a related NFTS permissions account. In the first scenario above, you will need to grant each worker process identity *read* and *execute* permissions for the business web application contents.

You can assign each application at the website, virtual directory or directory level. To assign a virtual directory application to an application pool:

1. In the IIS MMC console, expand the local computer, expand the appropriate website, then right-click the **Virtual Directory** and select **Properties**.

2. In the **Virtual Directory** tab (shown in Figure 6.6), use the **Application Pool** drop-down list to select the name of the application pool to which you want to assign the application.

Figure 6.6 Configuring a Virtual Directory Application Pool – Virtual Directory Tab

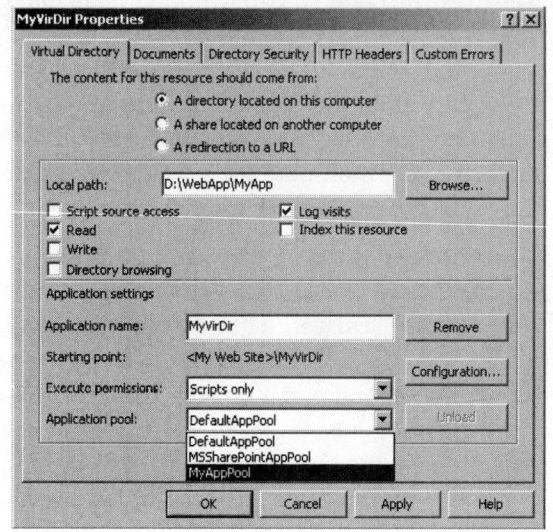

3. Click **OK**.

Refer to the following guidelines when considering application isolation:

1. Isolate applications to different application pools when you need higher system reliability.
2. Create a new application pool when the application requires a special configuration.
3. Secure your application isolation with the default Network Service account or a minimal-privileges user account.

REALITY CHECK...

Isolate applications only on an as-needed basis. Though you can create many application pools to isolate your application, you should only do it when it is required. Creating too many configuration application pools will not give you any advantage, as each worker process servicing the application pool requires a certain amount of system resources.

The bottom line regarding an application pool is this—focus on web application requirements, justifying the need to isolate the application, and always put security as the first consideration before making any decision.

Understanding User Impersonation

User impersonation occurs when a user pretends to be another user. User impersonation can occur when a user configures an application pool to allow his or her own account credentials to replace the original base identity. It is important to understand the relationship between worker process identity and user impersonation; you will use this information when you are doing security planning and securing the web applications.

BY THE BOOK...

The default worker process identity for an application pool is the Network Service account. This is a predefined low-level access account that runs the worker process. However, when a client requests to access the resource content, the current user account associated with the application will be the only effective user token accessing the resource. The process of replacing the user token to another user is called *Impersonation*.

Each application uses two identities; one for the worker process identity and one for the request user's identity. If the application allows anonymous access, the authenticated user's token will default to an IUSR_<COMPUTERNAME> account, and if the request is not anonymous, the authenticated user's token is associated with the current user's authenticated account.

In order to understand user impersonation, you must first understand the two identities involved when a web application processes a client's request. The *process identity* is responsible for running the worker process and the *request identity* is the user who actually accesses the resources. Another factor in impersonation is the *user token default interval* of cache time, which is 15mins by default. This cache time means that if you change a user password within the cached time, you are able to use the old and new passwords at the same time. Token caching can be cleared by restarting the IIS services. You can also control the default interval for user token by following these procedures to change the registry setting:

1. Run the **Registry Editor** (Regedt32.exe).
2. Select the **HKEY_LOCAL_MACHINE** sub-tree, and access the following key:
   \System\CurrentControlSet\Services\InetInfo\Parameters
3. Select **Add Value** from the **Edit** menu.
4. Enter **UserTokenTTL** in the **Value Name** field.
5. Enter **REG_DWORD** in the **Data Type** field.
6. Use the **Data** field to enter the number of seconds for the token to be cached. Set this to **0** to disable token caching.
7. Restart **IIS Admin** and dependent services.

By default, ASP.NET impersonation is turned off. Typically, you can enable impersonation to avoid dealing with authentication and authorization issues in the ASP.NET application code. You can configure impersonation so that the application code can be executed by a user account to which you have specifically granted the required access rights.

When impersonation is enabled, ASP.NET always impersonates the access token that IIS provides to ISAPI extensions. That access token can be either the IUSR_<COMPUTERNAME> default anonymous user token or an authenticated user token. Only application code is impersonated; compilation and configuration are read as the process identity.

REALITY CHECK...

By understanding the concept behind impersonation and the identities involved, securing the application and its content will be your next tasks. Again, the rules with securing web resource are granting the minimum permissions, and explicitly denying access to other resources when such access must be restricted.

Your A** is Covered if You…

- ☑ Configured the default application pool identity with minimal users rights.
- ☑ Secured user-configurable application pool identities.
- ☑ Isolated web applications that require special security access rights.
- ☑ Secured application access for user-configurable application pool identities.
- ☑ Secured process and request identity user accounts.

Chapter 7

Securing FTP Sites

In this Chapter

The File Transfer Protocol (FTP) component of the Internet Information Server (IIS) provides you with the ability to upload and download files to and from the IIS server, and allows you to manipulate files remotely. If you decide to enable the FTP component, be sure you carry out the following security guidelines and procedures outlined in this chapter to protect your FTP server.

- Configuring FTP Sites
- Securing FTP Resources
- Configuring FTP User Isolation
- Securing the FTP Connection
- Enabling and Securing the FTP Access Log File

Throughout this chapter, you will learn different ways to secure your FTP contents, along with methods for securing the FTP connection, as FTP transfer does not support its own security. You will also learn to customize passive mode connections on the FTP server for better firewall security support and finally, you will learn how to use some of the new FTP features in IIS 6.0 to isolate FTP users.

Configuring FTP Sites

FTP provides a simple way for transferring files between client machines and the IIS server. This typically involves sharing files over the Internet so that users can connect to their servers and download desired files, or allowing users to post their files onto your server. By default, the FTP component is not installed with IIS 6.0, which is shipped in default locked-down mode. Before configuring the FTP component, you must first correctly install it. Refer to Chapter 3 for FTP installation instructions.

> **BY THE BOOK...**
>
> While the IIS package includes the FTP service, by default the FTP component is not installed. To set up an FTP site, you must first install the FTP component through the Control Panel, then customize it to your needs using the IIS Manager.
>
> The FTP component in IIS version 6 includes two new features:
>
> **FTP User Isolation** prevents users from viewing or overwriting other users' directory by restricting user to their own directories.
>
> **FTP Restart** enables FTP file uploading to be resumed without the need to re-upload the entire file again if an interruption occurs during data transfer.

When creating the FTP site, you will have to relocate the default FTP root path, set up FTP messages, and configure the FTP directory output style. When you first install the FTP service, a *Default FTP Site* will be created. You can rename this site, customize it to suit your needs, or you can delete it and create your own FTP site. IIS 6.0 allows you to create multiple FTP sites, with the stipulation that each site must bind to a unique Internet Protocol (IP) address or port number. To create new FTP site, perform the following steps:

1. In IIS Manager, expand the local computer, right-click the **FTP Sites** node, point to **New**, and click **FTP Site**.
2. In the **FTP Site Creation Wizard** dialog box, click **Next**.
3. Enter a **Description** of your FTP site and click **Next**.
4. Use the **Enter the IP address to use this FTP site** field (shown in Figure 7.1) to enter a new **IP address**, and leave the **TCP port** setting at 21.

Figure 7.1 Creating an FTP Site – FTP Site Creation Wizard Dialog Box

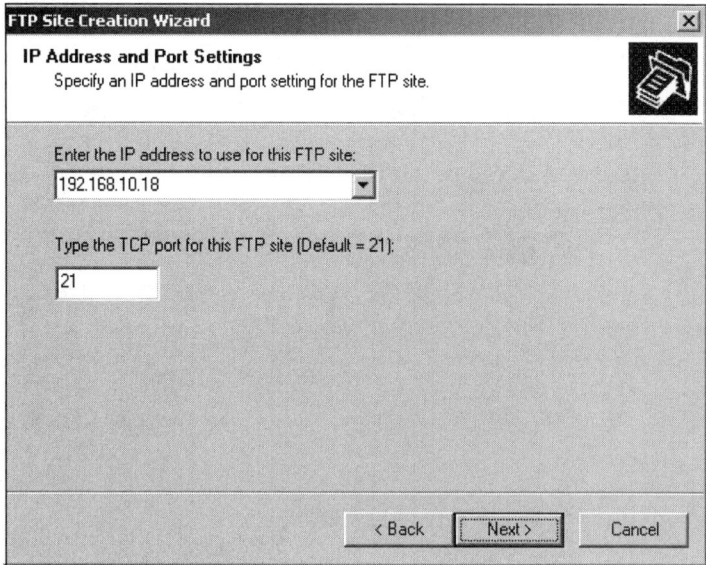

5. Click **Next**.
6. Select the desire mode of isolation and click **Next**. You will learn more about different user isolation modes later in the chapter, in the "Configuring FTP User Isolation" section.
7. Click **Browse** and select the appropriate directory path.
8. Click **Next**.
9. Select **Read** and click **Next**.
10. Click **Finish**.

Relocate the Default FTP Root Path

During installation, IIS will create a default FTP root path on your system drive, typically C:\Inetpub\Ftproot>. For security reasons, it is best to relocate this home folder to another partition or hard drive. In doing so, attackers who gain control over the new disk partitions will not be able to access system-related files located in the system drive. If you decided to customize the default FTP site or you would like to relocate the FTP home directory of your FTP site, perform the following steps:

1. In IIS Manager, expand the local computer, expand the **FTP Sites** node, right-click the FTP site whose home directory you want to change, and click **Stop**.
2. Right-click the FTP site again and click **Properties**.
3. Click the **Home Directory** tab (shown in Figure 7.2).

Figure 7.2 Changing the FTP Site Home Directory – Home Directory Tab

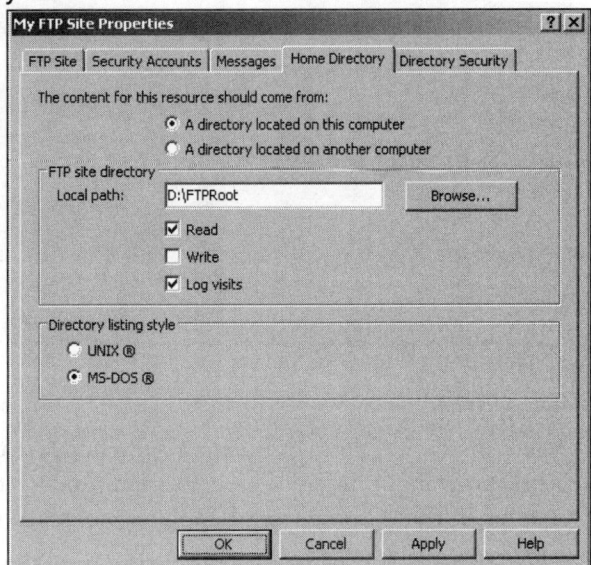

4. Under **The content for this resource should come from**, select the desired resource mode.
5. Enter the **Local Path** or click **Browse** to search for and select the path.
6. Click **OK**.
7. Right-click the **FTP site** you just modified and click **Start**.

Configure FTP Messages

You can configure the FTP site message to give more information when the user is connected to your FTP site. You can configure the FTP site to use the following message types:

- **Banner** Appears when users are connected to your FTP site.

- **Welcome** Appears when users log in to the FTP site.
- **Exit** Appears when users log off the FTP site.
- **Maximum connections** Displays a message stating that a user's connection attempt was refused because the FTP site has reached the maximum number of connections allowed.

To configure FTP messages, perform the following steps:

1. In IIS Manager, expand the **FTP sites** node, right-click the **FTP site** for which you want to change messages, and click **Properties**.
2. Click the **Messages** tab (shown in Figure 7.3).

Figure 7.3 Configuring FTP Messages – Messages Tab

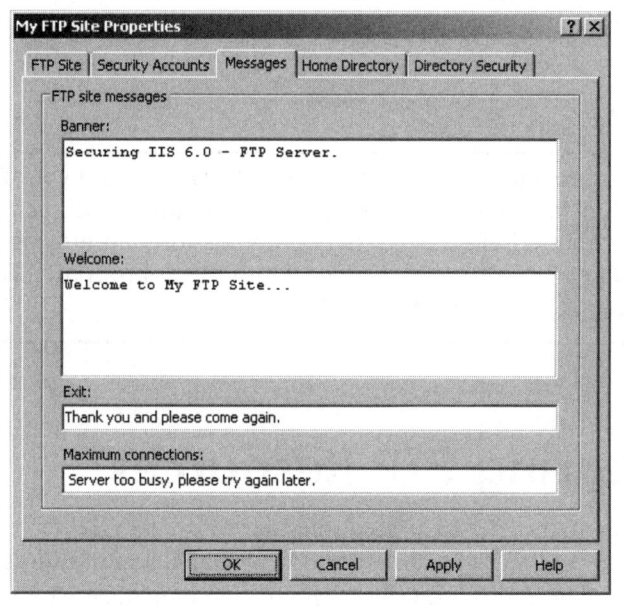

3. Type in the desired messages in the **Banner**, **Welcome**, **Exit**, and **Maximum connections** fields.
4. Click **OK**.

Configure the FTP Directory Output Style

When configuring the directory output style for directory listings, you can specify either MS DOS or UNIX style. In MS DOS style, directory listings display the year in a two-digit format while UNIX style shows a four-digit format when the file date is different from the current year on the FTP server. To configure the listing style, follow these steps:

1. In IIS Manager, expand the local computer, expand the **FTP Sites** node, right-click the **FTP Site** folder, and click **Properties**.
2. Click the **Home Directory** tab.
3. Under **Directory listing style**, select **UNIX** or **MS-DOS**.
4. Click **OK**.

REALITY CHECK...

To provide security, you should always relocate your FTP home directory to a new disk volume or partition and secure it with proper NT File System (NTFS) permissions. To provide ease-of-use and a user-friendly site, configure the appropriate FTP site messages and directory listing style.

Securing FTP Resources

FTP resources refer to content files served by the FTP server. To prevent unauthorized file uploading and downloading, you need to secure these content files. You can do this by protecting individual FTP files and/or controlling user access.

BY THE BOOK...

IIS FTP supports both anonymous and basic user authentication. By default, anonymous access uses the IUSR_<COMPUTER-NAME> user account as the authenticated user, and basic authentication allows users to login to the FTP server using their registered Windows user account.

For resource access, FTP provides two FTP site permissions—you can configure the FTP site to support *read-only* access or *read-write* access.

Notes from the Underground...

FTP Tagged

There is always the potential for attacks, or unauthorized file uploads, which are normally launched against FTP sites that allow anonymous access and do not have proper NTFS permissions set up to prevent anonymous user accounts. Attackers can create different unknown directories and files, and because most directories use a *Windows Reserved Name* such as COM1 and LPT1, these directories cannot be deleted using Windows Explorer or the del command. Attackers will use your FTP sites for file transfer purposes, including: illegal copies of movie files, unlicensed commercial software, hacker tools, and music files.

To prevent such attacks, always secure FTP content with strong FTP and NTFS permissions. Do not allow *write* FTP permissions if such access is not needed. If anonymous users are allowed to upload files, always create a separate directory for upload purposes. Grant *read* and *write* NTFS permissions to the upload directory and deny anonymous user *write* access for other directories. And finally, disable anonymous access if it is not needed.

Suppose, for example that you are hosting a public FTP site that allows anonymous uploads and downloads. You should create two different directories (one for uploading and one for downloading). You will configure FTP Site Permissions to allow *Read*, *Write* and *Log Visits*, this will ensure your FTP sites support both files downloading and uploading. The *log visits* enable you to capture each clients request send to FTP server and keep track of resources popularity and access detail. For NTFS permissions, you can configure physical folder NTFS permissions as follow:

> FTP root directory -> *D:\MyFTP* (System and Administrator: *Full Control*), (Anonymous user: *Read only*)
>
> Upload -> *D:\MyFTP\Upload* (System and Administrator: *Full Control*), (Anonymous user: *Read and Write*)
>
> Download -> *D:\MyFTP\Download* (System and Administrator: *Full Control*), (Anonymous user: *Read only*)

First, we will look into the two different authentications supported by the FTP component, and then we will focus on how to secure the FTP content using FTP site permissions and NTFS permissions.

When configuring IIS FTP, you can choose to support either anonymous or authenticated user access, or both. Anonymous access (which uses IUSR_<COMPUTERNAME> as the authenticated user) allows users to access the FTP site by supplying *anonymous* as the user name and entering any password they choose. From a security standpoint, this method is *not* recommended because it does not provide any access security to the FTP site.

In basic authentication access, users must login with a valid registered username and password. However, during the login process, the user's credentials are sent in plain text with *Base64* encoding, which can easily be intercepted and decoded. When you enable both anonymous and basic authentication access, IIS FTP will always try anonymous FTP authentication before basic FTP authentication. To configure FTP authentication, follow these steps:

1. In IIS Manager, expand the **FTP sites** node, right-click the desired FTP site and click **Properties**.
2. Click the **Security Accounts** tab (shown in Figure 7.4).

Figure 7.4 Configuring FTP Site Authentication – Security Accounts Tab

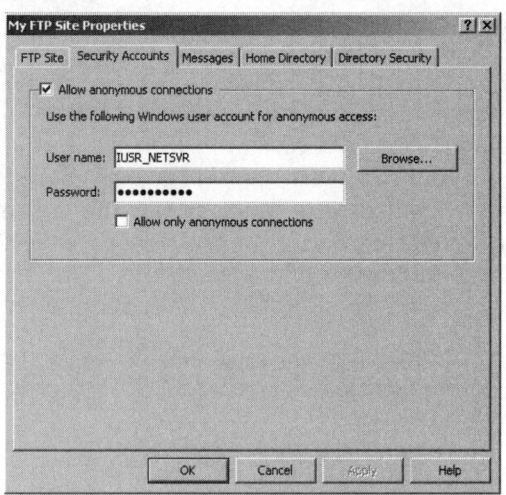

3. To allow anonymous authentication, enable the **Allow anonymous connections** checkbox and, if you will not be using the default IUSR_<COMPUTERNAME> user as the anonymous user, enter the **User name** and **Password** in the available fields.

4. To limit the site to anonymous authentication only, enable the **Allow only anonymous connections** checkbox; otherwise, to enable both anonymous and basic authentication, disable this option.

5. Click **OK**.

Once FTP authentication is configured, your next step should be to configure the FTP site permissions. FTP site permissions are similar to website permissions (discussed in Chapter 4), except that FTP site permissions are simpler to configure. FTP site permissions can be *read-only*, *write-only* or *read-write*. You can also configure *log visits* to specify whether site access activities will be logged to an FTP access log file.

It is important to note that *virtual directories*, rather than physical directories, are listed under the home FTP path in IIS Manager. FTP site permissions can be configured at the FTP site and/or virtual directory levels. To configure FTP site permission on a virtual directory, follow these steps:

1. In IIS Manager, expand the desired FTP sites node, right-click on the **Virtual Directory** you wish to configure, and click **Properties**.

2. Click the **Virtual Directory** tab (shown in Figure 7.5).

Figure 7.5 Configuring FTP Virtual Directory Permissions – Virtual Directory Tab

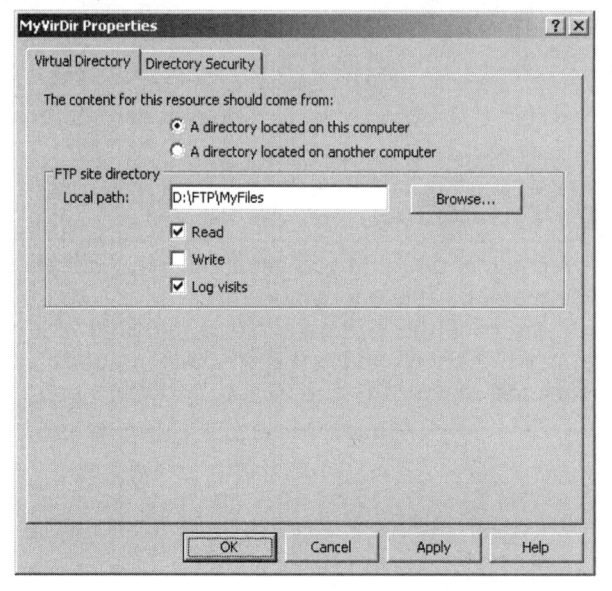

3. Enable the **Read** option to allow read access and enable the **Write** option to allow write access.
4. Enable **Log visits** to record log entries of FTP access.
5. Click **OK**.

To further secure the FTP resource, you must configure NTFS permissions in conjunction with FTP site permissions. FTP site permissions apply to every user, while NTFS permissions apply to individuals or groups of Windows user accounts. Where FTP permissions conflict with NTFS permissions, the more restrictive settings are applied. You can configure NTFS permissions using the Windows Explorer or via the command line tools discussed in Chapter 5.

A rule of thumb is that you should always grant minimum NTFS permissions to users. If you are using anonymous access, ensure that the IUSR_<COMPUTERNAME> account does not have write permission if you wish to disallow anonymous uploads (since attackers might use such access to upload malicious worms or viruses to sabotage the FTP server). If you must enable write access, you should always create different directories for uploading and downloading purposes.

You should follow these security practices when securing FTP resources:

- Disable anonymous access if it is not needed.
- Do not enable write access for the entire FTP site, rather, configure it at virtual directory level.
- Create separate directories for file uploads and downloads.
- Secure FTP contents by applying proper NTFS permissions.

REALITY CHECK...

It is recommended that you use basic FTP authentication on your FTP site and disable anonymous access if it is not needed. Next, configure minimum FTP permissions, ensuring that you do not enable write access unless it is absolutely required. Finally, always further secure your FTP site with proper NTFS permissions.

Configuring FTP User Isolation

IIS 6.0 introduces *FTP user isolation*, a feature that allows you to contain users to their own FTP directory. This is done by defining the user's home directory as their logical FTP root path, thus preventing users from accessing other users' contents. You configure FTP user isolation when you need to protect data access among different users.

BY THE BOOK...

There are three different types of FTP user isolation mode as defined by Microsoft:

Do not isolate users Does not enable FTP user isolation, and works similar to FTP components in previous versions of IIS. You are recommended to configure this mode if you do not wish to restrict user access or viewing of other users' directories.

Isolate users Authenticates users with a local or domain account database. Authenticated users will be restricted from accessing any directories outside of their home directory, and will be redirected back to their home directory. You should configure this mode when you need to limit a user's access to their FTP home directory.

Isolate users using Active Directory Authenticates users with Windows Domain Active Directory database. A user's FTP directory information is associated with the user object in the Active Directory. During the logon process, FTP service will query the Active Directory to obtain the user's FTP home directory information, and then redirect the user to the corresponding FTP directory. The *FTPRoot* and *FTPDir* properties hold the full path information for a user's FTP home directory.

You can configure FTP user isolation based on your needs. FTP user isolation is a *site level* property and you can easily create different FTP user isolations for each FTP site. You can specify the desired FTP user isolation mode when you create the FTP site (see Figure 7.6). FTP user isolation supports three isolation modes, each of which are described.

Figure 7.6 Configuring FTP User Isolation – FTP Site Creation Wizard Dialog Box

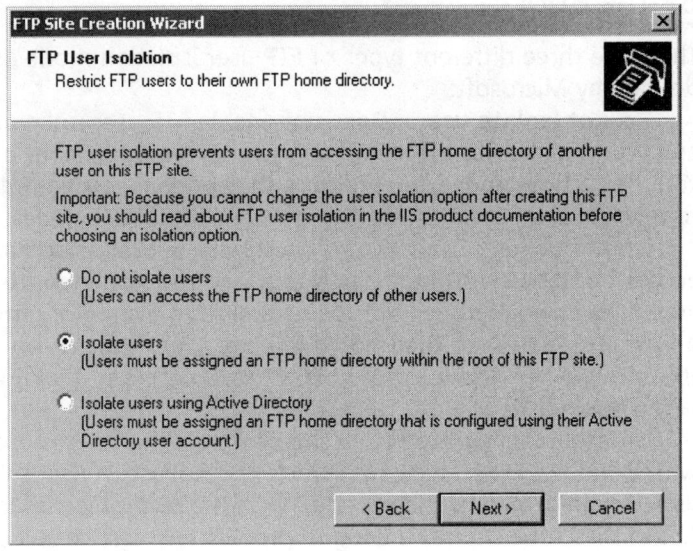

Do Not Isolate Users

Do not isolate users mode does not offer any user isolation, and when this option is selected, the FTP service functions in a manner similar to earlier versions of the IIS FTP service. This mode is ideal for a site that offers shared content downloads or does not require user isolation and data access protection. Users are able to navigate to the FTP root directory and access other users' directories. You can secure content access by configuring proper NTFS permissions in this mode, and you can also configure Access Control Lists (ACLs) based on user account identities to grant access to FTP sites.

When running in *Do not isolate users* mode, the FTP service first checks the default FTP root path specified in the FTP site. If the directory does not exist or if the user does not have permission to access the site, the connection will be denied. Next, the FTP service checks the username against a physical or virtual directory name under the FTP site. If the derived name matches the directory name and the user has the proper access permission, the directory will be the default log in home directory for that user. For anonymous users, the derived name will be *anonymous*, and if an *anonymous* directory does not exist, the user will be directory to the default FTP root path.

Isolate Users

Isolate users mode contains users to their own home directory, which serves as the FTP root path for that user. Users cannot navigate out of this folder, thus preventing them from accessing other users' directories. If users need to access a specific folder outside of their own directory, you can create a virtual directory on the FTP site and grant appropriate NTFS permissions.

In this isolation mode, users' home directories can be located either on the local computer or on a remote network share. You can isolate user based on local computer user or domain user, as long as the appropriate directories are created before you create the FTP site.

When creating the FTP root path and user folders, you must take the following into account:

- In local computer mode, users log in with individual account usernames. You must first create a folder called *LocalUser* under the FTP site root directory. Next, individual user directories must be created within the LocalUser directory. Therefore, the path for user SusanB would be D:\MyFTP\LocalUser\SusanB and the path for user Blitzco would be D:\MyFTP\LocalUser\Blitzco.

- In domains mode, users log in using their domain credentials. You must first create a subdirectory for each domain using the domain name under the FTP site root directory. Next, individual user directories must be created within the appropriate domain directory. For example, if the domain name is *accounts* and the user is *Nancy*, the full path is D:\MyFTP\accounts\nancy.

If anonymous access is allowed, you will need to create a directory called *Public* under the *LocalUser* directory, when anonymous users login, they will be directed to the *LocalUser/Public* folder.

To create a new FTP site with *isolate users* mode:

1. In IIS Manager, expand the local computer, right-click the **FTP Sites** node, point to **New**, and click **FTP Site**.

2. Provide an **FTP Site Description** and click **Next**.
3. Enter the **IP Address** and **TCP Port Setting** values, then click **Next**.
4. In the **FTP User Isolation** step, enable **Isolate users** and click **Next**.
5. In the **Path** field, enter the appropriate directory, or click **Browse** to search for and select the appropriate directory, then click **Next**.
6. Configure the **Access Permissions** you wish to assign to your users and click **Next**.
7. Click **Finish**.

Isolate Users Using Active Directory

Isolate users using Active Directory mode integrates the FTP service with Active Directory, as the user's home directory information is stored directly in Active Directory. Using this mode, you are able to distribute user home directories across different servers and disk volumes, giving you the full flexibility to customize and utilize your network resources.

User home directory information is stored in the *msIIS-FTProot* and *msIIS-FTPDir* user object properties in Active Directory. When a user accesses the FTP site, these two properties are retrieved from the Active Directory. If these properties are not found, the user will not be granted access to the FTP site. In Windows 2003 Server, these two properties have been included in the schema, and if you are planning to configure this isolation mode on a Windows 2000 Active Directory, you need to extend the schema to include *msIIS-FTProot* and *msIIS-FTPDir* properties. For details on how to extend the Active Directory schema, refer Windows 2000 Active Directory help documentation.

Before you can isolate user using Active Directory mode, you need to prepare the following:

- Configure the resource servers.
- Configure Active Directory.
- Create FTP site isolation using Active Directory.

You can configure users' home directories on a local computer or remote network shared path. When you are configuring users' directories to be on a remote network shared path, ensure users are granted minimum permission to access the shared directory.

Next, configure the default FTP root directory and the user home directory properties in Active Directory by running the **Iisftp.vbs** script, which is installed with IIS. You can view the existing properties by specifying **/GetADProp** when you run the script, and you can set the properties by specifying **/SetADProp** when you run the script. The following example demonstrates how to set the default FTP root path for user *Alex* on the remote server *MyFTPServer* and share path */Users*.

```
Iisftp.vbs /SetADProp Alex FTPRoot MyFTPServer\Users
```

To configure the user home directory for this user, use the following:

```
Iisftp.vbs /SetADProp Alex FTPDir Alexftp
```

For more details on how to configure msIIS-FTProot and msIIS-FTPDir properties using **Iisftp.vbs**, refer to the IIS 6.0 help document or type **Iisftp.vbs /SetADProp /?** at the command prompt.

To create a new FTP site that isolates users using Active Directory mode:

1. In IIS Manager, expand the local computer, right-click the **FTP Sites** folder, point to **New**, and click **FTP Site**.
2. Enter the **FTP Site Description** and click **Next**.
3. Enter the appropriate **IP Address** and **TCP Port** vaues and click **Next**.
4. In the **FTP User Isolation** step, enable the **Isolate users using Active Directory** option and click **Next**.
5. Enter the **User name** using domain\username format or click Browse to search for and select the appropriate username (Figure 7.7).
6. Enter a **Password**.

Figure 7.7 Configuring *Isolate User* Using Active Directory Mode – FTP Site Creation Wizard Dialog Box

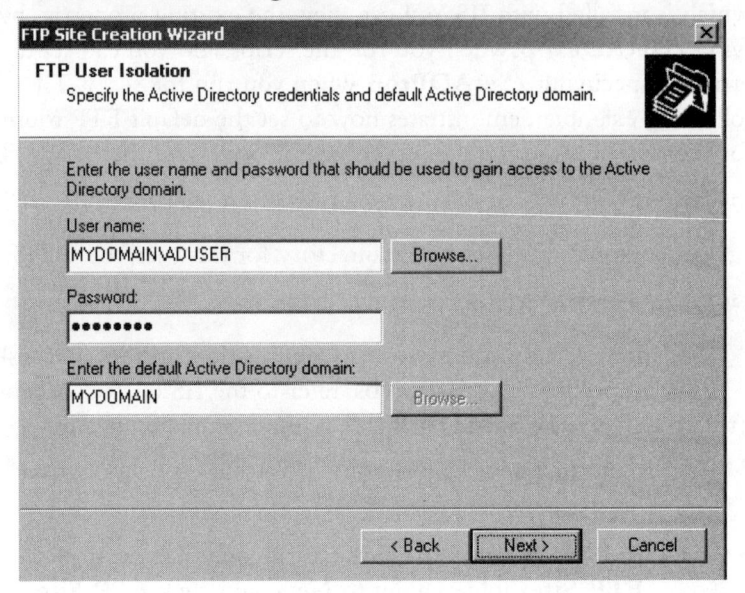

6. Use the **Enter the default Active Directory Domain** field to enter the default domain name or click Browse to search for and select the appropriate Active Directory domain, then click **Next**.
7. In the **Confirm Password** dialog box, re-enter the password and click **OK**.
8. Configure the **Access Permissions** you wish to assign to your users and click **Next**.
9. Click **Finish**.

REALITY CHECK...

FTP user isolation modes give you the ability to restrict data access and contain users to their home directories. It is recommended that you configure isolation based on your business needs. For example, if you are hosting an FTP site purely for content downloads, you would not isolate users.

On the other hand, if you provide dedicated web hosting and would like to provide your customers with direct FTP publishing, you can enable standard user isolation mode, restricting users from accessing other users' directories and data.

Isolating users using Active Directory give you full flexibility to configure different users' home directories across entire network resources. Typically, you would use this mode when you need to control different resource that are distributed across multiple servers for your domain users.

Securing the FTP Connection

FTP service itself does not offer any means of security for user credentials or data sent between the FTP server and the FTP client application. The implementation of IIS FTP service is based on the *RFC959* specification, which does not support any secure communication between FTP server and its client. We will look into different ways of securing FTP connection to protect sensitive data transferred.

BY THE BOOK...

According to Microsoft, IIS FTP implementation does not include any modes of security. The data transferred and exchanged between FTP clients and servers can easily be intercepted by attackers. Though users are required to enter user credentials during the logon process, the details are transmitted in plain text mode.

Inasmuch, attackers can interpret the unsecured data and gain further access to your FTP server. You can deploy Secure Sockets Layer (SSL) to secure the FTP connection and data transfer. Configuring SSL helps protect user credentials and transmitted data, as the details are encrypted using the SSL certificate.

If you intend to put sensitive data on your FTP server, you should secure the communication between the client application and FTP server to prevent the data from being analyzed or user credentials from being intercepted and re-used by attackers to gain access to the server.

As well as securing the FTP connection, , you can also limit access based on IP Address, which will reduce the possibility of channel attacks if the server is accessible by everyone in the network.

This restriction can be applied at the FTP site and virtual directory levels, and is similar to the website *IP Address and Domain Name Restriction* except that for FTP sites, you can only restrict access based on IP address (and not on domain name). It is recommended that you grant access only to those IP addresses that need to access the FTP site.

This restriction *does not* secure the communication between FTP server and client application, but it will reduce possibility of unauthorized access even when the user credential is being intercept and being used by attacker to attempt site access. To limit FTP site access by IP address, perform these steps:

1. In IIS Manager, expand the local computer, expand the **FTP Sites** folder, right-click the appropriate FTP site, and click **Properties**.

2. Click on the **Directory Security** tab (shown in Figure 7.8).

Figure 7.8 Limiting Access by IP Address – Directory Security Tab

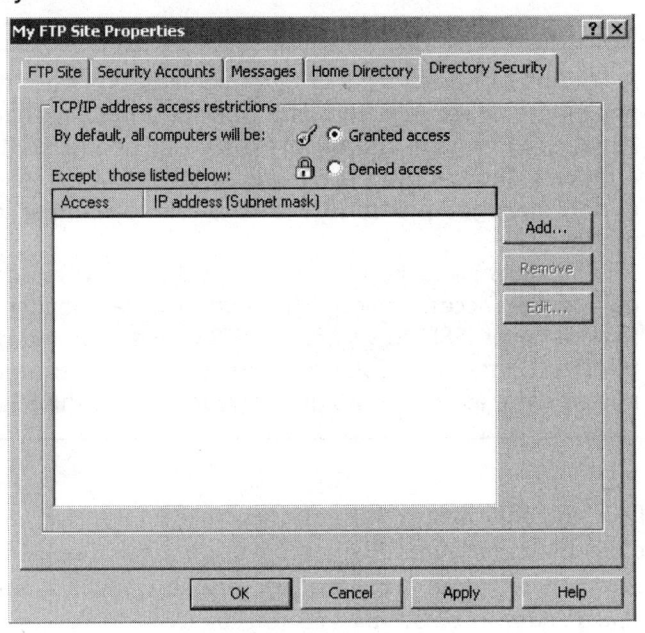

3. Click **Granted access** or **Denied access**. When you select **Denied access**, you deny access to all IP addresses except those listed in the **Except** list. When you select **Granted access**, you grant access to all IP addresses except those listed in the **Except** list.

4. To add addresses to the **Except** list, click **Add**.
5. Click **Single computer** to configure single IP address, or click **Group of computers** to configure groups of IP addresses with appropriate subnet mask ID.
6. Click **OK**.
7. Click **OK** again.

To hide your FTP server from normal attacks that try to gain access login via the default port, you can configure your FTP site to bind to ports other than TCP port 21. You also have the option to limit concurrent connections and to apply connection timeouts to ensure quality service from your FTP server. When you configure your FTP site to start on a port other than the default, you need to make sure that no other programs are using that port. Therefore, it is recommended that you use a high port range, for example, port 8000. To change default port for FTP site and connections related settings, follow the steps outlined here:

1. In IIS Manager, expand the local computer, expand the **FTP Sites** folder, right-click the FTP site whose home directory you want to change and click **Stop**.
2. Right-click the FTP site again, and click **Properties**.
3. Click the **FTP Site** tab (shown in Figure 7.9).

Figure 7.9 Configuring FTP Site Connection Properties – FTP Site Tab

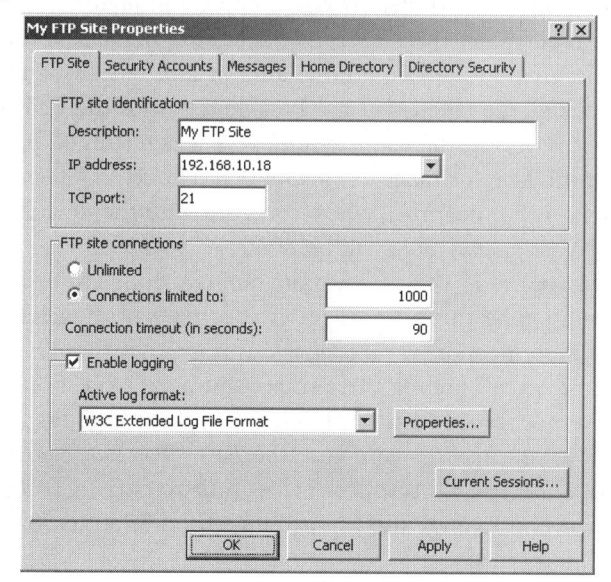

4. In the **TCP Port** field, enter the port number you wish to use.
5. Use the **Connections limited to** field to enter the maximum number of connections to allow.
6. Use the **Connection timeout** field to enter the desired timeout value (in seconds).
7. Click **OK**.
8. Right-click the **FTP site** you just changed and click **Start**.

When FTP client applications connect to FTP server, there are two things to consider; first, the connection mode, and second, the data transfer mode. FTP connection modes are can run in either *active* or *passive* mode. These modes are controled by the client application and cannot be disabled in the FTP service. Data transfer modes (specified in RFC959) are *stream*, *block* or *compressed*. Only stream mode is supported by the IIS FTP service.

In active mode, the FTP service uses TCP port 21 as its *control channel* port and TCP port 20 as its *data channel* port. The half-duplex *control channel* is for connection control messages and full-duplex *data channel* is for data transferring purposes.

In passive mode, once the client application has established the *control channel*, the client sends a passive (PASV) mode request and the FTP server replies with a unique port number and the client connects to that port (by default, the FTP server allocates ports for passive mode connection from WinSock dynamic port ranges, typically from port 1024 to 5000).

It is recommended that you have firewall implementation to protect the IIS server. When the FTP server is behind firewall, you need to ensure that the required FTP ports are not blocked. If such ports are being blocked, the client will not be able to access the FTP site properly.

In Active mode, the data channel port is determined by the control channel port. The formula is: if *control channel* port is X, *data channel* port will be $X - 1$. For example, when you configure the default FTP port to 8000, the *data channel* port will be $8000 - 1 = 7999$.

In passive mode, the default port range is from 1024 to 5000. However, opening this port range on your firewall to facilitate passive mode FTP connection is *not advisable* as it exposes the server to potential attacks. Instead of opening these important ports, you should customize the passive port range in IIS 6.0. To set the port range for a passive mode connection, you need to configure the *PassivePortRange* property in the metabase via Active Directory Services Interfaces (ADSI) scripts. To configure PassivePortRange using port range from 5500 to 5800, perform the following steps:

1. From the command prompt, navigate to **AdminScripts** folder (default path: C:\Inetpub\Adminscripts>).
2. Type **adsutil.vbs set /MSFTPSVC/PassivePortRange "5500-5800"** and press Enter.
3. Restart the FTP serviceby typing **net stop msftpsvc** followed by **net start msftpsvc** at the command prompt..

Now that you have configured basic connection properties for your FTP site, you will need to secure the connection. FTP itself does not provide security measurement when transferring data, so to secure the communication between client applications and FTP server, you need to configure other services to protect the communication.

There are two different ways of securing FTP connections:

- Virtual Private Network (VPN) with Point-to-Point Tunneling Protocol (PPTP)
- Virtual Private Network (VPN) with Internet Protocol Security (IPSec)

VPN extends the capabilities of a private network that cover links across public network such as the Internet. With PPTP, VPN enables secure transfer of data between client and server machines. Data is encrypted for confidentiality, so that even if data packets are intercepted, the information cannot be read without the encryption keys.

IPSec is an open framework standard to ensure private and secure communications over IP networks. This is a long-term direction for secure networking with objectives to protect the contents of IP packets and defend against network attacks via packet filtering and trusted communication. For more information on configuring VPN with PPTP or IPSec, refer to the Windows Server2003 help documentation.

REALITY CHECK...

FTP services send user credentials and file data across the network in plain text, which can be easily intercepted and analyzed. Therefore, it is recommended that you secure the FTP connection with VPN using either the PPTP or IPSec protocol.

Enabling and Securing the FTP Access Log File

Like the Web access log file, you can configure the FTP access log file, which provides details about each request sent to your FTP server. It is important that you enable FTP logging to keep track of each site activity. Log files will tell you how contents are being accessed, which user has uploaded which files, and much more.

> **BY THE BOOK...**
>
> Auditing server activities with log files is a good way to determine if unauthorized external users are attempting to access your virtual server, or if internal users are trying to access resources they do not have permissions to access.
>
> IIS 6.0 allow you to collect user access activity information by enabling the logging feature. The following logging formats are supported:
>
> **W3C Extended** A customizable format allowing you to configure the type of information to be collected when IIS writes the log entry. This format follows W3C Working Draft WD- logfile-960323 specifications.
>
> **IIS Log** A fixed format that records more information than NCSA common format.
>
> **ODCB Logging** A fixed set of data that can be recorded in a database source.
>
> The National Center for Supercomputing Application (NCSA) Common format is not supported, but IIS 6.0 includes a new remote logging feature. Remote logging allows you to redirect log files on a remote share network path using the Universal Naming Convention (UNC) method. This allows you to configure different log paths to a centralized log storage for backup and analysis purposes.
>
> Note that : UTF-8 logging, Centralized Binary logging, Http Error logging and Protocol substatus are not supported.

Essentially, FTP access logs are similar to Web access logs in that they both write an entry to the log file for each request the server served. However, FTP logs are not as comprehensive as Web logs and certain features that are supported in Web access logs do not exist in FTP access logs. FTP service supports the following logging formats:

- W3C Extended
- IIS Log
- ODBC Logging

It is important to note that FTP service does not support NCSA Common format. Out of the many new logging features introduced in IIS 6.0, you are able to utilize Remote Logging feature. UTF-8, Centralized Binary and HTTP Error logging are not availalbe in FTP access logging, nor is Protocol substatus. FTP site activity logging can be enabled and disabled at the FTP site and virtual directory levels only.

To enable logging on a FTP site, perform the following steps:

1. In IIS Manager, expand the local computer, expand the **FTP sites** node, right-click the **FTP Site** you wish to configure and click **Properties**.

2. On the **FTP Site** tab (shown in Figure 7.10), enable the **Enable logging** checkbox.

Figure 7.10 Enabling FTP Site Logging – FTP Site Tab

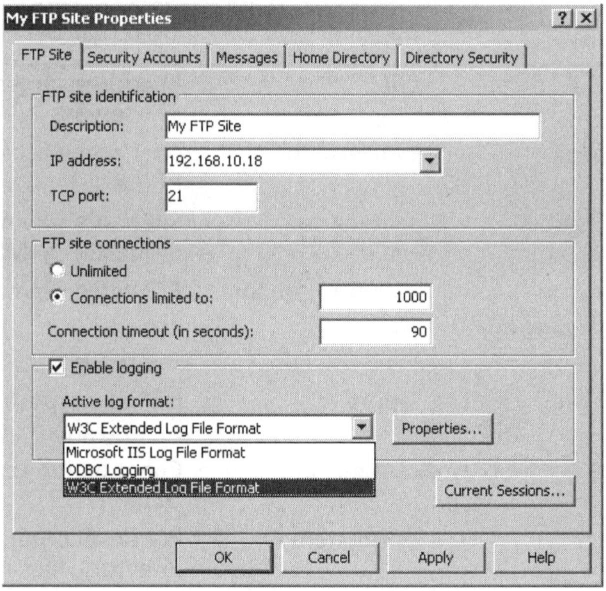

3. Select the desired **Active log format**. The default format is **W3C Extended Log File Format**.

4. Click **OK**.

It is recommended that you use W3C Extended format whenever possible. Although not all property fields in W3C Extended format are logged, this format will give you more comprehensive details than the other formats. The following properties are logged by default when you enable W3C Extended format:

- time
- c-ip
- cs-method
- cs-uri-stem
- sc-status
- sc-win32-status

To log more information, you can configure W3C Extended format to include more property fields. Table 7.1 illustrates W3C Extended properties fields that you can enable.

Table 7.1 FTP Site Logging – W3C Extended Logging Fields

Property	Field	Description
Client IP Address	c-ip	IP address accessed your FTP server
User Name	cs-username	User name accessed your FTP server
Service Name	s-sitename	Sitename serving the request. E.g. MSFTPSVC1
Server name	s-computername	FTP server name
Server IP Address	s-ip	FTP server IP address serving the request
Server Port	s-port	FTP server port number serving the request
Method	cs-method	Client action request. E.g. USER, PASS
URI Stem	cs-uri-stem	Request content name. E.g. directory, files name.
Protocol Status	sc-status	Status code of the request
Win32 Status	sc-win32-status	Status code in Windows terms
Bytes Sent	sc-bytes	Number of bytes sent by server

Continued

Table 7.1 FTP Site Logging – W3C Extended Logging Fields

Property	Field	Description
Bytes Received	cs-bytes	Number of bytes received by server
Time Taken	time-taken	Amount of time to process the request

To customize FTP server W3C Extended logging fields, you perform these steps:

1. In the IIS MMC console, expand the local computer, expand the **FTP sites** node, right-click the **FTP Site** you wish to configure and click **Properties**.

2. In the **Active log format** list box, select **W3C Extended Log File Format** and click on **Properties**.

3. In the **Logging Properties** dialog box, click on the **Advanced** tab (shown in Figure 7.11).

Figure 7.11 Customizing FTP W3C Extended Logging Fields – Advanced Tab

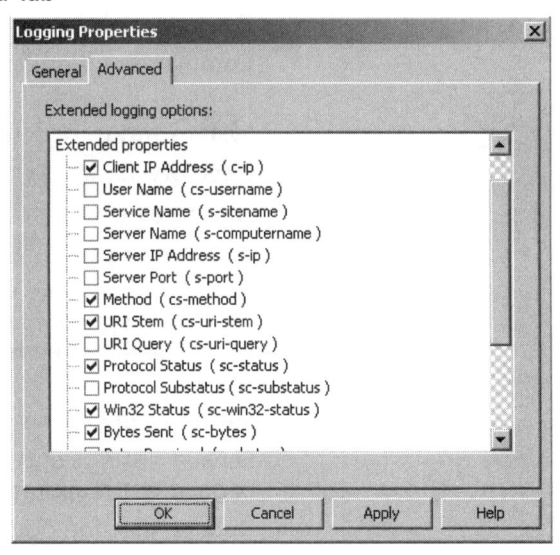

4. Enable the desired logging fields in the **Extended Properties** list.

5. Click **OK**.

Table 7.2 lists the IIS FTP status code. Status codes can help you identify whether or not the request is successful. They serve as troubleshooting hints and provide you with why a request may have failed. For example, a 257 'Directory' name status indicates that the request is successful and a new directory is created. It can also help you to identify any failed login when you see a 530 status code with a [5]PASS command.

Table 7.2 IIS FTP Status Codes

FTP Status Code	Description
1xx Positive Preliminary Reply	Initial action successful, continue new command
110	Restart marker reply
120	Service ready in X minutes
125	Data connection already open; transfer starting
150	File status okay; about to open data connection
2xx Positive Completion Reply	Client requests successfully accepted and command executed
200	Command okay
202	Command not implemented, superfluous at this site
211	System status, or system help reply
212	Directory status
213	File status
214	Help message
215	NAME system type, where NAME is an official system name from the list in the Assigned Numbers document
220	Service ready for new user
221	Service closing control connection. Logged out if appropriate
225	Data connection open; no transfer in progress
226	Closing data connection. Requested file action successful
227	Entering passive mode (h1,h2,h3,h4,p1,p2).
230	User logged in, proceed.

Continued

Table 7.2 IIS FTP Status Codes

FTP Status Code	Description
250	Requested file action okay, completed.
257	"PATHNAME" created
3xx Positive Intermediate Reply	Command succeeded, needs additional info to complete request
331	User name okay, need password.
332	Need account for login
350	Requested file action pending further information
4xx Transient Negative Completion Reply	Temporary error, client can retry the command
421	Service not available, closing control connection
425	Cannot open data connection
426	Connection closed; transfer aborted
450	Requested file action not taken. File unavailable
451	Requested action aborted: Local error in processing
452	Requested action not taken. Insufficient storage space in system
5xx Permanent Negative Completion Reply	Command failed, the error is permanent
500	Syntax error, command unrecognized
501	Syntax error in parameters or arguments
502	Command not implemented
503	Bad sequence of commands
504	Command not implemented for that parameter
530	Not logged in
532	Need account for storing files
550	Requested action not taken. File unavailable
551	Requested action aborted: Page type unknown

Continued

Table 7.2 IIS FTP Status Codes

FTP Status Code	Description
552	Requested file action aborted. Exceeded storage allocation
553	Requested action not taken. File name not allowed

For more details about FTP status code definitions, you can refer to section 4.2 of the FTP replies at www.w3.org/Protocols/rfc959/4_FileTransfer.html, from which this information was located.

The default FTP log path is located at %Windir%/system32/Logfiles/MSFTPSVC*X*, where *X* indicates the site ID the log file belong to. This is the identification number generated by IIS when you create the FTP site. In previous versions of IIS, these identification numbers are incremental, but with IIS 6.0, the site ID is randomly created by IIS based on the FTP site name. Now that you understand the differences between FTP and Web site logging, you should refer Chapter 4 – Enabling and Securing Web Access Log File section for details on how to secure FTP access log files.

REALITY CHECK...

Logging FTP site activity provides detailed information on access and usage of your FTP resources. It is recommended that you configure FTP site logging and protect the log files using NTFS permissions.

Your A** is Covered if You...

- ☑ Relocated your FTP content to a new disk volume.
- ☑ Configured FTP site messages and connection settings.
- ☑ Enabled FTP authentication.
- ☑ Secured your FTP contents with proper website permissions.
- ☑ Secured your FTP resources with proper NTFS permissions.
- ☑ Configured IP Address restrictions.
- ☑ Configured required ports range to passive FTP connections.
- ☑ Secured the FTP connection with VPN.
- ☑ Enabled FTP site activity logging.
- ☑ Secured FTP access log files.

Chapter 8
Securing SMTP and POP3 Services

In This Chapter

Windows Server 2003 provides e-mail services compromising both a Simple Mail Transfer Protocol (SMTP) server (for delivering mail), and a Post Office Protocol v3 (POP3) server (for hosting user mailboxes). Together these provide a complete e-mail service that allows users to send and retrieve mail. Like previous versions of IIS, the SMTP service is part of IIS. The POP3 server is new in Windows Server 2003, and is not part of IIS 6.0 itself. However many systems administrators will use the SMTP server in conjunction with the POP3 server, so we will examine it briefly here.

- Configuring SMTP Virtual Servers
- SMTP Virtual Server Security
- Configuring and Securing the POP3 Server

By the end of this chapter, you will know how to install and configure the SMTP and POP3 servers, and you will be familiar with the security options that each offers. We will also look at connection controls that can limit the machines that can connect to your servers, transport layer security for encrypting message delivery, and authentication mechanisms for your users.

Configuring SMTP Virtual Servers

SMTP is the protocol used to deliver e-mail across the Internet. When a user sends e-mail from an e-mail client, SMTP is used to convey the e-mail message from the user's computer to the organization's or ISP's SMTP server. This SMTP server then forwards the mail to the e-mail recipient's e-mail server using SMTP.

> **BY THE BOOK...**
>
> IIS 6.0 includes an SMTP service, which can be installed to facilitate the delivery of e-mail from users within your organization or from applications that you may develop. After installing the IIS 6.0 SMTP components, users can send e-mail using their standard e-mail client programs, such as Microsoft Outlook or Microsoft Outlook Express.
>
> The SMTP server can also accept e-mail for users in your organization. By using the Windows 2003 POP3 server, this received mail can be sorted into users' individual mailboxes ready to be viewed or retrieved by any standard POP3 e-mail client.

While the combination of SMTP server and POP3 server can provide a basic e-mail service, Microsoft sells a more advanced messaging system known as Microsoft Exchange Server. This product offer close integration with the Microsoft Outlook e-mail client, and supports mail, calendaring and task lists. Additionally, users can access their mail, calendars and tasks using MAPI (Messaging API), Hypertext Transfer Protocol (HTTP) (via a supplied web interface), as well as access mail via POP3 and IMAP (Internet Message Access Protocol). However, Microsoft Exchange requires an Active Directory environment and mailboxes can only be allocated to Windows users – you cannot create users that are only valid for messaging. For more information on Microsoft Exchange, visit the Exchange homepage at www.microsoft.com/exchange/.

The SMTP service is not installed by default (except on Windows Server 2003 Web Edition). To install the SMTP service, see Chapter 3. When you install the SMTP service, it creates an SMTP server called *Default SMTP Virtual Server* (shown in Figure 8.1). You can rename this server by right-clicking on it and selecting **Rename**.

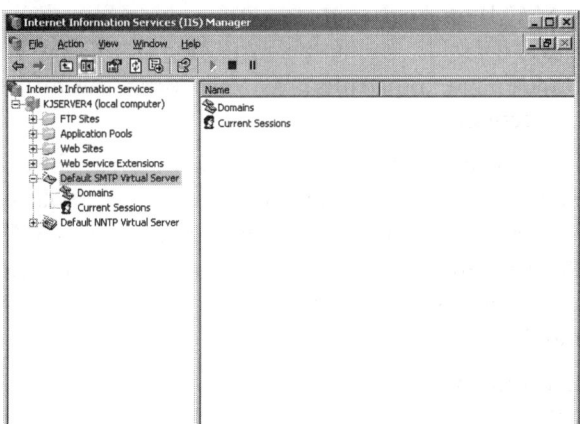

Figure 8.1 The Default SMTP Server

```
Internet Information Services (IIS) Manager
File  Action  View  Window  Help
Internet Information Services          Name
  KJSERVER4 (local computer)           Domains
    FTP Sites                          Current Sessions
    Application Pools
    Web Sites
    Web Service Extensions
    Default SMTP Virtual Server
      Domains
      Current Sessions
    Default NNTP Virtual Server
```

Creating Additional SMTP Servers

For most organizations, this single SMTP server should be sufficient; however, it is possible to create additional SMTP servers if required. Each SMTP server must bind to a separate IP address, or a unique Transmission Control Protocol (TCP) port (if running multiple SMTP servers on a single IP address). You might consider configuring multiple SMTP servers if:

- You accept mail for more than one domain (for example, example.com and myCompany.com), and mail for each domain will be received on a separate IP address.

- You require different settings for each SMTP server (for example, one server can be used anonymously and another requires all users to authenticate).

To create additional SMTP servers:

1. In the IIS Manager, right-click the local computer. Select **New | SMTP Virtual Server…**

2. In the **New SMTP Virtual Server Wizard**, enter a **Name** for your new virtual server and click **Next**.

3. Use the **Select the IP address for this SMTP virtual** server drop-down list to select an appropriate IP address. Click **Next**. Note that the address selected cannot be used by any other pre-existing SMTP server.

4. In the **Home Directory** field, enter the physical path where the SMTP server should store its working files, then click **Next**. This folder should be a partition other than your Windows system partition. We will discuss this further in the next section.

5. In the **Domain** field, enter the default domain for this SMTP server. This is the domain for which this server will accept e-mail (for example, if you enter example.com, then this SMTP server will accept mail addressed to <username>@example.com). You can use the IIS Manager to add additional domains later, if desired.

6. Click **Finish**.

Configuring Additional Domains

Each SMTP server can be configured to accept mail for multiple domain name system (DNS) domains. For example, if your organization owns both the myCompany.com and myCompany.net domains, then you can configure your SMTP server to accept incoming mail addressed to users of either domain. This is done by adding a *local alias* domain. Note that the *Default SMTP Virtual Server* created during installation of the SMTP service is automatically configured to accept mail addressed to the DNS name of the server.

Additionally, you can add *remote* domains that specify specific connection settings to be used when your SMTP server attempts to deliver mail to those domains.

To have your SMTP server accept mail for an additional domain (by creating a local alias domain):

1. In the IIS Manager, locate and expand the SMTP server.

2. Right-click the **Domains** icon and choose **New | Domain...** to launch the **New SMTP Domain Wizard**.

3. In the **Specify a Domain Type** field, select **Alias** and click **Next** (Figure 8.2).

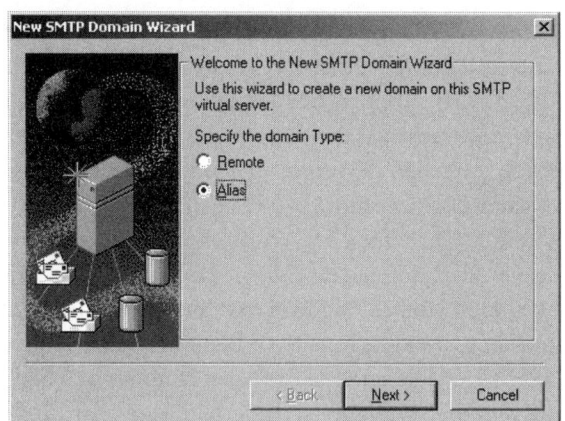

Figure 8.2 Add a New Local Alias Domain

4. Enter the **DNS domain name** (for example, myCompany.net) that the SMTP server should accept mail for, and click **Finish** to close the wizard.

To add a remote domain, follow the steps for configuring a local alias domain, but choose to add a **Remote** domain instead of an **Alias** domain. After you have added the new remote domain and closed the wizard, you can right-click on the domain and bring up its properties. This allows you to configure specific options to be used when delivering mail to this remote domain (Figure 8.3). These settings override any conflicting general settings for the SMTP server.

Figure 8.3 Remote Domain Settings

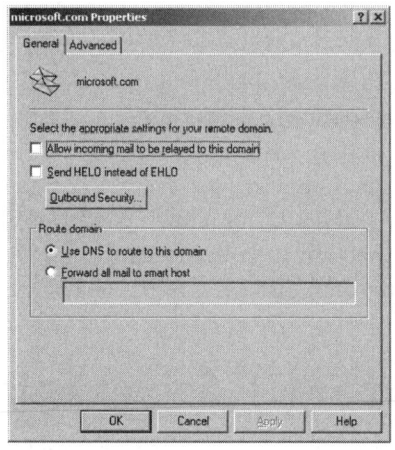

Two other settings that may be of interest are:

- **Send HELO instead of EHLO** When an SMTP server attempts to deliver mail it sends the EHLO command to indicate that it supports SMTP extensions (ESMTP). In some cases a remote host will not accept EHLO. If this is the case, you can force your SMTP server to send the older, universally supported HELO command instead. HELO is the opening command when a mail server attempts to deliver mail to a remote server. It is defined in RFC 821 Simple Mail Transfer Protocol www.ietf.org/rfc/rfc0821.txt. Since the initial standard, a number of extensions have been accepted (collectively known as Extended Simple Mail Transfer Protocol, or ESMTP). Mail servers that implement these extensions begin with EHLO rather than HELO. Some older mail servers may not understand the EHLO command.

- **Forward all mail to smart host** You can use this setting to force the SMTP server to deliver mail to a specific remote server, rather than relying on a DNS lookup. This may be useful if there is a low-cost route (for example, an internal route) to the remote domain that isn't published in the public DNS. You can enter either a Fully Qualified Domain Name (FQDN) or an IP address. If you enter an IP address, surround it with square brackets (for example, [192.168.100.100]).

On the **Advanced** tab, you can configure message queuing for remote mail servers. This is commonly used when you have a branch office that only periodically connects to the Internet or to the head office. A mail server at the branch office then collects any queued mail held for it at the central mail server by issuing an ATRN (Authenticated TURN) command. To enable this queuing, enable the **Queue messages for remote delivery** option. Add the user account(s) that are valid for collecting mail. The remote mail server will have to authenticate as one of these accounts. ATRN itself is part of open standard (RFC) called On Demand Mail Relay (ODMR) for allowing mail servers with an intermittent Internet connection to collect mail from a central holding server. For more information on ATRN see RFC2645 www.ietf.org/rfc/rfc2645.txt.

Configuring SMTP Server Folders

Each SMTP server uses a number of folders to hold its working files. These folders are created automatically whenever an SMTP server is created (either by installing the SMTP service or by manually creating additional SMTP servers). These folders are:

- **Badmail** This folder holds mail that the SMTP server is unable to deliver within its configured timeout limit (usually about 2 days). This may occur because the remote domain cannot be found in the DNS, or does not have a mail server that will accept mail. Additionally if your users or applications send out e-mail and the domain in the **From:** address cannot be found in the DNS, the message will end up in the Badmail folder.

- **Drop** This folder is used to store any incoming mail for a domain that the SMTP server accepts mail for. If you have the Windows 2003 POP3 server installed, this folder is not used. Instead, mail is passed to the POP3 server to be placed into user mailboxes.

- **Pickup** Any text files that contain valid SMTP headers and a message body dropped into this folder will be detected by the SMTP server and delivered. This method of having mail delivered is commonly used by applications that use the Microsoft CDONTS or CDOSYS components. These components can create an appropriately formatted text file and drop it into the Pickup directory.

- **Queue** This folder is used when the SMTP server cannot deliver a message right away (for example, due to network problems). Instead, the message is placed into the queue folder for subsequent retry.

It is possible that these folders may become quite large (for example, if a spammer attempts to deliver a large amount of mail to your organization). For this reason, it is recommended that you place these folders on a partition other than your Windows system partition. When creating additional SMTP servers, you can specify the location of these folders, however the Default SMTP Virtual Server places its folders in *system_drive:*\inetpub\mailoot\.

To move these folders to another partition, first create them on the preferred partition. You will then have to edit the IIS metabase to adjust the location the default SMTP server is using. To do this, you can use the graphical Metabase Explorer tool, which is part of the IIS 6.0 Resource Kit. You can download the IIS Resource Kit Tools from www.microsoft.com/downloads/details.aspx?FamilyID=56fc92ee-a71a-4c73-b628-ade629c89499.

Alternatively, you can use the command line adsutil.vbs script to edit the metabase. Adsutil.vbs is located in *system_drive*:inetpub\adminscripts\. You will have to replace *x:\mailroot* with the path to your preferred partition.

```
adsutil.vbs set smtpsvc/1/badmaildirectory x:\mailroot\badmail
adsutil.vbs set smtpsvc/1/dropdirectory x:\mailroot\drop
adsutil.vbs set smtpsvc/1/pickupdirectory x:\mailroot\pickup
adsutil.vbs set smtpsvc/1/queuedirectory x:\mailroot\queue
```

Enable Logging

By default, logging is not enabled on the Default SMTP Virtual Server, or on any additional SMTP server that you create. It is recommended that you enable logging for diagnostic and security auditing purposes. To enable logging for an SMTP server:

1. Locate the SMTP server in the IIS Manager, right-click it and select **Properties**.

2. On the **General** tab, enable the **Enable logging** option and select a log file format from the drop-down list. **W3C Extended Log File Format** is the default option and the most flexible.

3. Click the **Properties** button to customize the logging options.

4. On the **General** tab (Figure 8.4), choose when logfiles should be rolled over. Under the W3C Log specification, all events are logged in Greenwich Mean Time (GMT). If you want logfiles rolled over at midnight, local time rather than midnight GMT, enable **Use local time for file naming and rollover**. By default, log files are placed in %windir%\system32\logfiles\. Because logfiles can potentially become quite large, consuming space on your system partition, it is recommended that you place logfiles on a non-system partition.

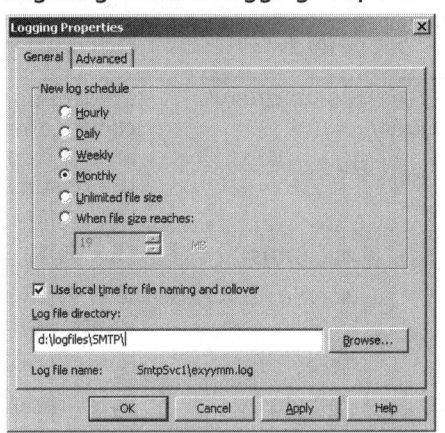

Figure 8.4 Configuring General Logging Properties

5. Select the **Advanced** tab to select the information that you want to log. Other than the date and time, which are self-explanatory, the a number of additional extended properties are available (Table 8.1).

Table 8.1 W3C Extended Logging Properties

Property	Field	Description
Client IP Address	c-ip	The IP address of the client connecting to the SMTP server, or the remote server being connected to for mail delivery.
User Name	cs-username	The name of the machine connecting to the SMTP server.
Service Name	s-sitename	The identifier of the SMTP server (for example, SMTPSVC1).
Server Name	s-servername	The name of the SMTP server.
Server IP Address	s-ip	The IP address of the SMTP server.
Server Port	s-port	The port used by the server (typically port 25).
Method	cs-method	The mail command sent from the client, for example, HELO, the RCPT or QUIT.

Continued

Table 8.1 W3C Extended Logging Properties

Property	Field	Description
Uniform Resource Identify (URI) Query	cs-uri-query	Information pertaining to the client command (for example, an RCPT command would log the destination address of the message).
Protocol Status	sc-status	The SMTP status code.
Win32 Status	sc-win32-status	The SMTP status code in Windows terms.
Bytes Sent	sc-bytes	Bytes sent by the SMTP server.
Bytes Received	cs-bytes	Bytes received by the SMTP server.
Time Taken	time-taken	Time taken to execute the command.

6. Click **OK** twice to exit and save your changes.

The SMTP status code can be helpful in diagnosing problems with mail delivery. The status codes listed in Table 8.2 are defined for SMTP.

Table 8.2 SMTP Status Codes

SMTP Status Code	Description
211	System status or system help reply.
214	Help message (for user).
220	<domain> Service ready.
221	<domain> Service closing transmission channel.
250	Requested mail action okay, completed.
251	User not local; will forward to <forward-path>.
354	Start mail input; end with <CRLF>.<CRLF>.
421	<domain> Service not available, closing transmission channel (for example, if the service is shutting down).
450	Requested mail action not taken: mailbox unavailable (for example, mailbox is busy).
451	Requested action aborted: local error in processing.

Continued

Table 8.2 SMTP Status Codes

SMTP Status Code	Description
452	Requested action not taken: insufficient system storage.
500	Syntax error, command unrecognized.
501	Syntax error in parameters or arguments.
502	Command not implemented.
503	Bad sequence of commands.
504	Command parameter not implemented.
550	Requested action not taken: mailbox unavailable (for example, mailbox not found).
551	User not local; please try <forward-path>.
552	Requested mail action aborted: exceeded storage allocation.
553	Requested action not taken: mailbox name not allowed.
554	Transaction failed.

For more information on SMTP and SMTP message formats, see RFC 821 – Simple Mail Transfer Protocol: www.ietf.org/rfc/rfc0821.txt, RFC822 - Standard for the Format of ARPA Internet Text Messages: www.ietf.org/rfc/rfc0822.txt, and RFC 1869 - SMTP Service Extensions: www.ietf.org/rfc/rfc1869.txt.

Other Configuration Options

We will briefly examine non-security-related configuration options. These options are managed by locating the SMTP server in the IIS Manager, right-clicking it and choosing **Properties**. Security-related configuration options are discussed in the next section.

The **Properties** dialog box for an SMTP server consists of a number of pages. The following options are available on each tab:

On the **General** tab you can:

- Choose the IP address that the server will listen on. To have the server listen on multiple IP addresses click the **Advanced** button.

- Limit the number of inbound connections. The minimum number of connections is 1. Limiting the number of connections can help avoid a Denial of Service (DoS) attack where a remote attacker opens thousands (or more) TCP connections to your SMTP server. You can also choose how quickly the server drops opened inactive connections. Choosing a lower number frees up resources more quickly, but performance may be degraded if the SMTP server continually has to open new connections that have been dropped.

- Enable and configure logging.

The **Messages** tab (Figure 8.5) contains the following settings:

Figure 8.5 SMTP Server Messages Tab

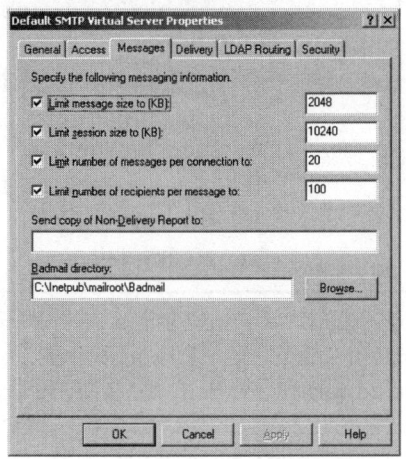

- Configure limits on the size of individual messages (by default, 2 MB), and on a session (a remote server may transmit a number of messages in a single session —the default limit is 20MB). If your users regularly send or receive messages that contain large attachments, you will need to increase these limits.

- Configure limits on the number of messages per connection (when this limit is reached, a new connection is opened), and the number of recipients per message (the default is 100, which conforms to the RFC 821 specification). If the message contains more recipients, the SMTP server opens another connection after processing the first 100.

- Enter an e-mail address where a copy of Non-Delivery Reports (NDRs) should be sent (for example, an administrative mailbox). An NDR is generated to the original sender of a message when it can't be delivered for some reason. The NDR typically includes some information as to why the message could not be delivered. You can also choose a directory to store badmail.

On the **Delivery** tab (Figure 8.6) you can configure the following options:

Figure 8.6 SMTP Server Delivery Tab

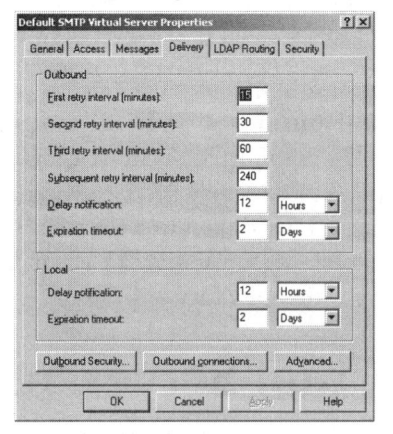

- How long the SMTP server will wait before attempting to retry delivery of messages that couldn't be delivered previously, as well as how long the SMTP server will attempt to deliver the message. This is configured separately for remote and local users.

- By clicking the **Outbound Security** button, you can configure the SMTP server to send particular credentials to the remote SMTP server. This is usually not set if your SMTP server connects to the Internet at large. However, if you have configured your SMTP server to forward all mail to a specified server (using the **Smart Host** setting, which we will encounter shortly), then the smart host may require your server to authenticate. You can also enable the **TLS** setting to have the SMTP server encrypt outbound mail using a secure sockets layer (SSL) certificate.

- By clicking the **Outbound Connections** button, you can choose to place limits on outbound connections from your SMTP server to remote SMTP servers, including the number of connections and how long idle connections are kept open.

- By clicking the **Advanced** button you can set advanced properties. You can override the server name that the SMTP server declares itself to be when connecting to remote servers. You can also configure a smart host (all mail will be forwarded to the smart host, either after attempting direct delivery, or immediately, depending on whether the **Attempt direct delivery before sending to smart host** checkbox is selected). You can also verify the DNS name of incoming connections by doing a reverse DNS lookup. If the client's declared DNS name does not match the name in the DNS, then the SMTP server adds *Unverified* to the SMTP header. Be aware that reverse DNS lookups incur a performance penalty.

On the **LDAP Routing** tab you can configure the SMTP server to get routing and mailbox information from a Lightweight Directory Access Protocol (LDAP) directory, such as Microsoft Active Directory. For example, clients can send mail to a distribution list, and have the SMTP server automatically expand it to each individual address based on information stored in the directory.

SMTP Virtual Server Security

By default, each SMTP server will accept mail for its default domain only. The Default SMTP Virtual Server created during installation only accepts mail addressed to <user>@<SMTP Server FQDN>. Additionally, only authenticated users are able to send mail out (to non-local domains) via the SMTP server.

BY THE BOOK...

The SMTP server has a number of configurable security options to help secure and protect your SMTP server, including:

Authentication, which allows you to determine which users can access the services of the SMTP server. The SMTP server supports anonymous authentication, basic authentication and integrated windows authentication.

Connection Controls, which allow you to determine which IP addresses or DNS-named machines are allowed to connect to the SMTP server.

Transport Layer Security, which allows you to secure the transmission of e-mail by encrypting it using technology similar to SSL. TLS also allows for machine authentication, as the TLS certificate contains the machine's name.

Relay Controls, which allow you to determine which IP addresses or DNS-named machines can relay through the SMTP server. Relaying allows delivery of mail to non-local e-mail addresses.

Configuring Authentication

The SMTP service supports three authentication mechanisms. By default, only anonymous access is enabled. When anonymous access is enabled, users do not have to supply a username or password to connect to the SMTP server. However, because relaying is (by default) only permitted for authenticated users, no mail will be delivered to remote (non-local) domains. To adjust relay restrictions, see the "Configuring Relay Controls" section later in this chapter. Alternatively, you can enable one of the other authentication mechanisms.

The SMTP server also supports basic authentication. When using basic authentication, the user supplies a username and password, which is passed, unencrypted, across the network to the SMTP server. This account can be either a Windows account local to the SMTP server, or an Active Directory domain account. Because the username and password are passed unencrypted, it is recommended that you also enable TLS to secure the transmission of credentials. To enable basic authentication:

1. In the IIS Manager locate the desired SMTP server. Right-click it and select **Properties**.
2. On the **Access** tab, click the **Authentication** button.
3. In the **Authentication** dialog box (Figure 8.7), enable the **Basic authentication** checkbox. Windows will present a warning that credentials will be transmitted in clear text. Click **OK**.

Figure 8.7 Enabling Basic Authentication

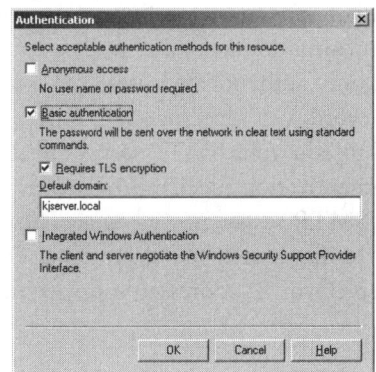

4. If desired, enable the **Requires TLS Encryption** checkbox to encrypt the transmission of username and password. TLS encryption requires the installation of a server certificate. See the "Configuring Transport Layer Security" section later in this chapter.

5. If desired, enter a default domain. This is the domain that will be used to authenticate users if they do not supply a domain as part of their credentials.

The SMTP server also supports integrated windows authentication, which provides greater security than basic authentication, as user credentials are not transmitted unencrypted across the network. The actual authentication exchange between server and client uses NTLM v2, and is covered in Chapter 5. To use integrated windows authentication, you must have an e-mail client that supports this authentication mechanism, such as Microsoft Outlook Express. To enable integrated windows authentication, follow the steps to enable basic authentication, but enable the **Integrated Windows Authentication** checkbox rather than the **Basic authentication** checkbox in the **Authentication** dialog box.

Note that if you disable anonymous access, any applications that you use that connect to the SMTP server using TCP sockets will have to authenticate in order to send mail. Applications that create formatted text files and drop them into the SMTP server's pickup directory (these applications typically run directly on the SMTP server itself) do not have to authenticate.

Configuring Connection Controls

The SMTP server allows you to configure connection controls, which let you specify which IP addresses or DNS-named machines can connect to the SMTP server. All other machines will be denied access.

By default, all machines are permitted access to the SMTP server. This means that any machine can open a connection to the SMTP server. However, by default, further access is limited. Unauthenticated users can only deliver mail to local domains (that is, they can deliver mail to your organization), and only authenticated users (who supply a valid Windows username and password) can send mail out. Furthermore, to allow authentication, you need to edit your SMTP server's settings and configure one or more of the authentication mechanisms mentioned earlier.

Thus, if your SMTP server is used to accept mail for your organization from the world in general, you do not want to implement connection controls except from IP addresses you specifically do not want to

Securing SMTP and POP3 Services • Chapter 3   255

receive mail from. However, if your server is only used internally (for example, to send mail out, and incoming mail from the world in general is handled by another machine), then you may wish to restrict connections to only your internal IP addresses.

To configure connection controls:

1. Open the IIS Manager and locate the desired SMTP server. Right-click it and select **Properties.**
2. On the **Access** tab, click the **Connection** button.
3. In the **Connection** dialog box, select **All except the list below** to grant access to all clients except those in the list, or select **Only the list below** to allow access only to the clients in the list of IP addresses.
4. Click **Add** to add each desired IP address to the list.
5. In the **Computer** dialog box (Figure 8.8), select one of the available options. If you select **Single computer**, enter the IP address of the machine, or click the **DNS Lookup** button to perform a DNS lookup on a domain name. If you select **Group of computers**, enter the network address and subnet mask. If you select **Domain**, enter the DNS name of the domain. Note that if you enter a domain, the SMTP server will do a reverse DNS lookup for all connection attempts, which may have a severe impact upon performance.

Figure 8.8 Configuring Connection Controls

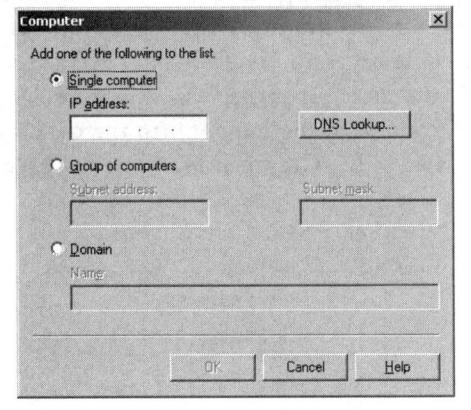

6. Click **OK** twice.

Configuring Transport Layer Security

The SMTP server supports the TLS protocol for encryption of data transmission. This can include both the message body and the authentication headers that are sent by clients that need to authenticate to access the SMTP server. TLS should be used if your SMTP server requires basic authentication, as credentials are passed unencrypted when using basic authentication.

TLS requires the installation of a server certificate. The technology works in the same way that SSL works for securing web traffic. The process for requesting, and installing a certificate is exactly the same as for requesting and installing a certificate for a website. In fact, the title on the dialog box for generating the certificate request is "Welcome to the Web Server Certificate Wizard"! To generate your server certificate request:

1. Open the IIS Manager and locate the SMTP server that you'd like to configure for TLS. Right-click it and select **Properties**.

2. On the **Access** tab, click the **Certificate** button to start the **Welcome to the Web Server Certificate Wizard**. Despite the name, this wizard can be used to install a certificate for your SMTP server. The subsequent steps to be followed are exactly the same as those outlined in Chapter 5, so we won't outline them here again.

If you already have a certificate allocated to a website and the DNS name of that website matches the DNS name of your SMTP server, then you can use the same certificate, rather than requesting a new certificate. To do this, select **Assign an Existing Certificate** rather than **Create a New Certificate** at step 2 of the wizard (Figure 8.9). Select the matching certificate from the list, confirm the details and close the wizard. Otherwise, select **Create a New Certificate**.

Figure 8.9 Assign an Existing Certificate

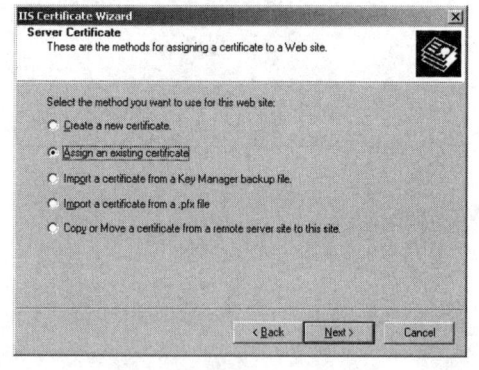

Once you have installed a certificate, you can configure TLS options:

1. Open the IIS Manager and locate the desired SMTP server. Right-click it and select **Properties**.
2. On the **Access** tab, click the **Communication** button.
3. In the **Security** dialog box (Figure 8.10) enable the **Require secure channel** option to force clients to use encryption. If you have a 128bit certificate, you can also enable **Require 128-bit encryption** to force clients to use the higher encryption level. If you do not enable this option, clients that do not support 128-bit encryption can use the lower security 40-bit encryption. Note that 40-bit encryption is no longer considered unbreakable as it can be broken by brute-force using modern computing power.

Figure 8.10 Setting TLS Options

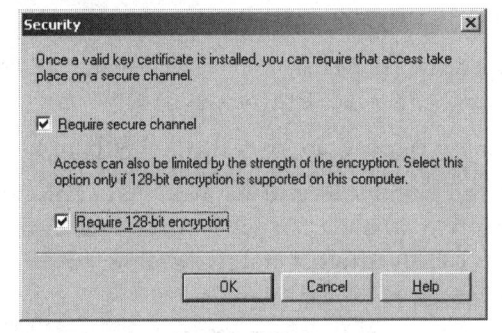

4. Click **OK**.

You should be aware that enabling TLS encrypts all traffic. This imposes a significant burden on the CPU of the SMTP server, and can markedly degrade performance.

Configuring Relay Controls

Relaying occurs when the SMTP server delivers mail to a non-local e-mail address (that is, to an account that is not hosted on the server). Mail that is destined for local domains hosted on the local server (whether the message originates from outside the organization or not) is not relayed mail.

The difficulty in setting relay controls is that you want users that are internal to your organization to be able to send mail to recipients outside your organization. However you do not want users outside your organization to use your SMTP server to send mail to other non-local addresses. This is known as third-party relay, and it involves outside users using your bandwidth and your server's processing power to handle their e-mail delivery. Typically, malicious users seeking SMTP servers that allow third-party relay are spammers seeking to offload delivery and processing responsibilities to someone else's server.

Even if you don't mind someone else using your SMTP server to deliver his or her mail (and there must be some administrators out there that don't, judging by the amount of spam being delivered by unsecured SMTP servers), you may find your e-mail server being added to one of the many SMTP server "blacklists". Other mail server administrators use these blacklists to prevent mail being delivered from an address contained in the blacklist. If your server ends up on such a blacklist, you may find that your legitimate outgoing e-mail will not be accepted by remote SMTP servers.

To configure relay settings:

1. Open the IIS Manager and locate your SMTP server. Right-click it and select **Properties**.

2. On the **Access** tab, click the **Relay** button.

3. In the **Connection** dialog box, select **All except the list below** to grant access to all clients except those in the list, or select **Only the list below** to allow access only to the clients in the list of IP addresses.

4. By default, **Only the list below** is selected, and no computers are listed. It is recommended that you leave this setting as is, and add only those IP addresses that should be allowed to relay. It is strongly recommended that you do not use the **All except the list below** unless the machine is not connected to the Internet.

5. Click **Add** to add each desired IP address to the list.

6. In the **Computer** dialog box, select one of the available options. If you select **Single computer**, enter the IP address of the machine or click the **DNS Lookup** button to perform a DNS lookup on a domain name. If you select **Group of computers**, enter the network address and subnet mask. If you select **Domain**, enter the DNS name of the domain. Note that if you enter a domain, the SMTP server will do a reverse DNS lookup for all connection attempts, which may have a severe impact upon performance.

7. If desired, you can choose to allow users who authenticate to relay regardless of the IP address restrictions you have set. To allow this, enable the **Allow all computers who authenticate to relay, regardless of the list above** option. Ensure that you have selected at least one authentication mechanism.

Notes from the Underground...

Allowing Authenticated Computers to Relay

Allowing authenticated computers to relay is useful for allowing users outside the corporate network (for example, home workers or sales personnel who do not VPN into your network) to utilize your SMTP server to relay. However, if you do allow this, you should ensure that well known accounts have strong passwords. Automated tools exist to scan IP addresses for SMTP servers and attempt to guess weak passwords for common accounts. If a spammer can get hold of an account and password, he or she can use your SMTP server to relay mail.

The user account being used to send mail is not logged in the SMTP server log files. Logon attempts (failed or otherwise) are logged in the Windows Security Event Log.

If you have no external users who need to relay mail (or all external users VPN into your internal network prior to sending mail), then you should consider disabling the Allow all computers who authenticate to relay... setting.

REALITY CHECK...

Ensure that you have followed the steps outlined above to secure your SMTP server and to ensure that your SMTP server does not adversely affect your Windows system.

You should move your SMTP server's folders off the system partition to avoid problems in the event that the SMTP server consumes large amounts of disk space. You should enable logging on your SMTP server.

If you require clients to authenticate, enable authentication. If you use basic authentication, ensure that you have installed a server certificate and enabled TLS to encrypt the user credentials as they are transmitted to the server.

If you allow anonymous relay, ensure that you allow only authorized computers from within your organization to do so. If you use the **Allow all computers who authenticate to relay...** option, then ensure that your user accounts have strong passwords. Monitor your Windows Security Event Log for failed logon attempts that may indicate an external attacker attempting to guess passwords.

Configuring and Securing the POP3 Server

The POP3 protocol allows mail to be retrieved by a user from his or her individual mailbox. An SMTP server receives mail for a domain and passes it across to a POP3 server to be sorted into individual mailboxes. Users then connect to the POP3 server to view or retrieve their mail.

By the Book...

Windows Server 2003 includes a basic POP3 server. While the POP3 server is not itself part of IIS 6.0, it can integrate with the SMTP server included as part of IIS 6.0 to allow your organization to receive mail and have it sorted into individual user mailboxes. These user mailboxes are defined using the POP3 Server Administration tools, and can be either Windows user accounts or standalone accounts valid only for use with the POP3 server. Users can then retrieve their mail using a standard POP3 e-mail client, such as Microsoft Outlook Express or Microsoft Outlook.

The POP3 server is not installed by default. To install it:

1. Access the Windows **Control Panel** and open **Add/Remove Programs**.
2. Select **Windows Components**.
3. Enable the **E-mail Services** option. This includes the core POP3 service and an optional web-based administration interface. To see these options, click the **Details** button when **E-mail Services** is highlighted.
4. Click **OK**.

The web-based administration option integrates with the IIS 6.0 HTML Administration website (Figure 8.11). For more information about this IIS 6.0 administration tool, see Chapter 3. Otherwise, the POP3 server can be administered via its own Microsoft Management Console (MMC). You can access this console by selecting **Start | Administrative Tools | POP3 Service** (Figure 8.12). Finally, the POP3 server can be administered using the command line winpop.exe tool, which is located in %windir%\system32\. For information on how to use this tool, consult the online POP3 help file, or type **winpop /?** at a command prompt.

Figure 8.11 E-mail Administration Integrates with IIS 6.0 Administration Website

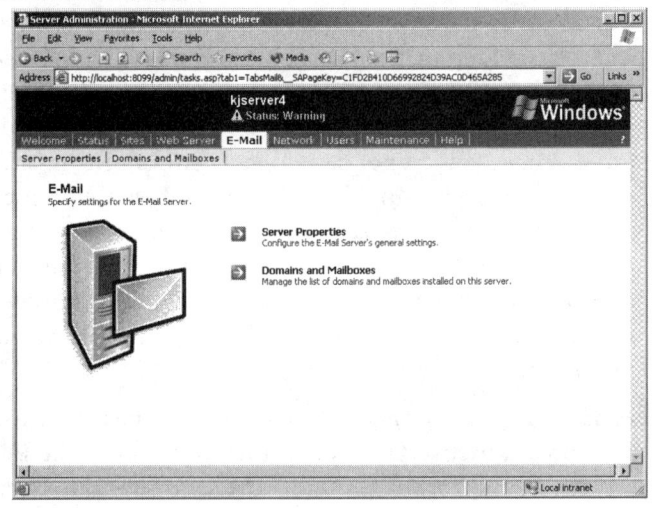

Figure 8.12 Administering the POP3 Server via the MMC Console

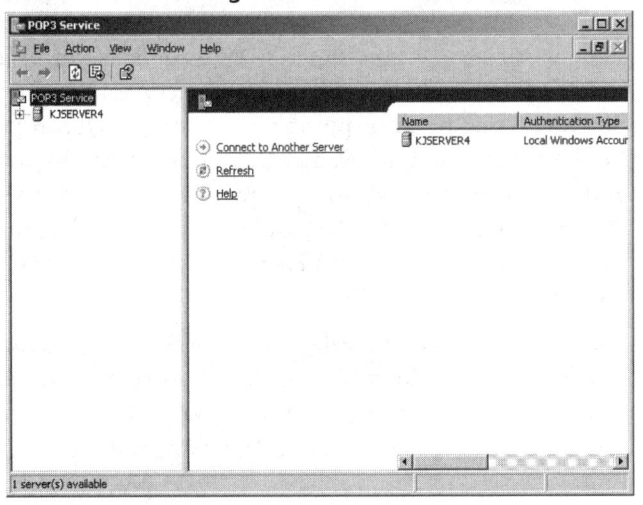

Initial Configuration

After installing the POP3 server, you will need to perform the several steps prior to creating any user mailboxes.

First, you will need to choose the authentication method. Once you have created domains that this POP3 service will handle, you cannot change the authentication method without deleting all the domains, so choosing an authenication mechanism should be your first step.

The POP3 server supports three authentication methods:

- **Local Windows Accounts** Here, user accounts and passwords are stored in the machine's local Security Accounts database. Each mailbox has an associated Windows account. This means that users can have a single password for logging onto the server and for accessing their mailbox. However, because Windows user account names must be unique, you cannot create two mailboxes with the same name, even if they are for different DNS domains (for example, you cannot have john@company1.com and john@company2.com). If you use this authentication method, you can require secure password authentication (SPA) for connecting clients. This uses the NTLM authentication mechanism. The user will have to be using a client, such as Microsoft Outlook Express, that supports SPA. The NTLM authentication mechanism is explained in Chapter 5.

- **Active Directory Integrated** User accounts and passwords are stored in Active Directory. To use this option, the POP3 server must be part of an Active Directory domain. User account properties are managed using the Active Directory Users and Groups MMC Console. If the forest encompasses multiple sub-domains, then you can create accounts with the same username in those different sub-domains (for example, if the AD forest includes europe.bigCorp.com and n-america.bigCorp.com, then it is possible to create john@europe.bigCorp.com and john@america.bigCorp.com). If you use this authentication method, you can require SPA for connecting clients. This uses the NTLM authentication mechanism. The user will have to be using a client, such as Microsoft Outlook Express, that supports SPA.

- **Encrypted Password File** User mailboxes are created independently of Windows. The mailbox password is hashed and stored in the user's mailbox. When user wishes to access his or her mail, he or she provides the password and the POP3 server repeats the hashing process and compares the two values. If they match, the user is granted access. This authentication mechanism is useful in a hosting environment or any other environment where you wish to give users POP3 accounts, but do not wish to give them associated Windows accounts. You would use this option in a hosting environment, or similar environments, because you may not wish to give out or manage thousands of Window accounts.

Use the following steps to change the authentication method (this is only possible prior to creating any domains or if at all existing domains are deleted):

1. Open the POP3 Server MMC Console.
2. Right-click on the desired computer name and select **Properties**.
3. Select the desired **Authentication Method** from the drop-down list (Figure 8.13).

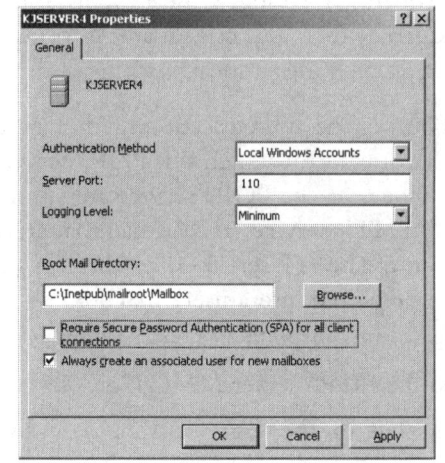

Figure 8.13 Setting the Authentication Method

4. If you wish to require connecting clients to use SPA, enable the **Require Secure Password Authentication (SPA) for all client connections** option. You can only select this option if you are using the **Local Windows Accounts**, or **Active Directory Integrated** authentication methods. The users will have to be using an e-mail client, such as Microsoft Outlook Express, that supports SPA.

5. If you are using either the Local Windows Accounts or Active Directory Integrated authentication methods, you can optionally, choose to have Windows automatically create a Windows local or domain user account when you create a mailbox in the POP3 server. To do so, enable the **Always create an associated user for new mailboxes** option.
6. Click **OK**.
7. Restart the POP3 server for the changes to take effect.

The following additional settings may be of interest:

- Prior to creating mailboxes, you should set the location of the **Root Mail Directory**. By default, this is set to *system_drive:\inetpub\mailroot\mailbox*. However, if you are storing a large amount of mail, this may consume excessive disk space on your system partition. You should move the root mail directory to an alternate partition by entering the desired path. The path must already exist; it will not be created for you here.

- You should choose an appropriate logging level. The default is **minimum**, which logs critical events. You can choose **medium**, which logs critical and warning events or **maximum**, which logs critical, warning and informational events.

After configuring the authentication method, you will next configure the DNS domains for which this POP3 server will handle mail. DNS domains added via the POP3 service are automatically registered with the IIS 6.0 SMTP service, so that mail that arrives for that domain is not placed into the SMTP server's drop directory, but is handed to the POP3 server to be placed into a user's mailbox.

Perform the following steps to create a new domain:

1. Open the POP3 server MMC Console.
2. Right-click on the desired computer and select **New | Domain**.
3. Enter the **DNS domain** (for example, myCompany.com) for which the POP3 server will handle mail.
4. Click **OK** to add the domain.

The display in the POP3 MMC Console will automatically be updated to display the newly added domain. You will see information about the number of mailboxes, number of messages, and the total disk space being used by the domain. The display includes an additional property called **State**, which indicates whether the domain is locked or not.

When the domain is locked, no users can retrieve mail, though incoming mail will still be sorted into their mailboxes. To lock a domain, right-click the domain in the POP3 server MMC Console and select **Lock**. To unlock a domain, right-click it and select **Unlock**.

If you wish to delete a domain, right-click it the POP3 server MMC Console and select **Delete**.

Configuring Mailboxes

After adding domains that the POP3 server will handle, you now need to add mailboxes for your users. To add a mailbox:

1. Open the POP3 server MMC Console.
2. Expand the server's node and highlight the domain under which you wish to create the new mailbox. The user's e-mail address will become <user>@selectedDomain.
3. Right-click the desired domain and select **New | Mailbox**.
4. Enter a name for the user in the **Mailbox Name** field.
5. If you are using one of the Windows authentication methods and you wish to create a user account for the user, enable the **Create associated user for this mailbox** option. If you are using the Active Directory integrated authentication method, you will have to be logged into the domain to create the domain account.
6. Enter a password for the user in the **Password** and **Confirm Password** fields.
7. Click **OK**.

If you are using the Active Directory integrated authentication method and a naming conflict occurs when creating the user's pre-Windows 2000 user account name (the Domain\Username account name), then the POP3 server will ensure that a unique pre-Windows 2000 user name is created in Active Directory. If your e-mail clients are using SPA to connect to the POP3 server, they will need this pre-Windows 2000 username to log on (not their Windows User Principle Name). You will need to note the altered pre-Windows 2000 username and pass it onto the user.

To delete a mailbox, perform the following steps:

1. Open the POP3 server MMC Console.
2. Expand the server's node and highlight the domain that contains the mailbox you wish to delete.
3. In the right-hand pane, right-click the mailbox you wish to delete and select **Delete**.

4. If you are using one of the Windows authentication mechanisms, you can delete the associated Windows user account by enabling the **Also delete the user account associated with this mailbox** option. If you are using the Active Directory integrated authentication method, you will have to be logged into the domain to delete the domain account.

5. Click **Yes** to delete the mailbox. All mail contained in the mailbox will be deleted.

If you need to change a password for a mailbox, perform the following steps:

1. Open a command prompt (you can do this be selecting **Start | Run** and entering **cmd.exe**).

2. Type **winpop changepwd username@domain_name new_password**, where <username>@<domain_name> is the mailbox whose password you wish to change and new_password is the new password. If you are using the Active Directory integrated authentication method, you will have to be logged into the domain to change the password of a domain account.

If you are using one of the Windows authentication methods, you can also change the password using the native Windows tools (for example, by using the Active Directory Users and Groups MMC).

You can enable quotas (disk space limits) for mailboxes to prevent users from consuming excessive amounts of disk space on your server. To do so, perform the following steps:

1. Select **Start | Run** and enter **cmd.exe**.

2. Enter **winpop createquotafile username@domain [/user:username]**.

The optional [/user:username] associates an existing user with this quota file. Quota files are automatically created when using either of the Windows authentication methods. The createquotafile parameter is only necessary when using the encrypted password file authentication method.

The actual disk quota is enforced by the Windows disk quota system. To enable disk quotas, perform the following steps:

1. Access **My Computer**. Right-click the desired drive and select **Properties**.

2. On the **Quota** tab, enable the **Enable Disk Quotas** option.

Disk quotas are enforced in Windows on a user-by-user basis. If you are using the encrypted password file authentication method, mailboxes are not automatically associated with Windows user accounts. The **winpop createquotefile** command associates a mailbox with a Windows user account to which a disk space quota can be applied. For more information on configuring Disk Quotas in Windows Server 2003, consult the Windows Server 2003 online help.

Your A** is Covered if You…

- ☑ Configure logging on your SMTP server and move its working folders to a non-system partition.

- ☑ Configure appropriate authentication mechanisms if required. If you choose to use basic authentication, install a server certificate and configure TLS to encrypt transmission of user credentials.

- ☑ Evaluate your relay requirements and only allow specific IP addresses or authenticated users to relay mail. If you allow authenticated users to relay mail, ensure that you use strong passwords to stop malicious users from guessing those passwords and using your SMTP server as a third-party relay. Monitor your Windows Event Logs for failed logon attempts that may indicate someone trying to guess user passwords.

- ☑ Configure connection controls if you would like to limit the IP addresses that can connect to your SMTP server.

- ☑ After installing the POP3 server, choose an authentication method prior to creating any domains. If you create domains, then wish to change the authentication method, you will need to delete all domains before doing so.

- ☑ If using local Windows or Active Directory user accounts, evaluate the use of SPA so that user credentials are not transmitted in clear text between e-mail clients and the POP3 server. The user's e-mail client will need to support SPA.

- ☑ Choose an appropriate logging level for the POP3 server. You should choose, at a minimum, the *minimum* logging level, which will log critical events.

- ☑ Move the mailroot directory off the system drive to prevent problems if user mailboxes start consuming an excessive amount of space.

Chapter 9

Securing NNTP Virtual Servers

In this Chapter

The Windows 2003 Network News Transfer Protocol (NNTP) component enables you to create news servers to host newsgroups or discussion groups. If you decide to enable this component, be sure you follow the security guidelines and procedures outlined in this chapter to protect your NNTP virtual server.

- Configuring NNTP Virtual Servers
- Managing NNTP Newsgroups
- Securing NNTP Newsgroups
- Enabling and Securing NNTP Access Log Files

By the end of this chapter you will have learned different ways to secure your NNTP newsgroups and manage newsgroups effectively. You will also be able to secure NNTP connections between your users and the NNTP virtual server.

Configuring NNTP Virtual Servers

NNTP is the protocol for distributing, posting and reading news messages between news servers and clients. NNTP gives you the ability to host online discussion groups, allowing users to collaborate and participate in discussions about different interest topics. By default, this component is not installed with IIS 6.0 because IIS 6.0 is shipped in a default locked-down mode. For details on how to install the NNTP component, refer to Chapter 3.

BY THE BOOK...

IIS includes an NNTP service, with which you can create newsgroups and host discussion groups on a server. By using any standard news reader client (such as Microsoft Outlook Express), users in your organization can read articles from others who have similar interests, post articles to other users, and participate in conversation threads.

The IIS 6.0 NNTP service introduces the *newfeed* service, which sends articles to and from other NNTP virtual servers. With newsfeeds, the news items that are posted on one server can be read by users on the other servers. However, IIS 6.0 NNTP only supports pulling feeds, and news server replication is not supported. For full push and pull newsfeeds, you need Microsoft Exchange server.

After creating an NNTP virtual server, you should relocate the default NNTP root path, configure the connection settings, and configure NNTP posting settings. When you first install the NNTP service, a *Default NNTP Virtual Server* will be created. You can rename this default virtual server, customize it to suit your needs, or you can delete it and create your own NNTP virtual server.

The IIS server will support multiple NNTP virtual servers as long as each virtual server binds to a unique IP address or port number. By default, the NNTP virtual server uses TCP port 119 for communication between NNTP clients and servers and uses TCP port 563 when Secure Socket Layer (SSL) is deployed. Deploying SSL helps secure the connection and encrypts data transmitted between the NNTP server and its clients and prevents unauthorized users from decoding data contents during transmissions.

To create a new NNTP virtual server, perform the following steps:

1. In IIS Manager, expand the local computer, right-click the local computer, point to **New** and click **NNTP Virtual Server**.
2. In the **New NNTP Site Creation Wizard** dialog box, enter the NNTP virtual server's **Name** and click **Next**.
3. Use the **Select the IP address for this NNTP virtual server** drop-down list (Figure 9.1) to select the appropriate IP address.
4. Enter **119** in the **TCP port this NNTP virtual server should use** field.

Figure 9.1 Creating an NNTP Virtual Server – New NNTP Virtual Server Wizard Dialog Box

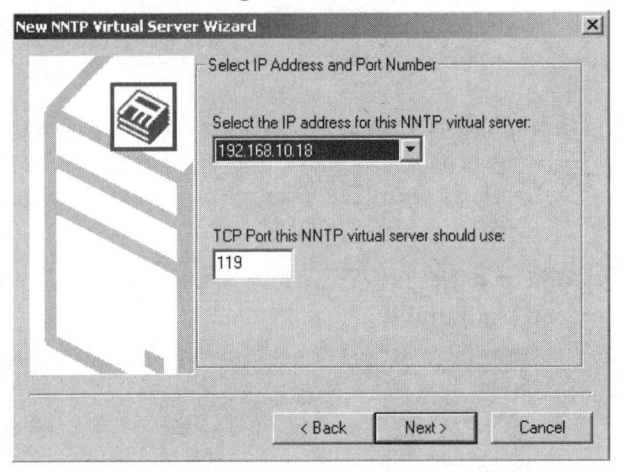

5. In the **Select Internal Files Path** dialog box (Figure 9.2), browse to the location where the NNTP internal files will be stored and click **Next**. Do not try to remove any of these files, as missing internal files can cause the NNTP virtual server to function improperly.

Figure 9.2 New NNTP Virtual Server Wizard – Configuring NNTP Internal Files Path

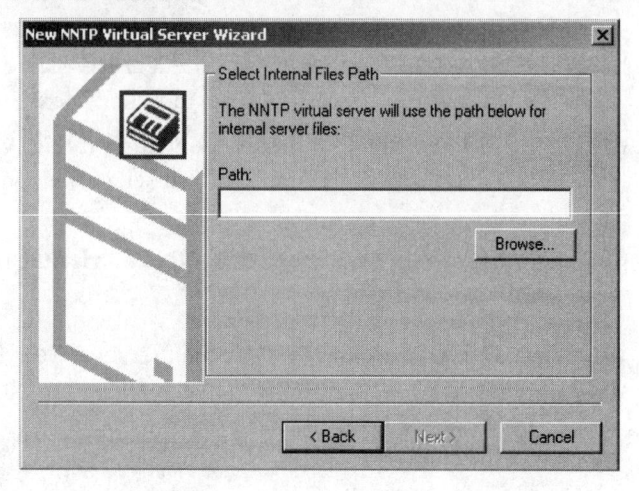

6. In the **Select Storage Medium** dialog box (Figure 9.3), select **File System** if you want to store news items locally, or select **Remote Share** if you plan to store news items on a remote network share, then click **Next**.

Figure 9.3 New NNTP Virtual Server Wizard – Configuring Storage Medium

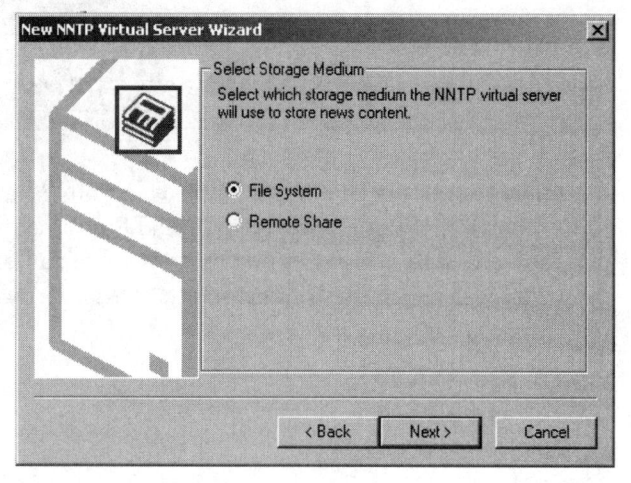

7. In **Path** field, enter the content path or click **Browse** to search for and select the path.
8. Click **Finish**.

IIS creates a default NNTP root path to your system drive, typically *C:\Inetpub\Nntpfile/root>* during installation. When you create a new NNTP virtual server, the default control files are located at *C:\Inetpub\Nntpfile/root/control>* and newsgroup files are located at *C:\Inetpub\Nntpfile/root>*. It is recommended that you move these two paths to different new disk volumes or partitions. By moving NNTP internal files and news contents out of default system drive, you can prevent illegal access to system drive information in the event that the NNTP virtual server is compromised. Furthermore, you should not relocate these two paths on the same disk partition, as internal files can be corrupted if the disk partition runs out of disk space. If you are running a high volume newsgroup server, you can deploy these paths and files to a redundant array of independent disks (RAID) to improve performance and to prevent any loss of data due to a bad disk drive.

An NNTP virtual directory is a directory that serves as the root of a part of the newsgroup hierarchy. It enables you to store newsgroup contents to different local disks or remote shared drives. By default, virtual directories will be created for the Default NNTP Virtual Server at …\root (for posting items) and at …\root\control (for control messages). Figure 9.4 shows these default virtual directories.

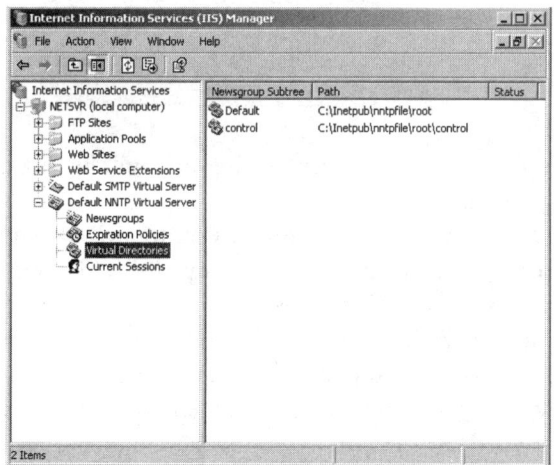

Figure 9.4 Default NNTP Virtual Directories

You have the option to relocate NNTP files and folders to local disk partitions or to a remote network shared path. It is important to note when you are using remote shared paths, you need to make sure the NNTP service has *read* and *write* NTFS permissions to the shared path. If not, news items cannot be written to the designated directory and postings will be rejected. Use the following steps to customize the default NNTP virtual server or to relocate the NNTP virtual directory path of your NNTP virtual server:

1. In IIS Manager, expand the local computer, expand the appropriate NNTP virtual server, and click **Virtual Directories**.

2. In the **Newsgroup Subtree** panel, right-click the **Default** or **control** virtual directory, and click **Properties**.

3. In the **Default Properties** dialog box (Figure 9.5), click **Contents**.

Figure 9.5 Configuring the NNTP Contents Path – General Tab

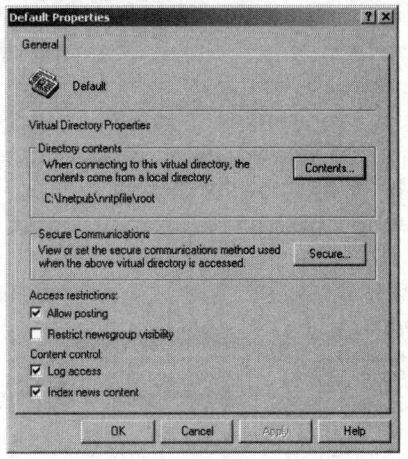

4. The **Directory Contents** dialog box will be displayed (Figure 9.6).

    If you wish to store contents on the local computer, select **Directory located on this computer** and enter or browse to the local path. Click **OK**.

    If you want to relocate the contents to a network drive, select **Share located on another computer** and enter or browse to the remote path. Next, enter a **Username** and **Password** for the remote connection, ensuring that the user has both read and write NTFS permissions on the network shared drive. Click **OK**.

Figure 9.6 Configuring the NNTP Contents Path – Directory Contents Dialog Box

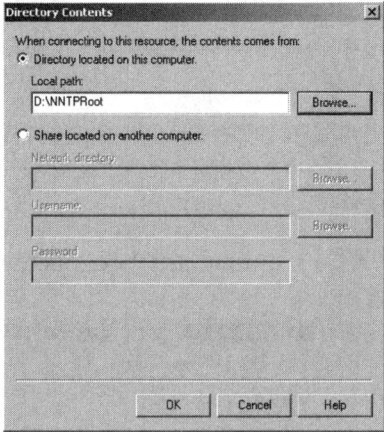

5. Click **OK** again to apply the changes.

The IIS NNTP service uses several file and message types, including:

- **Message files** News item files that are posted to newsgroups with the *.nws* file extension. These are stored in the newsgroup directory name under the NNTP root path.

- **Internal files** A variety of system-related files required by the NNTP service to function properly. For example, *.xix* files hold a list of stored news item subjects; NNTP creates one .xix subject file for every 128 news messages in a newsgroup. Others data structure files, including *.hsh*, *.hdr*, *.lst* and *.txt* are essential for NNTP to function correctly, and it is not recommended that you remove these files.

- **Control messages** Specially-formatted messages to control the NNTP service. For example, you can send special messages to the NNTP virtual server to remove or create newsgroups or to delete particular news postings from a newsgroup.

Now that you have created the NNTP service and relocated the default paths, you can move on to configuring the NNTP service's connection settings in order to benefit you and your users. You have two connection settings; you can configure concurrent settings to limit the number of simultaneous user connections to NNTP virtual server. For example, by limiting the number of concurrent connections, you can ensure better service to the connected users. You can configure the connection timeout to disconnect idle or inactive client connections to free-up server resources. Finally, you also have the option to configure a *Path*

Header, which displays the path a message has taken to reach its destination. By default the *Path Header* is the Fully Qualify Domain Name (FQDN) of the NNTP virtual server.

Use the following steps to configure basic connection settings for your NNTP virtual server:

1. In IIS Manager, expand the local computer, right-click the appropriate NNTP virtual server, and click **Properties**.
2. Click the **General** tab (Figure 9.7).

Figure 9.7 Configuring NNTP Connection Settings – General Tab

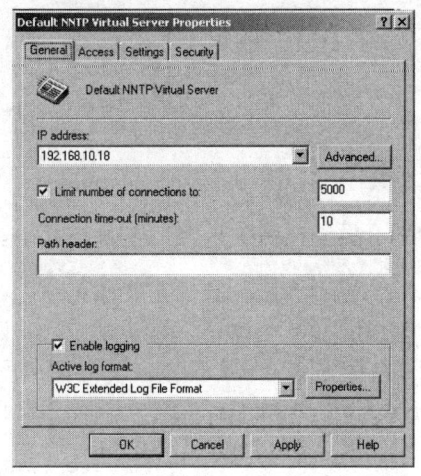

3. To limit the number of concurrent connections, enable the **Limit number of connections to** option and enter the desired number in the available textbox. By default, this value is **5000** connections.
4. To change the connection time-out, enter the new value in the **Connection time-out** field. By default, this value is **10** minutes. NNTP virtual server will disconnect client connections when the client has been idle or inactive after this configured time.
5. In the **Path header** field, enter the text that you wish to display in the path line. By default, this value is the hostname of the NNTP virtual server.
6. It is recommended that you turn on the **Enable logging** option and set the **Active log format** to **W3C Extended Log File Format**. NNTP logging is discussed in more detail later in the chapter..

7. Click **OK**.

You can also benefit by configuring the NNTP service's posting-related settings, such as message posting size and whether other NNTP servers can pull news items from your NNTP virtual server. By properly configuring posting settings, you can protect your newsgroups from attackers who try may try to steal unauthorized information or decrease the performance of your server by posting large messages and consuming server resources.

Posting settings can be applied to both client postings (in which NNTP clients post news articles directly to the NNTP virtual server) and to feed postings (in which news articles are fed from another NNTP server). By default, feed posting are enabled, but if you do not require this option, it is recommended that you disable it.

It is important to note that when an NNTP server pulls a news message, it will incur system resource usage. If there are thousands of messages pulled by another NNTP server, it may consume an unacceptable amount of bandwidth. To avoid network congestion on the NNTP virtual server, you should disable this feature unless it is required. If it is required, you can ask the parties involved to reduce the frequency at which they pull news messages. This will avoid unneeded traffic in the NNTP virtual server.

To configure the posting settings on an NNTP virtual server, perform the following steps:

1. In IIS Manager, expand the local computer, right-click the desired NNTP virtual server, and click **Properties**.
2. Click the **Settings** tab (Figure 9.8).

Figure 9.8 Configuring NNTP Posting Settings – Settings Tab

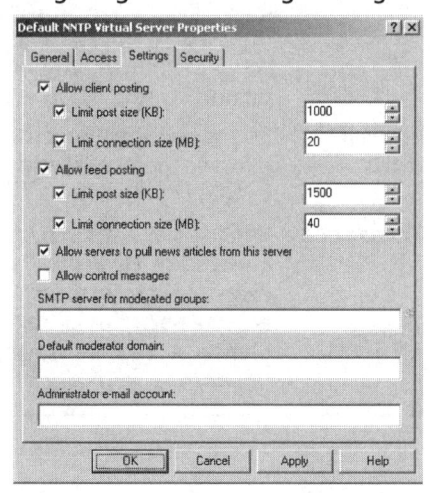

3. Using Table 9.1 as a guide, select the desired options and/or enter the desired values.

Table 9.1 NNTP Posting Related Settings

Option	Description
Allow client posting	Specifies whether users are allowed to post messages to this NNTP virtual server.
Limit post size (KB)	Specifies the largest single message size that a user can post to a newsgroup. To use this option, ensure it is enabled, then enter the desired maximum size in the available field. Disable this option to remove the size restriction.
Limit connection size (MB)	Specifies the maximum amount of data that user can post to a newsgroup during a connection. To use this option, ensure it is enabled, then enter the desired maximum size in the available field. Disable this option to remove the size restriction.
Allow feed posting	Specifies whether users are able to post messages to newsfeeds on this NNTP virtual server.
Limit post size (KB)	Specifies the largest single message size that a user can post to a newsfeed. To use this option, ensure it is enabled, then enter the desired maximum size in the available field. Disable this option to remove the size restriction.
Limit connection size (MB)	Specifies the maximum amount of data that users can post to a newsfeed during a connection. To use this option, ensure it is enabled, then enter the desired maximum size in the available field. Disable this option to remove the size restriction.
Allow servers to pull news articles from this server	Specifies whether other NNTP servers are allowed pull message feeds from this NNTP virtual server.
Allow control messages	Specifies whether control messages are allowed in this NNTP virtual server. For example, **newgroup 'mycorp.com.projects.seaport'** will instruct NNTP server to create new newsgroup named *'mycorp.com.projects.seaport'*.

4. Click **OK** to apply the changes.

REALITY CHECK...

Always relocate the NNTP posting contents and internal control files to new disk partitions, and configure connection-related settings to protect and improve your NNTP virtual server connections response.

Configure posting settings to restrict posting message size. Limit newsfeed posting if you do not need it (as it will occupy bandwidth resources), and prevent articles from being pulled to other NNTP servers if you do not want your newsgroup data to be copied.

Managing NNTP Newsgroups

Now that you have installed and configured the NNTP virtual server, you need to create the newsgroups that the server will host. You can create and remove newsgroups, and you can configure the way they behave. You can also configure *moderation* to monitor and control the news items that will be accepted in the newsgroups.

BY THE BOOK...

A *newsgroup* is the organizational structure of a group of related news articles. For example, if you are creating departmental newsgroups, then you may have accounting, project, support and other newsgroups to suit your organization's needs. You can further divide the newsgroup hierarchy if you wish to create more specific areas of discussion within your newsgroups.

You can change the properties of an existing newsgroup or delete the newsgroup if you no longer need it. You manage newsgroups in the *Newsgroups* node under the NNTP virtual server. You can also configure *expiration policies* in NNTP virtual server, which instruct the NNTP service to delete articles based on time or space limits.

Notes from the Underground...

Unwanted Posting

Any time a user posts an unsolicited message to a newsgroup, it is considered an *unwanted posting*. This can be a danger if sensitive or confidential details are posted and made known to users subscribing to the newsgroup. An unwanted posting may also take the form of unnecessarily large files or messages, which will take up bandwidth resources and degrade newsgroup performance for other users.

To prevent unwanted postings, you should limit the message posting size. The default client posting size is 1000KB (nearly 1MB). Imagine, if an attacker posted 10 news articles with 1000KB each, it would consume nearly 10MB of content storage and 10MB of bandwidth usage every time a user downloaded the news item. If you are hosting a discussion that does not require a large message size or does not require any file attachments, it is recommended that you configure the posting size to less than 20KB (typical pure text message will not exceed 5KB).

In addition to limiting file size, you can also configure moderated newsgroups to monitor and filter out unwanted messages. News articles posted to moderated newsgroups will only appear in the newsgroup after they have been approved by a designated moderator. By moderating newsgroups, you can control which messages can be seen in the newsgroups, and you can filter out junk or messages that violate your newsgroup's discussion rules.

When you first install NNTP, four predefined newsgroups are created (Figure 9.9), including control.cancel, control.newgroup, control.rmgroup, and microsoft.public.ins.

Figure 9.9 Default Newsgroups in Default NNTP Virtual Server

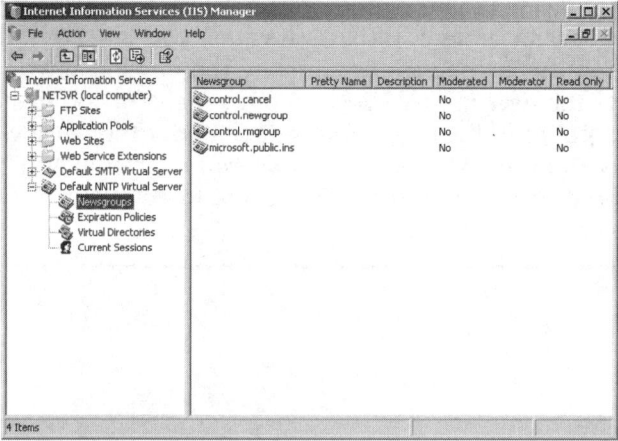

The *microsoft.public.ins* group is a sample predefined newsgroup, and you can rename it or simply remove it. However, the other three control newsgroups are related to NNTP service control messages and deleting these newsgroups will interfere with the proper operation of control messages. These control newsgroups are:

- **control..cancel** Can remove news items based on their message IDs. A message ID is the identification number that NNTP assigns to the message when it is posted to the newsgroup, and these IDs are unique throughout the entire NNTP virtual server.

- **control.newgroup** Responsible for creating new newsgroups when control messages contain the *newgroup* syntax.

- **control.rmgroup** Responsible for removing existing newsgroups when control messages contain the *rmgroup* syntax.

When creating a newsgroup, you should first decide on its name, which will consist of the discussion group name followed by any company departmental structures that you may be supporting. For example, the newsgroup name *mycorp.com.accounts* indicates that the newsgroup belongs to *mycorp.com* and it is related to the *accounts* department. Because newsgroup names can become quite long, you can use a *pretty name* (alias) for your newsgroup when you create it. To create a newsgroup on the NNTP virtual server, follow these steps:

1. In IIS Manager, expand the local computer and expand the desired NNTP virtual server.

2. Right-click the **Newsgroups** node, point to **New**, then click **Newsgroup**.

3. The **New Newsgroup Wizard** will open. Enter the newsgroup **Name** and click **Next**.

4. Enter a **Description** and **Pretty name** for the newsgroup (Figure 9.10).

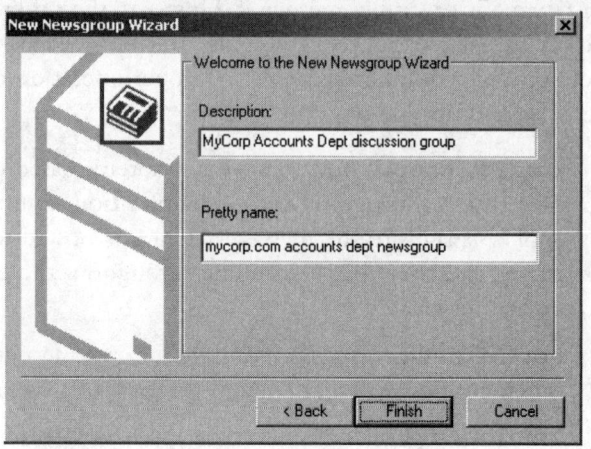

Figure 9.10 Creating Newsgroup – New Newsgroup Wizard

5. Click **Finish**.

Once you have created a newsgroup, you can rename it, change its description, change its pretty name, or delete it from the server. Use the following steps to edit or delete a newsgroup:

1. In IIS Manager, expand the local computer, expand the desired NNTP virtual server, and click **Newsgroups**.
2. In the details pane, right-click the desired newsgroup.
3. To rename the newsgroup, select **Rename** from the shortcut menu. To remove the newsgroup, click **Delete** in the shortcut menu. To change the newsgroup's description or pretty name, click **Properties**.

An NNTP virtual server can potentially store up to thousands of newsgroups. It might take a long time to enumerate all the newsgroups, so you may want to filter the newsgroups that will be enumerated. You can filter newsgroups by type using naming conventions, by number to control total number newsgroups, or both. To configure newsgroup enumeration, perform the following steps:

1. In IIS Manager, expand the local computer, then expand the desired NNTP virtual server.
2. Right-click **Newsgroups** and select **Limit groups enumeration**.
3. In the **Newsgroups** field (shown in Figure 9.11), enter the kind of the newsgroup you want to display in the newsgroup

list. To specify all newsgroups within a particular category, use the asterisk (*) wildcard. For example, use **projects.*** to specify that you want to view only the newsgroups in the projects hierarchy.

Figure 9.11 Enumerating Newsgroups – Find Newsgroups Dialog Box

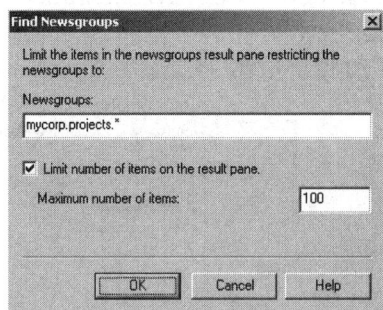

4. Use the **Limit number of items on the result pane** option to specify whether the result pane will contain a limited number of newsgroups. If so, enter the maximum number of items to display.

5. Click **OK**.

To keep your NNTP virtual server healthy, you should configure newsgroup limits and article expirations. Expiration policies specify how long news items are kept in NNTP newsgroups before they are automatically removed. It is recommended that you apply at least one expiration policy to each newsgroup.

An expiration policy can be applied to one or more newsgroups, and you can configure more than one expiration policy for a single newsgroup. When a newsgroup has more than one expiration policy, the more restrictive policy is applied. To configure newsgroup expiration, perform the following steps:

1. In IIS Manager, expand the local computer, then expand the desired NNTP virtual server.

2. Right-click **Expiration Policies**, point to **New**, and click **Expiration Policy**.

3. In the **New NNTP Expiration Policy Wizard** dialog box, enter the policy name and click **Next**.

4. In the **Newsgroups** dialog box (Figure 9.12), click **Add** to include desired newsgroups and click **Delete** to remove newsgroups from the list. Use the **Move Up** and **Move Down** buttons to control the order in which the policy will be applied to the newsgroups.

Figure 9.12 Configure NNTP Expiration Policy – Newsgroups Selection box

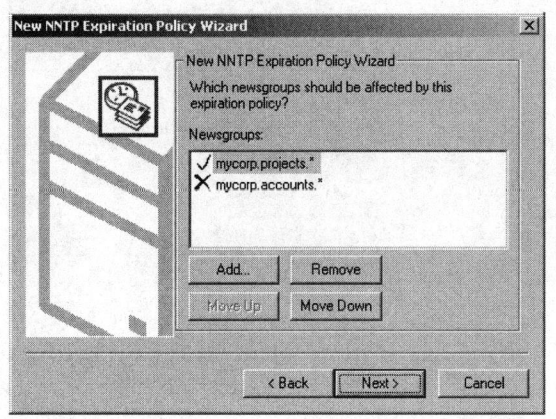

5. Click **Next**.
6. In the **Remove articles older than (Hours)** field, enter the age at which old articles will be removed. By default, this value is **168** hours, which is equivalent to **7** days.
7. Click **Finish**.

Once an expiration policy has been created, you can change the newsgroups to which the policy applies and the expiration time. To do this, double-click on the policy you wish to change and configure the desired expiration policy properties.

It is important to note that news articles that are deleted by the expiration policy are not recoverable. If you want to archive a newsgroup's contents, you can either have another NNTP virtual server pull all newsgroup messages on a specified schedule, or you can back up the entire NNTP virtual server. You can configure the NTBACKUP utility included in Windows Server 2003 family to back up NNTP contents, and ensure you back up both internal files and news content directories. For more details on using NTBACKUP for backing up and restoring data, refer to the Windows Server 2003 help documentation.

To secure your newsgroup and protect if from unwanted or unrelated news items, you can configure moderation to control which messages will be accepted in the newsgroup. A moderated newsgroup will direct user postings to a moderator who will either approve or reject the article before it is posted to the newsgroups. To use moderation in a newsgroup, you must specify either a Simple Mail Transfer Protocol (SMTP) mail server for sending news items directly to the moderators, or a directory where the news items are stored for the moderators.

It is important to note that any NNTP client application can be used to post messages to a moderated newsgroup. However, the moderator needs to use an NNTP client application that supports moderating functions. You can also specify a default moderator domain. If you decide to use the default moderator for a newsgroup, messages are sent to *newsgroup_name@default_domain*, where *newsgroup_name* is the name of the newsgroup and *default_domain* indicates the domain name that you specified. For example, when a message is posted to newsgroup *mycorp.com.projects.migration* with default domain name *mycorp.com*, the message is sent to *mycorp_com_projects_migration@mycorp.com*.

Before you can moderate newsgroups, you must first enable the moderation feature on the NNTP virtual server, then configure individual newsgroups to be moderated. To enable newsgroup moderation, perform the following steps:

1. In IIS Manager, expand the local computer, right-click the desired NNTP virtual server, and then click **Properties**.

2. On the **Settings** tab (shown in Figure 9.13), use the **SMTP server for moderated groups** field to enter the DNS name or IP address of the SMTP server, or enter the path to the directory where messages will be stored for the moderator(s). The default delivery directory is \Inetpub\Mailroot\Pickup.

Figure 9.13 Enabling NNTP Moderated Newsgroups – Settings Tab

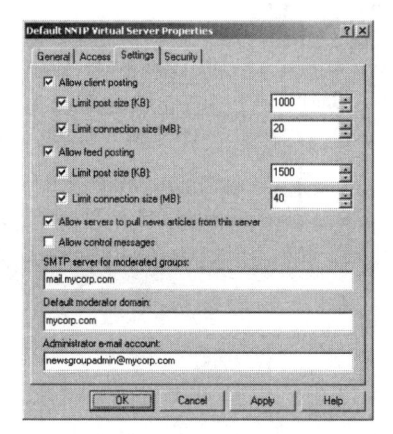

3. In the **Default moderator domain** field, enter the e-mail domain for default moderators. This is the Fully Qualified Domain Name (FQDN) of the e-mail domain, for example, mycompany.com.

4. In the **Administrator e-mail account** field, enter the administrator's e-mail address for receiving the non-delivery reports (**NDRs**) of moderated newsgroup messages that cannot be delivered to the specified moderator.

5. Click **OK**.

When you specify an SMTP server to deliver news items to moderators, you need to make sure that the process identity that the NNTP service is running is defined as an account on the SMTP server. The NNTP service will use this account identity to connect to the SMTP server when sending messages. By default, the NNTP service process identity is the *System* account.

If you configured NDR e-mail to be sent to the administrator e-mail account, you must configure the Windows registry:

1. Run the **Registry Editor** (Regedt32.exe).

2. From the **HKEY_LOCAL_MACHINE** sub-tree, go to the following key: **\System\CurrentControlSet\Services\NntpSvc\Parameters**

3. Click **Add Value** on the **Edit** menu.

4. Enter **MailFromHeader** in the **Value Name** field.

5. Enter **REG_DWORD** in the **Data Type** field.

6. Enter **1** in the **Data** field.

7. Restart the NNTP service by entering **net stop nntpsvc** at the command prompt, followed by the **net start nntpsvc** command.

Now that moderation has been enabled on the server, you can go ahead and configure individual newsgroups to use moderation. To configure an existing newsgroup to use moderation, perform these steps:

1. In IIS Manager, expand the local computer, expand the desire NNTP virtual server, and click **Newsgroups**.

2. In the details pane, right-click the desired newsgroup and select **Properties**.

3. On the **General** tab (shown in Figure 9.14), enable the **Moderated** option.

Figure 9.14 Configuring NNTP Moderation – General Tab

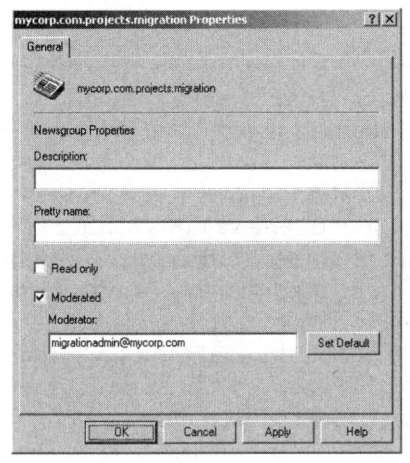

4. In the **Moderator** text field, enter the e-mail address of the moderator, or click **Set Default** to use the default moderator.
5. Click **OK**.

Reality Check...

Proper configuration of your newsgroups provides the basis for healthy and user-friendly discussion groups. Configuring an expiration policy allows you to recover disk space as old articles are removed from the server. To prevent unsolicited messages from reaching your newsgroup, enable the moderation feature. Messages posted to a moderated newsgroup are first sent to moderators for approval before they are actually listed in the newsgroup. This allows you to control message postings, directly protecting you from junk and unrelated posts.

Securing NNTP Newsgroups

By default, the NNTP service allows anonymous clients to connect and post messages to newsgroups. These messages are transferred from client machines to the server in plain text mode, meaning they are not secured.

To secure your newsgroups, you can configure different authentication modes to authenticate users when connecting to the NNTP virtual server and secure the communication with Secure Sockets Layer.

> **BY THE BOOK...**
>
> The NNTP service provides many built-in security features that you can configure to secure and protect your NNTP virtual server, including:
>
> **Authentication** Allows you to authenticate users before they can post and retrieve news articles. NNTP supports three different types of authentication mode, including anonymous, basic, and Integrated Windows Authentication.
>
> **Connection** Allows you to control access by granting and denying client access based on their IP address or domain name. By default, all IP addresses have access to NNTP virtual server. You can configure connection restrictions to limit NNTP virtual server access.
>
> **Certificate** Server certificates facilitate SSL in providing a secure and encrypted connection between the NNTP virtual server and the client computer. Implementing SSL secures data transmission, as it encrypts the data so that attackers will not be able to see the actual content. Besides protecting the data, SSL certificates are used to prove the identity of the NNTP server, as it holds the digital signature validated by a trusted certificate authority (CA).
>
> **Access Control** To further restrict access to NNTP newsgroups, you configure NTFS permissions for newsgroup contents. By creating Access Control Lists (ACLs) for the newsgroup directory, you can specify which users can authorize which contents.

Recall that default control newsgroups are created when you create the NNTP virtual server. You should hide these newsgroups and secure them with proper NTFS permissions. Restricting access and visibility to these groups will prevent unauthorized users from changing your newsgroups or deleting messages. To hide the default control newsgroups, perform these steps:

1. In IIS Manager, expand the local computer, expand the desired NNTP virtual server, and click **Virtual Directories**.

2. Under the **Newsgroup Subtree** panel, right-click the desired control directory, and click **Properties**.

3. In the **Properties** dialog box (Figure 9.15), enable the **Restrict newsgroup visibility** option.

Figure 9.15 Hiding Control Newsgroups – General Tab

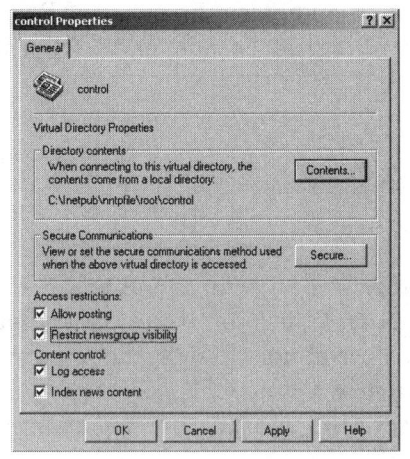

4. Click **OK**.

When the NNTP service receives *cancel*, *newgroup* and *rmgroup* control messages, it will post them into their respective control newsgroups for processing. It is important to note that by allowing control messages on the NNTP server, you open the door for potential malicious attacks. However, if you decide to allow control messages, perform the following steps:

1. In IIS Manager, expand the local computer, right-click the desired NNTP virtual server, and click **Properties**.
2. On the **Settings** tab, enable the **Allow control messages** option.
3. Click **OK**.

You can further restrict control message postings by configuring NTFS permissions on the control newsgroup's physical directory that is mapped to the control virtual directory. For example, suppose that you would like to control message postings for a certain group of users. To further protect your NNTP virtual server from being abused by anonymous control messages, you can configure NTFS permissions to restrict access to the control newsgroups. You will grant a specific group of users Full Control NTFS permission of a control newsgroup and Deny access for the rest of users. *Default NNTP Virtual Server control newsgroups* is mapped to C:\Inetpub\Nntpfile\root\control. In addition, you need to ensure the Access Control Lists (ACLs) for this directory include *Full Control* for *System* accounts.

Now that you have taken care of the control newsgroup security issues, you can move on to securing the NNTP virtual service itself. You can do this by applying one or more of the following security configurations:

- Authentication
- Certificate
- Connection

Note that these security settings are applied at the server level, which means you cannot place them on individual newsgroups. You can, however, apply NTFS permissions to different newsgroups in order to configure them separately.

Table 9.2 shows the authentication methods supported by the NNTP service.

Table 9.2 NNTP Authentication Methods

Method	Description
Anonymous	No username or password is required to access the NNTP virtual server. The default anonymous user is IUSR_<COMPUTERNAME>.
Basic	Users are required to have a valid Windows user account. User credentials are sent in plain text mode.
Integrated Windows	Users are required to have a valid Windows account, and user credentials are sent in encrypted mode.

It is recommended that you turn off anonymous access if it not required. If you want to host members-only newsgroups, you must turn off anonymous access and configure NNTP authentication. To configure NNTP authentication, perform these steps:

1. In IIS Manager, expand the local computer, right-click the desired NNTP virtual server, then click **Properties**.
2. On the **Access** tab, click **Authentication**.

3. In the **Authentication Methods** dialog box (Figure 9.16), enable the desired options (SSL authentication is discussed later in the chapter):

- Select **Allow Anonymous** if you want to grant access to anonymous users.

- Select **Basic Authentication** if you plan to authenticate the user via a valid Windows user account in plain text mode.

- Select **Integrated Windows Authentication** if you plan to authenticate the user via a valid Windows user account in encrypted mode.

Figure 9.16 Configuring NNTP Authentication Methods – Authentication Methods Dialog Box

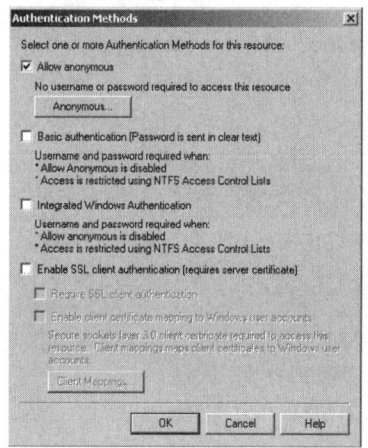

5. Click **OK**.

As well as user authentication, you also have the option to enable SSL client authentication. SSL provides a secure, encrypted connection between the NNTP service and the client computer. It protects private information when users connect across a public network such as the Internet. Basic authentication is often paired with SSL authentication to ensure that plain text user credentials are encrypted by SSL when they are transferred from clients to the NNTP server.

The downside of implementing SSL is the server overhead, since encrypted messages must be decrypted before they can be read by users. SSL connections also use additional bandwidth for the exchange of encryption key information when clients first connect to the NNTP server, so the connection and response times are typically slower when compared with non-SSL connections. Use the following steps to enable SSL authentication for clients. Note that the server certificate feature must be installed on the NNTP server before you can configure SSL authentication.

1. In IIS Manager, expand the local computer, right-click the desired NNTP virtual server, then click **Properties**.
2. On the **Access** tab, click **Authentication**.
3. In the **Authentication Methods** dialog box, enable the **Enable SSL client authentication** option.
4. If you want to force SSL client authentication, enable the **Require SSL client authentication** option.
5. Click **OK**.

To require a secure channel for newsgroup access once a valid SSL connection is made, use the following steps:

1. In IIS Manager, expand the local computer, expand the desired NNTP virtual server, then click **Virtual Directories**.
2. In the details pane, right-click the virtual directory that you want to modify and click **Properties**.
3. On the **General** tab, click **Secure**.
4. In the **Security** dialog box (Figure 9.17), enable the **Require secure channel** option.

Figure 9.17 Enabling Newsgroups SSL Connection – Security Dialog Box

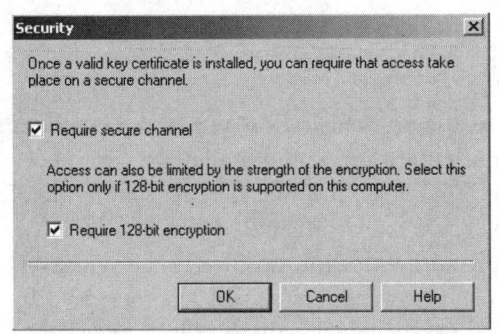

5. If desired, enable the **Require 128-bit encryption** option.
6. Click **OK**.

7. Click **OK** again.

As stated earlier, there are three types of security settings. We have already discussed authentication and certificate authentication. The following information can be used to configure IP address and domain name restrictions. This option allows you to restrict or allow access to the NNTP virtual server based on the IP address or domain name of the client. By default, all IP addresses have access to the NNTP virtual server. You can only configure this type of restriction at the server (but not the individual newsgroup) level. To limit NNTP access by IP address or domain name, perform these steps:

1. In IIS Manager, expand the local computer, right-click the desired NNTP virtual server, then click **Properties**.
2. On the **Access** tab, click **Connection**.
3. In the **Connection** dialog box, click **All except the list below** to grant access to all clients except those in the list, or click **Only the list below** to allow access only to the clients in the list of IP addresses.
4. Click **Add** to add each desired IP address to the list.
5. In the **Computer** dialog box (shown in Figure 9.18), select one of the following options: **Single Computer**, **Group of computers**, or **Domain**.

Figure 9.18 Limiting NNTP Access by IP Address – Computer Dialog Box

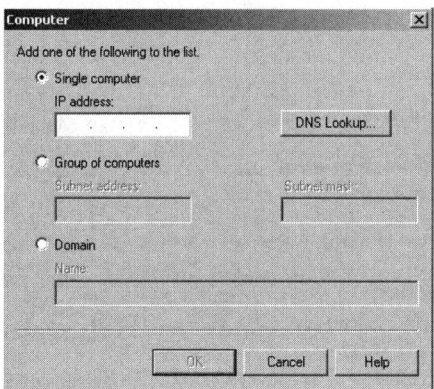

6. Continue as follows:

   - If you selected **Single Computer**, enter the **IP address** of the computer, or click **DNS Lookup** if you do not know the IP address.

- If you selected **Group of computers**, enter the **Subnet address** and subnet mask for the group of computers.
- If you selected **Domain**, enter the domain name of the computer you wish to add to the list.

7. Click **OK** in all dialog boxes to save your settings.

To help you further secure and restrict access to newsgroups, you can configure NTFS permissions on NNTP resources. Because each user is associated with a registered Windows user account, you can control the ACLs of the resources to restrict access.

For example, suppose that you are hosting public and private newsgroups on the NNTP virtual server. You would like to restrict anonymous access to the private newsgroups to a special group of members. In this scenario, you need to configure anonymous access and either basic or integrated Windows authentication; anonymous users will access the newsgroups using the default anonymous account, and special members will authenticate with their registered Windows user accounts. To restrict access, you can place the two newsgroups in different directories and configure proper NTFS restrictions for the private newsgroup to deny access for anonymous accounts and grant read and write access to the special member group. You can control access to individual newsgroups or sets of newsgroups based the directory hierarchy structure.

The NNTP service supports the use of a *site operator*, which is a designated individual who can act as a server administrator to change or reconfigure the NNTP virtual server. By default, site operators include members of the administrators local group and the local service and network service. It is not recommended that you add a new user to be a site operator unless the user is required to manage the NNTP server on your behalf. If you decided to grant site operator permissions to another user, perform these steps:

1. In IIS Manager, expand the local computer, right-click the desired NNTP virtual server, then click **Properties**.
2. On the **Security** tab (Figure 9.19), click **Add**.

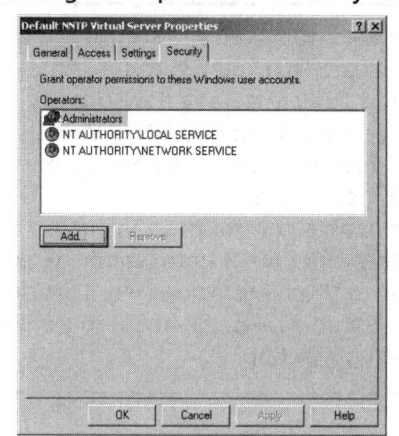

Figure 9.19 Adding Site Operator – Security Tab

3. In the **Select Users or Groups** dialog box, click **Locations**, then select the domain of the operator you want to add.
4. In the **Select Users or Groups** dialog box, click **Object Types** and select the desired operator or group, then click **OK**.
5. In the **Select Users or Groups** dialog box, enter the object name or click **Advanced** to search for and select a particular object.
6. Click **OK**.

You should follow these best security practices when securing NNTP newsgroups.

- Hide control newsgroups and only enable them when they are needed.
- Disable anonymous access if it is not required.
- Configure NNTP authentication to prevent unauthorized access.
- Secure basic authentication with SSL certificates.
- Create a hierarchy of different newsgroups so that you can isolate different areas of discussion.
- Configure SSL connections when accessing newsgroups.
- Secure the newsgroup's content directory with proper NTFS permissions.

REALITY CHECK...

Ensure you have followed the security guidelines outlined in this section to secure NNTP newsgroups. Analyze the user's requirements before you create any newsgroups, and determine if you need to have more than one NNTP virtual server. Design a proper newsgroup hierarchy give your newsgroups names that are both simple and meaningful.

Do not enable control postings unless you secure the newsgroups with proper NTFS permissions. Grant minimum access permissions to the newsgroups' content directories and secure communication between client computers and the NNTP server with an SSL connection.

Enabling and Securing NNTP Access Log Files

The NNTP access log files can provide details about each message posted and each action request of the NNTP virtual server. It is important that you enable NNTP logging to keep track of newsgroup access activity, as it keeps track of user connections and retrieval and posting of news items.

BY THE BOOK...

Auditing server activity with log files is a good way to detect if unauthorized external users are attempting to access your virtual server, or if internal users are trying to access resources they do not have permissions to access.

IIS 6.0 allows you to collect user access activity information by enabling the logging feature. IIS 6.0 supports the following logging formats:

W3C Extended A customizable format allowing you to configure the types of information to be collected. This format follows the W3C working draft specification.

NCSA Common National Center for Supercomputing Applications (NCSA) common format is an old specification of log file. Details that are logged are fixed and not customizable. Data captured includes remote host name, data, time, request type, HTTP status and number of bytes sent by the server.

IIS Log A fixed format that records more information than NCSA common format. These extra details include the time taken to process the request, bytes received by the server, and Win32 status.

ODCB Logging A fixed set of data that can be recorded in a database source.

IIS 6.0 supports a new feature, called *remote logging*. This feature allows you to redirect log files to a remote shared network path using the Universal Naming Convention (UNC) method. This allows you to configure different log paths to a centralized log storage for backup and analysis purposes. Note that UTF-8 logging, centralized binary logging, HTTP error logging and the protocol sub-status features that were supported in earlier versions of IIS are not supported in IIS 6.0.

Essentially, NNTP access logs are the same as web access logs, as both write an entry to the log file for each request the server served. However, NNTP logs are not as comprehensive as web logs and certain features that are supported in web access logs do not exist in NNTP access logs.

NNTP virtual server activity logging can be enabled and disabled at NNTP virtual server level only. To enable logging on a NNTP virtual server, perform the following steps:

1. In IIS Manager, expand the local computer, right-click the desired NNTP virtual server, then click **Properties**.
2. On the **General** tab (Figure 9.20), enable the **Enable logging** option.

Figure 9.20 Enabling NNTP Virtual Server Logging – General Tab

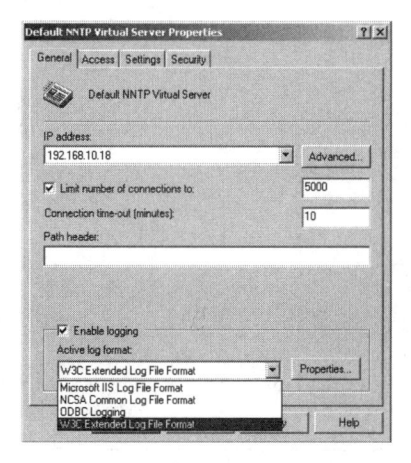

3. Select the desired format from the **Active log format** drop-down list. By default, the format is **Microsoft IIS Log File Format**.
4. Click **OK**.

The type of information logged in Microsoft IIS log format and W3C extended format is essentially the same. However, it is recommended that you use W3C extended format, as this format is easier to read and each property name is logged. Though not all property fields in W3C extended format are logged, this format will give you the most comprehensive details.

By default *no* field properties are logged when you select W3C extended format; you must configure the fields to be logged. Table 9.3 lists the W3C extended properties fields that you can enable.

Table 9.3 NNTP Virtual Server Logging – W3C Extended Logging Fields

Property	Field	Description
Client IP Address	c-ip	The IP address of the client that accessed your NNTP server.
User Name	cs-username	The username of the client that accessed your NNTP server. Anonymous users will appear as <user>.
Service Name	s-sitename	The sitename that served the request, for example, NNTPSVC1.
Server name	s-computername	The name of the NNTP server that served the request.
Server IP Address	s-ip	The IP address of the NNTP server that served the request.
Server Port	s-port	The port number of the NNTP server that served the request.
Method	cs-method	The requested client action, for example, POST or ARTICLE.
URI Stem	cs-uri-stem	The request's content name, for example, newsgroup or message ID.
Protocol Status	sc-status	The status code of the request.
Win32 Status	sc-win32-status	The status code in Windows terms.
Bytes Sent	sc-bytes	The number of bytes sent by the server.

Continued

Table 9.3 NNTP Virtual Server Logging – W3C Extended Logging Fields

Property	Field	Description
Bytes Received	cs-bytes	The number of bytes received by the server.
Time Taken	time-taken	The amount of time it took to process the request.

To customize the NNTP virtual server's W3C extended logging fields, perform these steps:

1. In the IIS MMC console, expand the local computer, right-click the desired NNTP virtual server, and click **Properties**.

2. Ensure **W3C Extended Log File Format** is selected in the **Active log format** drop-down list, and click on **Properties**.

3. In the **Logging Properties** dialog box, click on the **Advanced** tab (shown in Figure 9.21).

Figure 9.21 Customizing NNTP W3C Extended Logging Fields Advanced Tab

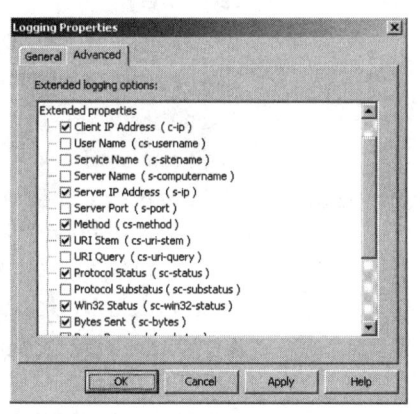

4. Enable all of the desired logging fields by clicking to place a check in their checkboxes.

5. Click **OK** twice to save your changes.

The status codes recorded in the NNTP log can help you identify whether a request was successful or failed, and can provide clues as to why a request may have failed. For example, the status 480 indicates that the request failed because a valid login was required for the request. This can indicate an attempted anonymous login. The NNTP log status codes are listed in Table 9.4.

Table 9.4 IIS NNTP Status Codes

NNTP Status Code	Description
1xx Informative Message	Initial action successful, continue new command
100	Help text
199	Debug out put.
2xx Positive Message	Client requests successfully accepted and command executed
200	Server ready - posting allowed
201	Server ready - no posting allowed
205	Closing connection - goodbye!
215	List of newsgroups
220	N <a> article retrieved - head and body follow (N = article number, <a> = message id)
221	N <a> article retrieved - head follows
222	N <a> article retrieved - body follows
223	N <a> article retrieved - request text separately
230	List of new articles by message-id
231	List of new newsgroups
235	Article transferred
240	Article posted
3xx Positive Intermediate Message	Command succeeded, needs additional info to complete request
335	Send article to be transferred
340	Send article to be posted
4xx Temporary Negative Message	Temporary error, client can retry the command
400	Service discontinued
411	No such news group
412	No newsgroup has been selected
420	No current article has been selected
421	No next article in this group
422	No previous article in this group
423	No such article number in this group
430	No such article found

Continued

Table 9.4 IIS NNTP Status Codes

NNTP Status Code	Description
435	Article not wanted - do not send it
436	Transfer failed - try again later
437	Article rejected - do not try again
440	Posting not allowed
441	Posting failed
480	Logon required
5xx Permanent Negative Message	Command failed, the error is permanent
500	Command not recognized
501	Command syntax error
502	Access restriction or permission denied
503	Program fault - command not performed

For more details about NNTP status code definitions, refer to section 2.4 NNTP Responses at www.w3.org/Protocols/rfc977/rfc977.html.

The default log path for NNTP is %Windir%/system32/Logfiles/NNTPSVC*X*, where *X* indicates the ID of the virtual server that the log file belongs to. This site ID is the identification number generated by IIS when you create the NNTP site. In earlier versions of IIS, these identification numbers are incremental, but with IIS 6.0, the site ID is randomly created by IIS based on the NNTP site name. Now that you understand the differences between NNTP and website logging, you should refer Chapter 4 for details on how to secure NNTP access log files.

REALITY CHECK...

Logging NNTP virtual server activity provides detailed information about server access and the usage of newsgroup resources. It is recommended that you enable and configure NNTP virtual server logging and protect the log files using NTFS permissions.

Your A** is Covered if You...

- ☑ Relocated your NNTP contents and control newsgroups to new disk partitions.
- ☑ Configured NNTP virtual server connection settings.
- ☑ Configured NNTP posting-related settings.
- ☑ Configured newsgroup enumeration and expiration policies.
- ☑ Configured newsgroup moderation to protect private newsgroups.
- ☑ Restricted the visibility of the control newsgroups secured them with NTFS permissions.
- ☑ Restricted NNTP anonymous access if it is not required.
- ☑ Configured NNTP user authentication.
- ☑ Configured SSL connections between the NNTP server and client computers.
- ☑ Configured IP address and domain name restrictions.
- ☑ Secured the newsgroup contents directory with proper NTFS permissions.
- ☑ Enabled NNTP virtual server activity logging.
- ☑ Secured NNTP access log files.

Chapter 10
Securing Certificate Services

In this Chapter

Certificate Services is a security technology that allows you to verify object identity and provide data security. The Certificate Services component is included in all members of the Windows Server 2003 family of operating systems except Web Edition. If you decide to enable this component, be sure you follow the security guidelines and procedures outlined in this chapter to protect your Certificate Services.

- Understanding Certificate Services
- Configuring Certificate Services
- Securing Certificate Authority Web Enrollment Support
- Monitoring Certificate Authority Web Enrollment Access

By the end of this chapter you will understand the role played by certificates, and you will know how to configure Certificate Services and secure and monitor your web enrollment certificate authority (CA).

Understanding Certificate Services

By default, Certificate Services is not installed during IIS 6.0 installation, as the operating system is shipped in default locked down mode. This section will instruct you on the basics of certificates and how to configure Certificate Services on the IIS server.

> **BY THE BOOK...**
>
> *Certificate Services* is a component included in most of the Windows Server 2003 family, which allows system administrators to make use of digital certificates.
>
> A *certificate* is a document that has been digitally signed by a certificate authority, and contains information that identifies the certificate owner. The certificate is useful when the users of the certificate trust the CA or issuer. Other usage of the certificate includes facilitating Secure Sockets Layer (SSL) for securing data transmission and providing authentication security.
>
> A *certificate authority* is responsible for issuing digital certificates. It uses an industry standard encryption method to hold certification information. This encryption method consists of two separate keys that are mathematically linked together. The *private* key is kept confidential, while the *public* key is freely available to all users. These keys will be applied to *message digest*, or hashing, which is a process of applying one-way mathematical formulas to a set of data to produce a new cipher. No other data can be hashed to produce the same unique instance. For more details about Windows Server Cryptography and PKI Basics, you can refer to www.microsoft.com/technet/prodtechnol/windows2000serv/deploy/confeat/cryptpki.mspx.

Before you install and configure Certificate Services, it is important to understand the concept behind certificates. As mentioned, the certificate is a digital document that is verified and issued by a CA. It is used to prove an object's identity and to secure information using the Public Key Infrastructure (PKI). A certificate can be used for:

- **Authentication** Proof of identity for users or machines. For example, when a user connects to a SSL website, the user can verify that the web server has the identity that it claims to have.

- **Digital Signatures** Ensures the integrity of a message and the identity of its sender. For example, a user can include a digital signature in an e-mail message so the recipient can be assured that the message has indeed been sent by the designated user, and that the message is valid and can be trusted.

- **Privacy and Encryption** Ensures that the information transmitted is only available to the targeted receiver. Encryption methods include Data Encryption Standard (DES) and Digital Signature Algorithm (DSA).

The Certificates Service works by using private and public keys that are related by a set of mathematical formulas. The public key is publicly available for all users to obtain. Its purpose is to encrypt data and verify digital signatures. The private key is kept confidential by valid certificate holders. Its purpose is to sign messages and decrypt data that has been encrypted by public keys. In a typical setup, the sender will encrypt a message using the receiver's public key and receiver will decrypt the message using his or her own private key. This is known as *asymmetric encryption*, whereby the encryption and decryption are carried out by two different keys.

Certificates are valid for a limited period of time. When this period expires, the certificate becomes invalid. Generally, certificates hold the following information:

- Public key information.

- Object's identifier details, such as name, location, and e-mail address.

- Validity period, which states the time when the certificate was created and when it will become invalid.

- CA's details, such as issuer identity and digital signature that verifies the certificate.

IIS server makes use of two main types of certificates that allow you to prove the identity of your Web server and users, as well as to secure the connection to protect transmitted data between client machines and the IIS server.

- **Client certificates** These certificates belong to clients and contain identity information about the client. They allow you to positively identify users as before allowing them to access your Web server. You can configure client certification authentication in IIS to further increase Web server security when clients are trying to access your web server.

- **Server certificates** Before you can configure SSL security on your Web server, you must obtain a server certificate. This certificate is digital identification that holds details about your Web server. It enables users to authenticate your Web server, validate web resources, and also to establish SSL secure connections to the server.

For example, when you buy and sell shares online with your security firm, you want to make sure that you are actually connecting to the firm's legitimate and secure Web server. You can verify the *server certificate* configured in the Web server is valid before you continue any transaction. The following occurs when you connect to the SSL-enabled online trading Web server:

- Your web browser connects to the online trading Web server.

- Normally, you will be redirected to Hypertext Transfer Protocol Secure (HTTPS) link, and the security firm's Web server will then send its server certificate to your web browser.

- Your web browser first checks the certificate validity period, and then it checks the certificate's issuer to see if the CA is legitimate. It will then check the certificate's common name with the domain name entered in the browser address bar. If any of these checkpoints fail, you will be prompted either to trust the server certification and continue or abort the connection.

- If the server certificate passes all the checkpoints, the server is authenticated and you will have a secure session established. Sensitive data traveling between your web browser and online trading Web server will be encrypted and protected by the SSL connection.

You can obtain certificates from a CA, although there are some trusted third-party commercial CA organizations, such as, Verisign.com and Thwate.com. Alternatively, you can create your own CA using Certificate Services included in Windows Server 2003. Before you configure your own CA, you first will need more details about CA and its structure.

Certificate Authority and its Structure

CAs accept certificate requests and verify the request information before the certificate is issued to clients. The CA is also responsible for revoking invalid certificates by publishing the details in a list called the *certificate revocation list* (CRL). Every CA has a certificate to confirm its own identity;

this certificate can be issued by another CA or by the CA itself (if the CA is a *root* CA). The following outlines CA types and their relationships:

- A *root* CA, also known as a *root authority* is the most trusted type of CA in its hierarchical structure.

- A *subordinate* CA is one that has been verified by the root CA and is trusted by users in the certification chain.

- A *certificate hierarchy* defines a model of trust for certificates in which the structure is created by parent-child relationships between certification authorities.

Microsoft Certificate Services allows you to create either *Enterprise* or *standalone* CAs, depending on your organization's needs. An *Enterprise* CA requires the existence of an Active Directory (AD), and should be used when you need to issue and manage certification through the entire enterprise Active Directory domain. *Standalone* CAs do not require the presence of an Active Directory. They are less automated than the Enterprise CA model, and user enrollment is typically conducted via web pages using *web enrollment support* (discussed later in the chapter).

Certificate hierarchies allow Certificate Services to scale to many levels. For example, in a big Enterprise organization, you can set up many CAs and define their roles accordingly. You can have different root CAs for different uses, such as server certificate and client certificate. Or you might want to have two different subordinate or intermediate CAs to handle different certificate requests. You may also want to create parent/child CA relationships when you need to grant organizational or geographical business units the ability to manage and issue certificates within that department or location.

To learn more about Certificate Services, refer to the Windows Server 2003 help documentation or the Windows Server 2003 PKI Operations Guide at www.microsoft.com/technet/prodtechnol/ windowsserver2003/technologies/security/ws03pkog.mspx.

Reality Check...

Microsoft Certificate Services allows you to create your own CA for issuing and managing digital certificates. Ensure you understand the concept behind Certificate Services such as certificate usage, types and information hold in the certificate. You are advice to understand your organization needs and its planning when you decided type of CA you will be configuring.

Configuring Certificate Services

Certificate Services allows you to create your own *Certificate Authority* (CA), enabling you to issue certificates for your organization. This component is available in Windows Server 2003 *Standard, Enterprise* and *Data Center* edition, if you are running Windows Server 2003 *Web edition*, you are not able to install Certificate Services.

> **BY THE BOOK...**
>
> When you install Certificate Services in Windows Server 2003, the following two components are included:
>
> *Certificate Services CA* This is the core component that enables you to establish your own CA. The component must be installed for CA to function properly. Once it's installed, you can manage certificates using Certificate Authority Microsoft Management Console (MMC) in Administrative Tools.
>
> *Certificate Services Web Enrollment Support* This component is optional; it enables clients to summit certificates requests via IIS server. This feature is made possible using Active Server Pages (ASP) scripts.

You will begin with establishing your own CA, and then you will learn detail related to certificate management using the certificate authority management console. Finally, you will get to know more about certificate services web enrollment support component and details about /*CertSrv* virtual directory in IIS server and files associated with the web based component.

Configuring Your Certificate Authority

Now that you understand the basic concepts about certificates, certification authorities and types, you are ready to configure Certificate Services and create your own CA. This section will focus on the installation and configuration of a standalone CA.

To install Certificate Services to support standalone CAs, perform these steps:

1. Click **Start**, and then click **Control Panel**.
2. Double-click **Add or Remove Programs** and click **Add/Remove Windows Components**.

3. In the **Windows Components Wizard** dialog box (Figure 10.1), enable the **Certificate Services** option.

Figure 10.1 Installing Certificate Services – Windows Components Wizard

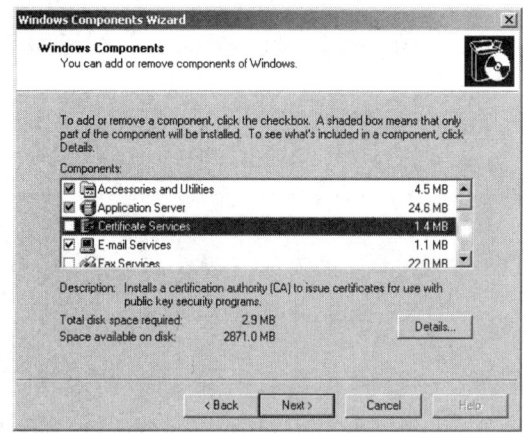

4. A warning dialog box will appear (Figure 10.2) to inform you that once Certificate Services is installed, you will not be able to change the machine's name or domain membership. Click **Yes**.

Figure 10.2 Installing Certificate Services – Microsoft Certificate Services Dialog Box

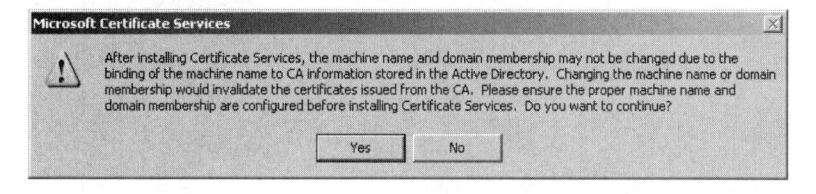

5. Click **Details** to view the Certificate Services subcomponents (Figure 10.3). You will see a new dialog box (Figure 10.3). **Certificate Services CA** is the component that allows you to issue and manage certificates, and **Certificate Services Web Enrollment Support** enables users to request certificates via the IIS server. This component is required when configuring a standalone CA. Ensure both options are enabled, and click **OK**.

Figure 10.3 Installing Certificate Services – Certificate Services Subcomponents

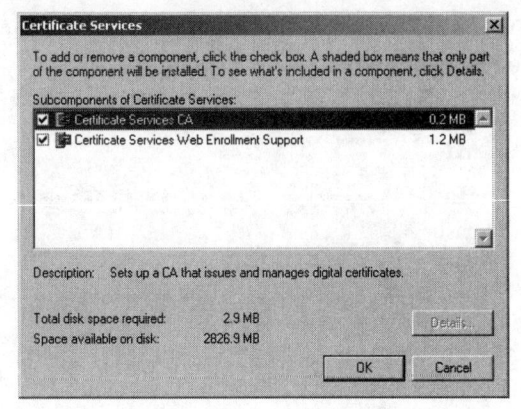

6. Click **Next** to continue with the installation.
7. Next, you will be prompted to select the **CA Type** (Figure 10.4). Select **Stand-alone root CA**.

Figure 10.4 Installing Certificate Services– Selecting CA Type

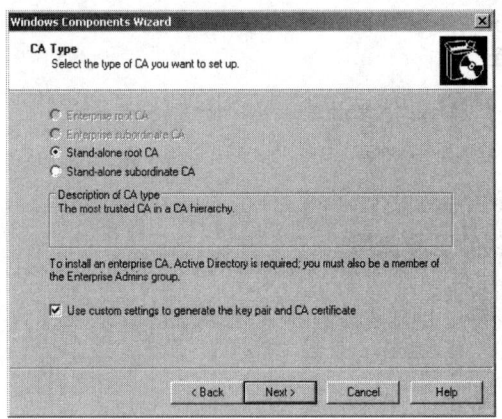

8. To customize a key pair and CA certificate, ensure the **Use custom settings to generate the key pair and CA certificate** option is enabled.
9. Click **Next**.
10. If you choose to customize a CA certificate, you will be prompted to customize it in the next step (Figure 10.5). Choose the desired **CSP** (Cryptographic Service Provider), **Hash algorithm** and **Key length**, then click **Next**.

- **Cryptographic Service Provider** CSP provides the Crypto Application Programming Interface (CryptoAPI), which is responsible for managing the keys used in the cryptographic process. There are many CSPs included in Certificate Services; each provider will have a different implementation of CryptoAPI. The default CSP setting is **Microsoft Strong Cryptographic Provider**.

- **Hash algorithm** A mathematical formula that creates a hash value from a piece of data. The algorithm is useful for detecting changes in the data object, as tampered data will not have the same hash value as original piece of data. The default hash algorithm setting is **Secure Hash Algorithm (SHA-1)**.

- **Key Length** This specifies the key length to be generated by the CSP; the longer the key length, the stronger the security, but longer key lengths require more resources to process. The default key length setting is **2048**.

Figure 10.5 Installing Certificate Services – Customizing a CA Certificate

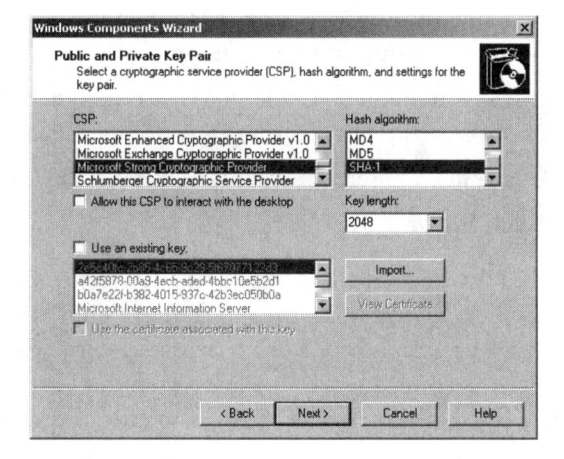

11. Next, you will be prompted for information to identify the CA (Figure 10.6). Enter the **Common Name for this CA** and **Distinguished name suffix**. Note that these names cannot be changed once Certificate Services is complete.

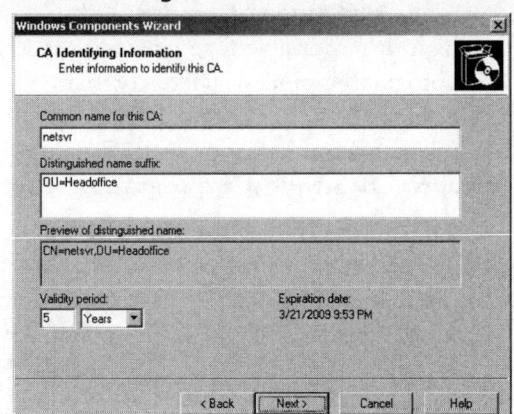

Figure 10.6 Customizing a CA Certificate – CA Identification

12. Use the **Validity period** fields to specify the validity duration for the root CA, then click **Next**.
13. Specify the storage location for the **certificate database, certificate database log** and the **certificate shared folder**, and then click **Next**. By default, certificate database and log is created at **%windir%/system32/certlog/** and the shared folders are **CertConfig** and **CertEnroll**.
14. If IIS is running, you will receive a notice that IIS must be stopped before installation can continue. Click **OK**.
15. If prompted, insert the Windows Server 2003 installation CD.
16. Click **Finish**.

Now that you have installed Certificate Services, you can issue and manage digital certificates using the CA. You can either request certificates via the Certification Authority Microsoft Management Console (MMC), or you can instruct your users to request certificates via the IIS Web server. To open the Certification Authority MMC, perform these steps:

1. Click **Start | Control Panel**, double-click **Administrative Tools**, then double-click **Certification Authority**.
2. In the Certification Authority MMC, expand the desired computer node (Figure 10.7).

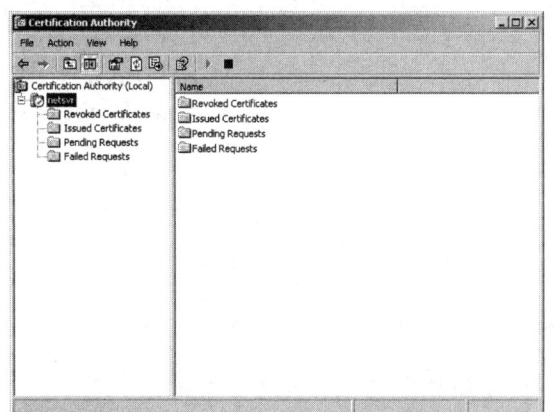

Figure 10.7 Certification Authority MMC

Four folders are shown:

- **Revoked Certificates** This folder keeps track of revoked certificates. Certificates can be revoked for several reasons, for example, if the key or CA has been compromised or has ceased operation. Revoked certificates will be published in a certificate revocation list. Revoked certificates are invalid and cannot be used. The lists are retrieved by clients and cached for a period of time until the lifespan of the CRL expires. At that time, clients will retrieve a new CRL from the CA. For more information about CRLs, refer to: www.microsoft.com/resources/documentation/WindowsServ/2003/standard/proddocs/en-us/sag_CS_CertRevoke.asp.

- **Issued Certificates** This folder holds certificates that have been issued by this CA. You can view the certificate details by double-clicking the desired certificate.

- **Pending Requests** This folder stores new certificate requests. As a system administrator, you will verify requester information and the details that have been submitted in the request. After that, you can either **approve** or **reject** the request.

- **Failed Requests** This folder contains failed certificate requests. If you cannot verify a requester's identity or a request submitted contains invalid information, you have the ability to deny and fail the certificate request.

For more details on how to manage and issue certificates in **Certificate Authority** MMC, you can refer to the Windows Server 2003 help documentation.

Once you have installed the Certificate Services Web Enrollment Support component, you will notice that the **Default Web Site** will contain a new **CertSrv** virtual directory (Figure 10.8). This virtual directory is mapped to %windir%/system32/CertSrv/ and contains ASP scripts that enable web enrollment support. It allows users to submit certificate requests via web pages, view request statuses and download issued certificates. Users can also download CA certificates, certificate chains, and CRLs using this virtual directory.

Figure 10.8 Certificate Services Virtual Directories – IIS Manager

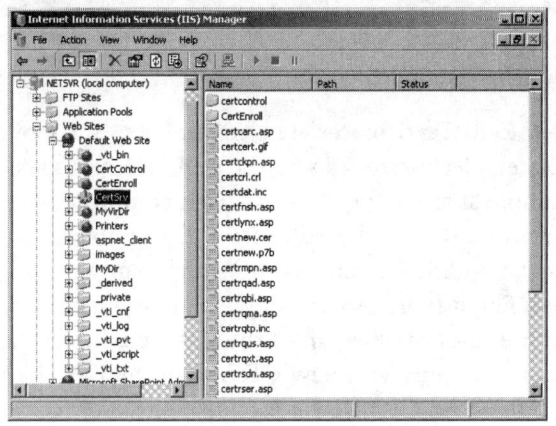

The CertSrv directory contains the **certcontrol** and **CertEnroll** subdirectories. certcontrol is mapped to %windir%/system32/CertSrv/certcontrol/, and keeps enrollment cabinet (cab) files for different operating systems. CertEnroll is mapped to %windir%/system32/CertSrv/CertEnroll/, and holds CRLs of revoked certificates, as well as a list of CA certificates that must be installed on the client's web browser in order to trust your CA.

To access the Certificate Services Web Enrollment Support component, open your web browser and select the **/certsrv/** virtual directory. For example, if your Web server name is called **netsvr**, enter **http://netsvr/certsrv/** in the browser's address bar (Figure 10.9).

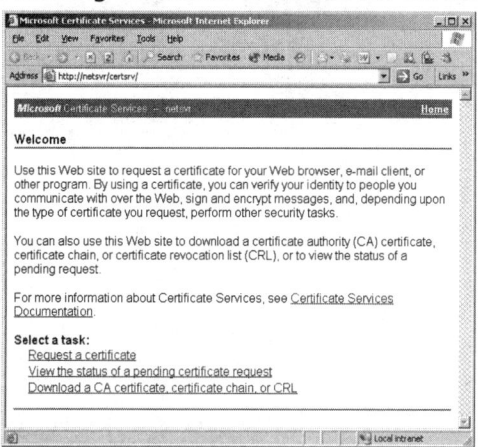

Figure 10.9 Browsing Certificate Services Web Enrollment

You can request a certificate by clicking the **Request a certificate** link. All new certificate requests will be stored in the **Pending Requests** folder in the Certificate Authority MMC. You can also view pending requests or download issued certificates by clicking on the **View the status of a pending certificate request** link. To download a CA certificates, click the **Download a CA certificate, certificate chain, or CRL** link.

For more details on requesting server certificates for an SSL connection, refer to Chapter 5. You can now generate the certificate signing request (CSR), which is an unsigned certificate request file containing your server information. Once this is submitted to the CA server, you can follow these steps to issue or deny the certificate request:

1. Click **Start | Control Panel**, double-click **Administrative Tools**, then double-click **Certification Authority**.

2. In the Certification Authority MMC, expand the desired computer node, then click on **Pending Requests**. All pending requests will be listed in the right-hand pane (Figure 10.10).

Figure 10.10 Viewing Pending Requests – Certificate Authority MMC

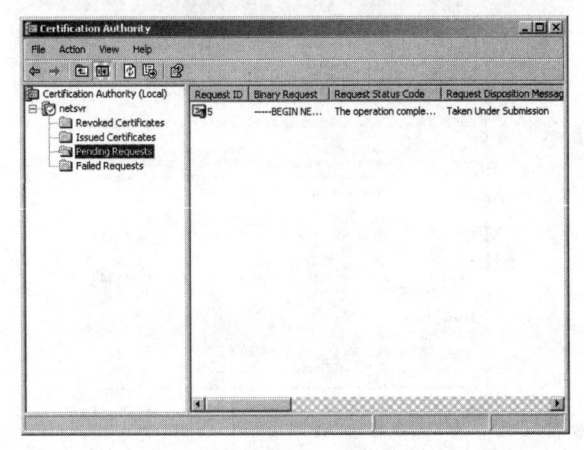

3. To view more details about a pending request, right-click it, point to **All Tasks**, and select **View Attributes or Extensions**. To grant or deny the certificate, right-click the certificate and select either **Issue** or **Deny** (Figure 10.11).

Figure 10.11 Issue a Pending Request

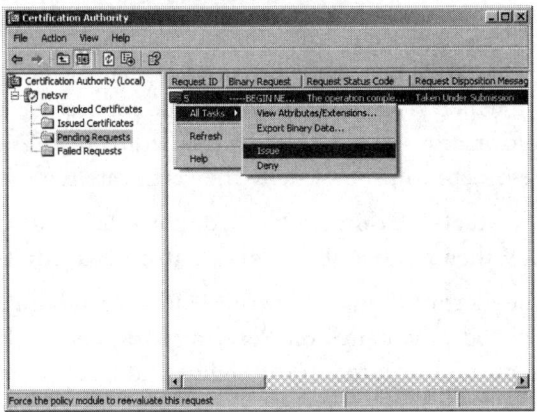

Once a certificate is issued, you can inform users to download the certificate at the CA server website. For more information about installing issued certificates to a website, refer to Chapter 5.

Finally, visit the best practices with Windows Server 2003 Certificate Services at http://www.microsoft.com/technet/prodtechnol/windowsserver2003/technologies/security/ws3pkibp.mspx.

> **REALITY CHECK...**
>
> Microsoft Certificate Services allows you to create your own CA for issuing and managing digital certificates. Once installed, you can issue and manage certificates with the Certificate Authority MMC. Users can use the Web Enrollment Support Component to request a certificate and download issued certificates.
>
> Web enrollment support is made possible using ASP scripts. You will need to enable ASP service extensions in the IIS Web Service Extensions list to facilitate this component. If you installed the *Urlscan* component, refer to chapter 5 for information on customizing *Urlscan* to allow web enrollment support.

Securing Certificate Services Web Enrollment Support

Certificate Services Web Enrollment Support is a series of ASP scripts that are hosted on a website, so you secure web enrollment the same way that you secure web resource contents. You can also refer to Chapter 4 and 5 for more details on securing website resources.

> **BY THE BOOK...**
>
> Certificate Services Web Enrollment Support is actually running as a web application on the IIS server. You can protect and secure web enrollment using:
>
> **Authentication** Allows you to authenticate users before granting them access to your CA certificate resources.
>
> **Connection** Controls access by granting and denying client access based on IP addresses and domain names. By default, all IP addresses have access to web enrollment support. You can configure connection restrictions to limit web enrollment access.

To help protect your CA web enrollment application, you need to configure various security settings to prevent malicious attacks to the application. When a client requests a certificate via the CA web enrollment, the client is actually sending a request to the website. IIS will communicate with the Certificate Services and place the request in your CA.

Web Enrollment Virtual Directory Permissions

As explained in the previous section, after the Certificate Services Web Enrollment Support is installed, a virtual directory named *CertSrv* is created under the default website. This virtual directory will then be the main entry point for the web enrollment component. Figure 10.12 outlines the virtual directory permissions for /*CertSrv*.

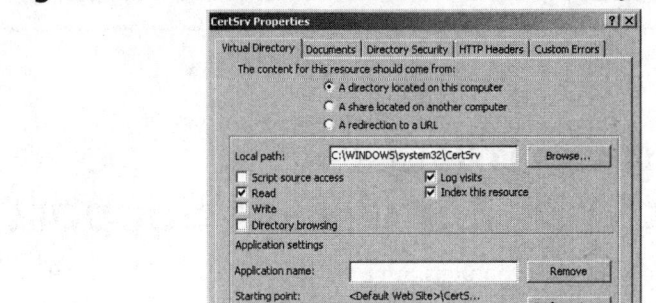

Figure 10.12 CA Web Enrollment Virtual Directory Permissions

Only the following general permissions are selected:

- **Read** Enabled by default, this permission allows users to view the directory or file resource.

- **Log visit** Enabled by default, this permission creates a log entry in the log file when users access it.

- **Index this resource** Indexes the resource's content for searching support. This option is enabled by default if the indexing service is installed on the IIS server.

For execution permissions, this virtual directory is configured for **Script Only**. This permission allows the execution of the ASP scripting engine, which is required for the web enrollment support component. You are not recommended to modify any of the preconfigured permissions. You can refer Chapter 4 Setting Website Permissions for more details.

Authenticating Web Enrollment

In Chapter 5, we discussed different website authentication methods supported in IIS 6.0. You can configure different authentication modes to authorize user access. Authentications protect CA web enrollment from being wrongly used or abused. For example, with authentication, users have to be authorized before they can submit new certificate requests or download issued certificates. You can make sure that only valid users can request certificates.

Table 10.1 lists the different authentication methods you can use to configure CA web enrollment. These authentication methods can be applied to any website application.

Table 10.1 Authentication Methods

Method	Description
Anonymous	No username or password is required to access this server. The default anonymous user is the IUSR_<COMPUTERNAME> account.
Integrated Windows	Authentication for valid Windows user account is required, and user credentials are sent in encrypted mode.
Digest	Authentication for valid Active Directory user account is required, and user credentials are sent in encrypted mode.
Basic	Authentication for valid Windows user account is required, and user credentials are sent in plain text mode.
Microsoft .NET Passport	Authentication for valid .NET passport user account is required, and user credentials are sent in encrypted mode.

By default, only anonymous authentication is configured for CA web enrollment. It is recommended that you disable anonymous access and configure another authentication mode. With anonymous access enabled, any user can submit a new request. Although you need to approve the request and issue the certificate before it can be used, limiting anonymous access will help you avoid unneeded administrative tasks. To configure another authentication mode, perform these steps:

1. In IIS Manager, expand the local computer, expand the **Web Sites** folder, expand the desired website, right-click on the **CertSrv** virtual directory, and then click **Properties**.

2. On the **Directory Security** tab, under **Authentication and access control**, click **Edit**.
3. In the **Authentication Methods** dialog box (Figure 10.13), enable the desired authentication method.

Figure 10.13 Configuring CA Web Enrollment Authentications – Authentication Methods Dialog Box

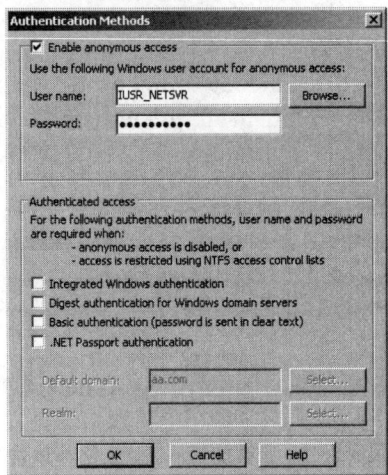

4. Deselect the **Enable anonymous access** option.
5. Click **OK**.

You can refer to Chapter 5 for more details on configuring website authentication. It is important to note that basic authentication sends user credentials in plain text mode, and it is recommended that you configure SSL to secure the connection and protect transmitted data.

Restricting Access to Protect your Web Enrollment

To further protect your CA web enrollment, you can use connection control to block or grant access based on client IP addresses or domain names. This allows you to restrict access if a client IP address or domain name is not on the permitted access list. For example, if you have a CA issuing certificates for a few external vendor users, you should limit CA web enrollment access to the vendors' network IP addresses. This will ensure only valid vendor users are able to access your web-based CA and submit new certificate requests. To secure CA web enrollment, you will first configure authentication and require users to supply their usernames and passwords before they can gain access to the CA web enrollment; you can either have one common user login account for all users, or you can create different user accounts for each user. Next, you can configure IP address restriction to further protect your web-based CA. You should deny all IP access and grant access only to specified users or networks. For more details on how to configure connection restrictions, refer to Chapter 4.

To raise the security bar, you can apply various security measures to your CA web enrollment using built-in security features such as SSL to secure the connection between clients and the server. You are also able to further restrict access by configuring permissions based on users or user groups in the Certificate Authority MMC. The default user groups and their permissions are listed in Table 10.2.

Table 10.2 Default User Rights in Certificate Authority

User / Group	Access Rights
Administrators	Issue and Manage Certificates
	Manage CA
Everyone	Request Certificates

For example, if you only want to allow users in the Accounting department to request certificates, you can remove the **Everyone** group and grant the **Request Certificates** permission to the Accounting department user groups. Or if you wish to deny users from the Projects department from accessing the CA web enrollment, you could specifically deny access to the Project department's users. If you need other users to help you manage and issue certificates for this CA, you can grant the **Issue and Manage Certificates** permission to that user.

To configure user access permissions in the Certificate Authority MMC, perform the following steps:

1. Click **Start** | **Control Panel**, double-click **Administrative Tools**, and double-click **Certification Authority**.

2. In the Certification Authority MMC, right-click the computer node and click **Properties**.

3. Click the **Security** tab (Figure 10.14).

Figure 10.14 Configuring CA Web Enrollment Access Permissions

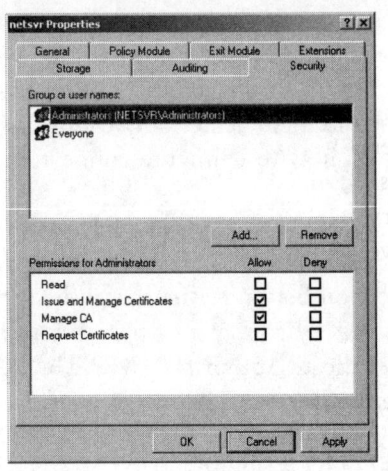

4. To add a new user or group, click **Add**.
5. To remove a user or group, select the desired user or group and click **Remove**.
6. To modify user or group permissions, enable the **Allow** or **Deny** options for the listed permissions.
7. Click **OK**.

For more details on configuring security settings, please refer to the Windows Server 2003 help documentation.

REALITY CHECK...

After enabling CA Web Enrollment Support, you must ensure you have followed the guidelines discussed in this section to protect your web-based CA. It is not recommended that you allow anonymous access for CA web enrollment. If you need to change the authentication methods, be sure you have gone through the Chapter 5 for more details about each authentication mode. Finally, to further restrict access, it is recommended that you configure access control to grant and deny access based on client IP addresses and domain names.

Monitoring Certificate Services Web Enrollment Access

Monitoring web access log files can help you keep track of access to your CA web enrollment component. By default, /CertSrv virtual directory logging is enabled. You can analyze log entries to understand how web enrollments are being accessed and to learn which users are accessing the server and which web browsers they are using. Access log files will also give you hints to help you troubleshoot web-based CA problems if there are connection issues. One more benefit of enabling activity logging is that it allows you to detect if there are unauthorized users trying to gain access to your web enrollment support component.

BY THE BOOK...

IIS 6.0 allows you to collect user access activity information by enabling the logging feature. Information can be logged using the following formats:

W3C Extended A customizable format that allows you to configure the types of information to be collected when IIS writes the log entry. This format follows the W3C working draft specification. You can visit www.w3.org/TR/WD-logfile for information about the working draft.

NCSA Common National Center for Supercomputing Applications (NCSA) common format is an old log file specification whose details are fixed and not customizable. Data captured includes remote host name, data, time, request type, HTTP status and number of bytes sent by the server.

IIS Log A fixed format that records more information than NCSA common format. These extra details include time taken to process the request, bytes received by server, and Win32 status.

ODCB Logging A fixed set of data that can be recorded in a database source.

New log file features introduced in IIS 6.0 include:

UTF-8 logging In earlier IIS versions, log files are logged in ASCII text or local codepage mode. In IIS 6.0 you can configure the logging in Universal Transformation Format (UTF) 8 mode. UTF-8 mode logging allows you to log every request in UTF-8 encoding characters, which support more text characters than standard ASCII format. For example, with UTF-8 logging, you can have request log entries that are in Unicode text, such as Japanese content filenames.

Remote logging In IIS 6.0, you can redirect log files on a remote share network path using the Universal Naming Convention (UNC) method. This allows you to configure a different log path to centralized log storage for backup and analysis purposes.

Centralized Binary logging This format allows multiple websites to write unformatted binary log data to a single file.

HTTP Error logging This log file format captures HTTP API errors record by the HTTP.SYS driver.

Protocol substatus This is only available in W3C extended format, and provides further detail in addition to standard protocol status to help you further understand request statuses.

To find out more about logging web enrollment component access activities, please refer to Chapter 4's *Enabling and Securing Web Access Log File* section.

REALITY CHECK...

By default, logging is enabled for the */CertSrv* virtual directory and you are not advised to disable it, as logging access allows you to monitor access to your web enrollment activity such as client request new certificate, viewing pending request, downloading issued certificates and CA certificates. You can also audit log files to check if any unauthorized user is trying to gain access to the web based CA. Finally, be sure you follow the guidelines in Chapter 4 to protect the log files using NTFS permissions.

Your A** is Covered if You...

- ☑ Configured web enrollment user authentication support.
- ☑ Configured user access rights for CA.
- ☑ Configured an SSL connection between the CA server and client computers.
- ☑ Configured IP address and domain name restrictions.
- ☑ Enabled web enrollment virtual directory logging.

Chapter 11
Securing Web Publishing

In This Chapter

Traditional Web publishing has involved utilizing the File Transfer Protocol (FTP), whereby users upload new content to their Web server via a dedicated FTP client. This process has a number of downsides. IIS 6.0 offers two Web publishing technologies that overcome many of these disadvantages. The first is Web Distributed Authoring and Versioning (WebDAV), an open protocol defined in RFC standards 2518 and 3253, and the second is FrontPage Server Extensions (FPSE), a proprietary publishing mechanism that offers additional flexibility over WebDAV. In this chapter we will cover:

- Configuring and securing WebDAV Publishing
- Configuring and securing FrontPage Server Extensions publishing

By the time you reach the end of this chapter, you should be familiar with the steps involved in enabling both WebDAV and FPSE publishing. Additionally, you should be aware of the security options that each publishing mechanism offers and how to tailor these to the your organization's needs.

Configuring and Securing WebDAV Publishing

Traditional Web publishing has involved the use of FTP clients and servers. This method has a number of downsides. It requires an extra server (FTP) on the Web server, it requires additional ports to be opened in firewalls, it requires a dedicated FTP client on the user's machine, and updating content cannot be done "in place" on the server. Instead, it must be downloaded to the user's machine, edited, and uploaded again. WebDAV obviates these problems by allowing editing over HTTP. Additionally, it supports a rudimentary file-locking system that prevents two users attempting to write to the same file at the same time.

> **BY THE BOOK...**
>
> WebDAV is an open publishing protocol defined in RFCs 2518 and 3253. It allows publishing over standard HTTP protocols and the use of the same robust authentication mechanisms that can be used for normal Web site authentication. Because WebDAV is an open standard, clients can use any WebDAV client, either from Microsoft or from a third party. Both Windows XP and Windows Server 2003 have built-in WebDAV clients that allow authoring from within Windows. Additionally, products from Microsoft Office 2000 support WebDAV. Users with Internet Explorer v5 or later can also use WebDAV publishing.
>
> *Note:* Utilizing the WebDAV client in Windows XP or Windows Server 2003 requires the Webclient service to be started. This option is set to *Disabled* by default in Windows Server 2003 . It must be started before you can use Windows Server 2003 as a WebDAV client.

Installing and Enabling WebDAV

WebDAV Publishing is not enabled by default when you install IIS 6.0. If you did not already install and enable WebDAV publishing when you installed IIS 6.0, you need to follow these steps:

1. Open the **Add/Remove Programs Control Panel**. Select **Add/Remove Windows Components**.

2. Under **Application Server | Internet Information Services | World Wide Web Service**, check the **WebDAV Publishing** component. *Note:* WebDAV Publishing is always installed as part of IIS 6.0. This procedure merely enables the WebDAV Publishing components.

3. Click **OK** to exit the dialog boxes, and click **Next** to enable WebDav Publishing.

Alternatively, the WebDAV Publishing Web Service Extension can be enabled via the IIS Manager. (For more information on Web Service Extensions, see Chapter 4, "Web Server Security.") To enable the WebDAV Publishing extension:

1. Open the **IIS Manager**, and locate the **Web Service Extensions** node.

2. Select **WebDav Publishing** in the right-hand pane, and click the **Allow** button (see Figure 11.1).

Figure 11.1 Enabling the WebDAV Publishing Web Service Extension

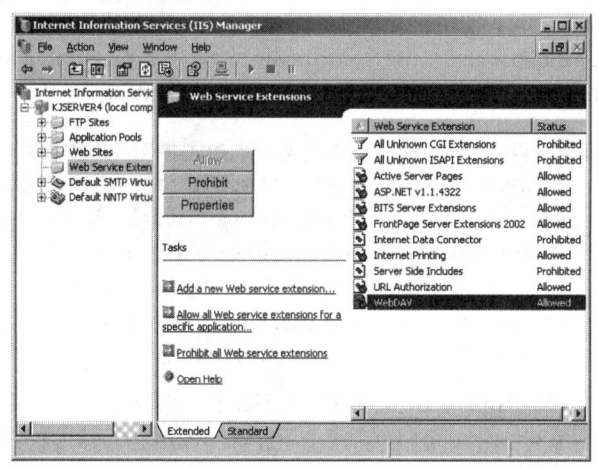

The preceding steps enable WebDAV Publishing on your Web sites. You should note the following:

- WebDAV Publishing cannot be selectively enabled or disabled on a site-by-site basis. It is enabled or disabled for all Web sites on the server. However, what users can do is restricted by IIS Web permissions and NTFS file permissions. If you do not enable appropriate permissions, users will not be able to perform publishing actions. You need to rely on these permissions if you want to allow publishing on one Web site but not on another.

- If you are running URLScan, you need to edit the default urlscan.ini configuration file to allow the HTTP verbs that WebDAV Publishing uses. In addition to standard HTTP headers such as *PUT* (to copy data to the server), *DELETE* (to delete a resource on the server), and *GET* (to retrieve a file), you need to allow WebDAV-specific headers such as *PROPFIND* (return properties of the object, such as file size, author, or the like), *LOCK* (place a lock on the resource to allow editing), *UNLOCK* (release a lock), and *COPY/MOVE* (copy or move a resource). You can find a full list of WebDAV headers in section 8 of RFC 2518 at www.ietf.org/rfc/rfc2518.txt.

Configuring and Securing WebDAV

After enabling WebDAV, you need to configure appropriate security permissions to allow authorized users an appropriate level of access while denying unauthorized users permissions to perform publishing actions. To do this requires configuring three sets of settings:

- **Decide on an appropriate authentication mechanism** If all users of the Web site are required to authenticate using a valid Windows account, you can disable **Allow Anonymous Authentication** and enable one (or more) of the authentication mechanisms that IIS 6.0 supports. For more information on the authentication mechanisms that IIS 6.0 supports, see Chapter 5, "Advanced Web Server Security."

- **Configure appropriate IIS 6.0 Web permissions for the Web site, folder, or file you want to expose for publishing** These settings determine the maximum possible rights that users can utilize. If an IIS 6.0 Web permission (e.g., Write) is not enabled, no users are able to write data to the server via WebDAV. For more information on IIS Web permissions, see Chapter 4, "Web Server Security."

- **Configure NTFS permissions** These determine the permissions that individual users and groups have when performing publishing actions. You can use NTFS permissions to further restrict the IIS Web permissions (for example, to allow one group to perform writing actions while allowing another group only read actions). However, NTFS permissions are subordinate to IIS Web permissions. If an NTFS permission is granted (e.g., Write), the user will not be able to perform a write action if the corresponding IIS Web permission is not enabled. For more information on NTFS permissions, see Chapter 4, "Web Server Security," and Windows 2003 Online Help.

When choosing an authentication mechanism, decide whether your Web site needs to allow anonymous visitors. If it doesn't, disable **Allow Anonymous Authentication** in the IIS Manager, and enable one (or more) of the available authentication mechanisms. This ensures that all users require valid Windows credentials to access the Web site, and it means that anonymous visitors to your site cannot perform any authoring actions.

For an intranet environment, consider enabling Integrated Windows Authentication. For an external-facing environment, consider the use of Advanced Digest/Digest Authentication or Basic Authentication. If you are using Basic Authentication, you should secure the transmission of user credentials by utilizing Secure Sockets Layer (SSL), because user credentials are passed unencrypted when Basic Authentication is used. For more information on each authentication mechanism, see Chapter 5, "Advanced Web Server Security."

There is a security risk if you enable *Script Source Access* whilst allowing anonymous access to your site. You can deny the anonymous user account permissions to write new content to the server, but you can't deny the anonymous user the NTFS *read* permission (this is required to browse pages on the site). If you allow anonymous access, the combination of NTFS *read* permission plus IIS *Read* and *Script Source Access* web permissions allows all users to view the source code of your dynamic files.

It may be best to create two separate websites that point to the same content; one for anonymous access (enable IIS *Read* web permissions), and one for authenticated access (enable IIS Script Source Access web permissions).

After choosing your authentication mechanism, you need to configure IIS Web permissions. These can be applied to all Web sites, an individual site, or an individual folder or file. To configure IIS Web permissions:

1. Open the **IIS Manager**, and locate the website, folder, or file you for which you want to change the permissions. If you want to change the permissions on all Web sites, select the **websites** node. Right-click and choose **Properties**.

2. On the **Home Directory**, **Directory**, or **File** tab, select the appropriate Web permissions (see Figure 11.2). The available Web permissions are shown in Table 11.1.

Figure 11.2 Configuring IIS Web Permissions to Allow WebDAV Publishing

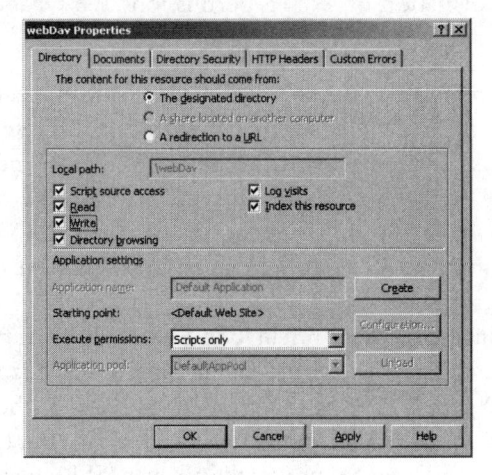

Table 11.1 IIS 6.0 Web Permissions

Permission	Explanation
Read	Allows users to read static files (including the ability to copy them off the server). If Script Source Access is enabled, users can read dynamic files as well.
Script Source Access	Allows users access to dynamic files. If Read permissions are also enabled, users can read the files (including the ability to copy them off the server). If Write permissions are also enabled, users can write dynamic files to the server. If neither Read nor Write permissions are enabled, this setting has no effect.
Write	Allows users to write static files to the server. If Script Source Access is enabled, users can write dynamic files (e.g., ASP or ASP.NET files).
Directory Browsing	Allows users to get a list of files in a folder. This setting is not available when setting permission on a single file.
Log Visits	Although this setting is available in the same section, it does not grant or revoke any WebDAV publishing privileges. It is used to determine whether requests (WebDAV or otherwise) for this resource are logged in the IIS request logs.

Continued

Table 11.1 IIS 6.0 Web Permissions

Permission	Explanation
Index this resource	Allows the resource to be index by Index Server. If the resource is indexed and Index Server is running, users can search based on the text contained in the resource.

3. Grant only those permissions that are required for the particular Web site, folder or file. Click **OK** to exit the dialog box and save your settings.

Note: If the *Execute* permissions are set to *Scripts Only*, executable files (.exe) are treated as static files (similar to HTML files or images). If *Execute* permissions are set to *Scripts* and *Executables*, executable files are treated like dynamic files (such as ASP scripts), and accessing these requires allowing Script Source Access. This only applies to executables that do not have an associated Web Service Extension. Any executable that has a Web Service Extension is always treated as dynamic content.

After configuring IIS Web permissions, you need to determine appropriate NTFS permissions (as shown in Table 11.2). These NTFS permissions determine what actions each user on your Web site is capable of performing, subject to the limits of the IIS Web permissions. For information on how to configure NTFS permissions, using either Windows Explorer or command-line tools, see Chapter 4, "Configuring Web Server Security."

Table 11.2 NTFS Permissions

Give the User…	To Allow…
Read (R)	Users to read files located on the Web site, folder, or the individual file. If **Script Source Access** is enabled in the IIS Web permissions, users can access the source code of dynamic files (such as ASP or ASP.Net files).
Read+Execute (RX)	Users to run executable (.exe) files in addition to being able to read files.
Write (W)	Users to write files to the server (including copying and moving existing files). If **Script Source Access** is enabled in the IIS Web permissions, users can write dynamic files to the server (such as ASP or ASP.NET files).
Delete (D)	Users to delete files from the server.

Continued

Table 11.2 NTFS Permissions

Give the User...	To Allow...
List Folder Contents	Users to obtain a list of files in a folder.
Modify (RWXD)	Users to make modifications to any files. Users can read files, copy or move files, write files, and delete files.

After configuring appropriate NTFS permissions, you are now ready to utilize WebDAV Publishing. On a Windows Server 2003 you need to start the Webclient service manually to utilize the built-in WebDav client. To test your WebDAV folder:

1. Open **Internet Explorer**. From the **File** menu, choose the **Open** option.

2. Enter your WebDAV-enabled URL (for example, http://yourserver.com/webDavFolder/) and check the **Open as Web Folder** check box.

3. Alternatively, you can open your Windows **Network Places** folder. Start the **Add a new network place** wizard, and enter the same URL as the network place to be created.

Your WebDAV-enabled folder should now appear, assuming that you enabled the IIS Directory Browsing Web permission. If you did not, you need to enter the exact name of a file to read it (see Figure 11.3).

Figure 11.3 Viewing a WebDAV-Enabled Folder

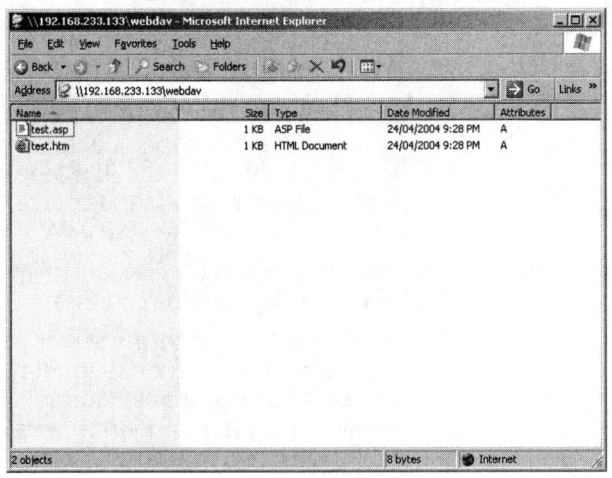

> **REALITY CHECK…**
>
> WebDAV is an open, widely supported standard. It allows a number of diverse clients to connect to your Web site and perform authoring actions. However, the WebDAV implementation on IIS 6.0 requires that you configure appropriate NTFS and IIS Web permissions to allow authoring. These permissions may include granting users NTFS Write permissions to a Web site or enabling IIS Directory Browsing Web permissions. Allowing this type of access constitutes a security risk because it increases the attack surface of your Web server. Additionally WebDAV Publishing cannot be selectively enabled for individual Web sites (only prevented by configuring restrictive NTFS/IIS permissions). For a more flexible and secure publishing system, you might want to examine Microsoft's FrontPage Server Extensions (FPSE).

Configuring and Security FrontPage Server Extensions

An alternative publishing technology to WebDAV is Microsoft FrontPage Server Extensions (FPSE). FPSE, however, extends beyond authoring. Using FPSE, clients can create and manage site themes (a common look for all pages) and utilize server-side FPSE components that allow dynamic content to be created without the user having to write much, if any, code. Multiple authors can work on a Web site utilizing the FPSE source control features.

> **BY THE BOOK…**
>
> Microsoft FrontPage Server Extensions is a set of server-side technologies that allow FrontPage clients (such as Microsoft FrontPage 2003 and Visual Studio.Net) to author (or publish) content to a FPSE extended Web site. Additionally, FPSE exposes a set of application technologies that allow users to create dynamic content without needing to write much (or any) code—for example connecting to databases, creating contact forms, or hosting online polls.
>
> FrontPage authoring is available over HTTP (or over HTTPS) and supports standard authentication mechanisms for authenticating users. FPSE supports the concept of *roles,* which are similar to Windows groups. Roles can be granted particular rights,

and then users (or groups) can be placed into one or more roles. Users and groups can be either Windows users and groups or users created within FPSE that are only valid for FPSE authoring. Windows XP and Windows Server 2003 both include a simple FrontPage client. Access to the full feature set of FPSE requires a more complete client, such as Microsoft FrontPage or Visual Studio.Net.

FPSE technology also underlies Microsoft's Sharepoint products, such as Windows Sharepoint Services (WSS), Sharepoint Portal Server (SPS), and Sharepoint Team Services (STS). For more information about Windows Sharepoint Services, a free add-on for Windows Server 2003, visit www.microsoft.com/windowsserver2003/technologies/sharepoint/default.mspx.

Complete coverage of FPSE would require a book in itself, so we examine only two areas in this chapter. First, we will install and enable FPSE to allow authoring. Then we will look at securing your FPSE extended Web site. The security section has information relevant to securing FPSE, whether you use it merely for allowing users to publish content or you use the full gamut of services provided by FPSE.

Installing FrontPage Server Extensions

Before installing FPSE, you should be aware of the following installation requirements and restrictions. If your server does not meet the requirements, attempting to configure FPSE may fail or have unexpected results:

- **FPSE requires NTFS formatted drives** This includes the system drive to which FPSE's files will be installed and any drives that contain Web site content that you would like to make available for authoring. NTFS provides performance, reliability, and security enhancements over FAT formatted drives, and Microsoft recommends formatting all drives in a server using the NTFS file system. Windows Server 2003 has a command-line tool, convert.exe, that you can use to convert FAT formatted drives to NTFS formatted drives. Please consult the Windows Server 2003 Online Help for more information on using this tool.

- **FPSE does not support nested Web sites** If a folder available in one Web site is available in another Web site (either as a virtual directory or as the root of the second Web site), unexpected behavior may result. This is caused by the FPSE security and permissions settings of one Web site overriding those configured on the other.

- **WebDAV authoring is not supported on any FPSE enabled Web site** If you configure a Web site for FPSE authoring, WebDAV clients will not be able to connect. Windows XP and Windows Server 2003 include a FPSE client and will automatically switch between WebDAV and FPSE as required.

FPSE are not installed by default. If you did not already install and enable FPSE when you installed IIS 6.0, follow these steps:

1. Open the **Add/Remove Programs Control Panel**. Select **Add/Remove Windows Components**.

2. Under **Application Server | Internet Information Services**, check the **FrontPage 2002 Server Extensions** component.

3. Click **OK** to exit the dialog boxes, and click **Next** to install and enable FPSE.

If you have previously installed FPSE but disabled the associated Web Service Extension, enable it by opening the IIS Manager, expanding the Web Service Extensions node, and choosing to allow FrontPage 2002 Server Extensions in the right-hand pane (refer back to Figure 11.1).

If you are running URLScan, you need to make the following changes to your configuration:

1. Edit the urlscan.ini file to allow URLScan to load as a low priority filter. This allows the FPSE ISAPI filter to process incoming requests prior to URLScan. Urlscan.ini, by default, is located in %systemroot%\system32\inetsrv\urlscan\. Open the urlscan.ini file in Notepad (or similar text editor) and set **AllowLateScanning=1**.

2. Ensure that you are not removing the IIS 6.0 Server header or substituting your own. FrontPage publishing may fail if you are doing this. To prevent problems, set RemoveServerHeader=0 in the urlscan.ini file.

3. Optionally, you can use urlscan.ini to provide further protection to FPSE's publishing folders (these are special folders used by FPSE for various purposes, including keeping track of files that are locked for editing, FPSE configuration files, and FPSE authoring log files). To do this, add the following code to the [DenyURLSequences] section of your urlscan.ini file:

```
/fpdb/      ; holds FrontPage database files
/_private   ; holds FrontPage private files (usually
FPSE form/poll results)
/_vti_pvt   ; holds FrontPage configuration files
/_vti_cnf   ; holds FrontPage metadata files
/_vti_txt   ; holds FrontPage catalogs & indices (for
FPSE searching)
/_vti_log   ; holds FrontPage authoring log files
```

4. After making these changes, you must restart IIS to reload the URLScan filter with its new settings. For more information on ensuring that FPSE works with URLScan, see Microsoft KB Article 318290 at http://support.microsoft.com/?kbid=318290.

Enabling FPSE Authoring

Enabling FrontPage clients (such as Microsoft FrontPage and Visual Studio.Net) to author against your Web site requires *extending* an existing Web site. Once the Web site (known as a *virtual server* in FrontPage terms) has been extended, your clients can connect and start publishing and editing files. In IIS 6.0 terms, an *extended Web site* is the same as a FrontPage *virtual server*. You might see both terms used in documentation, depending on whether the documentation is geared toward IIS 6.0 administrators or FrontPage authors.

Before extending a Web site to allow FPSE authoring, it is useful to configure FrontPage server defaults. These default settings will be used by all Web sites that you choose to extend, unless you explicitly choose to set alternate settings for a particular Web site. To configure these default settings:

1. Open the **Microsoft Sharepoint Administrator** Web site located in the Administrative Tools folder of your Start menu (see Figure 11.4).

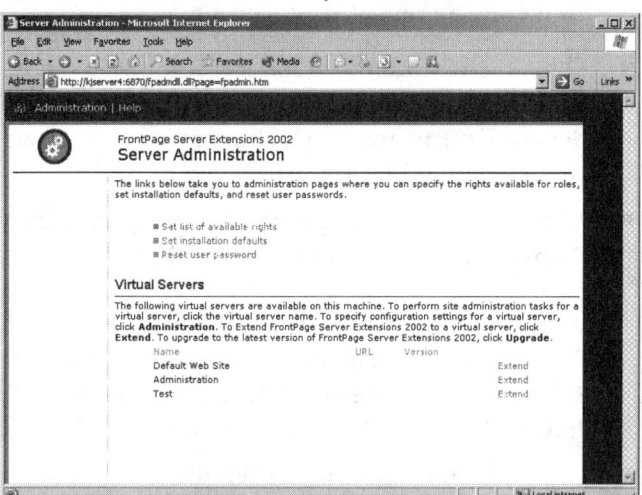

Figure 11.4 The Microsoft Sharepoint Administrator Web site

2. Click the **Set Installation Defaults** link.

On the Set Installation Defaults page (see Figure 11.5), you can enter mail settings if your users will be using any of the mail-enabled features of FrontPage. Additionally, you can choose whether to log authoring actions, require SSL for authoring, and whether authors can upload executable content (.exe files). SSL requires the installation of a server certificate. See Chapter 5, "Advanced Web Server Security," for more information on installing a server certificate. Authoring actions are logged for each *virtual host* and are stored in the /_vti_log folder of each Web site.

Figure 11.5 Set Installation Defaults

After setting server defaults, we can now proceed to extending a Web site. To do this, do one of the following:

- Open the **IIS Manager** and locate the Web site you want to extend. Right-click and choose **All Tasks**, then **Configure Server Extensions 2002**. This will open the Sharepoint Administration Web site asking you to confirm the extension.

- Alternatively, you can open the **Microsoft Sharepoint Administrator** Web site located in the Administrative Tools folder of your Start menu. This tool lists all Web sites defined on your Web server. For Web sites that have not been extended, an Extend link exists. For already extended Web sites, an Administration link exists (refer back to Figure 11.4). Click the **Extend** link for a Web site that has not already been extended.

- On the **Install** page, enter a Windows user account that will be the administrator of this Web site. (You can add more administrators later.) Click the **Submit** button to extend the Web site.

When you return to the Microsoft Sharepoint Administrator Web site homepage, your extended Web site will now have two links (see Figure 11.6).

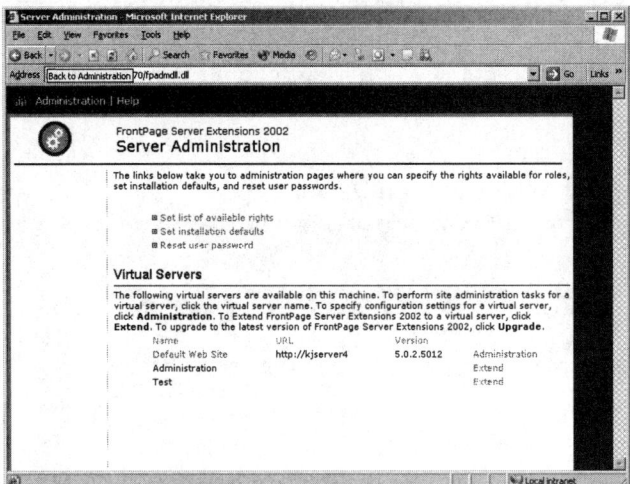

Figure 11.6 Extended Default Web Site

The Administration link allows you to configure various site-wide settings (overriding the defaults specified earlier), configure a maximum number of user accounts for the Web site, or to uninstall FPSE from this site. The Web site name is also a hyperlink, and this link takes us to a Site Administration Web site where most of our settings will be configured. Click this link to load the Site Administration Web site (see Figure 11.7).

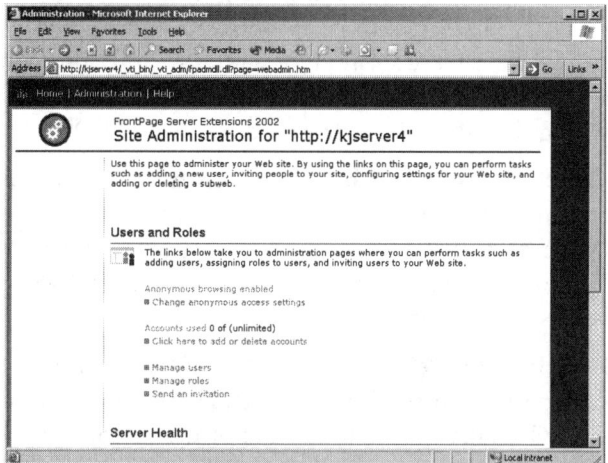

Figure 11.7 The Site Administration Homepage

The Site Administration homepage contains the following links and options:

- **Change Anonymous Access Settings** Click this link if you want to enable or disable anonymous browsing of your Web site. Additionally, you can elevate the privileges of anonymous users. Normally, anonymous users can only browse your Web site. However, you can give them authoring or administration privileges—neither of which is recommended.

- **Add/Delete User accounts** This option allows you to add or delete user accounts defined for this Web site. If you want to add existing Windows accounts or groups (or remove permissions for previously added Windows users or groups), you should use the next option, Manage User Accounts.

- **Manage User Accounts** This option allows you to decide what privileges each user or group has within the site. This is done by assigning users or groups to *roles*. FPSE comes with some predefined roles, or you can define additional roles (with custom privileges) using the next option. This option also lets you add Windows users or groups to the FPSE site.

- **Manage Roles** This option allows you to define what *roles* exist on the server. Each role has a set of rights. FPSE comes with some predefined roles, or you can create a new role and an add a custom set of rights.

- **Send an Invitation** A three-step wizard allows you to send an invitation e-mail to users who you want to notify about this FPSE Web site. You can, through the wizard, add these users automatically to your FPSE Web site and choose the roles into which they should be placed.

- **Check Server Health** This option has FPSE run diagnostic checks on its configuration information and verifies your NTFS permissions to ensure that they are securely configured. This option can also be used to alter the NTFS permissions of your site so that they are secure.

- **Recalculate Web** Use this option if the FPSE metadata about content in your site is no longer in synch with the actual content. (This may occur if you add or delete content without using FPSE, for example, by using Explorer to copy files directly into the Web site's folders.) Performing this operation forces FPSE to examine all folders and files and recalculate its metadata.

- **Configure Version Control** If you enable version control, users can check out (and check in) files. Checked-out files cannot be edited by other users. Checkout information is stored in the _vti_cnf directories created by FPSE.

- **Create a Subweb** This option allows you to designate separate sections of the Web site as subwebs. Each subweb can have its own configuration and security information, just like its parent Web site. This is useful if you have a single Web site but need to partition sections of it among different groups within your organization.

Securing your FPSE Virtual Host

To secure your FPSE Virtual Host (or Extended Web site), you should perform the following steps. Similar steps can be performed if you are securing a subweb created within a virtual host/extended Web site.

First, determine if you will allow anonymous (unauthenticated) access. Anonymous access is useful if you have an external-facing Web site viewable by the general public. Alternatively, if you require all users to authenticate, you should disable anonymous access. To enable or disable anonymous access:

1. Open the **Site Administration** homepage (refer back to Figure 11.7).
2. Click the **Change Anonymous Access Settings** link.
3. Choose whether to allow anonymous access or not. If you do allow anonymous access, determine what role anonymous (unauthenticated) users will be placed into. The Browser role (the default) allows anonymous users to browse your site. It is not recommended that you place unauthenticated users in any other role that has greater privileges than this role.

Now determine the authentication mechanism that you will use. Unless you allow anonymous (unauthenticated) users to perform authoring actions (not recommended), users will need to provide credentials if they want to perform authoring actions. IIS 6.0 supports a number of authentication mechanisms, including Integrated Windows Authentication (IWA), Digest/Advanced Digest authentication, and Basic authentication. If you choose Basic authentication, you should use SSL to encrypt the transmission of user credentials between client and server. To enable authentication, you need to use the IIS Manager. For more information on enabling authentication, see Chapter 5, "Advanced Web Server Security."

The next step involves determining the types of roles you will need within your Web site or subweb. You need at least one user (or group of users) that has full control over the Web site. Additionally, you most likely have users who can browse the Web site and users who can author content. However, you might want to have administrators that can create new user accounts but cannot change other server settings. To do this, you need to create a custom role.

After determining the user roles you need (and the rights each of these users roles requires), you should compare them to FPSE's predefined roles . If there are no built-in roles that meet your needs, create new roles. To do this:

1. Open the **Site Administration** homepage (refer back to Figure 11.7).
2. Click the **Manage Roles** link.
3. Select any existing role if you want to see detailed information on the user rights that the role has. If you need to create a custom role, click **Add a Role**.

4. On the Add a Role page, enter a name of the role and (optionally) a description. Choose the user rights that this role should have (see Figure 11.8).

Figure 11.8 Creating a New Role

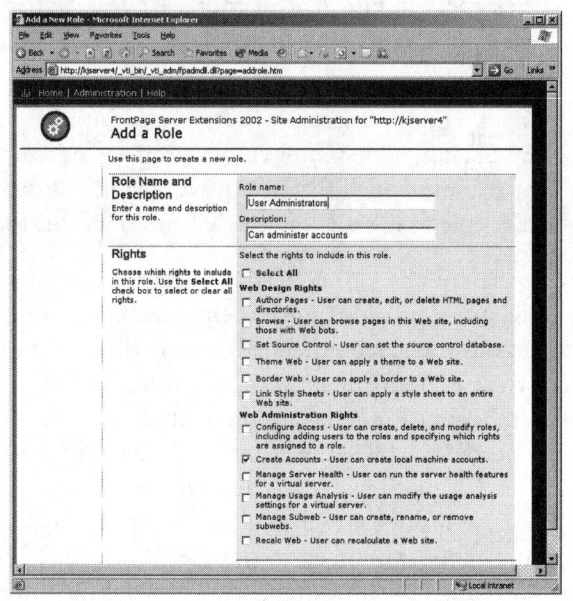

5. Click **Submit** to create the new role.
6. Repeat this process for each role you need to create.

After creating all the roles you will require, you now need to add user accounts to your FPSE Web site. To add Windows users or groups, use the **Manage Users** link on the Site Administration homepage. Alternatively, you can create non-Windows accounts (which are valid only for use with FPSE-related tasks such as publishing content) using the **Add a User** link. To add a Windows user or group and assign them to a role:

1. Open the **Site Administration** homepage (Figure 11.7).
2. Click the **Manage Users** link.
3. Click **Add a User**.
4. On the **Add a User** page, select **Add user or group name** (for example, DOMAIN\name) and enter the user account name or group.

5. Check the roles that this user account should be assigned to, and click the **Submit** button to add the new user or role.

6. This same process can be achieved using the **Send an Invitation** link on the Site Administration homepage. The **Send an Invitation** link also allows you to enter an e-mail address for the user (plus an invitational message) that will be e-mailed to the user, in addition to creating the new user account and assigning the user a role or roles.

7. Repeat this process of each user or group you need to add to the Web site.

Run the FPSE Tighten Security wizard. This wizard applies appropriate NTFS permissions to your FPSE extended Web site. It will, for example, set restrictive read permissions on all folders for users in the browser role. If you are using the FPSE database publishing tools, it will configure appropriate access on the special /fpdb folder where you store database files. If you have any special file or folder requirements, you might need to adjust your NTFS permissions after running this wizard. For example, if you have a third-party Perl CGI script that requires execute permissions, you might need to adjust the NTFS permissions to allow that.

To run the wizard:

1. Open the **Site Administration** homepage (refer back to Figure 11.7).

2. Click the **Check Server Health** link.

3. Check **Repair** next to **Reapply File Security Settings**. Check **Repair** next to **Tighten Security**. Click **Submit** to run the wizard.

Finally, determine if you will require FPSE to log authoring actions in a log file. This requirement can be set for all Web sites or an individual Web site. To do this:

1. Open the **Microsoft Sharepoint Administrator** in the Administrative Tools folder of your Start menu.

2. To configure logging for all Web sites, click the **Set Installation Defaults** link, and check **Log Authoring Actions**.

3. To configure logging for an individual Web site, click the **Administration** link next to the Web site's name on the Sharepoint Administrator homepage. Then select **Change**

Configuration Settings and check the **Log Authoring Actions** setting.

Now you are ready to have your users publish content to your Web site. If you have a FrontPage client (such as Microsoft FrontPage or Visual Studio or Visual Studio.Net), you can connect directly to the Web site. To do this in Microsoft FrontPage, choose **File | Open Site...** and enter your site URL into the dialog box. You might then need to enter appropriate credentials. If you are authorized to view the site, you should see the site structure in the site browser (see Figure 11.9).

Figure 11.9 Connecting Using Microsoft FrontPage 2003

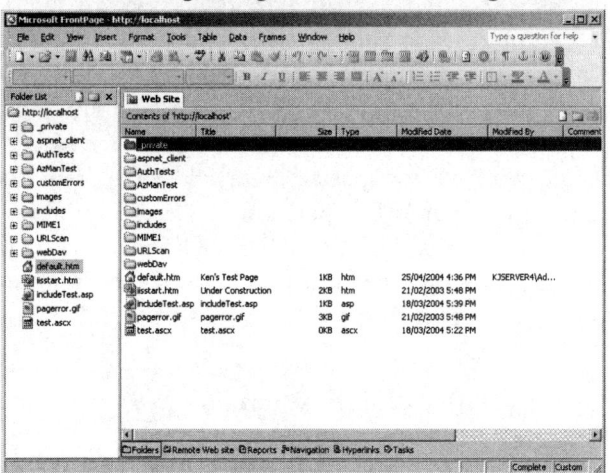

If you have Windows XP or Windows Server 2003, you can also connect using the in-built FPSE client. To do so, open **My Network Places**, and start the **Add Network Place** wizard. Enter the URL of your FPSE enabled Web site, and it should be accessible directly from Explorer (see Figure 11.10). On a Windows Server 2003, you need to start the Webclient service manually to utilize the built-in FPSE client.

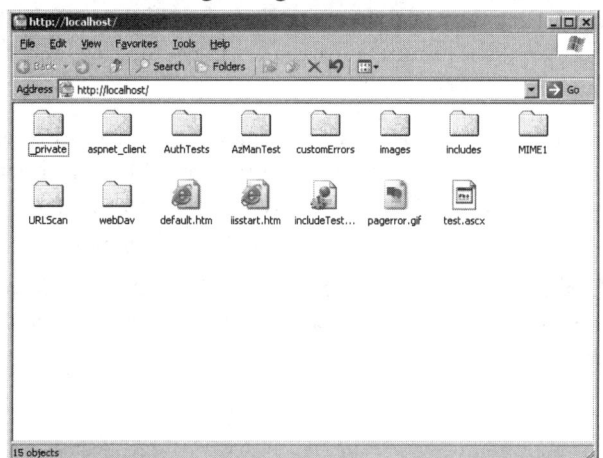

Figure 11.10 Connecting Using Windows 2003 Client

REALITY CHECK...

Microsoft FrontPage Server Extensions provides a flexible and feature-rich method of publishing content to FPSE extended Web sites. In addition to publishing content, users can also utilize the various FPSE components that allow for dynamic content without requiring experience in writing server-side code. On the other hand, administering an FPSE extended Web site is a more complex task than administering many other publishing technologies. To secure an FPSE extended Web site, an administrator is required to plan and implement authentication, roles, and users, in addition to having FPSE configure NTFS permissions.

Your A** Is Covered If You...

- ☑ Choose an appropriate publishing system. If you need to support non–Windows clients, you can utilize WebDAV, an open publishing standard. If you have Microsoft FrontPage clients, you can utilize Microsoft FrontPage Server Extensions.

- ☑ Designate appropriate IIS Web and NTFS file and folder permissions for WebDAV Publishing. Additionally, you need to choose an appropriate authentication mechanism. If you are using Basic authentication, ensure that you use SSL to encrypt the transmission of user credentials.

- ☑ Develop an appropriate permissions plan if you're using FrontPage Server Extensions. You should determine the roles that you will require, create roles if appropriate, and add users into those roles.

- ☑ Utilize an appropriate authentication mechanism to allow users to authenticate if they want to perform FPSE authoring actions. If using Basic authentication, ensure that you use SSL to encrypt the transmission of user credentials.

- ☑ Enable FPSE author logging on FPSE extended Web sites if you want to generate an audit trail to track users' authoring actions.

Chapter 12
Securing Internet Printing

In this Chapter

Internet printing was first introduced in Internet Information Server (IIS) 5.0. By using Internet Printing Protocol (IPP), it allows you to print documents and manage printers via a web browser, as if the printer was connected locally to your machine. If you decide to enable this component, be sure you follow the security guidelines and procedures outlined in this chapter to protect your Internet printing.

- Configuring Internet Printing
- Securing Internet Printing
- Monitoring Internet Printing Access

When you are finished with this chapter you will have learned different ways to secure your Internet printing, as well as improved upon your overall knowledge of configuring Internet printing. You will also be able to restrict access and protect your shared printers.

Configuring Internet Printing

Internet printing allows you to share printers via the IIS server, making it available for users to connect and print their documents using a web browser. Internet printing also allows you to administrate printers via this method. You can manage documents in the print queue, delete partially printed jobs, and pause and resume printers. For example, suppose your company has ten sales executives, each of whom receives orders everyday from different locations and is required to submit daily sales reports via e-mail to the sales manager at headquarters. The sales manager then prints out each report and hands it to the stock control department. By using Internet printing, the sales manager can instruct sales executives to print their report via the Internet at the end of each business day, thus precluding the need for the sales manager to read every e-mail and print out each report.

By default, the Internet printing component is not installed with IIS 6.0, which is shipped in default locked down mode. For details on how to install the Internet printing component, refer to Chapter 3.

> **BY THE BOOK...**
>
> IIS 6.0 supports the Internet Printing Protocol and the Internet printing component, which makes all shared printers on the IIS server available for users to print documents using Hypertext Transfer Protocol (HTTP).
>
> Web browsers with IPP support, such as Microsoft Internet Explorer 4.01 and later, can print to these Internet printers. Clients will connect to these printers via HTTP in a manner similar to requesting web resource contents from the IIS server. To secure the connection and protect sensitive data, you can configure Secure Sockets Layer (SSL) on the Internet printing virtual directory. The client can then connect to these printers via HTTP Secure (HTTPS). Internet printing is made available through Active Server Pages (ASP) that process and fulfill each client's request.

In this chapter, you will first learn how Internet printing works, and then you will configure your own Internet printers. We will also look at the administrative tasks that allow you to manage Internet printers and the details associated with this component.

When a client connects to an Internet printer via a web browser, the IIS server automatically sends a cabinet (cab) file that contains the appropriate printer driver to the client's machine. If the printer driver cannot be located by the IIS server, the client will be prompted to install the appropriate driver before he or she can connect to the printer. For more details on how to configure operating system printer drivers, refer to the Windows Server 2003 help documentation at www.microsoft.com/windowsserver2003/technologies/fileandprint/print/default.mspx.

Internet printing makes use of ASP scripts, which will query shared printers installed on the IIS server and publish the results within the IIS server. Any web browsers that support IPP, such as Microsoft Internet Explorer 4.01 or Netscape Navigator 4.06, will able to connect to the Internet printers.

To enable Internet printing, you must first add shared printers in Windows Server 2003, then install the Internet printing component using the **Add or Remove Programs** feature in the Windows **Control Panel**, and finally allow the Internet printing component to run in the web service extensions lists. For details on installing the Internet printing component, refer Chapter 3. To turn on the Internet printing function after you install the component, perform these steps:

1. In IIS Manager, expand the local computer and click **Web Service Extensions**.

2. In the details pane (Figure 12.1), click on **Internet Printing,** then click **Allow**.

Figure 12.1 Enabling Internet Printing Service Extension – Web Service Extensions Node

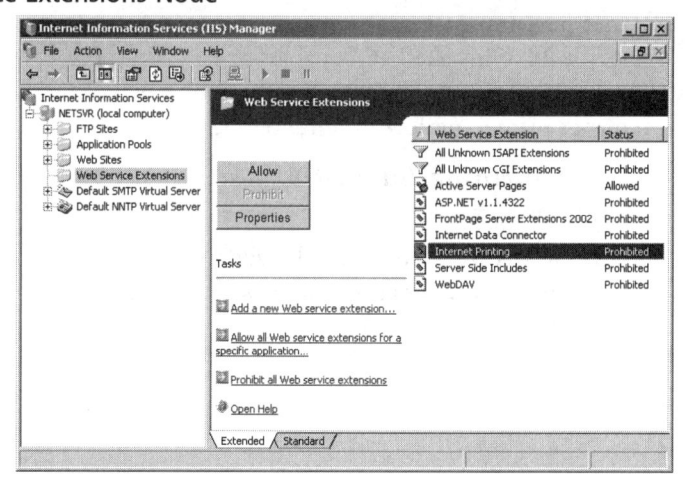

3. Close IIS Manager.

It is important to note that Internet printing functionality is dependent on ASP scripts, so you must enable the **Active Server Pages** web service extension in order use Internet printing. By default, after you install Internet printing, you will see a virtual directory named *Printers* created under the *Default Web Site* (Figure 12.2)

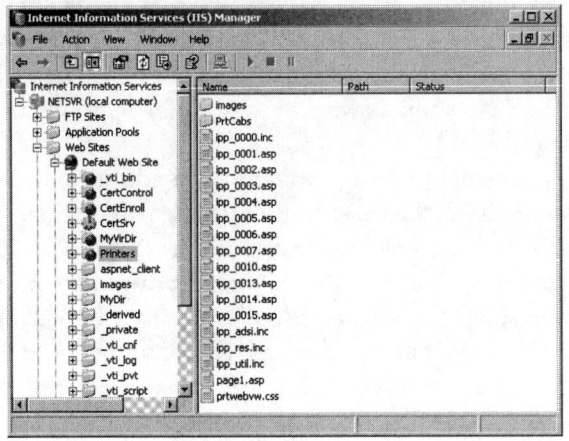

Figure 12.2 Printers Virtual Directory – IIS Manager

This virtual directory is mapped to the %windir%/web/printers/ folder. The *images* sub-folder stores image files used by the ASP scripts and the *PrtCabs* sub-folder stores the printer driver cab files. The printer driver cabinet files will be downloaded by clients when they connect to the Internet printers.

Once you have installed and enabled the Internet printing web service extension, you are ready to use the Internet printers. To connect to an Internet printer, perform the following steps:

1. Start **Microsoft Internet Explorer** or any web browser with IPP support.

2. In the **Address** box, type the address of the printer, for example **http://netsvr/printers/**. All existing printers will be listed (Figure 12.3).

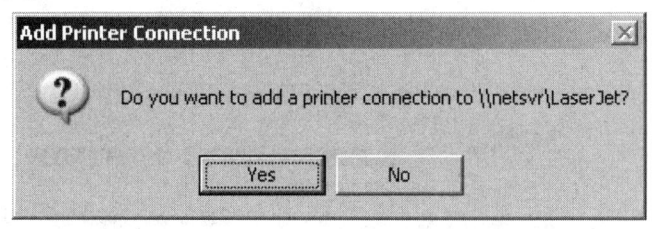

Figure 12.3 Browsing Internet Printers – Microsoft Internet Explorer

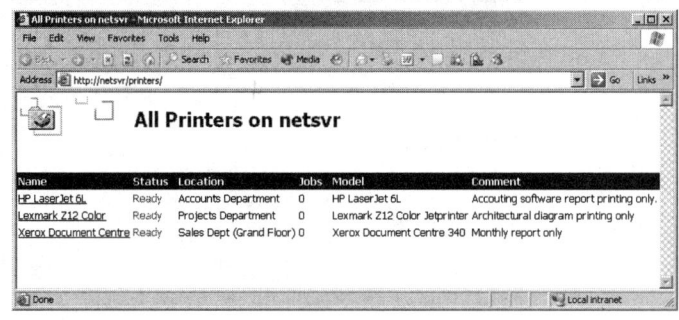

3. In the printers list, click the name of the printer that you want to connect to.
4. To connect to the printer, click **Connect** under **Printer Actions**.

If the client has not previously used the selected printer, or if for some other reason no printer driver exists for the selected printer, you will have to follow these additional steps:

1. You will be prompted to add the printer. In the **Add Printer Connection** dialog box (Figure 12.4), click **Yes** to install the printer driver remotely via the web browser. When the installation is finished, you will see the message, "The printer has been installed on your machine" (Figure 12.5).

Figure 12.4 Installing a Printer Driver – Add Printer Connection Dialog Box

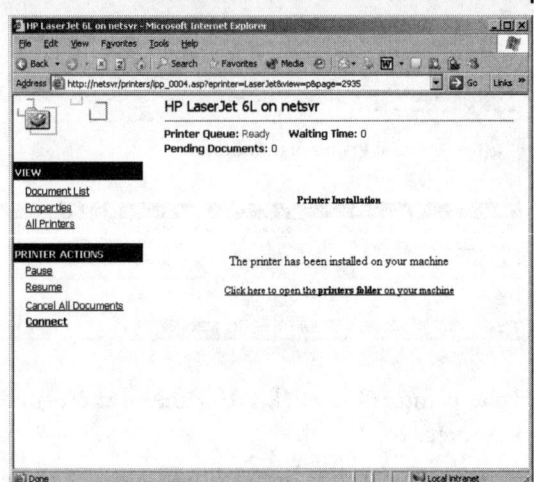

Figure 12.5 Printer Installation – Microsoft Internet Explorer

2. To verify printer driver installation, you can click on the **Printers Folder** hyperlink. This will open the **Printers and Faxes** folder in your local computer, where you can verify the printer's details by double-clicking the newly installed printer.

Once you are connected to the desired printer, you can either manage the printer or connect and print your document. Figure 12.6 shows the available options for managing the printer.

Figure 12.6 Managing an Internet Printer – Microsoft Internet Explorer

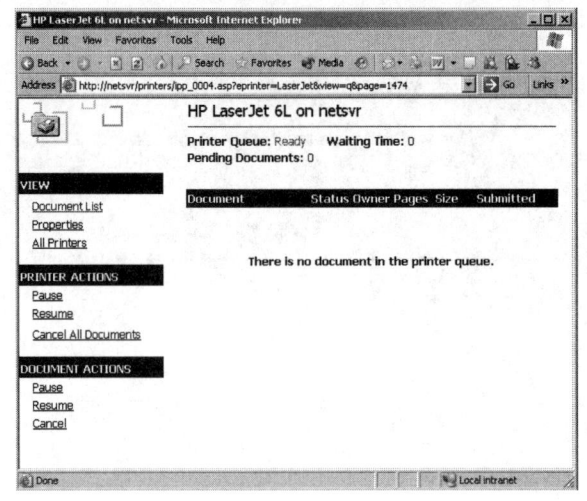

Depending on your access permissions, you may be able to manage the printer in a variety of ways. By default, administrators have full permissions on the printer. Administrators will able to pause printing, resume printing, and manage documents in the print queue. Non-administrator users will only be able to manage their own documents; they can either pause or resume printing or cancel their own print jobs. Table 12.1 lists the default users and their access rights.

Table 12.1 Internet Printing Default User Rights

User / Group	Access Rights
Administrators	Print Manage Printers Manage Documents
Creator Owner	Manage Documents
Everyone	Print
Power Users / Print Operators	Print Manage Printers Manage Documents

Creator Owner refers to the user who creates and owns the resource content. In this context, users who submit the print request to the printer own the print job, and with the *manage documents* access permissions, users are allowed to control their own print jobs.

☞ REALITY CHECK...

To enable Internet printing features, first you must install and configure shared printers on the Windows Server 2003. Shared printers are automatically included as Internet printers when an Internet printing component is installed in the IIS 6.0 server. In order for Internet printing to function properly, ensure that ASP and Internet Printing service extensions are enabled in IIS web service extensions list.

When clients first connect to Internet printers, the Internet printing component will send related operating system printer driver files to the client's browser. After the print driver installation, clients will be able to print documents to the Internet printer. To ensure smooth deployment of Internet printers, configure different client's operation system printer drivers for the shared printers. This will avoid a situation where no suitable printer drivers can be found when clients connect to the printers.

Securing Internet Printing

Internet printing is a web resource, and you should secure Internet printers the same way you secure web resource contents. Refer to Chapters 4 and 5 for more detail on different security configuration to secure website resources.

> **BY THE BOOK...**
>
> Internet printing actually runs as a web application on the IIS server. You can protect and secure Internet printing using the built-in security features listed below:
> **Authentication** Allows you to authenticate users before they can send print jobs and manage Internet printers.
> **Connection** Control access by granting and denying client access based on their IP addresses or domain names. By default, all IP addresses have access to Internet printing.

To help protect your print server, you need to configure various security settings to prevent malicious attacks on the printers. You secure Internet printers in the same way that you configure security for the website. Internet printers are simply a form of web content in which clients will send requests to print documents and IIS will process and redirect print jobs to the appropriate printers.

In Chapter 5, we discussed different website authentication methods supported in IIS 6.0. You can configure different authentication modes to grant or deny user access. Authentications protect the print server from being wrongly used or abused. For example, if your print server allows anonymous access, attackers can sabotage the printers by sending lot of junk documents to print. The printer's resources (such as paper and ink cartridges) are wasted and legitimate users are not able to print their documents, as the printers are busy handling the non-legitimate print jobs.

Table 12.2 lists different authentication methods you can use to secure Internet printing.

Table 12.2 Authentication Methods

Method	Description
Anonymous	No username or password is required to access the server. Default anonymous users use the IUSR_<COMPUTERNAME> account.
Integrated Windows	Authentication for a valid Windows user account is required, and user credentials are sent in encrypted mode.
Digest	Authentication for a valid Active Directory user account is required, and user credentials are sent in encrypted mode.
Basic	Authentication for a valid Windows user account is required, and user credentials are sent in plain text mode.
Microsoft .NET Passport	Authentication for a valid .NET passport user account is required, and user credentials are sent in encrypted mode.

By default, only Integrated Windows authentication is configured for Internet printing. This ensures that no anonymous access is allowed. Users are required to provide a valid username and password before they are allowed to connect to the print server. To configure other authentication modes, perform these steps:

1. In IIS Manager, expand the local computer, expand the **Web Sites** folder, and expand the desired website.

2. Right-click on the **Printers** virtual directory, then click **Properties**.

3. On the **Directory Security** tab, click **Edit**.

4. In the **Authentication Methods** dialog box (Figure 12.7), enable the desired authentication method(s). It is not recommended that you select **Enable anonymous access**, as this will allow anonymous user to connect to the print server without any authentication process.

Figure 12.7 Configuring Internet Printing Authentications – Authentication Methods Dialog Box

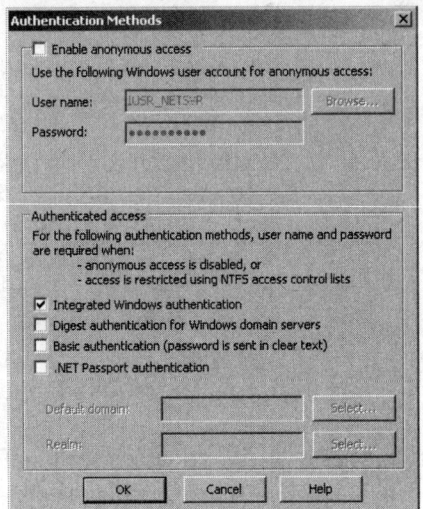

5. Click **OK**.

To further protect your print server, you can use connection control to block or grant access based on the client's IP address or domain name. For example, suppose your company's sales manager (who has a fixed IP broadband connection) will connect to the print server every night around 9:00 P.M. to print out sales reports for operation planning. To secure Internet printing, you can first configure authentication so that the sales manager is required to supply his username and password before he can gain access to the printer. Next, you can configure IP address restriction to further protect your print server; you can deny all IP access except to the broadband IP address that the sales manager is using. For more details on how to configure connection restrictions, refer to Chapter 4.

To add more security, you can also apply various security measurements for Internet printing using built-in security features such as SSL to secure the connection between the client and the print server.

You can also restrict access permissions by configuring printer access permissions based on users or user groups in **Printers and Faxes** folder in the Windows **Control Panel**. For example, suppose you have a few printers shared over company corporate network using Internet printing service, and two of the printers can only be accessed by the Accounts and Projects departments. Even though these printers are listed on the Internet printing page, if connected users do not have the require permissions, they will not be able to download the printer driver and print documents to that printer. To allow printing, users must at least have *print* permissions.

If you do not wish to have the printer listed on the Internet printing page, you can stop sharing the printer. For details on configuring printer access permissions and sharing settings, please refer to the Windows Server 2003 help documentation.

> **REALITY CHECK…**
>
> After enabling Internet printing, you must ensure that you have followed the guidelines discussed in this section to protect your print server. It is not recommended that you allow anonymous access for Internet printing. If you need to change the authentication methods, be sure you have gone through the Chapter 5 for details about each authentication mode. Finally, to further restrict access, it is recommended that you configure access control to grant and deny access based on a client's IP address and/or domain name.

Monitoring Internet Printing Access

Monitoring web access log files can help you keep track of the access details of your print server. By default, */printers* virtual directory logging is enabled. You can analyze log entries to understand how Internet printers are being accessed, as the log provides you with details of when and which user accessed the server and which web browser the user is using. Access log files will also give you hints to help you troubleshoot the print server if there are connection issues. One more benefit of enabling activity logging is that it allows you to detect if there are unauthorized users trying to gain access to your Internet printers.

> **BY THE BOOK…**
>
> IIS 6.0 allows you to collect user access activity information by enabling the logging feature. Information can be logged using the following formats:
> **W3C Extended** A customizable format that allows you to configure the types of information to be collected when IIS

writes the log entry. This format follows the W3C working draft specification. You can visit www.w3.org/TR/WD-logfile for information about the working draft.

NCSA Common National Center for Supercomputing Applications (NCSA) common format is an old specification of log file. Details logged are fixed and not customizable. Data captured includes remote host name, data, time, request type, HTTP status and number of bytes sent by the server.

IIS Log A fixed format that records more information than NCSA common format. These extra details include time taken to process the request, bytes received by server, and Win32 status.

ODCB Logging A fixed set of data that can be recorded in a database source.

New log file features introduced in IIS 6.0 include:

UTF-8 logging In earlier IIS versions, log files are logged in ASCII text or local codepage mode. In IIS 6.0 you can configure the logging in Universal Transformation Format (UTF) 8 mode. UTF-8 mode logging allows you to log every request in UTF-8 encoding characters, which support more text characters than standard ASCII format. For example, with UTF-8 logging, you can have request log entries that are in Unicode text, such as Japanese content filenames.

Remote logging In IIS 6.0, you can redirect log files on a remote share network path using the Universal Naming Convention (UNC) method. This allows you to configure a different log path to centralized log storage for backup and analysis purposes.

Centralized Binary logging This format allows multiple websites to write unformatted binary log data to a single file.

Http Error logging This log file format captures HTTP API errors record by the HTTP.SYS driver.

Protocol substatus This is only available in W3C extended format, and provides further detail in addition to standard protocol status to help you further understand request statuses.

To find out more about logging Internet Printing access activities, please refer to Chapter 4's *Enabling and Securing Web Access Log File* section

REALITY CHECK...

Logging Internet printing activities provides detailed information on access and usage of Internet printer resources. By default, logging is enabled for the */printers* virtual directory and you are not advised to disable it, as logging access allows you to monitor access to your Internet printers. You can also audit log files to check if any unauthorized user is trying to gain access to the Internet printers. Finally, be sure you follow the guidelines in Chapter 4 to protect the log files using NTFS permissions.

Your A** is Covered if You...

- ☑ Configured Internet printing user authentications.
- ☑ Configured user access rights for Internet printers.
- ☑ Configured SSL connections between the Internet printing server and client computers.
- ☑ Configured IP address and domain name restrictions.
- ☑ Enabled Internet printing virtual directory logging.

Chapter 13
Monitoring Internet Information Services (IIS) 6.0

In this Chapter

We have reached the final chapter of this book. You have a hardened IIS 6.0 server, but it doesn't end here. Securing IIS 6 not only pertains to configuration settings in IIS server, but to many tasks that must be performed in order to maintain a healthy and secured IIS server. These tasks include: a standard security control procedure for physical access to your server, a well-defined backup and disaster recovery plan, a combination of various security hardware (firewall) and software applications (antivirus, Intrusion Detection System (IDS)), guarding the entire network, and more. Once you have everything in place and running, your next tasks will be to monitor the activities of every component and audit and check the log files of every security element you have in place. In regard to IIS server, we will focus on various log sources that can help you to identify potential problem or signs of attack.

- Monitoring Site Activities Logging
- Monitoring Event Viewer Logging
- Monitoring HTTP API Error Logging
- Monitoring URLScan Logging

By the end of this chapter, you will understand how monitoring activities in IIS can give you a greater perspective of ongoing events on your server. You will learn how to identify possible unauthorized access and recognize potential attack hints using the various IIS server log files.

Monitoring Site Activities Logging

Logging site activities helps you to keep track of client access requests. This type of log provides you with details about who, when, where, and how contents are being accessed. Information that can be logged includes the visitor's IP address, the user account accessing the contents, a timestamp of when requests were made, the server status reply to the request, the requested resource location, the amount of bytes used in the request, and more. These log files also provide you with a good troubleshooting channel to resolve any failure or error request, and can provide you with clues about possible attacker behavior and intrusion patterns.

By the Book...

IIS 6.0 provides site access logging for every component. Each component has support for a few logging formats, ranging from fixed format (such as IIS, National Center for Supercomputing Applications (NCSA) and Open Database Connectivity (ODBC) to customizable versions of World Wide Web Consortium (W3C) extended format.

IIS 6.0 includes many new features in site logging, including:

UTF-8 logging Universal Transformation Format (UTF) logging allows you to log every request in UTF-8 encoding characters, which support more text characters than standard ASCII format. For example, with UTF-8 logging, you can have request log entries that are in Unicode text such as Japanese content filename.

Remote logging Redirect log files on a remote share network path using the Universal Naming Convention (UNC) method. This allows you to configure a different log path to centralize log storage for backup and analysis purposes.

Centralized Binary logging This format allows multiple websites to write unformatted binary log data to a single file.

HTTP Error logging This log file format captures Hypertext Transfer Protocol (HTTP) application programming interface (API) errors recorded by the HTTP.SYS driver.

Protocol substatus This is only available in W3C extended format and provides further detail in addition to standard protocol status to help you understand request statuses.

Monitoring site activity log files allows you to monitor client requests sent to related services. It is recommended that you enable logging for every request made to your IIS server. You will not only be able to understand how contents are being accessed, you will also be able to determine why a particular request has failed by looking at the service's reply status in the log file. Previously, in Chapter 4, we discussed the example of a 404.2 HTTP status code indicating a failed request due to the disabled dynamic content service extension in web service extensions list. This not only helps you to troubleshoot IIS server if users keep getting a 404 reply from your server, but it also provides you with hints that attackers may be trying to gain unauthorized access via that particular service extension.

Let's recap the various formats supported by these IIS services. Table 13.1 outlines services and their supported log formats:

Table 13.1 IIS Services and Logging Formats

Type of Service	IIS	NCSA	ODBC	W3C Extended	Centralized Binary
FTP	Yes	No	Yes	Yes	No
Web	Yes	Yes	Yes	Yes	Yes
SMTP	Yes	Yes	Yes	Yes	No
NNTP	Yes	Yes	Yes	Yes	No

It is important to know that the current Post Office Protocol 3 (POP3) service only supports *Event Viewer* logging and does not support any logging formats in other IIS components. Take note that the new logging features, including UTF-8, centralized binary and HTTP error logging, are only available in website activity logging. Protocol substatus, the new W3C extended property field, is also only available for website W3C extended logging format. On the other hand, the remote logging feature, which was not available in previous versions of IIS, is now available for all IIS services.

It is recommended that you review and check your access log files on a routine basis. By doing so, you will understand a content's popularity and how often it has been accessed. You can utilize log analyzer software such as Analog, LiveStats, and other third party utilities. Log analyzers normally produce graphical reports to illustrate different details derived from the log files. Reports include page view, number of hits, IP address' registrar, bandwidth, and more. You can then use these reports to work on related market projects, infrastructure planning, and others. Some sophisticated analyzers allow you to create customized reports. For example, reports may involve a number of failed requests such as 404, 500 and 403 HTTP status code for websites, and failed login (530 File Transfer Protocol (FTP) status code) for FTP sites. These reports can help you determine the next course of action to take to remedy any problems that exist.

You can also analyze logs by using Microsoft Log Parser 2.1, included in the IIS 6.0 Resource Kit. You can download IIS 6.0 Resource Kit for free at www.microsoft.com/downloads/details.aspx?FamilyId=56FC92EE-A71A-4C73-B628-ADE629C89499. Log Parser is a command line utility (Figure 13.1) that allows you to parse different log files in Windows Server 2003. It is capable of parsing different IIS logging formats, Event Viewer, HTTP errors, generic text files and more. For example you can run Log Parser to check how many 404 requests exist in the IIS web access log. The output of the Log Parser query can be redirected to a text file like SQL server, XML, Comma Separated Value (CSV), W3C and IIS log files. For more details on how to use the Log Parser, please refer to the IIS 6.0 Resource Kit help documentation.

Figure 13.1 Log Parser Command Line Utility

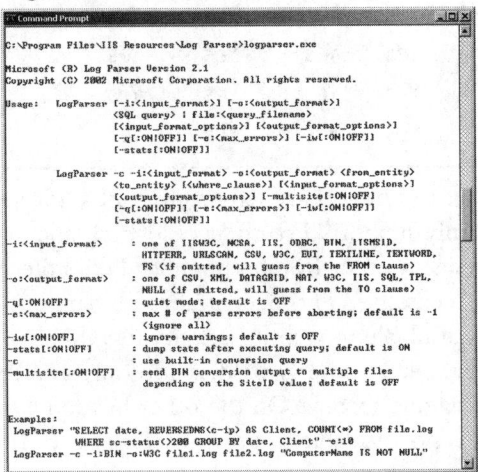

It is recommended that you configure W3C extended format for all IIS services. The main reason for this is that W3C extended format is the most comprehensive log format in IIS and it allows you to customize different logging property fields. For professional system administrators, there are a few items that may deserve more attention than others in the log files. These details include:

- **Status Code** The reply status code tells you whether the request was successfully fulfilled by IIS or why the request failed. Again, this not only helps you to troubleshoot IIS server, but it also provides clues about whether someone is trying to gain unauthorized access to your IIS server.

- **Client IP Address** This indicates where the request originated from. If you suspect malicious attacks coming from a certain IP addresses, you can configure IP address restriction to protect your server.

- **User name** This shows which user account made the request. If an anonymous access is allowed, the default IUSR_<COMPUTERNAME> account will be the request identity. If the site is configured to use user authentication, users will be required to provide a valid username and password, and IIS will log the username in the log file. From the log, you will know the name of the user accessing the contents.

- **Time Taken** The amount of time IIS took to fulfill the request. This is helpful in determining how long a request was served. For example, if an active server page (ASP) script took more than 2 minutes to complete, you might want review the coding to determine if there is a problem with logic flow.

- **Bytes Sent and Received** The amount of bytes IIS used to accept and reply to a request. This can give you bandwidth usage information about IIS server, allowing you to plan for future network bandwidth upgrades. It can also tell you when something is wrong with your server. For example, if there is a sudden increase in bytes sent or received by the FTP server, you might want to check if there are users uploading or downloading a huge file that could be compromisingdisk and bandwidth resources.

The following is a sample log entry:

```
#Software: Internet Information Services 6.0
#Version: 1.0
#Date: 2004-2-18 07:46:15
#Fields: date time s-sitename s-computername s-ip cs-method cs-uri-stem cs-uri-query s-port cs-username c-ip sc-status sc-substatus sc-win32-status sc-bytes cs-bytes time-taken
2004-02-18 07:46:15 W3SVC1 192.168.10.18 GET /printers/ - 80 ali 192.168.10.44 401 1 1326 1777 422 80
```

This log entry indicates that user **ali** is trying to access the **printers** directory of the website whose ID is **1**, but that the request was not successful (status code **401.1**) because the login failed.

In a network load balancing (NLB) environment, like the Windows Server 2003 NLB components, each NLB web host will generate its own log files. Most log analyzer applications support multiple log sources, whereby a different set of log files are combined to produce overall website access analysis reports.

As demonstrated in previous chapters concerning site activity logging, in addition to configuring logging, it is recommended that you also protect and secure the log files. Because attackers who have gained access to your server will try to cover their tracks by deleting the log files, it is always recommended that you move the log files to a new disk volume and secure it with proper NT file system (NTFS) permissions. If you have a centralized disk array on your network, it is recommended that you configure remote logging to relocate the log files to a centralized storage where you have frequent backup and a different analysis tool to analyze the log files. For more detailsabout each site's access logging, you can refer to chapters 4 (website logging), 7 (FTP logging), 8 (SMTP and POP3 logging), and 9 (NNTP logging).

Reality Check...

You have learned about site access logging and features supported in different IIS components. You have also learned how to configure different log formats and secure the log files. Your next task is to establish standard procedures to frequently backup and archive old log files, as well as to audit and analyze the log files to identify potential threats against your IIS server.

Ensure that you pay attention to details such as status code, client IP address, username, time taken, and bytes consumed when analyzing log files. The status code helps you to determine whether the request was successful or not, and the client IP address and username tell you where the request was sent from and which user identity was used to access the content. Time taken and bytes consumed indicate system resources in time and bandwidth spent by IIS to fulfill the request.

Monitoring Event Viewer Logging

Event viewer is another log source that records related service events in IIS and Windows operating systems. These events can be logged in three different categories: system, security, and application. If IIS server is configured as an Active Directory Domain Controller (DC) and Domain Name Server (DNS), you will see additional log types in the event viewer. The Directory Server and File Replication Service logs are related to Active Directory operation events, and the DNS server log captures domain name zone-related events.

> **BY THE BOOK...**
>
> When the Windows operating system starts, it will load up the event log service. This service is responsible for writing log entries to different log types in the Event Viewer. There are three main log types for IIS6 in a stand-alone Windows 2003 server:
>
> **Application** Contains events logged by services and applications running on the server. Software developers are able to determine which information is logged. For example, you may want to write an entry to this log type when your component object is writing to the content directory.
>
> **Security** Captures events related to security aspects. For example, if you configure failed attempts for logon auditing, the security log will capture the event of a user's failed logon.
>
> **System** Records events related to operating system components. For example, if a specific Windows service failed to load during startup, the events will be captured in the system log.
>
> There are five types of events that can be generated in different logs. Out of those five different events, there are two events available in the security log. The event types include:
>
> **Error** Indicates that a problem has occurred, for example, the hardware driver failed to initialize.
>
> **Information** Provides information about a particular action or event, for example, the event service started when the operating system initialized.
>
> **Warning** Gives you warning signs of insignificant problems. For example, if the performance monitor can't load an object's required counter, it will generate a warning message in the log file.
>
> **Success Audit** Only available in the security log, and indicates the successful security events. For example, if the logon

audit is enabled when a user successfully logs into the system, a "success" audit entry is written to security log.

Failure Audit Only available in the security log, and indicates the failed security events. For example, if the logon audit is enabled, a failure audit event will be generated if an attacker tries to login to the system.

Monitoring the Event Viewer log entries generated by IIS allows you to gather information about a particular IIS service. Each service has related sets of predefined events that will be logged in the Event Viewer. It is important to be familiar with these events and their causes. These logs not only help you to identify why an event occurred, they can also assist you in troubleshooting the IIS server and taking the appropriate measures to deal with the event. For example, Event ID 3 logged by the IISLOG component indicates that the component cannot create an access log file due to permissions-related settings. Based on this log detail, you can determine that you should grant system account Full Control NTFS permissions at the log path. Event Viewer also alerts you to possible attacks. For example, when you audit an account logon policy, you may be alarmed to find an an increasing number of *Failure Audit* entries in the security log with different logon account names. This tells you that attackers are guessing different username and password combinations to gain access to your system. You can then further investigate the IIS access log file to determine the requested content and the attacker's IP address. You can then protect your server from further abuse by blocking the attacker's IP address using the IP address restriction feature or by filtering the traffic at your router access list or firewall policies.

Let's look in more detail at the event logs and log entry structure. By default, the event logs are stored in the %windir%/system32/config/ directory and have an .evt (Event) extension. The logs include:

- **Application** AppEvent.Evt
- **Security** SecEvent.Evt
- **System** SysEvent.Evt

To open the Event Viewer, click the **Start** menu, point to **Administrative Tools**, then click **Event Viewer**. You can also start the Event Viewer by typing **eventvwr** at the command prompt. Figure 13.2 shows the Event Viewer Microsoft Management Console (MMC).

Figure 13.2 Event Viewer MMC

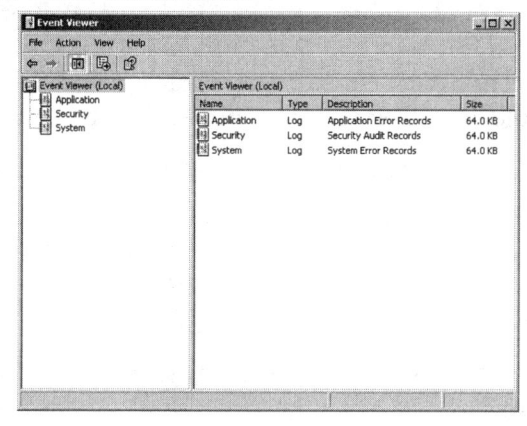

Table 13.2 outlines the format and structure of the event log entries.

Table 13.2 Event Entry Structure

Field	Description
Date	The date that the event occurred.
Time	The time that the event occurred.
Type	Type of event: application and system logs include Error, Information, or Warning types, and the security log includes Success Audit and Failure Audit.
User	The user account that triggered the event.
Computer	The name of the computer where the event occurred.
Source	The application that logged the events. In IIS context, it can be IIS services or its components, for example the IISLOG component.
Category	Classification of events, primarily used in the security log. For example, an audit account logon will be listed in the Account Logon category.
Event ID	Identification number associated with the event. You can use this Event ID to search the Microsoft website for more details about the event.
Description	The full details of the event. Additional details of the event will be recorded in this field and normally, the error code will be included here.
Data	Data associated with the event. You can either view this field in bytes or words mode. This data is usually useful when you need to further analyze the course of the event.

The event log file size must be a multiple of 64 KB. By default in the Windows Server 2003 family, the log size is 16384KB or 16 MB, and the default action to take when the maximum log size is reached is to overwrite events as needed. To configure the log file size and the action to take when the log file reaches its maximum size, perform these steps:

1. Click the **Start** menu, point to **Administrative Tools**, and click **Event Viewer**.
2. In the console tree, click the log you want to change. In this example you are changing the **System** Log.
3. Select **Properties** from the **Action** menu.
4. On the **General** tab (Figure 13.3), set the desired **Maximum log size**.

Figure 13.3 Configuring Event Log Properties

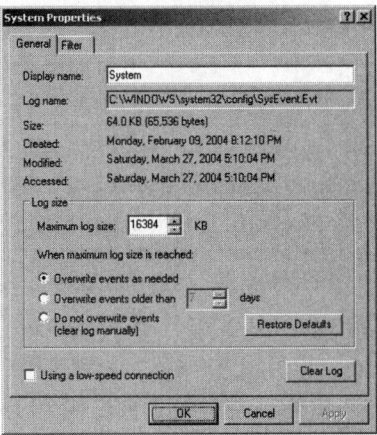

5. In the **When maximum log size is reached** section, select one of the following:

    - **Overwrite events as needed** This option will overwrite the oldest log entry when the log file reaches its maximum file size. This is the default option.
    - **Overwrite events older than [X] days** This option allows you to retain log information for the number of days you specify. If a log file reaches the maximum file size but is still within the retention period, new events will be discarded. The default number of days to retain events is **7** days.

- **Do no overwrite events** This option requires logs to be cleaned manually, as the Event Log service will not overwrite any old event entries. When the log reaches its maximum size, new events will be discarded.

6. If you wish to restore the default settings, click **Restore Defaults**. This will reset the log options to the default settings.

7. If you want to remove all existing log entries, click **Clear Log**. This will permanently remove all event log entries. If you want to retain the information currently in the log, click **Yes** when prompted to save the original log before clearing it, and then click **OK**. You are advised to archive log files on a regular basis.

8. Click **OK**.

It is recommended that you configure the system to audit account logon events and monitor these events in the security log. If you need to monitor special contents access, you must first turn on file or folder access auditing to capture request events made to the special contents. For more details on configuring security auditing for logon and contents access, please refer to the Windows Server 2003 help documentation.

Figure 13.4 shows a typical event log entry. In this example, a **Failure Audit** event was triggered in the security log. It has an event ID of **680** and it is from the **Security** component. This entry shows that user **ali** has failed to send correct user credentials and that the authentication process was not successful.

Figure 13.4 Event Properties Dialog Box

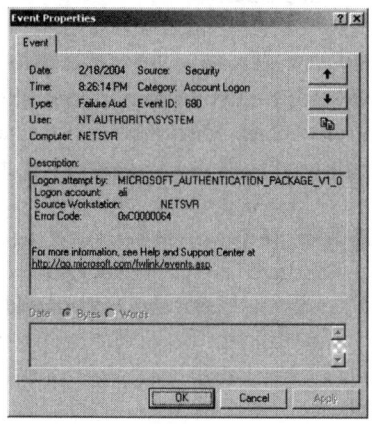

Now that you have learned about the Event Viewer, you will need to focus on IIS-related events. Table 13.3 lists common event types generated by related components.

Table 13.3 IIS Events

Component Events	Description
ASP	Errors and events triggered by the ASP scripting engine.
ASP.NET	Errors and events triggered by the ASP.NET scripting engine.
FTP	Events triggered by the FTP service.
WWW	Events triggered by the WWW service.
ODBC Log Driver	Events triggered by the IIS ODBC logging component.
Server-Side Include	Events triggered by SSI include files.
WWW Performance Counter	Events triggered by the WWW-related performance counter.
Core WWW Service component.	Events triggered by the Core Web server

To learn more about each event, you can refer to www.msdn.microsoft.com/library/en-us/iissdk/iis/iis_event_messages.asp. These events are vital for you to know the status and health of your IIS server. Each event log provides you with valuable information about the events occurring on the IIS server, and it is recommended that you review and audit event log entries on a regular basis.

You can use log analyzers to analyze event log contents, and you can configure filters in the Event Viewer to limit the types of events that you. By parsing the log, you can produce important analysis reports to help you determine server status as well as security risks. For example, you can use the Log Parser tool to generate a list of log entries that are all related to failed logon requests, and then you can combine this information with the site activities log file to determine which resource the request intended to access and from what IP address the request originated.

To find out more details on particular events and errors, you can click the Microsoft website link in the Event Properties dialog box (Figure 13.2), or you can view third-party events and errors at www.eventid.net.

REALITY CHECK...

By default, all IIS events and errors are captured in the Event Viewer. You can analyze the log entries to check the status and performance of your IIS server. It is recommended that you configure security auditing for logon events. To avoid too many entries for successful account logon events, you can configure auditing so that only failed attempts are logged. A failure audit log entry will be captured in the security log if there is an unsuccessful logon attempt.

You are advised to monitor Event Viewer logging on a regular basis. You can analyze event logs with Log Parser by Microsoft, or another third-party tool. If you need to find more information about a particular error or event, visit the resources mentioned in this section.

Monitoring HTTP API Error Logging

HTTP API error logs are generated by HTTP.SYS. This new kernel-mode driver handles HTTP requests and routes them to the related application pool. Errors occurring in this driver will trigger a log entry in the HTTP API error logs. By default, HTTP API error logging is enabled, and you can monitor this log file to troubleshooting client HTTP request errors. For example, a 503 status code indicates that the requested application was not available. This log file also captures illegal requests sent to IIS, including bad requests, forbidden access, and more.

BY THE BOOK...

In IIS 6.0, HTTP requests are now handled in kernel mode. This is a new network subsystem introduced in Windows Server 2003. Requests are now directly routed from the kernel mode driver HTTP.SYS to the correct application pool worker processes. This increases performance because it bypasses context-switching between user mode and the kernel mode driver, utilizing the cache mechanism to return cached content without the need for user mode interaction.

Any error that occurs during request receiving, routing and sending replies will trigger an error log entry in the HTTP API error log file. The log file is in pure ASCII plain text fixed format, and any text editor such as Notepad can be used to open and read the log file.

This section will recap the role played by HTTP.SYS in IIS 6.0 architecture, discuss how to properly configure HTTP.SYS, and will wrap up with information on configuring and analyzing the HTTP API error log.

HTTP.SYS has the following roles in IIS 6.0:

- Keeps track of all client connections to the server.
- Accepts HTTP requests and routes them to their respective application pool request queues.
- Facilitates Quality of Service (QoS) features, including connection limits, timeouts, request queue lengths and throttling bandwidth usages.
- Sends responses back to clients and implements kernel mode caching. Kernel mode caching allows HTTP.SYS to reply to client requests using cached responses without the need to call the application pool. This improvement allows fulfilled client requests in kernal mode to bypass routing to the user mode.
- Responsible for generating text-based logging for websites.

By default, HTTP API error logging is enabled. Log files are created in the %windir%/system32/LogFiles/HTTPERR folder and use the httperrX.log format. X refers to the running number of the log file, and X is automatically increased to X+1 when the log file reaches the maximum file size (default is 1MB). For example, if the first HTTP API error log file is httperr1.log, httperr2.log will be created when httperr1.log reaches 1MB.

You can configure HTTP.SYS behavior by manipulating the registry parameter. If the registry key does not exist in system registry, HTTP.SYS will use the default value specified in the kernel mode driver. HTTP API registry settings are loaded into the kernel mode driver whenever the HTTP service restarts. To reload HTTP API driver settings after making changes, you can restart the driver by issuing the **net stop HTTP** and **net start HTTP** commands at the command prompt. Table 13.4 outlines the HTTP.SYS settings in the system registry; these keys are located at Hkey_Local_Machine\System\CurrentControlSet\Services\HTTP\Parameters. All key values are in DWORD format.

Table 13.4 HTTP.SYS System Registry Settings

Registry Key	Description
AllowRestrictedChars	Hex-escaped characters that HTTP.SYS will accept in request URLs. Default value is 0 (disabled).
EnableErrorLogging	Enable HTTP API error logging. Default value is True.
EnableNonUTF8	Value 0, instructs HTTP.SYS to accept only UTF-8 encoded URLs. By default, the driver accepts American National Standards Institute (ANSI) and Double Byte Character Set (DBCS) encoded URLs in requests. Default value is 1 (enabled).
ErrorLogFileTruncateSize	Maximum file size (MB) of HTTP API error log. Default value 1MB.
ErrorLoggingDir	HTTP API error log path. Default log path is %SystemRoot%\System32\LogFiles.
FavorUTF8	By default HTTP.SYS always decodes a request URLs as UTF-8 first; if it fails, it will try to decode with ANSI and DBCS. Default value is 1 (enabled).
MaxConnections	Maximum connections allowed in HTTP.SYS. Default value is calculated automatically by HTTP.SYS.
MaxEndpoints	Maximum number of current endpoint objects allowed. Default value is 0, which indicates that the maximum endpoints will be determined by available memory.
MaxFieldLength	Maximum header size per request. Default value is 16KB.
MaxRequestBytes	Maximum total size of request content and header. Default value is 16KB.
PercentUAllowed	Specifies whether HTTP.SYS should accept %uNNNN notation in request URLs. NNNN is a Unicode number that represents Unicode characters. Default value is 1 (enabled).
UrlSegmentMaxCount	Maximum URL path segment allowed in one request. Default value is 255.
UrlSengmentMaxLength	Maximum number of characters in a request URL path segment. Default value is 260 characters.

Continued

Table 13.4 HTTP.SYS System Registry Settings

Registry Key	Description
UriEnableCache	Determines kernel mode cache status. Default value is 1 (enabled).
UriMaxUriBytes	Specifies the size of the response that will not be cached in kernel mode. This registry key instructs kernel mode driver control what content to be cached. If content size is lesser than the predefined size, the content will not cached. Default value is 262144 bytes (256KB).
UriScavengerPeriod	Frequency of time period to check cached response. If response has not been accessed after the specified time, the response will be flushed. Default value is 120 seconds.

It is important to note that the system registry holds the configuration settings of the operating system. An invalid configuration can damage the system or cause the operating system to malfunction. It is recommended that you back up the registry file before you start configuring registry settings. For more details about HTTP.SYS registry settings you can refer www.support.microsoft.com/?id=820729.

Table 13.5 lists the HTTP API error log fields and their descriptions.

Table 13.5 HTTP API Error Log Fields

Field	Example	Description
Date	2004-02-14	Date when the error occurred. Uses W3C format. YYYY-MM-DD.
Time	03:32:22	Time when the error occurred. Uses W3C format. HH:MM:SS.
Client IP Address	192.168.10.44	The IP address of the client that sent the request.
Client Port	2588	The source socket port number of the machine that sent the request.
Server IP Address	192.168.10.18	The IP address of the server that accepted the request.
Server Port	80	The server socket port number of the server that accepted the request.

Continued

Table 13.5 HTTP API Error Log Fields

Field	Example	Description
Protocol Version	HTTP/1.1	HTTP protocol version used in the request. Uses HTTP/X.X format.
Verb	GET	HTTP verb action sent in the request. The verb size cannot exceed 255 bytes.
CookedURL+Query	/../../cmd.exe	Targeted request content and query parameters sent along the request. Field will be truncated if it exceeds 4096 bytes.
Protocol Status	403	The protocol replies status assigned by IIS. Uses HTTP status code.
SiteID	-	The ID of the website from which the client made the request.
Reason Phrase	Forbidden	Explanation of why the error occurred.

If the field value is not available, it will be replaced by a hyphen (-). Whenever you view an HTTP API error log, you should pay attention to the Protocol Status and Reason Phrase fields. The following is a sample HTTP API error log entry:

```
2004-02-18 06:03:47 192.168.10.44 3897 192.168.10.18 80 HTTP/1.1
GET / 400 - Hostname
```

This log entry indicates the request was not successful (status code **400** bad request) because an error occurred when passing the **Hostname**. Typically, this is related to the host header sent in the request. The following is another example showing that the request was restricted by the kernel mode driver (status code **403** forbidden), because access to the requested resource is prohibited by the system.

```
2004-02-14 03:32:22 192.168.10.44 4534 192.168.10.18 80 HTTP/1.1
GET /../../cmd.exe 403 - Forbidden
```

By understanding all possible reasons for an error, you will be able to resolve the error and take the next course of action to deal with similar requests in the future. For example, if you notice that a certain group of IP addresses is sending requests to access cmd.exe or other command line utilities, you can configure IP address restriction in IIS to prevent further abuse. You can also report to the respective ISPs to file a complaint about the attack. Table 13.6 outlines the Reason Phrase field entries in HTTP API error log.

Table 13.6 HTTP API Error Log – Reason Phrase Details

Reason Phrase	Description
AppOffline	Indicates that the application is offline. Server responds with a "503 status code service unavailable" message.
AppPoolTimer	Indicates that the application is not available because the application pool is too busy. Server responds with a "503 status code service unavailable" message.
AppShutdown	Indicates that the application is being shutdown. Server responds with a "503 status code service unavailable" message.
BadRequest	Error occurred during request processing.
Connection_Abandoned_By_AppPool	Error occurred while the application worker process was processing the request.
Connection_Dropped	Not used. Reserved for future.
ConnLimit	Indicates that the connection limit was reached at the site level. Server responds with a "503 status code service unavailable" message.
Disabled	Similar to AppOffline, except that the application was taken offline by an administrator.
EntityTooLarge	Requested entity exceeded the permitted size limit. Refer to the MaxFieldLength and MaxRequestBytes registry key settings for HTTP.SYS.
FieldLength	Requested field length exceeded the permitted limit. Refer to MaxFieldLength and MaxRequestBytes registry key settings for HTTP.SYS.
Header	Error occurred when processing request header.
Hostname	Error occurred when processing request hostname.
Invalid_CR/LF	Error in request carriage return or line feed.

Continued

Table 13.6 HTTP API Error Log – Reason Phrase Details

Reason Phrase	Description
LengthRequired	Missing length value in request.
N/A	Internal error occurred while processing the request, such as kernel driver restart or memory allocation failed.
N/I	Unsupported encoding format.
Number	Error occurred when processing number.
Precondition	Request precondition detail missing.
QueueFull	Indicates that the application request queue is full. Server responds with a "503 status code service unavailable" message.
Timer_AppPool	Request connection timeout waiting in application pool. By default this value is 2 minutes.
Timer_ConnectionIdle	Request connection timeout after idle or inactive for certain period of time. By default, this value is 2 minutes.
Timer_EntityBody	Request connection timed out before the entity body was received by HTTP.SYS. By default, this value is 2 minutes.
Timer_HeaderWait	Request connection timed out when the header could not be processed within the predefined time frame. By default, this value is 2 minutes.
Timer_MinBytesPerSeconds	Request connection timed out when the response was not received by the client in a reasonable transfer time. By default, reasonable rate is 150 bytes/seconds or above.
Timer_Response	Not used. Reserved for future.
URL	Error occurred when processing request URL.
URL_Length	Request URL length over permitted limit.
Verb	Error occurred when processing request HTTP verb.
Version_N/S	Unsupported HTTP protocol version in request.

Now that you have learned about HTTP API error logging and what to monitor in the log files, you can further customize the log file and secure it with proper NTFS permissions. As mentioned earlier, the default log path is located at %windir%/system32/Logfiles/HTTPERR/. You can edit the registry key *ErrorLoggingDir*, described in Table 13.4, to relocate the log path. Remember, after you change the registry settings, you need to restart the HTTP service before the changes become effective. Next, if you decide to relocate the HTTP API error log path, ensure you grant administrators and system accounts Full Control NTFS permissions at the log path. If HTTP.SYS cannot create the log file in the new path, it will trigger an error in the Event Viewer system log.

Reality Check...

The HTTP error log contains critical information regarding errors occurring in HTTP.SYS. This error log is created when the kernel mode driver tries to process an incoming request, but fails. You can review the log file to find out why the request was not accepted.

It is important to note that this kernel mode error logging only pertains to HTTP requests. Other IIS components such as FTP or NNTP do not utilize this kernel mode driver for request routing. By default, HTTP API error logging is enabled. It is not recommended that you disable this error logging.

Monitoring URLScan Logging

URLScan is an Internet Server API (ISAPI) filter that can be installed in IIS 6.0. URLScan monitors incoming HTTP requests based on a set of rules. If requests do not comply with the URLScan rule sets, IIS replies with a "404 File Not Found" error to the client and writes an entry in the URLScan log file. To customize the rule sets, you can edit the URLScan.ini configuration file using a normal text editor such as Notepad. IIS 6.0 has similar built-in features provided by URLScan, so this filter is not included in IIS 6.0. You should assess your needs when determining whether a URLScan is needed. For example, IIS 6.0 does not have the capability of denying specific HTTP verbs such as HEAD, OPTION, DELETE and so on. The URLScan, however allows you to configure the DenyVerbs setting to filter certain HTTP verbs. By default, URLScan filter and configuration files are located at %windir%/system32/inetsrv/urlscan/. For more detail about URLScan and rule sets configuration, refer to Chapter 5.

By the Book...

URLScan was first introduced in IIS 5.0 to combat various worm attacks such as CodeRed and Nimda. It was designed to run in IIS 4.0 and IIS 5.0. The first two versions, 2.0 and 2.1, were equipped with the IIS Lockdown Tool. This tool includes a series of security templates and configuration programs capable of locking down the server. It secures and protects the server by reducing server functionality so that attack surfaces are minimized. This helps the system administrator disable unwanted IIS components and secure it with proper access permissions. It is recommended that you install IIS Lockdown with URLScan if you still have servers running older versions of IIS.

URLScan version 2.5 was first released as a seperate package. A couple of enhancements were introduced in this version, but it did not work with IIS 6.0. At the insistence of their clientele, Microsoft re-released a new version of 2.5 URLScan that was compatible with IIS 6.0. Most of the features included in URLScan are built-in in IIS 6.0. So, you need to analyze and determine whether your network necessitates URLScan. For more information about IIS 6.0 built-in security features and the differences between them and URLScan, you can refer to www.microsoft.com/technet/security/tools/urlscan.mspx?#XSLTsection123121120120.

Monitoring URLScan log files allows you to detect rejected requests or malicious attacks against your server. If you suspect your application request was blocked by URLScan, you can customize URLScan.ini to suit your application needs based on the log entry. Though logged details may indicate that the URLScan successfully thwarted a security strike, you are advised to further analyze attack patterns and take proactive measures to prevent attackers from further abusing the server.

Table 13.7 shows a subset of URLScan logging configuration parameters.

Table 13.7 URLScan Logging Settings in URLScan.ini

Parameter	Description
EnableLogging = 0 | 1	If set to 1, URLScan will log rejected requests to the URLScan logfile. If set to 0, logging is not enabled. Default value is 1.

Continued

Table 13.7 URLScan Logging Settings in URLScan.ini

Parameter	Description
PerProcessLogging = 0 | 1	If set to 1, URLScan will create separate log files for each w3wp.exe worker process. The log filename includes the Process ID (PID) of each worker process. This is required in IIS6 to ensure that separate worker processes do not attempt to lock the log file at the same time. If set to 0, all rejected requests are logged to the same file. Default value is 1.
PerDayLogging = 0 | 1	If set to 1, URLScan will create separate log files each day. The log filename will contain (in MMDDYY format) the day pertaining to the log file. If this setting is used in conjunction with PerProcessLogging then the filename will contain both the date and the PID in the format: Urlscan.DDMMYY.<processID>.log. Default value is 1.
LoggingDirectory = <path>	A full path that indicates where URLScan logs should be stored. By default, this is the *logs* folder in the location where URLScan is installed: %windir%/system32/inetsrv/urlscan/logs/

With these default configurations, URLScan will create daily log files for each worker process. By default, log files are created in the %windir%/system32/inetsrv/urlscan/logs/ folder. An example of a log file's saved name would be urlscan180204.2480.log, whereby the log file is created on 18th Feb 2004 by the worker process ID 2480. If the log path is secured with proper NTFS permissions, normal users will not be able to read the contents of the log files. Table 13.8 outlines the default user NTFS permissions for the URLScan log directory.

Table 13.8 Default NTFS Permissions for URLScan Logging Directory

User / Group	Permissions
Administrators	Full Control
IIS_WPG	Read, Write
Local Service	Read, Write
Network Service	Read, Write
System	Full Control

It is important to note that the application pool identities, such as Local Service and Network Service, are able to write log entries to this log directory. This is because these identities will be the user accounts that load up the URLScan filter, so these accounts require write permissions to the log file. If you decide to change the log path, you can edit URLScan.ini as discussed in Chapter 5. You must restart the IIS services before the changes will take effect.

Now, let's look at log entry format in URLScan log files. This log file is fairly simple and easy to understand. You will see the following details in a log entry:

- **Date and Time** Records the date and time when the request was blocked. The time is in local machine time.

- **Client IP Address** The IP address of the client who made the request.

- **Reason** The reason the request was rejected. This field will mention the rule that is disallowed.

- **Site ID** The ID of the website that the request was sent to.

- **Raw URL** The requested URL in raw format. This will be the URL path and the requested content name.

URLScan only monitors and screens HTTP requests. It does not inspect other IIS components such as NNTP and FTP requests. Consider the following log entry:

```
[02-18-2004 - 12:25:28] Client at 192.168.10.44 : URL contains
extension '.exe', which is disallowed. Request will be rejected.
Site Instance='1', Raw URL='/aa.exe'
```

This shows that website ID **1** rejected a client request from **192.168.10.44** because the URL request contained an **.exe** extension, which is not allowed in the URLScan.ini rule sets. Consider another example:

```
[02-18-2004 - 21:01:23] Client at 192.168.10.44: Sent verb
'PROPFIND', which is not specifically allowed. Request will be
rejected.
```

This request was rejected because HTTP verb **PROFIND**, which is related to Web Distributed Authoring and Versioning (WebDAV) is not allowed in the rule sets. Notice that there is no Site ID or Raw URL in this entry because this is a preliminary query request for IIS server to return more detail before WebDAV can continue the next request.

Finally, as mentioned in the previous section, you can utilize the Log Parser tool to help you analyze and parse important log entries in URLScan log file. You are advised to audit URLScan log files on a regular basis to detect any malicious attacks.

> **REALITY CHECK...**
>
> URLScan is an ISAPI filter that is hosted on the IIS server to inspect incoming HTTP requests. If a request does not meet the criteria in URLScan.ini, the request will be blocked and the client will receive a 404 response. It is important to note that URLScan only monitors HTTP requests, and that FTP, NNTP and other IIS components requests are not bound to the same rule sets.
>
> By default, URLScan logging is enabled, and it is not recommended that you disable this logging, as it can provide valuable information and hints about possible attacks to the IIS server. Since IIS 6.0 is shipped in default locked down mode, many URLScan features have been built in as IIS 6.0 core components. You should determine your needs and understand the differences between the built-in and URLScan features before you deploy URLScan on your IIS server. For more information on configuring URLScan, refer to Chapter 5.

Your A** is Covered if You...

- ☑ Enable different log sources, including Site, Events, HTTP API, and URLScan.
- ☑ Monitor and audit site activities logging.
- ☑ Monitor and audit Event Viewer logging.
- ☑ Monitor and audit HTTP API error logging.
- ☑ Monitor and audit URLScan logging.
- ☑ Take proactive actions based on various log sources.
- ☑ Secure and protect different log sources.

Index

404 error response, 33, 71, 106, 175, 364, 380

A

access
  configuring to authorization store, 166
  restricting based on IP addresses, 228
access control
  configuring permissions in Certificate
    Authority MMC, 321–322
  and Internet Printing, 354
  NNTP service, 288
Access Control Entries (ACEs), 163
Access Control Lists (ACLs), 23, 92, 116, 222
AccessURL, creating role for, 169–172
accounts
  administrative privileges, 60
  IIS 6.0 built-in, 136–137
  selecting for application pool identify, 200–202
  user. *See* user accounts
Active Directory
  configuring FTP user isolation, 221–227
  installation, 40
  POP3 accounts and passwords storage, 262
Active Directory Domain Controller (DC), log types in event viewer, 367
Active Directory Service Interface (ADSI)
  classes, 3
  scripts, 230
Active Server Pages. *See* ASP
Add Network Place wizard, 344
Add/Remove Programs, installing IIS6 with, 44–49
adding
  MIME types, 71, 72–75
  printer connections, 351
  remote domains, 243
addresses, IP. *See* IP addresses
Admin Base Objects (ABO), 13
administrative accounts, 60
administrative tools
  locating after IIS6 installation, 59–63
  Manage Your Server tool, 40–43
ADSI (Active Directory Services Interface), 59
advanced digest authentication
  configuring, 125–126
  mechanism described, 116
  support for (table), 9
alerts, creating special, 176
All Unknown CGI Extensions, enabling, 71
All Unknown ISAPI Extensions enabling, 71
Analog log analyzer software, 363
anonymous access
  creating, changing account, 96, 139
  disabling, 72, 254
  disabling for WebDAV Publishing, 329
  and Internet Printing, 354, 357
  and NTFS permissions, 89
  preventing default, 93
  website permission, 84
  when to grant, 99
anonymous authentication
  configuring, 117–120
  mechanism described, 116
  and web enrollment, 319
anonymous user name and FTP access, 218
answer files for installing IIS6, 50–53
antivirus programs, 31, 68
AppEvent.Evt, 368
application health monitoring, and worker process isolation mode, 16
application pools
  configuring identifies, 200–202
  described, using, 196–198
  IIS 6.0 improvements (table), 2–3
  and increased scalability, performance, 15
  isolating web applications, 203–206
  processor affinity, 17
Application Server, configuring your server as, 40–43
Application Server Console, 45
Application Server Manager, installing, 42
Application Server MMC described, using, 61–62
applications
  creating for URL authorization, 166–169
  enabling and disabling dynamic, 67–71
  logging events, 367
  restricting file types served by IIS, 76
  web. *See* web applications
  and worker process isolation mode, 15
architecture of IIS 6.0, 10–14
.ascx files, 186
ASP (Active Server Pages)
  and authentication, 116
  directives in, 184
  error messages, 176–179
  IIS subcomponent in Control Panel hierarchy (table), 46
  pages, paths for, 187–189
  scripts for Internet Printing, 349
ASP method Parent Path, 89
ASPError object, 181
ASP.NET
  configuring custom error message, 182–184
  described, 45
  errors, 176
  impersonation, 78
  installing, 42
  and IUSR_<machinename> account, 139

385

386   Index

user controls, 186
and user impersonation, 208
ASP.NET account IIS 6.0 running in IIS5 isolation mode, 142
aspnet_wp.exe, 140
attacks
   attack surface of servers, reducing, 49
   Denial of Service (DoS), 25, 250
   FTP port security, 230
   against FTP sites, 217
   hijacking threats, 162
   HTTP request, 192
   packet filtering, 231
   parent paths, 188
   on printers, 354
   profiling and worms, 68
   and restricting access to web content, 99
   risks of information disclosure, 177–178
   Sadmind/IIS worm, 54
   unauthorized access, 72
   and URLScan, 381
auditing
   best security practices, 32–34
   enabling FPSE log authoring, 346
   printer log files, 359
   server activity, 232, 296
authentication
   benefits and drawbacks of different mechanism, 134–1161
   and Certificate Services, 304
   configuring anonymous, 118–120
   configuring for FPSE, 341
   configuring on SMTP servers, 252–254
   described generally, 117–118
   FrontPage support, 333
   and FTP access, 217, 220
   IIS 6.0, new features, 88
   Internet Printing (table), 354
   Kerberos v5, 127–129
   NNTP service, 288, 290
   POP3 server methods, 262–265
   and relaying, 257–259
   and SSL, 150, 292
   Subauthentication, configuring, 132–133
   web enrollment, 319–320
authentication servers (ASs) and Kerberos v5, 127–128
Authorization Manager
   configuring URL authorization with, 163–175
   linking IIS to, 172–174
authorization store, creating, 164–166, 175
azman.msc, 163

B

back doors, 34
backups, system, 37

bandwidth
   limiting used by websites, 6
   logging IIS server, 365
basic authentication
   benefits and drawbacks of, 134–135
   configuring, 120–122
   configuring SMTP servers, 253–254, 259
   described, 116
   and web enrollment, 319
batch command files, browser handling of, 75
blocking HTTP requests, 143, 148
browsers
   and authentication, 117–118
   authentication method selection bug, 125
   controlling how data files are handled, 75
   digest authentication support, 122
   and Internet Printing, 349
   redirection to HTTP, 306
bugs
   alerting users with error page, 183–184
   browser authentication method selection, 125

C

cabinet files, 348
Cacls.exe, 93
CAs. *See* certificate authorities
centralized binary logging, 100, 112
Centralized Binary Logging, 324, 358
.cer files, 158
certificate authorities (CAs)
   configuring, 308–312
   described, structure, 151, 306–307
certificate requests
   generating SSL, 153–156
   submitting, 156–158
certificate revocation lists (CRLs), 151, 306–307, 312
Certificate Services
   best practices, 316
   certificate authorities, 306–307
   configuring, 308–317
   described, 303–306
   monitoring web enrollment access, 323–324
   opening Certification Authority MMC, 312
   securing, 303–307
   Web Enrollment Support component, 314–322
certificates
   and Certificate Services, 304–306
   configuring for SMTP servers, 256–257
   installing issued, 158–160
   managing website, 160–161
   and NNTP service, 288

Index   387

and SSL, 150
CertSrv directory, 314
CGI (Common Gateway Interface), 70
client access requests, monitoring, 362–366
client certificates, Certificate Services, 305
client IP addresses logging, 365
client nonce, 122
cmd.exe, 266
cmdlines.txt, 54
cnonce, 122–123
Code Red worm, 68, 192, 381
command-line tools, permissions for (table), 8
Common Gateway Interface (CGI), 70
Configure Your Server wizard, 40–43
configuring
   Access Control Lists (ACLs), 222
   advanced digest authentication, 125–126
   anonymous authentication, 118–120
   application pools, 198–202
   ASP error messages, 178–184
   authentication for Internet Printing, 355
   authentication, IIS mechanisms, 115–116
   basic authentication, 120–122
   Certificate Services, 308–317
   default documents, 91
   delegation, 133–134
   digest authentication, 122–125
   DNS domain for POP3 e-mail, 264
   event log properties, 370
   FrontPage Server Extensions (FPSE), 333–345
   FTP messages, permissions, authentication, 214–218
   host header names, 192
   HTTP.SYS, 374
   IIS 6.0, 172–174
   IIS Web permissions, 329–331
   Internet Printing, 347–353
   IP address restrictions, 76–82, 189–192
   IWA, 126–131
   mailboxes, POP3 servers, 265–267
   MIME, 71–75
   NNTP authentication, 270–279, 290–292
   NTFS permissions, 220
   ODCB logging, 108–112
   POP3 servers, 260–267
   remote logging, 113
   Secure Socket Layer (SSL), 348
   servers to use SSL, 150–163
   SMTP connection controls, 252, 254–257
   SMTP virtual servers, 240–252
   Subauthentication, 132–133
   UNC authentication, 131–132, 163–175
   URLScan, 142–150
   web application pool identities, 138–139
   web service extensions, 67–71
   WebDAV, 328–333
   website identities, 189–192
   websites' SSL options, 161–162
   worker isolation mode, 196–197
connecting Internet printers, 350–352
connections
   changing FTP ports, 229–230
   configuring NNTP virtual server settings, 276
   securing FTP, 227–231
constrained delegation, 9
control channel ports, 230
control code access security, 36
control messages, NNTP service, 275
Control Panel, IIS6 components hierarchy (table), 45–48
CPU monitoring, configuring for, 199
creating
   anonymous access account, 96
   application pools, 198
   certificate requests, 153–156
   default Web site, 43
   FTP site, 212–213
   local alias domain, 242
   new NNTP virtual server, 270–273
   newsgroups on NNTP virtual server, 281–282
   SMTP servers, 241–242
   virtual directory applications, 203–206
   web applications, 203
   web service extension access lists, 67
Creator Owner (Internet Printing), 353
CRLs. *See* certificate revocation lists
Cryptographic Service Provider (CSP), 310–311
customizing
   default NNTP virtual server, 274
   error messages, 175–184
   NNTP virtual server's W3C extended logging fields, 299
   W3C extended logging fields, 106–107
   web service extensions, 70

D

data
   channel ports, 230
   nonce, 122
Data Encryption Standard (DES), 305
data transfer modes, 230
debugging. *See* troubleshooting
default document, defining for website, 90
delegation
   constrained, 9
   described, configuring, 133–134
deleting
   See also removing

default Web site, 43
MIME types, 72, 75
newsgroups, 282
Denial of Service (DoS) attacks, 25, 250
Deny write permission, 95
DES (Data Encryption Standard), 305
digest authentication
    benefits and drawbacks of, 135
    configuring, 122–125
    mechanism described, 116
    support for (table), 9
    and web enrollment, 319
Digital Signature Algorithm (DSA), 305
directives, and include files, 184
directories
    attacking, 217
    configuring FTP output style, 216
    FTP, configuring user isolation, 221–227
    relating default FTP root path, 213–214
directory browsing, website permission, 83
Directory Listing Denial error, 91
disabling
    anonymous access, 119, 254
    behaviors with IISLockDown tool, 56–57
    default Web site, 43
    parent paths, 187–189
    Remote Registry service, 31
    token caching, 208
    URLScan logging, 384
    web service extensions, 67–71
    Windows services, 28–29
Distributed Transaction Coordinator. See DTC
Domain Controllers (DCs)
    configuring your server as, 40
    and advanced digest authentication, 125
Domain Name Server (DNS)
    domains and SMTP configurations, 242–244
    log types in event viewer, 367
    names, sample configuration (table), 190
domain names
    accessing Internet Printing, 354
    Fully Qualified Domain Name (FQDN), 154
    limiting NNTP access by, 293
    and IP address restrictions, 82
domains
    adding remote, 243
    configuring IP address restrictions for, 81
    configuring SMTP server, 242–244
DoS (Denial of Service) attacks, 25, 250
download sites
    Authorization and Profile Application Manager, 164
    IIS 6.0 Resources Kit, tools, 133, 364
    IIS6 Migration tool, 58

security bulletins, Windows updates, 27
SSLDiag, 160
URLScan, 143
Windows Server 2003 security and deployment guides, 34, 49
drivers, printer, 349
DSA (Digital Signature Algorithm), 305
DTC, 42, 45
DWORD format, 374
dynamic applications, enabling and disabling, 67–71

E

e-mail
    configuring DNS domain for POP3, 264
    mailboxes. See mailboxes
    and SMTP, 240
    SMTP relay controls, 257–260
    SMTP server configuration, 286
editing
    IIS6 installation answer file, 50–53
    newsgroups, 282
    URLScan log files, 380
EHLO command, 244
enabling
    Active Server Pages, 349–350
    ASP in IIS web service extensions list, 353
    delegation in Windows 2003 domain, 133–134
    file-level security, 30–32
    FPSE authoring, 338–342
    FTP access log file, 232–238
    Internet Printing, 349
    IPSec, 114
    NNTP access log files, 296–301
    parent paths, 187–189
    SMTP logging, 246–249
    SSL authentication for clients, 292
    W3C extended format logging on website, 101
    web access log files, 98–114
    web service extensions, 67–71
    WebDAV, 326–328
    Windows services, 28–29
    worker isolation mode, 196–197
encryption
    128-bit, enabling, 161
    PPTP data security, 231
    and SSL, 150
    symmetric and public/private key, 152
    TLS, enabling on SMTP servers, 254
enhancements to IIS 6.0, 1–19
enrollment support. See web enrollment support
Enterprise CAs, 307
error logs. See logging

Index

error messages
  '404 File Not Found,' 175
  ASP, configuring, 176–179
  configuring custom, 175–184
  'Unauthorized: Logon failed due to server configuration,' 117
errors
  404 error response, 71, 175, 364
  Directory Listing Denial, 91
  HTTP API error logging, 374–380
  logging in Event Viewer, 367
ESMTP (SMTP extensions), 244
event log service, 367
Event Viewer, 33, 367–373
events
  configuring log entries, 370
  IIS (table), 372
.evt log files, 368
exceptions, unhandled, creating error messages for, 176
executables, website permission, 83, 84
Execute permissions, 331
expiration policy for newsgroups, 283–284, 287
Extended Simple Mail Transfer Protocol (ESMTP), 244

F

Failure Audit log entry, 368
file-level security, server application of, 30
File Transfer Protocol. *See* FTP
filename extensions, blocking and allowing, 149
files
  controlling browser handling of data, 75
  include, securing, 184–187
filters
  configuring in Event Viewer, 372
  ISAPI. *See* ISAPI
  URLScan, 380
firewalls
  in networking environments, 24
  protecting IIS server with, 230
folders, configuring SMTP service, 244–246
FPSE. *See* FrontPage Server Extensions
FPSE authoring, enabling, 336–340
FPSE Tighten Security Wizard, 343
FPSE Virtual Host (Extended Web site), 340
FQDN (Full Quality Domain Name), 76
FrontPage Server Extensions (FPSE)
  configuring and securing, 333–345
  enabling Web Service Extension, 335
  IIS5 and IIS6, 56
  installing, 42, 334–336
  managing with Microsoft Sharepoint Administration, 62

securing virtual host, 340–345
FTP (File Transfer Protocol)
  configuring access log file, 232–238
  configuring directory output style, 216
  configuring messages, 214–215
  configuring server root folder, 54
  configuring user isolation, 221–227
  IIS status codes (table), 236–238
  IIS subcomponent in Control Panel hierarchy (table), 46
  IIS6 component described, 211
  relocating default root path, 213–214
  securing connections, 227–231
  securing resources, 216–220
  security summary, 238
  user isolation, IIS 6.0 improvements (table), 9
FTP connections, securing, 231
FTP servers, IIS 6.0 service described, 10
FTP Site Creation wizard, 212–213, 222, 226
FTP sites, creating new, 212–213
Fully Qualified Domain Name (FQDN), 76, 154

G

group policy, disabling IIS installations with (table), 8
groups
  hardening Windows Server 2003, 29–30
  IIS_WPG account, 137
  user rights, default (table), 98–99

H

Hardware Compatibility Lists (HCLs), Windows 2003, 55
hashed passwords, 122, 125, 127
.hdr files, 275
HELO command, 244
hosting discussion groups, 270
.hsh files, 275
HTTP (Hypertext Transfer Protocol), 401.2 error, 117
HTTP API error logging, 33, 324, 374–380
HTTP Error logging, 101, 358, 362
HTTP errors, configuring custom messages, 175–184
HTTP headers and SSL authentication, 163
HTTP and Internet Printing, 348
HTTP requests, 143, 153–156
HTTP status codes (table), 105–107
HTTP verbs, allowing for WebDAV Publishing, 328
httpext.dll, 47
httpodbc.dll, 47
HTTP.SYS, 5, 12, 88, , 374–376

Index

Hypertext Transfer Protocol. *See* HTTP

I

ICF (Internet Connection Firewall), 24
identities, application pool, Network Service, 202
idle timeout, configuring application pools to support, 199
IDSs (Intrusion Detection Systems), 25, 68
IIDC, IIS subcomponent in Control Panel hierarchy (table), 47
IIS 5.0
 isolation mode, 17–19, 139–142
 upgrading to IIS6, 55–59
 worker isolation mode in, 196–197
IIS (Internet Information Services) 6.0
 access control process, 76–78
 application isolation, 203
 application processing modes, 14–19, 135–136
 architecture, services described, 10–14
 availability and reliability improvements (table), 2–3
 configuring, 172–174
 Core files (table), 45
 enhancements to, 1–19
 events (table), 372
 FTP component, 211
 hierarchy of components in Control Panel (table), 45–48
 HTTP status codes (table), 105–107
 installing components on Microsoft Server 2003, 39
 installing using unattended setup, 49–54
 installing with Add/Remove Programs, 44–49
 Internet Printing. *See* Internet Printing
 locating administrative tools after installation, 59–63
 manageability improvements (table), 4–5
 migration tool, 58
 monitoring components generally, 361
 new security features, 88–90
 non-default installation (table), 7
 running in IIS5 isolation mode, 139–142
 running in worker process mode, 136–139
 security checklist, 35–37
 upgrading IIS5 to, 55–59
 vulnerabilities, reducing, 49
 Web permissions (table), 330–331
 website request handling, 190
 worker isolation mode, 59, 195
 WWW publishing service, 14
IIS 6.0 Resource Kit, downloading tools, 133
IIS Lockdown Tool, 56, 143, 381

IIS Log
 Certificate Services support, 323
 logging, 100, 232, 297, 358
IIS Manager
 IIS subcomponent in Control Panel hierarchy (table), 46
 installing, 42
 opening using administrative privileges, 60
IIS Metabase
 best security practices, 36
 editing to disable default Web fault, 43
 history, backup and restore (table), 4
 IIS support, 3
 and Inetinfo.exe, 12
IIS Services and logging formats (table), 363
IIS Web permissions and NTFS permissions, 328–329
IIS6. *See* IIS (Internet Information Services) 6.0
Iisftp.vbs, 225
IIS_WPG group account, 137
IMAP (Internet Message Access Protocol), 240
impersonation, user, 207–208
in-process web applications, hosting, 13
include files, securing, 184–187
indexing service
 and web enrollment, 318
 website permission, 83, 86, 331
Inetinfo.exe process and IIS Admin service, 12–13
.ini files, browser handling of, 75
installing
 Certificate Services to support standalone CAs, 308–312
 FrontPage Server Extensions (FPSE), 334–336, 42
 FTP service, 212
 IIS on Microsoft Server 2003, 39–43
 IIS6, 44–54
 POP3 server, 260–261
 printer drivers, 351
 shared printers, 353
Integrated Windows Authentication. *See* IWA
Internet Connection Firewall (ICF), 24
Internet Data Connector. *See* IDC
Internet Information Services. *See* IIS
Internet Message Access Protocol. *See* IMAP
Internet Printing
 configuring, 347–353
 monitoring, 357–359
 securing, 354–357
Internet Printing Protocol (IPP), 347, 348
Internet Protocol Security. *See* IPSec
Internet Security and Acceleration (ISA) servers, 24

Index

Internet Server Application Program Interface. *See* ISAPI
InternetServer section, installation answer file (table), 52–53
intranet security zone, 126
Intrusion Detection Systems (IDSs), 25, 68
IP addresses
  accessing Internet Printing, 354, 356
  configuring, 189–192
  configuring restrictions, 75–81
  limiting NNTP access by, 293
  restricting access based on, 227–228
  W3C Extended logging, 247–248
IPSec
  configuration, 114
  securing FTP connections with, 231
ISA servers vs. ICF, 24
ISAPI
  extensions, IIS5 and IIS6, 55, 57
  filters, IIS 6.0 improvements, 13
  filters, security recommendations, 36
  and Inetinfo.exe, 18
  installing, 42
  URLScan. *See* URLScan
Isolate user mode (FTP), 223–225
isolating web applications, 203–206
isolation mode
  See also worker process isolation mode
  benefits of, 14–19
  IIS5, 139–141
IUSR_<COMPUTER-NAME> user account, 216, 218
IUSR_<machinename> account, 139, 142
IUSR_<webserver-name> account, 119
IWA (Integrated Windows Authentication)
  benefits and drawbacks of, 134–135
  configuring, 126–131
  enabling in intranet environment, 328–329
  mechanism described, 116
  and web enrollment, 319
IWAM_<computername> account, 141–142
IWAM_<machinename> account and isolation mode, 18

J

JScript, 26

K

Kerberos Distribution Center (KDC), 128
Kerberos v5 authentication, 127–129
kernel, IIS 6.0's new HTTP.sys mode driver, 12

L

LDAP (Lightweight Directory Access Protocol) and SMTP configurations, 252
LiveStats log analyzer software, 363
Local Security Authority Subsystem (LSASS), 13
Local Service account, 136–137, 200–202
LocalSystem account, 18, 123, 136
locked-down mode, IIS installation, 8
Log Parser command line utility, 364
log visits, website permission, 83, 86
logging
  best security practices, 32–34
  centralized binary, 112
  Certificate Services, supported formats, 323–324
  configuring URLScan, 143–150
  disabling for directories, 101
  enabling for SMTP service, 246–249
  enabling FPSE log authoring, 343
  enabling ODBC, 108–112
  enabling on NNTP virtual server, 297–298
  Event Viewer event entry structure (table), 369
  FTP access, 232–238
  HTTP API error, 374–380
  IIS 6.0, improvements in (table), 7
  IIS6-supported formats, 362
  Internet Printing access, 357
  log analyzer software, 363
  monitoring event viewer, 367–373
  POP3 servers, choosing level for, 267
  site activities, 362–366
  supported by IIS Services (table), 363
  URLScan, 380–384
  W3C Extended, 103, 247–248
logins and access to FTP resources, 216
logons
  attempts, logging, 259
  configuring security of, 373
  risks of information disclosure, 177
  'Unauthorized' error, 117
.lst files, 275

M

mailboxes
  configuring, 265–267
  enabling quotas, 266
  POP3 server, encrypted password file, 262
man-in-the-middle attacks, 162
Manage Your Server tool, 40
managing
  NNTP newsgroups, 279–287

392 Index

patches and updates, 25–28
printers, 352
website certificates, 160–161
MAPI (Messaging API), 240
MBSA (Microsoft Baseline Security Analyzer), 27
mbschema.xml, 12–13
MDAC (Microsoft Data Access Component), 26
Message Queuing, IIS subcomponent in Control Panel hierarchy (table), 48
messages
  configuring FTP, 214–215
  configuring SMTP server, 250
  errors. *See* error messages
  NNTP service types, 275
  unwanted postings to newsgroups, 280
Messaging API. *See* MAPI
Metabase Explorer tool, 124, 245
Microsoft Baseline Security Analyzer (MBSA), 27
Microsoft Certificate Services, 153
Microsoft Data Access Component (MDAC), 26
Microsoft Exchange Server, 240, 270
Microsoft Log Parser 2.1, 364
Microsoft Management Console, 42
Microsoft Outlook and Microsoft Exchange Server, 240
Microsoft Passport, 88, 117, 132
Microsoft Server 2003, various installation components, 39
Microsoft Sharepoint products, 334
Migration tool (IIS5 to IIS6), 58
MIME (Multi-Purpose Internet Mail Exchange)
  configuring, 71–75
  creating access lists, 76
  recognized types served, 8
MMC (Microsoft Management Console), 42
monitoring
  applications' health, 16
  Certificate Services Web Enrollment access, 323–324
  CPU, configuring application pools to support, 199
  event viewer logging, 367–373
  HTTP API error logging, 373–380
  Internet Printing, 357–359
  site activities logging, 362–366
  URLScan logging, 380–384
MS DOS, directory output style, 216
Multi-Purpose Internet Mail Extension. *See* MIME

N

National Center for Supercomputing Applications (NCSA), 100, 296, 362
NCSA Common logging format, 100, 232, 296, 323, 358
.NET framework, 26, 36
NetBIOS names and HTTP requests, 189
Network COM+, 42–43
network load balancing (NLB), 366
Network News Transfer Protocol (NNTP), 35
Network Service
  account, 136
  application pool identity, 202
networking environment, securing, 23–25
New NNTP Virtual Server Wizard, 270–273
New SMTP Domain Wizard, 242
New SMTP Virtual Server Wizard, 241–242
newfeed service, 270
newsgroup message files, 275
newsgroups
  configuring expiration, 283–284
  NNTP. *See* NNTP newsgroups
  preventing unwanted postings, 280
  requiring secure channel with SSL connection, 292
  using moderation in, 285–287
NIMDA worm, 192, 381
NLB (network load balancing), 366
NNTP (Network News Transfer Protocol)
  IIS subcomponent in Control Panel hierarchy (table), 46
  posting related settings (table), 278
  protocol described, 35
  servers. *See* NNTP virtual servers
NNTP newsgroups
  best security practices, 295
  managing, 279–287
  planning security for, 296
  securing, 287–296
NNTP virtual servers
  authentication methods (table), 290
  creating, configuring, 270–279
  enabling logging on, 297–298
  IIS 6.0 service described, 10
  posting settings, 277–279
  status codes (table), 300–301
nonce described, 122
NT file system permissions. *See* NTFS permissions
NTFS formatted drives and FPSE, 334
NTFS permissions
  and authentication, 116, 120
  basic access control lists (table), 92

Index   393

best security practices, 36
combining with website permissions, 87
configuring, 220
configuring FTP site logging with, 238
configuring for WebDAV Publishing, 326–332
default (table), 97
file type recommendations (table), 96
formatting operating system partitions with, 30
and FTP sites, 216–217
IIS5 and IIS6, 56
protecting log files with, 115
restricting control message postings, 289
and unauthorized access attacks, 72
viewing and modifying, 93
and website permissions, 82
NTLM v2 authentication, 127
.nws files, 275

O

ODBC logging, 297, 362
  Certificate Services support, 323
  format described, 100
  logging format described, 232
  printer activity, 358
  properties (table), 108–109
Open Database Connectivity. *See* ODBC logging
operating system
  registry settings, 376
  Windows Server 2003. *See* Windows Server 2003
out of process web applications, 141
Outlook Web Access (OWA), 149

P

packet filtering attacks, preventing, 231
parent paths, disabling, 187–189
PassivePortRange property, configuring, 230–231
passport authentication, 88, 117, 132
passwords
  See also permissions, user rights
  changing for mailboxes, 266
  hashing described, 122
  impersonation, and anonymous authentication, 120
  storing in Active Directory, 262
  and token caching, 207
patches and updates, managing, 25–28
per binary basic setting, web service extensions, 67

performance
  and application isolation, 204
  application pools and, 196–197
  encryption's effect on, 150
Perl scripts, 70
permissions
  See also passwords, user rights
  for business web application contents, 205–206
  CA Web Enrollment virtual directory, 318
  configuring access, in Certificate Authority MMC, 321–322
  configuring for WebDAV Publishing, 328–335
  default registry (table), 98
  Deny write, 95
  NTFS, 30–32, 216–217, 220
  setting website, 82–88
  and unauthorized access attacks, 72
  using Event Viewer to help configure, 368
PKI (Public Key Infrastructure), 304
plaintext and FTP credentials, 227
Point-to-Point Tunneling Protocol (PPTP), 231
POP3 servers
  choosing logging level, 267
  configuring and securing, 260–265
  configuring mailboxes, 265–267
  described, 49
  and e-mail, 240
  logging format, 363
ports
  configuring FTP, 229–230
  well-known IIS (table), 24
Post Office Protocol 3. *See* POP3
printer drivers, 349, 351
printing, Internet. *See* Internet Printing
process identity and user impersonation, 207
process recycling
  configuring application pools to support, 199
  described (table), 3
  and worker processes, 16
processor affinity, 17
profiling, attacker's use of, 68
Protocol Substatus, 101, 104, 358
protocols
  See also specific protocol
  enabling firewall control, 24
public key cryptography
  and Certificate Services, 305
  and SSL, 151, 152
Public Key Infrastructure (PKI), 304
publishing services

deciding upon appropriate, 345
Web, described, 14

Q

Quality of Service (QoS) functionality and HTTP.sys, 12

R

RAID and NNTP virtual servers, 273
rapid-fail protection, configuring application pools to support, 199
Read, website permission, 83
redundant array of independent disks. *See* RAID
registry
  default permissions (table), 98
  disabling token caching, 207
  HTTP.SYS system settings (table), 375–376
relaying
  evaluating requirements, 267
  and SMTP servers, 257–259
reliability and application isolation, 204
Remote Administration
  IIS subcomponent in Control Panel hierarchy (table), 47
  website described, using, 61–62
Remote Desktop Web Connection, IIS subcomponent in Control Panel hierarchy (table), 47
Remote logging, 100, 113, 324, 358
Remote Procedure Call (RPC), 28
Remote Registry service, 31
removing
  See also deleting
  MIME types, 72, 75
  unwanted application mapping at website level, 87
renaming SMTP servers, 240
reports based on log files, 363
request identity and user impersonation, 207
request queue limit, configuring application pools to support, 199
requests
  file-level security, 30
  IIS access control process, 76–78
resources
  Certificate Services, 307
  Default Permissions and User Rights, 99
  FPSE and URLScan, 336
  FTP, securing, 216–220
  FTP status code definitions, 238
  FTP user isolation, 221–227
  IE intranet security zone, 126
  IIS events, 372
  Kerberos authentication, 129

MBSA information, 28
Sadmind/IIS worm, 54
securing ASP.NET applications, 36
security bulletins, Windows updates, 27
Setspn.exe tool, 130
Trustworthy Computing, 21
URLScan logging, 381
Windows 2003 Server Deployment Guide, 49
Windows Server 2003 Security Guide, 34
Windows Server Cryptography, 304
writing secure code recommendations, 37
restricting
  access to protect web enrollment, 320–322
  SMTP server messages, 249–250
role-based authorization, 163, 193, 333
roles
  creating for FPSE, 340–342
  managing for websites, 340
root CAs, 307
routers in networking environments, 23
routing, LDAP, 252
RPCs (Remote Procedure Calls), 28
runas command, 60

S

Sadmind/IIS worm, 54
scalability improvements in IIS 6.0, 5–7
scope, creating for URL authorization, 168–169
scripts
  ASP, for printing, 349–350
  Perl, 70
  website permission, 83, 84, 86, 88
SecEvent.Evt, 368
Secure Hash Algorithm (SHA-1), 311
Secure Password Authentication (SPA), 263
Secure Sockets Layer (SSL)
  authentication. *See* SSL authentication
  configuring, 150–163, 348
  deploying, 270
  use of certificates, 151
securing
  Certificate Services, 303–323
  FPSE virtual host, 340–345
  FrontPage Server Extensions (FPSE), 333–345
  FTP connections, 227–231, 231
  FTP resources, 216–220
  include files, 184–187
  IIS 6.0 improvements, 7–9
  Internet Printing, 354–357
  log files, 33, 366
  NNTP access log files, 296–301
  NNTP newsgroups, 287–296
  POP3 server, 260–267

Index 395

SMTP and POP3 services, 239
SMTP virtual servers, 252
web access log files, 99–115
web publishing generally, 325
web resources, 87
WebDAV, 328–333
security
   advanced web server configuration, 115
   application pools, 16–17, 203
   auditing and logging, 32–34, 373
   bulletins, 27
   FTP home directory relocation, 216
   IIS 6.0 improvements, 19
   log files, security guidelines, 114
   logging aspects of, 367
   minimizing dynamic contents for IIS processing, 67
   network, best practices, 25
   new IIS 6.0 features, 88–90
   plaintext and FTP credentials, 227
   reducing server attack surface, 49
   Trustworthy Computing, 21
   WebDAV vulnerabilities, 333
   website permissions, best practices, 83–85
   Windows Server 2003 Security Guide download, 34
server certificates and Certificate Services, 305
Server Side Includes (SSI) web service extension, 47
servers
   See also specific server
   configuring NNTP virtual, 270–279
   configuring with wizard, 40–43
   POP3, 49
   SMTP. *See* SMTP servers
   upgrading to IIS6, 55–59
Service Principal Name (SPN) and authentication, 130
services used by IIS 6.0
   described (table), 11
   and ports (table), 24
   SMTP, 240
Setpn.exe, 130
SHA-1 (Secure Hash Algorithm), 311
shared printers, installing and configuring, 353
shared secrets, 128
Sharepoint Administration
   configuring FrontPage server defaults, 338–339
   website, 62–63
Sharepoint products, 334
Simple Mail Transfer Protocol. *See* SMTP
site activities monitoring, logging, 362–366

Site Administration homepage, and extended websites, 339
SMTP (Simple Mail Transfer Protocol)
   IIS subcomponent in Control Panel hierarchy (table), 46
   installing, 43
   and newsgroups, 285
   servers, IIS 6.0 service described, 10
SMTP extensions (ESMTP), 244
SMTP status codes (table), 248–249
SMTP virtual servers
   configuring, 240–252
   configuring authentication, 252–254
   configuring relay controls, 257–260
   configuring TLS, 256–257
   connection controls, 252, 254–255
   enabling logging, 246–249
   folders, configuring, 244–246
   LDAP routing, configuring, 252
   non-security-related configuration options, 249–252
   renaming, 240
   security, 252
snooping attacks, 162
SPA (Secure Password Authentication), 263
spammers and SMTP folders, 245
SPN. *See* Service Principal Name
SQL injection vulnerabilities, 37, 177
SSL. *See* Secure Sockets Layer (SSL)
SSL authentication
   configuring website SSL options, 161–162
   creating and configuring roles, 169–172
   enabling for clients, 292
   encryption limitations, 162
   generating certificate requests, 153–156
   installing issued certificate, 158–160
   managing website certificates, 160–161
   SSL diagnostics tool, 160
   submitting certificate requests, 156–158
SSLDiag diagnostic tool, 160
standalone CAs, 307
status codes
   analyzing in log files, 366
   IIS NNTP (table), 300–301
   reply status, 365
   SMTP (table), 248–249
.stm, shtm, shtml files, 184
SubAuthentication
   configuring, 132–133
   installation of, 9
svchost.exe, 14
symmetric encryption, 152
SysEvent.Evt, 368
sysocmgr.exe, 54

T

TCP ports, configuring, 189–192
testing
   authorization store, 175
   WebDAV folder, 332
TGTs (ticket granting tickets) in Kerberos v5, 127–128
TLS (Transport Layer Security), SMTP virtual server security, 252, 256–257
token caching, clearing, 207
Transport Layer Security. *See* TLS
troubleshooting
   client HTTP request errors, 373
   Inetinfo.exe failures, 17
   with log files, 32, 362
   request error issues, 114
Trustworthy Computing, 21
.txt files, 275

U

unattended setup, IIS6, 49–54
unauthorized access attacks, 72
UNC authentication
   configuring, 131–132
   mechanism described, 117
Universal Naming Convention (UNC) method, 100
Universal Transformation Format. *See* UTF
UNIX directory output style, 216
updates
   and patches, managing, 25–28
   security, 34
   Windows, downloading, 27
upgrading
   IIS5 to IIS6, 55–59
   Windows 2000 Server running IIS 5.0, 19
URL authorization, configuring with Authorization Manager, 163–175
URLScan
   and FrontPage authoring, 335
   logging, 33, 380–384
   tool described, 142–143
UseDigestSSP metabase key and digest authentication, 123–126
user accounts
   access control lists and NTFS permissions, 92
   delegation and, 133
   enabling certificate mapping, 162
   hardening Windows Server 2003, 29–30
   IUSR_<COMPUTER-NAME>, 216
   managing for websites, 339
   permissions for command-line tools, 8
   storing in Active Directory, 262
user controls, ASP.NET, 186
user impersonation, 207–208
user names, logging, 365
user rights
   application pool Network Service identity, 200–202
   for common IIS 6.0 accounts (table), 137–138
   default, in CA (table), 321
   default (table), 98–99
   held by common IIS 5.0 isolation mode (table), 140–141
   Internet Printing default (table), 352
   permissions. *See* passwords, permissions
UTF-8 logging, 100, 323, 358, 362

V

VBScript, error handling, 182
Virtual Private Networks (VPNs) and FTP security, 231
viruses
   and antivirus programs, 31
   Sadmind/IIS worm, 54
   worms. *See* worms
Visual Studio.Net, 62, 333
VPNs (Virtual Private Networks), 231
vulnerabilities
   in IIS, reducing, 49
   parent paths, 188

W

W3C Extended
   Certificate Services, supporting logging format, 323
   fields described (table), 234–235
   logging fields (table), 103–104
   logging format, 100, 232, 296, 363, 364
   logging printer activity, 357
   and MIME types, 75
   NNTP, logging fields (table), 298–299
warning messages in log files, 367
Web application pools, 15, 136, 138
web applications
   creating scope, URL authorization, 168–169
   hosting, 13
   isolating with isolation pools, 203–206
   out of process, 141
Web Distributed Authoring and Versioning. *See* WebDAV
web enrollment, 307, 320–322
Web Enrollment Support component, Certificate Services, 314–322
web gardens
   configuring application pools to support, 199
   described, 6
   and worker process isolation mode, 16

Index   397

Web permissions, IIS (table), 332–333
Web publishing service, 14, 325
Web Server Certificate wizard, 159–160
Web servers, IIS 6.0 service described, 10
Web Service Administration and Monitoring. (WSAM), 14
web service extensions
   enabling and disabling, 66–70
   wildcards in, 75
WebDAV (Web Distributed Authoring and Versioning)
   configuring, securing, 328–333
   described, security vulnerabilities, 333
   and FPSE, 335
   installing and enabling, 326–328
   publishing, IIS subcomponent in Control Panel hierarchy (table), 47
website identities, 189–190
websites
   and application isolation, 205
   Certificate Services, 307, 316
   configuring IP address, TCP port, host-header combinations, 189–192
   configuring SSL options, 161–162
   default, disabling, 43
   defining default document, 90
   enabling W3C extended logging format, 101
   extending to allow FPSE authoring, 336
   IE intranet security zone, 126
   IIS site activity logging, 33
   information on FPSE and URLScan, 338
   Kerberos authentication, 129
   MBSA information, 28
   Microsoft Server 2003 help documentation, 349
   PKI information, 304
   relocating web content, 89–90
   Remote Administration, 61–62
   restricting IP addresses and domain names, 76
   scalability improvements, 6
   secure ASP.NET applications, 36
   setting permissions for, 81–87
   Setspn.exe tool, 130
   Sharepoint Administration, 62–63
   Trustworthy Computing, 21
   W3C Extended logging, 238
   WebDAV publishing limitations, 333
   Windows 2003 protocol transition, 134
   Windows 2003 Server Deployment Guide, 49
   writing secure code recommendations, 37
Welcome to the Web Server Certificate Wizard, 256
Windows 2003 Server. *See* Windows Server 2003
Windows Components Wizard, 44, 309
Windows Explorer, assigning NTFS permissions with, 92–93
Windows Internet Name Service (WINS), 130
Windows Management Instrumentation (WMI), 3, 59
Windows scripting engine, 26
Windows Security Event Log, logon attempts, 259
Windows Server 2003
   hardening, generally, 21–23
   installing IIS6 during setup, 50–53
   securing user accounts, groups, 29–30
Windows Server Cryptography, 304
Windows services, enabling, disabling, 28–29
Windows Sharepoint Services (WSS), 334
winpop createquotefile command, 267
winpop.exe tool, 261
WINS (Windows Internet Name Service), 130
wizards
   Add Network Place, 344
   Configure Your Server, 40–43
   FPSE Tighten Security, 343
   FTP Site Creation, 212–213
   New NNTP Virtual Server, 270–273
   New SMTP Domain, 242
   New SMTP Virtual Server, 241–242
   Web Server Certificate, 159–160
   Welcome to the Web Server Certificate, 256
   Windows Components, 44, 309
WMI (Windows Management Instrumentation), 59
worker isolation mode, 195–199
worker process isolation mode, 14–17, 88–89, 136–139
World Wide Web Publishing service
   IIS subcomponent in Control Panel hierarchy (table), 48
   installing, 42
worms
   See also attacks
   described, protecting against, 68, 192
   Sadmind/IIS worm, 54
   and URLScan, 381
Write, website permission, 83, 84, 86
WSAM (Web Service Administration and Monitoring), 14
WWW, configuring server root folder, 54
WWW Publishing service, disabling, 56–57

X

Xcacls.exe, 93–95

Syngress: *The Definition of a Serious Security Library*

Syn·gress (sin–gres): *noun, sing.* Freedom from risk or danger; safety. See *security*.

AVAILABLE MAY 2004!
ORDER at
www.syngress.com

CYA: Securing IIS 6.0
The down and dirty guide to configuring, maintaining, and troubleshooting essential Exchange Server 2003 features. Network engineers operate in high-stress environments where competitive business demands often run counter to "best practices." Design and planning lead times are non-existent and deployed systems are subject to constant end-runs. But at the end of the day, they are held accountable if things go wrong. They need help. They need to guarantee they've configured their network professionally and responsibly. A highly portable, easily digestible road-map, ensuring that the reader has in fact covered his a**.

ISBN: 1-931836-24-8

Price: $$39.95 US $59.95 CAN

The Best Damn Windows Server 2003 Book Period
Susan Snedaker

Windows Server 2003 is certainly Microsoft's most robust, and complex, enterprise operating system developed to date. Any one of the component "services" in Server 2003 has more features and functionality than existed in the entire Windows NT 4 operating system! In addition, the audience of system administrators has now evolved to a highly professional, skills certified community of IT professionals with a need for the tens of thousands of pages of Microsoft documentation and web-based support to be distilled into a concise, applied format. This is the book that meets the needs of today's Windows Server 2003 professional.

ISBN: 1-931836-12-4

Price: $59.95 US $79.95 CAN

AVAILABLE JUNE 2004!
ORDER at
www.syngress.com

solutions@syngress.com